AF511676

VEDIC SACRIFICE
Challenge and Response

Vedic Sacrifice

Challenge and Response

ISRAEL SELVANAYAGAM

MANOHAR
2020

First published 1996
POD reprint 2020

© Israel Selvanayagam 1996

All rights reserved. No part of this publication may be reproduced or transmitted, in any form or by any means, without prior permission of the author and the publisher.

ISBN 978-81-7304-104-4

Published by
Ajay Kumar Jain *for*
Manohar Publishers & Distributors
4753/23 Ansari Road, Daryaganj
New Delhi 110 002

Printed at
Replika Press Pvt. Ltd.

To

SAM ANNAN

Contents

Foreword

It is an honour to be asked by Dr. Selvanayagam to write a foreword to his work on Vedic sacrifice, and a pleasure to accede to his request. Since the perspective of the present study is primarily historical, perhaps it may not be impertinent to make use of historical data in order to enquire, in this foreword, concerning some repercussions consequent on the vitality of Vedic tradition, or at least one aspect of it.

Anyone who is even casually concerned with understanding contemporary India is aware of the fearfully oppressive tyranny which *dalits* have and continue to suffer in the context of brahmanical religion, Vedism. The fearsome character of this suffering is not only experienced in its intensity but also in its durability. Why? What is it that makes this religious tradition so incredibly resistent, enduring, and influential? Perhaps an answer is to be had from an examination of the dominant central feature of vedic religion—the *yajna*. Let us, then, quickly and all too briefly survey some prominent examples in the history of its development of *yajna* as an explanatory category. This may help explain the durability of brahmanical religion by demonstrating how its cardinal element, *yajna*, has served throughout Indian religious history as a marker of traditional orthodoxy and hence a means for acceptable innovation.

It is generally agreed that the essential function of sacrifice the world over is to consecrate, to make sacred; and indeed, the etymology of the word *sacrifice* testifies on behalf of this understanding (L. *sacer-facio*, "to make sacred"). Sacrifice, as a category in Indian religious thought, does indeed make sacred; it projects traditional and canonical meaning on a potentially infinite set of human religious activities and doctrines, thereby consecrating and legitimising them. One might even say that the imaginary entity called the "Indian mind" frequently thinks with a dominant "sacrificial consciousness".

The Vedic sacrifice in post-Vedic India has been pronounced dead by Indologists often and early, perhaps too early. The pioneers of Western knowledge of the Vedic ritual—Hillebrandt, Levi, Caland, and others—assumed their subject matter was speaking to them from the grave. These experts regarded performance of Vedic sacrifices recorded in the nineteenth and early twentieth centuries as, at best, a kind of necrophiliac theatre performed by Brahmans reading from a script.

However, scholars more recently—C.G. Kashikar, Frits Staal, Frederick Smith, Asko Parpola, Michael Witzel, David Knipe and Brian K. Smith, to mention a few—have demonstrated that *yajña* was relegated to a historical tomb somewhat prematurely. Certainly Vedic rituals are in no sense popular or widespread in contemporary South Asia, but fieldwork data are now being accumulated which reveal a surprisingly large number of living traditions of Vedic ritualists throughout India.[1]

Too often, however, fieldwork on current performances and performers of Vedic *yajnas* has tended merely to repaint the death mask rather than strip it off. Contemporary exempla of Vedic ritualism have too frequently been presented as surviving fossils of the distant past, wholly irrelevant to the religions of India now—and to those of the past two millennia. The *yajna*, it is said with a certain commonsensical persuasiveness, is at most an antique relic of post-Vedic religious traditions. When it is not simply ignored as a museum piece of no contemporary interest or usefulness, it is radically misunderstood. Perhaps *yajna* as it has transmigrated throughout the history of post-Vedic Indian religious history, in a variety of historical settings and divergent traditions, needs to be viewed not so much as a ritual act or set of acts (the purpose of which might be constructive, expiatory, propitiary, purifying or cathartic) but rather as a category that acts to provide explanatory power, and hence consecrating and legitimising authority in Indian culture and religion.

We begin with an all too brief, but hopefully not totally inadequate, survey of *yajna* as an explanatory category: a mode of classification that renders phenomena explicable by connecting them to an already assimilated precedent. For Indian writers and thinkers from Vedic times to the present, *yajna* is, contrary to some

Western opinions, in a real sense a datum of known quantity. It might well appear that, in all of this, sacrifice functions as a metaphor in Indian religious discourse, but it could equally be said that from the Indian point of view other beliefs, actions, and phenomena are metaphors of the sacrifice. That is to say, it is quite as reasonable to regard *yajna* as a model *for* understanding other phenomena as it is to assume that it is only a model *of* other phenomena.[2]

The projection of the sacrifice from its ritual confines onto various aspects of human life and the world at large begins, of course, in the Veda itself. The theory of ritual in Vedic texts centres on the notion that sacrifice is not only the activity of priests, but is also the means for explaining the workings of the cosmos and the human self.[3] *Yajna* is thus the primary category of knowledge in both Vedic cosmology and Vedic anthropology, as is indicated in the frequently encountered phrase *puruso vai yajnah,* "man [cosmic and human] is the sacrifice."

The sacrifice as an explicatory model for understanding the cosmos is dramatically exemplified in the well-known Purusa Sukta (RV 10.90) in which the creation of the universe is represented as the primordial sacrifice and dismemberment of the cosmic *Purusa.* This myth, as well as the related cosmogonic myths of Prajapati's fragmentation of sacrificial construction[4]—provides a blueprint etched by the *yajna* for tracing the origins of the cosmos.

But it is the epistemological function of the Vedic sacrifice, in the cosmological mode, that interests us at this juncture. This function of the sacrifice serves to explain the cosmos in both its origins and its ongoing operations. These latter are also comprehended through application of the sacrificial paradigm, as the early Upanisad testifies.

> The world (of heaven) over there, Gautama, is a fire. The sun is its fuel, the rays of the sun are its smoke, the day is its flame, the moon its coals, the stars its sparks. Into this fire the gods offer faith, and from that oblation king Soma is born. The rain cloud, Gautama, is a fire. The wind is its fuel, the mist its smoke, lightning its flame, the thunderbolt its coals, and the roar of the thunder its sparks. Into this fire the gods offer king Soma, and from this oblation rain is born. The earth, Gautama, is a fire. The year is its fuel, space its smoke, night its flame, the four directions its coals, the four intermediate directions its sparks. Into this fire the gods offer rain, and from that oblation food is born.[5]

Such a sacrifical comprehension of the workings of the cosmos often assumes a reciprocal arrangement among the cosmic forçes, one sacrificing to another in order to keep the universe functioning in its regularity:

The fire here (on earth) offers itself in the rising sun; the setting sun offers itself in the fire; the night also offers itself in the day, and the day in the night; the in-breath [offers itself] in the expiration, and the expiration in the in-breath. These six sacrifices themselves each in the other.[6]

Indeed, as the Satapatha Brahmana puts it, "this all (*tat sarvam*) participates in (*abhakta*) the sacrificer"[7] and "this all" is made explicable when conceived in such a manner.

The sacrificial arena as the model both of and for the organisation of the cosmos persists long after the Vedic age has come to a close, providing us with examples of the post-Vedic exercise of the "sacrificial consciousness." The Buddhist *stupa,* a cosmological mapping centered on a cosmic man of another sort, the Buddha, is made up of parts whose names are borrowed from the terminology of the Vedic *yajna.*[8] So, too, when Hindu temples appear in the middle of the first millennium A.D., dedicated to gods propelled to glory by the *bhakti* movement, they, too, patterned themselves on the plan of the Vedic sacrificial arena.[9] The Vedic sacrifice as the Indian *ur*-model of the cosmos, thus is superimposed on post-Vedic worship centres and microcosmos of both Buddhist and Hindu varieties.

But it is at the level of *adhyatman,* making sense of the human self and human life, that the Vedic *yajna* most obviously and continually reappears throughout the history of Indian religions. The projection of the sacrifice onto the human *purusa* and his/her existence, the meaningful overlay of the concept of sacrifice onto human existence, also begins in the Veda itself. The human body is understood as a reduplication of the sacrificial arena, for at the microcosmic level, too, *puruso vai yajnah:*

Man, Gautama, is a fire. Speech is his fuel, breath his smoke, the tongue his flame, the eye his coals, the ear his sparks.[10]

The sacrificial site (*vedi*) is indeed his breast, the sacrificial grass is his hair. The *garhapatya* fire is his heart, the *daksina* fire is his mind, the *ahavaniya* fire is his mouth.[11]

The generation of human bodies depicted sacrificial terms under this paradigm is envisioned as a process of sacrificial oblations of male seed into the "fire" that is woman. Into the "fire" that is man, the gods make an "offering of food", from which semen is produced. The semen, in turn, is poured into the woman to produce new life. For not only is man depicted as a sacrifice, but

> Woman, Gautama, is a sacrificial fire. The vagina is her fuel, foreplay her smoke, the womb her flame, the penetration her coals, and the pleasure her sparks. Into this fire the gods make an offering of semen, and from that oblation the embryo is born.[12]

The body's dissolution at death is likewise regarded in sacrificial terms in Vedic texts and the related *antyesti samskara*—a final complete offering of the body into the cremation fire. Replicating the cosmogonic sacrificial dispersion of the body of Purusa/ Prajapati, the human body, too, is sacrificially disintegrated, and reintegrated into the cosmos.

> The voice of the deceased enters the fire, his breath [enters] the wind, his eye the sun, his mind the moon, his ear the cardinal directions,.his flesh the earth, his *atman* the atmosphere, his body hair the plants, the hair on his head the trees, and his blood and semen are deposited in the waters.[13]

As Bruce Lincoln writes by way of summarising this and other related Indo-European visions of death as sacrifice, "Like all sacrifice, death is a repetitive act. Each death repeats every other death and every other sacrifice: above all the first death, which was also the first sacrifice."[14]

When the new doctrine of *samsara* first appears in the early Upanisads, it is, not surprisingly, cast in the mould that is *yajna*. Indeed, the earliest formulation of transmigration and the reincarnation of the *atman* explains the process of rebirth as a series of oblations in five fires, culminating in the oblation of male seed into the womb fire of the female.[15]

And just as both the origins and the ongoing functions of the cosmos are represented in sacrificial tones in the Veda, so is the ongoing process of human life—in addition to the origins and ends of that life—depicted as a *yajna*. According to the Chandogya Upanisad, human existence is to be understood as a kind of *soma* sacrifice, with its three periods of youth, maturity and old age corresponding to the three *soma* pressings in the morning, midday, and evening.[16]

The sacrificial paradigm is also applied in discussions of the critical moments of that sacrifice which is the life of humans. The "second birth" or initiation into Vedic society (*upanayana*)—a significant symbol of *dalit* oppression—is one of the few rituals of Vedism that persists more or less unchanged throughout the history of Vedism, and has always been represented as a sacrifice.[17] *Upanayana* also inaugurates the study of the Veda (*brahmacarya*), which is likewise understood as a kind of sacrifice.[18]

The conclusion of the period of Veda study is, as might well be expected, homologised with the conclusion of the Vedic sacrifice: the gift to the teacher presented by the departing student is specifically termed as *daksina* or sacrificial fee and the ceremonial bath at the end of *brahmacarya*, the *samavartana*, recalls the concluding bath of the sacrifice—the *avabhrtha*.

The notion that the accumulation of religious knowledge is a kind of sacrifice together with the conceptualisation of human physiology in sacrificial terms combines to make possible the representation of world renunciation (in the Upanisads and other texts) as yet another version of the *yajna*. But the very act and subsequent life of renunciation—which includes renunciation of sacrifice, of ritual action or *karman*—is presented in the texts as a "higher" or "truer" sacrifice. The renouncer, or "sacrificer", "sacrifices" only in himself (*atmanneva yajati*),"[19] and such a sacrifice is envisioned by the monistic Upanisadic thinkers as a means to obtain mystical union in a pantheistic conception of that oneness: "His offering is made in all worlds, in all beings, in all selves."[20]

This identification of the life and physiology of the renouncer—who has resumed himself the sacrificial fires which are then extinguished[21]—and the ritual of sacrifice creates homologies between all the functions of life and the functions of ritual. The consumption of daily meals becomes an *atmayajna* or "sacrifice to and in the self."[22] Even the breathing of the renouncer is considered to be an "inner sacrifice" (*antara-agnihotra*) or "sacrifice to and in the life-breaths" (*prana-agnihotra*).[23]

In this way, every moment of the life of the world renouncer is regarded as sacrifice, every breath and "oblation", and life as whole is considered a "continuous" and "uninterrupted" *yajna*.

In the Upanisads the *yajna* was transformed and redefined, as Dr. Selvanayagam has demonstrated, but nevertheless preserved. This was accomplished by equating new religious practices—meditation, yoga, and contemplation on the ultimate nature of the self—to it. All are not agreed as to how these data are to be interpreted, but we need not enter into this controversy. Indeed, regardless of whether the representations of the practices of world renouncers in sacrificial terms is interpreted by its scholars as the organic development of Vedic ritualism or as a strategy for incorporating within the orthodox tradition practices of extraneous origin, the function is the same: to conceptualise and articulate the new in terms of the old. The category of *yajna* thus serves to *explain the unknown* (its explicative function as a category); and we might safely say, it also acts to *traditionalise the innovative.*

By the time of the *Bhagavadgita* (*c.* second century B.C. or later), a text that manifests a syncretistic and emergent Hindu orthodoxy, and number of traditional as well as heterogeneous and non-Vedic practices are synthesised into Hindu religious life by identifying them with *yajna.*

Some *yogins* offer only sacrifice to the gods; others offer the sacrifice with the sacrifice in the fire of *brahman.* Others offer the senses beginning with hearing in the fires of self-restraint; and others offer the objects of sense, beginning with sounds, in the fires of the senses. Others [offer] all acts of the senses and acts of the breaths in the fire, kindled by wisdom, of the yoga of self-restraint. Others [offer] material sacrifice, the sacrifice of austerities, or the sacrifice of yoga; and [others offer] sacrifices of Veda recitation (*svadhyaya*) and mystical knowledge (*jnana*)—world renouncers whose vows are keen. Some offer the inhalation of breath in the exhalation of breath, and the exhalation of breath in the inhalation of breath, controlling them both, intent on breath control. Others restrict their meals and offer the breaths in the breaths. All these are knowers of the sacrifice, their defilements erased by sacrifice.[24]

And with the *Gita* we also witness a new extension of the category of sacrifice. Isolating and generalising the component of the ritual called the *tyaga* (the "giving up" or "renunciation" of the offering), the Gita teaches the doctrine of *karma-yoga* as sacrificially oriented everyday action whereby "all attachment and all the fruits [of action] are renounced."[25] For, the text says, "this world is bound by the bonds of *karma* except where that action is done sacrificially."[26]

In yet another move that will have consequences for the subsequent development of devotional Hinduism, the Gita introduces the new teaching of *bhakti* in the guise of the reinterpreted "true sacrifice."

A leaf, or a flower, or a cup of water that a pious soul may offer Me with *bhakti*, that do I accept, for it was *bhakti* that made the offering. Whatever you do, whatever you eat, whatever you offer or give away, whatever austerity you may perform, consign it to me. You will be liberated from those bonds which *karma* creates, whose fruits are good and bad. Your *atman* yoked by renunciation, fully liberated, you will come to Me.[27]

In later texts of Hindu sectarian and devotional traditions, sacrifice continues to be a leitmotif long after it has ceased to be performed by anyone other than the occasional kings (seeking Vedic legitimacy) or Brahmans stuck in the backwaters of South Asia. The ritual of *puja* to the image of Visnu, Siva, the Goddess, or one of their *avataras* simultaneously replaces the *yajna* while it incorporates within itself many rites from the Vedic sacrifice. The *smarta* Hindu *puja* ritual structure encompasses within its Vedic rites of the fire sacrifice (mostly at the *grhya* level) but makes them subservient to more recent principal rites of service to the image. Vedic ritualism, recapitulated in its most compact form now functions as merely a subsidiary rite within a ritual oriented around a different centre and purpose.[28]

Certain Hindu texts do indeed teach a sort of "cult at a discount," procuring the same fruits as the great sacrifices. Thus, the rewards that the Vedic ritualists aimed for can now be obtained at a smaller expense.[29] In these cases, the Vedic sacrifice provides the later Hindu tradition with a kind of standard of worth by which non-Vedic religious practices might be measured. In the Mahabharata,[30] to cite an example of this frequently encountered phenomenon, the rewards of visiting various Hindu pilgrimage spots are couched in terms of the old sacrificial system. The mere appearance at one or another *tirtha* wins for the pilgrim "the fruit of a soma sacrifice" or "the fruit of a horse sacrifice". Results which once entailed great expense and painstaking labour, and which were in all likelihood available only to the religious, political, and economic élite, are now easily acquirable by all, thanks to the full equation of the later version to the original. In this way the new and relatively simple religious practices of Hindu worship are said to resume in themselves the power of the most complex Vedic sacrifices, just as certain domestic rites came to contain the essence of the *mahayajnas*. And identification of the simple and the complex puts the former in a better light. Why bother to undertake massive and obsolete sacrificial endeavours when their "fruits" can be efficiently (and economically) obtained through new and improved techniques?

However, the purpose of shrouding new Hindu practices in sacrificial clothing is not simply to prove the superiority of the new to the old, but first and foremost to present the new *as* the old. Sacrifice has functioned throughout Indian religious history as a marker of traditionalism and as a means of acceptable innovation.[31]

Sacrifice thus serves as a stake for traditionalism and as a means for acceptable innovation within the boundaries of orthodoxy, and the strategy of reforming by appeal to the category of *yajna* is still at work in the modern period. Tagore preached his secularised humanism in a dramatic vehicle entitled "sacrifice"[32] and Gandhi's redefinition of *yajna* in light of his own philosophy summarises a process that has been at work throughout Hindu history—the search to find a "deeper" and new meaning in the archaic Vedic concept.

> *Yajna* has a deeper meaning than the offering of ghee and other things in the sacrificial fire. *Yajna* is sacrifice of one's all for the good of humanity, and to me these offerings of *ahutis* have a symbolic meaning. We have to offer up our weaknesses, our passions, our narrowness into the purifying fire, so that we may be cleansed.[33]

Perhaps enough has been said to indicate that the Vedic sacrifice is indeed a candidate for inclusion in the repertoire of entities constitutive of Hindu cultural and religious continuity. In all times and in the most diverse traditions comprising the Hindu religious configuration, the concept of sacrifice has been an old skin into which new wine is poured.

But there is even greater significance, for the deployment of the category of *yajna* is also a means to make Hinduism Vedic; and to make something Vedic in the Hindu tradition, is to make it canonical and orthodox. It is in this sense that the Vedic sacrifice in the Hindu tradition might be regarded as one mode of defining Hindus. Indeed, it is because of the integral connection between *yajna* and Veda that sacrifice might be termed a canonical category in the Hindu tradition. This being the case, it is hardly surprising to find *yajna* freighting an incredibly resistant and durable Vedism.

In the final analysis, however, Vedism—and Hinduism insofar as it took to itself certain definite and possibly defining features of Vedism—is a system based on hierarchically calibrated distinction. It is, in other words, a system based on judgements of better and worse, more and less complete, higher and lower realisation of form. And the hierarchical yardstick was unfailingly applied to human beings—the most obvious, and heinous result being the caste system. Whether it is possible to reimagine/reform Vedism and Hinduism in an egalitarian mode, without ceding the right to make hierarchical value judgements, is probably the existentially dominant, and as yet unsolved, problem that plagues the contemporary Hindu religious tradition, indeed all religious traditions.

Professor & Head DAVID C. SCOTT
Department of Religion & Culture
United Theological College
Bangalore

NOTES

1. See, e.g., C.G. Kashikar and Asko Parpola, "Srauta Traditions in Recent Times," in Frits Staal, ed., *Agni: The Vedic Ritual of the Fire Altar,* 2 vols. (Berkeley: Asian Humanities Press, 1983), II: 199-251. Also to be noted is the work—yet to be published—being done by David Knipe with an enclave of Vedic *brahmans* on the Andhra coast.
2. *Model of* and *model for* are, of course, Clifford Geertz's terms for what he regards as the two principal functions of religion in cultural life: to provide both intellectually plausible and emotionally satisfying modes of living. See his essay "Religion as a Cultural System," in *The Interpretation of Cultures: Selected Essays by Clifford Geertz* (New York: Basic Books, 1973), 87-125.
3. Jean Filliozat argues that Vedic philosophy turns on the assumption that it is possible to correlate corresponding elements lying on three discrete planes of reality: the macrocosmos (whose contents and forces are collectively called *adhidevata*, "relating to the godly"), the ritual sphere (*adhiyajna*, "relating to the sacrifice") and the microcosmos (*adhyatman*, "relating to the self"). Further, the connections made and found among cosmos, ritual, and self were not designed solely to reduce these levels to any one, nor were they simple metaphors. Such homologies were to express metaphysical truth and to make all three levels mutually explicative. See Henri Hubert and Marcel Mauss, *Sacrifice: Its Nature and Function,* trans. by W.D. Halls (Chicago: University of Chicago Press, 1964), 48-56.
4. In the post-Rigvedic texts, the locus classicus of the developed ritualism typifying Vedism, the function and pride of place of creater gods in the Rig Veda Samhita (and most especially, the god

Purusa) is usurped by the deity Prajapati. Or, rather, the imagery, philosophical speculations and implications of the mythology of Purusa are extended to and developed in the myths of Prajapati. There can be no doubt that in the minds of the authors of the later texts the two deities are the same; they are explicitly identified in several places (e.g. SB 6.1.15, 6.1.1.8, 7.4.1.1.5, etc.), and the characteristics and functions of Prajapati are obviously of a piece with those of Purusa as he appears in the Purusa Sukta.

5. ChU 5.4.1-5.6.2
6. KB 2.8.
7. SB 3.6.2.26.
8. Cf. L.A. Govinda, *Psycho-Cosmic Symbolism of the Buddhist Stupa* (Emeryville, CA: Dharma Publishing, 1976).
9. See Stella Kramrisch, *The Hindu Temple*, 2 vols. (reprint ed., Delhi: Motilal Banarsidass, 1976), I: 1-17, 67-97, 139-44; and also L.A. Ravi Varma, "Rituals of Worship," in Haridas Bhattacharya, ed., *The Cultural Heritage of India*, 4 vols. (Calcutta: Ramakrishna Mission Institute of Culture, 1956).
10. ChU 5.7.1.
11. ChU 5.18.2
12. ChU 5.8.1-2
13. BAU 3.2.13.
14. Bruce Lincoln, *Myth, Cosmos, and Society: Indo-European Themes of Creation and Destruction* (Cambridge, MA: Harvard University Press, 1986), 127.
15. ChU 5.3.1-10.
16. ChU 3.16-17.
17. As Jan Gonda has demonstrated, the *upanayana* is both conceived as and modelled on the initiation and consecration of the sacrificer, the *diksa*; and initiation into the cult throughout the history of Indian religions, orthodox and heterodox alike, preserves and reduplicates this sacrificial origin. See Jan Gonda, *Change and Continuity in India Religion*. Disputation Rheno-Trajectinae, vol. 9 (The Hague: Mouton, 1965), 79-80.
18. SB 11.3.3.2.
19. Maitri Upanisad 6.9.
20. ChU 5.24.2.
21. For the rite of the "interiorisation" of the sacrificial fires, see, e.g. Baudhayana Dharma Sutra 2.10.17.19.
22. For the *atamayajna*, see Ananda K. Coomaraswamy, "Atmayajna: Self-Sacrifice." *Harvard Journal of Asiatic Studies* 6 (1941); 358-88.
23. For the *prana-agnihotra*, see H.W. Bodewitz, *Jaiminiya Brahmana* (Leiden: E.J. Brill, 1973), and the following texts: ChU 5.19-24, BAU 1.5.23, Kausitaki Upanisad 2.5, etc.
24. BG 4.25-30.

25. BG 18.6.
26. BG 3.9.
27. BG 9.26-28.
28. See T. Goudriaan, "Vaikhanasa Daily Worship," *Indo-Iranian Journal* 12 (1970), 161-215.
29. Kamaleswar Bhattacharya, "Le 'Vedisme' de certains texts hindouistes," *Journal asiatique* 225 (1967), 200-231.
30. Mbh. 3.80-83.
31. The radical movement of Tantricism too does not neglect to codify its practices in orthodox sacrificial terminology. The partaking of the five "forbidden" (to the orthodox, that is) substances is represented in Tantric texts as oblations to various deities located within the body of the practitioner. See Agehananda Bharati, *The Tantric Tradition* (New York: Samuel Weiser, 1975), 260-62.
32. Rabindranath Tagore, "Sacrifice," in *A Tagore Reader*, ed. by Amiya Chakravarty (Boston: Beacon Press, 1966), 125-48.
33. Mohandas Gandhi, *In Search of the Supreme,* comp. and ed. by V.B. Kher (Ahmedabad: Navajivan Publishing House, 1961), 276.

Preface

THIS BOOK is the modified version of a dissertation submitted to the Senate of Serampore College in 1989 for the degree of Doctor of Theology. Since then a number of studies on Vedic sacrifice have appeared. In perspective and methodology my work may yet contribute to an understanding of the post-Vedic development of the concepts of *yajña* or sacrifice.

Some of the suggestions made by the examiners of the dissertation have been incorporated; so also a few insights from new material and dialogue with scholars of Hinduism. The more aware I am of the vast area covered in this book and of the extensive studies on Vedic sacrifice the more modest I become about acknowledging its limitations. Studying all the original texts of the *Vedas, Sūtras, Darśanas,* epics and the *śramaṇa* literature is impossible given the limited scope and time of the research. Only the principal *Upaniṣads, Mānavadharma Śāstrā* and sections of the *Mahābhārata* including the *Gītā* could be studied in their original. Admittedly, I am not a Sanskritist to make linguistic analysis of every verse of these texts. I have consulted all the major translations of them. For most of the rest I have relied on secondary sources, yet not 'secondary' in terms of their sound scholarship and reputation. To keep the book readable for average students of Hinduism I have avoided obscure Sanskrit terms. Further, I seem to proceed fast at some junctures mentioning issues and giving the references in footnotes without dealing with them in detail. There are reasons for this. First, I assume that the readers are already familiar with the basic issues. Second, I did not want to go beyond the present size of the book. Third, my main purpose is to suggest a new line of reading the development of ancient religious thought in India. All these reasons make me claim no more than an outline for this work which needs extensive discussion and far more detail. It is my hope that this outline will stimulate students to study and present the pan-mythic religious traditions of India with adequate clarity.

It is my duty to acknowledge help from different persons during my research for this book. Two-thirds of the time (1986-88) was spent in Bangalore at the United Theological College and one-third in Cambridge, U.K. Following are the most notable ones who were closely associated with my work.

It was Dr. Eric Lott who, at the initial stages of my research struggled with me in shaping directions, focusing on the issues concerned and formulating the topic. Before leaving Bangalore in March 1988 he was able to go through the major part of the preliminary draft and make valuable comments. Even after his return to England he continued to be an encouraging consultant. I am deeply grateful to him.

Dr. David Scott, who succeeded Dr. Lott as my official supervisor, drew my attention to some important areas for further consideration after reading the revised preliminary draft. During my ten months period of intensive research in Cambridge his prompt replies answering my questions and giving practical suggestions greatly facilitated the process of finalising the draft in time. Subsequently he vigorously encouraged me to publish the work. Further, he has graced this book with an insightful foreword. I owe to him immensly.

During my stay in Cambridge Dr. Julius Lipner, going through the pre-final draft very minutely, made many good suggestions for further refinement. He also directed me to new source material in Cambridge and London. My sincere thanks are due to him.

Besides, brief consultations I had with Professors Gispert-Sauch of New Delhi, Ria Kloppenborg of Utrecht and Diana Eck of Harvard gave some good insights into the concerns of this book. I am thankful to these scholars.

I also wish to acknowledge the kind assistance provided by the librarians and library staff of the following institutions: United Theological College, Bangalore; Tamilnadu Theological Seminary, Madurai; Vidyajyoti, Delhi; the University Library, the Divinity School, the Centre for South Asian Studies, the Faculty of Oriental Studies and Wesley House, all in Cambridge; the School of Oriental and African Studies and India Office Library in London. An additional bursary made available by the Spalding Trust helped me to have easy access to libraries in London.

I place on record my appreciation and gratitude for the patient assistance of my wife Gnanaleelal in various ways including in typing the draft. Along with her my two daughters Ani Esther and Arulkani deserve appreciation for their cheerful cooperation while I was away from Madurai for more than two years.

Manohar Publishers & Distributors deserve appreciation for the excellent job in producing the book.

Tamilnadu Theological Seminary
Arasaradi, Madurai 625 010
5 July 1995

ISRAEL SELVANAYAGAM

Abbreviations

AiĀr	*Aitareya Āraṇyaka*
AiB	*Aitareya Brāhmaṇa*
ABORI	*Annals of the Bhandarkar Oriental Research Institute*
ADLR	*Abingdon Dictionary of Living Religions*, ed. Keith Crim
AG	*Anugītā*
ALB	*The Adyar Library Bulletin*
AS	*Asian Studies*
AS/EA	*Asiatische Studien/Etudes Asiatiques*
AV	*Atharva Veda*
BhG	*Bhagavad Gītā*
BhPur	*Bhāgavata Purāṇa*
BṛU	*Bṛhad-āraṇyaka Upaniṣad*
CHI	*The Cultural Heritage of India*
ChU	*Chāndogya Upaniṣad*
DH	*A Dictionary of Hinduism* by Margaret and James Stutley
ER	*Encyclopedia of Religion*, ed. Mircea Eliade
ERE	*Encyclopaedia of Religion and Ethics*, ed. James Hastings
HDhś	*History of Dharmaśāstra* by P.V. Kane
HJAS	*Harvard Journal of Asiatic Studies*
HIL	*A History of Indian Literature*, ed. J. Gonda
HR	*History of Religions*
IA	*Indian Antiquary*
IC	*Indian Culture*
IHQ	*The Indian Historical Quarterly*
IIJ	*Indo-Iranian Journal*
JAAR	*Journal of the American Academy of Religion*
JAOS	*Journal of the American Oriental Society*
JBBRAS	*Journal of the Bombay Branch of the Royal Asiatic Society*
JOIUB	*Journal of the Oriental Institute*, M.S.University of Baroda

JRAS	*The Journal of the Royal Asiatic Society*
JSBhG	*Journal of Studies in the Bhagavad Gītā*
KaiU	*Kaivalya Upaniṣad*
KauU	*Kauṣitāki Upaniṣad*
KeU	*Kena Upaniṣad*
KU	*Kaṭha Upaniṣad*
MaiU	*Maitrī Upaniṣad*
Manu	*Mānavadharmaśāstra*
MāU	*Māṇḍūkya Upaniṣad*
MuU	*Muṇḍaka Upaniṣad*
NIA	*New Indian Antiquary*
PEW	*Philosophy East and West*
PrU	*Praśna Upaniṣad*
RS	*Religious Studies*
RSR	*Religious Studies Review*
ṚV	*Ṛgveda*
SV	*Sāma Veda*
ŚB	*Śatapatha Brāhmaṇa*
SBE	*Sacred Books of the East,* ed. Max Muller
SHS	*Studies in the History of Religions*
SR	*Studies in Religion*
ŚvU	*Śvetāsvatara Upaniṣad*
TB	*Taittirīya Brāhmaṇa*
TU	*Taittirīya Upaniṣad*
WZKSAIP	*Wiener Zeitschrift für die Kunde Sudasiens und Archiv für Indische Philosophie*
YV	*Yajur Veda*
ZKT	*Zeitschrift für Katholische Theologie*

A Note on Transliteration

The transliteration of Sanskrit terms is in accordance with the standard system followed internationally. It follows, for example, that of Monier-Williams' *Sanskrit-English Dictionary*, with a few exceptions: the letter *ṛ* replaces his *ṛi*, *ṣ* his *sh* and *ś* his *s*. The pattern followed in quotations, however, remains unaltered.

Introduction

Yajña, WHICH is usually translated as sacrifice,[1] is the most central element of Vedic religion. It was the heart of the religious and social life of the Vedic Aryans. From a simple gift or food offering to gods, *yajña* developed into a complex ritual mechanism for generating the power to create and recreate the universe and all forms of its life as we see in the *saṃhitā* and *brāhmaṇa* parts of the *Vedas*. Dominant ideas of Indian religious thought such as *karman, brahman, tapas, kāma, artha, ahiṃsā* and *dharma* originated in the context of ritual *yajña*. But in course of time there were changes in the understanding of *yajña* within the Brāhmaṇic-Hindu tradition. This book aims to examine the nature of these changes and identify the historical factors that contributed to them.

The post-Vedic period is taken to start from the time of the *Āraṇyakas* and the *Upaniṣads* in which radical departures in the understanding of *yajña* are discernible. Along with and following these departures great changes seem to have taken place in the spheres of religion, society and economy in the Gangetic valley. The interaction between different religious traditions and socio-economic factors produced what may be called "the most creative period of the history of Indian religious thought" covering roughly the period between 600 and 200 B.C. This book tries to focus on the understanding of *yajña* during this period.

Yajña is one of the recurring themes in the *Bhagavad Gītā*. New forms of *yajña* and new interpretations of its meaning mixed with old ideas seem to reflect the changes in the understanding of *yajña* that took place in post-Vedic times. Futher, the attempt of the *Gītā* to synthesise different forms and meanings of *yajña* seems to reveal the kind of tension involved in the transition from Vedic brāhmaṇism to Hinduism.

This book is an inquiry into an historical-hermeneutical process, a search for the patterns of change in a particular context. As *yajña* is the essence of the *Vedas*, changes in the understanding of the authority of the *Veda* are closely connected with changing attitudes to *yajña*. The particular focus of this inquiry will be the nature of the post-Vedic developments in the understanding of *yajña* and the response of the *Bhagavad Gītā*. As the *Gītā* stands on the threshold of Vedic brāhmaṇism and brāhmaṇic Hinduism, this may help to understand certain distinctive characteristics of the Hindu religious tradition.

Some Striking Issues

1. To start with the *Bhagavad Gītā*, *yajña* is one of its most difficult themes, as many interpreters have recognised. The opinions of scholars as to the exact position of the *Gītā* concerning Vedic sacrifice are divided, as we shall point out later. This is not without reason. There is no particular view of sacrifice found in this text. On the one hand, the *Gītā* seems to reaffirm the Vedic *yajña*. For this it uses new expressions like the *yajña cakra* (wheel of sacrifice, 3.14-16). It raises new questions, e.g. whether one should continue to perform *yajña* in the stage of *saṃnyāsa* (renunciation, 18.3, 5). It has added to the practice of *yajña* the practices of *dāna* (giving gifts or alms), *tapas* (austere practice) and *svādhyāya* (study of scriptures) as equally effective and meaningful (e.g.11.48, 53). It makes new connections, for example with the *triguṇa* category of *Sāṃkhya* (17.11-13). On the other hand, it undermines the significance of ritual *yajña* by introducing new forms like *jñāna yajña* (sacrifice of knowledge) and *japa yajña* (sacrifice of uttering sacred formulas) and giving them a superior status (4.33;10.25); further, it relates the idea of *yajña* to *karman* (action), particularly to the famous ideal of *niṣkāma karman* (action without desire) and describes all actions as forms of sacrifice (3.9; 9.27). Above all Kṛṣṇa, the new Lord and enjoyer of *yajña*, cannot be attained by *yajña* (5.29; 7.30; 1;1.48). The important question is to understand these new forms and find a connection between all such different meanings of sacrifice.

While many commentators on the *Gītā* do not worry about the nature and distinctive meanings of the different forms of *yajña*, or their interconnections, some tend to reduce them to a particular strand, thereby undermining all others. In the Vedāntic approaches, it is obvious that particular metaphysical positions colour interpretations of the *yajña* verses of the *Gītā*. Those who have tried to find different literary pieces in the *Gītā* classify the text into different sections. While this attempt seems to be highly conjectural, the literary critics themselves differ widely and do not help to clarify matters pertaining to the *yajña* verses. The allegorical interpretation of *yajña* as devotion to God and dedicated service to humanity, given by the theosophists in the early part of this century and elaborated further by modern thinkers and reformers of Hinduism in the later decades, is dominant in the minds of many who study the *Gītā*. All these approaches seem to have obscured the meaning of the *yajña* verses and hindered an in-depth study of them.

The historical-hermeneutical approach we propose in this study is expected to shed light for a clearer understanding of *yajña* in the post-Vedic period which is reflected in the *Gīta*. Within the limited scope of this study we shall try to trace the origins of new ideas, the exigencies for their accommodation and problems of their synthesis. This will help to identify the historical context of the *Gītā*, the structure of its literature, and the nature of its message all controversial issues. In the same way, this may help us to examine popular claims about the synthesis of the *Gītā* and the universal appeal of its message.

2. How the *Bhagavad Gītā* affirms all the major aspects of the Vedic *yajña* will become clear when we delineate them at the beginning of our discussion and see the verses concerned in their light. But to trace the development of *jñāna yajña* we need to go through the early *Upaniṣads*. So far the *Upaniṣads* have been studied as a philosophy of the ultimate reality in terms of *brahman* and *ātman*; what is ignored (except for passing references) in this approach, however, is the Upaniṣadic view of sacrifice, which is very significant for changes in the understanding of sacrifice. Opinions are divided whether the *Upaniṣads*, as true end or goal of the *Vedas* (i.e. *Vedānta*), affirm or deny the Vedic *yajña* and its world-view, for although the *Upaniṣads* are full of sacrificial language, there is no clear-cut view of their attitude to Vedic *yajña*. The aspects of ritual *yajña* and new development of *jñāna yajña* and *ātmayajña* (self-sacrifice) are so mixed as to create what is seen as 'a puzzle'. In this aspect certain fundamental questions have to be raised: in what way do the *Upaniṣads* present the ritual *yajña* of the *Vedas*? Are the underlying notions of the ritual *yajña* and *jñāna yajña* similar or different? Can we establish a logical link between these two types of *yajña* which

are presented sometimes in diametric opposition? The *Upaniṣads* refer to a new type of *yajamānas* (sacrificers or patrons of sacrifice) who deny the authority of the *Vedas* and deride their ritual. The question arises whether these people are part of the ritual system or 'outsiders' who challenged the traditional complicated ritual system and infused new ideas into it using the language of sacrifice. Such questions may call for a new approach to the *Upaniṣads* from the perspective of Vedic *yajña.*

3. To identify those who infused new ideas into the ritual system, we need to consider perhaps the most powerful force in the history of ancient India, namely the *śramaṇa* movement. Although glimpses of the presence and thought of strange figures like *munis* are discernible in the *Vedas,* more prominently in the *Upaniṣads,* the Buddhist and Jaina literature tells much about them. Actually the Buddhists, Jainas and *Ājīvikas* were the most established of several *śramaṇa* groups. In their view of *yajña,* they seem to resemble the teachers of the *Upaniṣads* who propounded the idea of *ātma yajña.* The tension between ritual and interiorisation is intensified further by the *śramaṇas,* although as religious communities they share certain concerns of the brāhmaṇic tradition. Socio-political upheavals seem also to have played their part. Particularly, the kind of relationship maintained between the political rulers and the religious groups apparently contributed much to the change in sacrificial system and propagation of new ideas. While, the process of interaction was obviously complex certain major trends are identifiable. For example, we may ask in what way the *yajña*-oriented brāhmaṇic *dharma* had to broaden its scope so as to incorporate new ideas like *mokṣa* and *ahiṃsā* as they appear, for instance, in the *Mahābhārata.* What prompted the writers of the *Dharma Sūtras* and *Śāstras,* basically law-givers for social life, to emphasise the authority of the *Vedas,* the validity of sacrifice and the superiority of the brahmins? Can we find connections between Aśoka banning the killing of animals in all forms including sacrifice and the concern to exempt killing for the purpose of sacrifice from this law? To push the issue further, in what way can the tendency to renounce ritual *yajña* and war that was regarded as the *yajña* of kṣatriyas, in the name of *ahiṃsā,* help us to understand the desperate condition of Arjuna in the *Bhagavad Gītā*? A consideration of the above issues may greatly help to understand the dynamics of a context marked by contrary views on sacrifice.

4. Hindu religious tradition is known for its composite and encyclopaedic nature. But its complex development from the Vedic religion needs more systematic study than is available. This study presupposes that the best starting point to understand some major systems of Hindu life and thought is Vedic *yajña.* The system of *catur varṇa* (fourfold 'colour' division), the prototype of later caste divisions, is closely associated with the system of Vedic *yajña,* brahmins being the executors of performance and kṣatriyas the rich patrons. The concern about *varṇa* and the danger of its *saṃkara* (mixture) can be recognised through the process of our study of changes in *yajña.* In the formulation of the fourfold *puruṣārtha* (goals of human life), *mokṣa* is added to the *yajña*-oriented *artha, kāma,* and *dharma,* and tension seems to have been created about the order of precedence of these components. Likewise in the formulation of the fourfold *āśrama dharma* (fourfold stages in life), the place of *saṃnyāsa* (renunciation) and the duties attached to it, including the question of *yajña,* was so ambiguous that some *sūtrakāras* were not able to accept it as an authentic stage of life. Usually studies dealing with these formulations do not acknowledge sufficiently the tension involved in such formulations, which is necessary to understand later phases of Hinduism in its encounter with other cults and traditions.

Not only the incorporation of new ideas, but also, more significantly, new images of transcendence or God, seem to have played an important role in the process of change. Thus new visions, old traditions and new interpretations are integrally related. To be specific, the figure of Kṛṣṇa is important in the background of the *Bhagavad Gītā*. The process of his relation to Vedic *yajña,* first as its opponent and then its supporter, is a very interesting moment in the subject of our study. How do we account for the change in Kṛṣṇa's relationship to *yajña*? In what way does he provide an integrating focus of old and new meanings of sacrifice? Does the figure of Kṛṣṇa solve the problem of integration without further tension, or does the *Gītā* leave scope for reconsideration? This we have to see in the light of the *yajña* verses of the *Gītā* and some subsequent developments. Thus the concept of sacrifice, the central concern of the Vedic texts, may provide a unifying perspective on brāhmaṇic-Hindu continuity.

5. Interpretation is one of the important dimensions of a religious tradition. In this study we highlight the interpretative process of one of the early phases of Hindusim by considering *yajña.* This would

mean that radical and new interpretations in Hinduism have taken place not only in the last two centuries, as usually highlighted with reference to the impact of the West, but also in much earlier periods. Further, every interpretation has its own exigency, pattern, conceptual tools and principles, even though resemblances between interpretations, especially within a particular tradition, may be present. The *Upaniṣads*, for instance, have developed allegorical interpretations of sacrifice and its interiorisation. As noted, it is very difficult to understand the nature of this pattern since it is not clear whether it confirms the Vedic ritual or denies it. This pattern seems to have been modified further as we find its influence in the challenges of Buddha and Jaina traditions. The *Gītā*, without showing any interest in the allegorical interpretations, states differently its position with the use of the thought forms of its day by relating *yajña* to its fundamental categories of *karman, jñāna* and *bhakti.* Those who allegorise the *yajña* of the *Gītā* or repeat the Upaniṣadic allegorisation today, do not however see the difference between various types of allegorisation. Therefore, the context of a particular pattern of interpretation and the development of new patterns need to be investigated so that the distinctive positions of apparently identical patterns may become clear.

The interpretative process around *yajna* cannot be reduced to allegorical interpretation. We need to look for other types of interpretation as well. As far as the theme of our study is concerned, we do not meet exegetic principles except in Jaimini's *Mīmāṃsā Sūtras* which develop principles of selection, connection and meaning. Their forceful affirmation of the categorical imperative of *yajña* performance will be our main focus. Similar affirmations with different styles are many in, for example, *Manu-smṛti, Mahābhārata* and *Bhagavad Gītā.* They seem to have been necessitated by the context. Moreover, mythological reformulations may also represent a type of interpretation. For example, in its final shape, what does the main story of the *Mahābhārata,* which starts and ends with *yajña,* tell about sacrifice? Do the dual motifs in it like *deva* and *asura* and *dharma* and *adharma* reveal anything about *yajña*? Likewise, what does the incorporation of the Buddha, an opponent of Vedic sacrifice, as an *avatāra* mean? Another element, as we have already noted, is assimilation of new ideas. The substitutory practices of *yajña* like *dāna, tīrtha* (visiting holy places) and *pūjā* have been accepted by the brāhmaṇic orthodoxy. But it is to be asked whether there is a discussion in the early brāhmaṇic tradition about the way in which these new practices fulfil the function of *yajña* even as the latter is not replaced. Likewise, is there any explanation for retaining *hiṃsā* in *yajña* while the principle of *ahiṃsā* is incorporated? And did the *śramaṇas* fail to give an alternative vision in which *hiṃsā* in any form was totally avoidable? Answers to these questions may not be explicitly available in the texts. What is important to note is that we need to understand interpretation in a broad way as affirmation, assimilation and reformulation while not necessarily agreeing with arguments for their inter-connections and inner coherence.

Attitude to scriptures is an important aspect in the hermeneutical process of a religious tradition. By studying changes in the understanding of *yajña*, the essence of *śruti* (heard or revealed) i.e. the *Vedas*, we may understand more fully the attitude of certain subsequent religious texts to the *Vedas*. For example, while the *Upaniṣads* have points of radical departure from the Vedic view of sacrifice, in what sense can one accept them as the end and goal of the *Vedas* (i.e. *Vedānta*)? Is the *Mahābhārata*, called the fifth *Veda* faithful to the four *Vedas* in understanding sacrifice while it incorporates ideas that seem to go against the *Vedas*? In what way do the *Vedas* form the primary sources of the *Śāstras*? How do the orthodox *darśanas* accept the authority of the *Vedas* when most of them give least importance to sacrifice? Further, what are the unique characteristics of the *Gītā* which have led it, originally a text that comes under *smṛti* (remembered, interpreted tradition), to gain the status of a *śruti* or *Veda*?

PREVIOUS STUDIES

The last generation of Indologists like A.B. Keith, Monier Williams and M. Winternitz produced massive works on Indian literature which provide insights into the centrality and nature of *yajña* in the Vedic tradition. Subsequently, several theories about the origin of sacrifice mention the Vedic idea of sacrifice. In recent years, there has been a new enthusiasm concerning the study of Vedic sacrifice. Of the continental writers J. Gonda is outstanding in his massive work on Vedic ritual although his works are mainly based on linguistic analysis. J.C. Heesterman's novel theory of Vedic ritual has provoked much discussion; so also has that of Fritz Staal in America. One more notable American scholar, especially for conceptual treatment of the Vedic sacrifice through profound essays, is Brian K. Smith. Scholars like G.V. Devasthali and G.U. Thite in India, influenced by the continental scholars, have made extensive studies on sacrifice in the *Brāhmaṇa* texts. Besides, R. Panikkar and a group of scholars influenced by him (e.g. H. Aguilar and Uma Vesci) have made efforts to interpret the Vedic *yajña* as a "primal vision" which may provide important insights for a meaningful and authentic life. There have also been comparisons between the Vedic and, for instance, Christian concept of sacrifice, as made by Jose Thachil and Louis Maliekal. Monographs on Hinduism usually refer to Vedic sacrifice in passing; there are, however, a few exceptions of which Thomas Hopkins' monograph on Hindu religious tradition is the most remarkable: it sets the foundation of this tradition by describing the fundamental aspects of Vedic sacrifice. We shall discuss the work of these scholars in the course of our study.

Most of the above studies, however, lack a historical perspective or an attempt to make coherent connections with later developments. Those who make passing references to sacrifice in the *Upaniṣads* and the *Gītā*, for example, seem to be unfair in their treatment and conclusions of the idea of sacrifice, as we shall point out later. On the whole, in fact, post-Vedic developments in the understanding of sacrifice have not been given adequate scholarly attention. Even the famous study of J. Gonda, *Change and Continuity in Indian Religion,* though it contains ideas related to *yajña,* has not given sacrifice a separate treatment. Perhaps it is too complex for a mere descriptive analysis.

At the same time, a few works on post-Vedic developments in the understanding of sacrifice need to be acknowledged. Thomas Goman and Ronald Laura in their essay, "A Logical Treatment of some Upaniṣadic Puzzles and Changing Conceptions of Sacrifice",[2] point out certain tendencies in the *Upaniṣads* such as the superiority of *jñāna* and *tapas,* interiorisation of ritual and an attempt to redefine the meaning of sacrifice within the overall religious structure. T.G. Mainkar is said to have pointed out in a Marathi booklet the continuation of the elements of Vedic sacrifice in the *Upaniṣads.* Similarly, G.U. Thite in his essay on "The Magico-religious Elements in the Principal *Upaniṣads*",[3] shows the ritualistic ideas found in the *Upaniṣads* with an acknowledgement of a few anti-ritualistic thoughts. More recently, Y. Wadhwani-Shah, in her essay on "Sacrificial Ritual and the *Upaniṣads*"[4] reviews the above. She gives more weight to the anti-ritualistic tendencies of the *Upaniṣads* and suggests a mixture detail is of course beyond the scope of these essays.

The most substantial study done so far on the subject of our study is that of the French scholars Madeleine Biardeau and Charles Malamoud on sacrifice in ancient India.[5] In the first major part of this work, Biardeau identifies the cosmic significance attached to Vedic sacrifice, the interaction of two poles in the *Upaniṣads*, i.e. ritual and material well-being on the one hand and interiorisation and renouncement on the other, development of systems and formulations like *varṇa* and *puruṣārtha*, and finally the idea of a supreme God who can integrate different views. But she does not deal in detail with the problems involved in these developments. Sufficient recognition of tension between ritual and interiorisation and between ritual and God in the Upaniṣadic texts, *Mahābhārata* and *Gītā* will come from more textual study. Biardeau's thesis that Viṣṇu and Śiva played complementary roles, the former identified with the ritual and the latter with interiorisation, before they were made opponents by sectarianism, needs evaluation by reference to all the major aspects of Vedic *yajña* and changes effected on them. This would apply to her studies on the *Mahābhārata* too. What makes Biardeau's work distinctive is the structuralist approach of the French sociological tradition. Then it is natural that she rejects history as an inadequate guide, identifies basic structural relationships of high and low, pure and impure, ritual and interiorisation, and highlights *bhakti* as the summit which expresses an hierarchical system of values.[6] Although important insights may be gained from this study, for our inquiry, its use is minimal.

The full history of the *śramaṇa* movement in ancient India including its impact on Vedic religion and society, its merits and failures, has yet to be written. Nevertheless, the pioneering works of Rhys Davids, R.G. Bhandarkar, A.L. Basham, G.C. Pande, A.K. Warder and P.S. Jaini provide significant insights into the interaction between the brāhmaṇic tradition and the *śramaṇa* movement, particularly into the question of changes in the idea and practice of sacrifice during the period we cover in this study. Relatedly, the socio-economic-political changes and how the impact of the *śramaṇa* movement on them contributed to changes in the understanding of sacrifice are pointed out in the writings of people like R.C. Majumdar on Indian history and with more critical analysis in the writings of D.D.Kosambi and Romila Thapar. Our attempt to trace certain referent historical factors will be based on the writings of these historians.

As the focal point of our study is the interpretation of sacrifice in the *Bhagavad Gītā,* studies to this effect need to be acknowledged. The survey made by M. Callewaert and S. Hemraj of numerous translations, of commentaries on and approaches to the *Gītā*[7] may give the impression that it is an "overdone" topic. It needs to be stated, however, that "the quantity is remarkably disproportionate to the actual quality of the work that has been produced, and a fresh approach seems both warranted and desirable".[8] We suggest that the best way of approaching the *Gītā* is from the perspective of Vedic sacrifice and its changes. We have a few studies on *yajña* in the *Gītā* to be acknowledged. Thirty-eight years ago Josef Neuner published an essay in German on the religion and rites of the *Bhagavad Gītā.*[9] Recognising briefly the fundamental ideas of Vedic sacrifice and the new departure of the *Upaniṣads* developing what he calls *yoga yajña,* he moves on to the teaching of the *Gītā* on sacrifice. He points out that the Gita on the one hand acknowledges the power of Vedic *yajña* to sustain the cosmos and all living beings and on the other criticises false motives in *yajña* and the exclusive claims for the *Vedas.* He also points out how the *Gītā* turns the *triguṇa* category of *Sāṃkhya* towards a ritual system. But without dwelling further on the significance of new forms of affirmation and connections of the text, Neuner moves to the main concern of his essay, i.e., a discussion on ritual and religion in Christianity in comparison with Hinduism. Fourteen years later J.F.T. Jordens wrote a rather brief essay, "Yajña in the *Bhagavad Gītā*".[10] This is the only study that tries to bring together all the *yajña* passages of the *Gītā* and identify their interpretative nature. Jordens' conclusions, however, lack exactitude and perspective mainly because his study has shown no interest in post-Vedic developments in the understanding of matters pertaining to sacrifice, to which the *Gītā* seems to respond. Moreover, none of the studies mentioned above has touched upon the impact of the *Gītā* on under-standing sacrifice in subsequent times. Hence the need for a comprehensive perspective of change and continuity in a religious category of importance.

An Historical-Hermeneutical Process: Methodological Considerations

We need to attempt an analysis of the assumptions and logical limitations that undergird the overall perspective to be taken and the procedures to be followed in this study. It may be useful to see how our approach relates or does not relate to other important approaches known in the science of religion in general and in the study of Indian religious traditions in particular.

We start with the recognition of 'dynamic process' as one of the fundamental dimensions of a religious tradition. This is a historical process and a hermeneutical process too in which we may recognise tradition, continual change and even mutation. Eric Lott writes:

> In general this mutable, processive character of religion's ongoing life has tended to be overlooked as much as it will be denied by the devotees of a tradition.[11]

Nowhere is the dynamic process so prominent as in India. But its nature needs to be defined on the basis of changes in fundamental ideas like sacrifice.

The idea and practice of *yajña* in fact is not only fundamental but also central to brāhmaṇic Hinduism. Sacrifice and the *Vedas* are the two fundamental components of the dynamic process in Hinduism. As Mircea Eliade observes, although the *Vedas* and sacrifice are pre-eminently static as primal categories "the religious history of Indo-Aryan India proves to be essentially dynamic in perpetual transformation".[12] Along with the domination of caste, Eliade points out, the hermeneutical process of the brāhmaṇic orthodoxy can be reduced to two fundamental denominators, the *Vedas* and ritual around which cohere the complexities of absorption of extra-orthodox cults and ideas which have continued to the present day. It is this complexity that makes it difficult to define Hinduism; what is possible is only working definitions. Brian Smith suggests such a working definition that "*Hinduism is the religion of those humans who create, perpetuate and transform traditions with the legitimising reference to the authority of the Veda*".[13] This legitimising reference is applicable to *yajña*, the central concern of the *Vedas*.

The next question is how far the science of religion has taken seriously such changes and the apparent tension that ensues. Although it is not our special concern, we need to be aware of the wide range of meanings attached to phenomenology and its various types.[14] Before we view its methodological assumptions, the basic attitudinal principle that phenomenology provides should be acknowledged. Though its essentialist approach is to a large extent outmoded the typology it provides helps to identify religious activities, attitudes and systems. It warns researchers, particularly those who approach religious traditions other than their own, to guard themselves from intrusion of their personal faith and value judgements. It emphasises further an impartial inquiry which requires penetrative insight into the context of the object studied and meticulous care with the sources. The nature of this process is described in many ways by different scholars. To sum up the essential characteristic of such an inquiry, it requires

> an empathetic understanding on the part of the investigating subject... in the process of 'objective' inquiry, the inquirer must strike a delicate balance between the centripetal force of empathetic identity with the object focused upon, and the centrifugal force of impartial scrutiny. The result of such balanced investigation can well be expected to be balanced conclusions.[15]

We need not enter a discussion on the nature of objectivity or phenomenological epoch or suspension of judgement here. Hindu scholars themselves express the need for objectivity. B.G. Tilak, for example, with reference to identifying the context of the *Bhagavad Gītā*, emphasises "an unprejudiced and unprepossessed mind".[16] But a comparative study of different views of the context of the *Gītā* alone may reveal the influence of personal viewpoints. Yet it should be imperative for an inquirer to be as fair and as penetrative as possible with the object of his/her study. We shall describe soon the presuppositions of the historical-hermeneutical perspective we are taking in this study.

Coming to the perspective and procedures suggested by the phenomenology of religion, it should be noted that phenomenology in general aims at "capturing the meaning of religious phenomena without committing itself to an analysis of the historical, cultural, social and psychological setting of those phenomena. It thereby neglects the study of diachronic, formative processes that give a religious phenomenon its depth and endow it with the colours of real life".[17] Nevertheless, in a modified phenomenology, the complementarity between history and phenomenology is desired. Accordingly, while the former provides data, the latter injects insights and intuition.[18] Moreover, the typology can be descriptive as well as evocative if "it can deal with types of changes and types of relationships during changes between different materials and non-religious milieu".[19] If this is developed further, we may expect studies that may bring out distinctive processes of development in understanding such religious categories as sacrifice.

As far as the historical approach to Indian religious traditions is concerned, two extreme positions need to be pointed out: ahistorical outlook and historical reductionism. The ahistorical perspective is operative on different grounds. First, there is repeated emphasis on religious experience (*anubhava*) which tends to undermine not only other dimensions of religion like ritual, and myth but also a rigorous study of historical developments.[20] At the same time, respect for reason is expressed as value judgements without in any way defining its nature and implications for the study of religion.[21] Further, it is suggested that "the Indian mind loves to retain the mystery rather than to lay it too bare. There is even a vernacular proverb which says, it is wrong to trace the ancestry of a sage or to follow up a river to its very source".[22] This is a rather typical Hindu attitude. Much study of Hinduism in India is influenced by this tendency.

Second, related to the emphasis on experience and reason in the sense of value judgements, there are those who claim for the *Gītā* perennial and universal appeal, and are not concerned about the historical questions around it. For them one can live the life and spirit of such texts without any dispute.[23] One can find such a tendency in the writings of S. Radhakrishnan, although he could not but consider historical developments some way or the other. But this view fails to define the nature of life and spirit with all its religious dimensions or to identify the tension involved in changes in the understanding of ritual or ethics and their inter-connections.

Strong emphasis on specialisation in Sanskrit has something to do with the slow maturation of scholarly inquiry into the origins of Indian thought. As Kees Bolle points out, "while among Indian scholars no strong stimulus existed for a wider interest in historical developments, for Indologists educated in Europe and America every man-hour was needed to master Sanskrit texts". The consequence, he feels, is "a feeble and round about linguistic introduction".[24] As we have already noted most studies of Indologists are loaded with linguistic analysis.

Fourth, those like Biardeau and L. Dumont, who have taken a structuralist approach reject history in principle as an inadequate guide. For them historical change is mere surface change and structural relationships are more fundamental. But this approach cannot account for changes which have inextricable relationship with historical changes in religious ideas.

Last, there is a tendency to view religious ideas as developing naturally. For example, in 1942, Franklin Edgerton suggested that concepts like *artha*, *kāma*, *dharma*, *bhakti* and *nirvāṇa* of classical

Indian culture may all be reasonably derived by *natural internal development* of the earlier Vedic culture we know. Though the possibility of the influence of other cultures on Classical Hinduism cannot be denied, he said "it is not necessary, and equally certainly it cannot be proved, because we know practically nothing about any such culture in ancient India. Speculation on the subject therefore seems to me idle".[25] In Edgerton's time there were no substantial studies on the interaction between Vedic culture and non-Vedic cultures as have been made in recent years. But if he tried to relate his examples to *yajña*, in the context of which they originated, he could identify at least certain problems in understanding their development. Further, the claim for 'natural internal development' is still made with reference, for instance, to the development of Upaniṣadic interiorisation as a logical conclusion of Vedic ritual. We shall point out later the shortcomings of this claim as it fails to recognise the tension between these two.

At the other extreme, however, there is a historical perspective which reduces the religious consciousness to social conditioning. Some historians of Indian tradition, especially those oriented to Marxian dialectical materialism, have done this. Thus, Kosambi views changes in the understanding of sacrifice from the perspective of class struggle between the brahmin priests and the laity; *bhakti* merely perpetuates feudalism; the only value of the *Gītā*, is in aesthetic pleasure derived from its beauty of expression.[26] Admittedly, religious consciousness cannot be divorced from socio-economic conditions. But to reduce it to a one-way traffic is unjustified because, first, transcendental awareness has been part of human history; second, new kinds of religious awareness have often contributed to the transformation of socio-economic conditions as we note in the development of religious traditions in India. Therefore we need to beware of reductionist tendencies when we consult the writings of people like Kosambi which may otherwise provide useful insights to making more convincing suggestions regarding the questions we have raised earlier.

In a balanced approach it is possible to avoid the temptation of ahistorical ultimate concerns on the one hand and anti-religious reductionism on the other. Both can interact in a dynamic process. As Lott points out,

> acceptance of 'historical' explanation for a religious tradition does not in itself preclude the trans-historical dimension. 'Sacred histories' are possible

along with secular histories, seen as in dynamic conjunction with the secular causal sequences in the historical process, perhaps as distinctive, meaning-shaping 'perspectives' of that secular history.[27]

Once the possibility of this conjunction is accepted, different views may be developed regarding the nature of the interaction between social change and spiritual perspectives. For example, Pande notes:

> The experience of social change and suffering is undoubtedly connected with the quest of new pathways in religion and philosophy. Social crisis, however, only indicates the need for fresh thinking without determining its nature. Social change is an "occasion" rather than a "cause" of spiritual change, providing its antecedent rather than logical reference.[28]

What is more significant for our purpose is, however, to note that only in the interaction between the causal factors of social history and spiritual perceptions new forms of interpretation become understandable.

Actually the *Gītā* may be a good example of the new interpretation of religious concepts in a dynamic conjunction of old vision and new circumstances. As a "child of historic Hinduism" the *Gītā* reflects both a period of conflicting views and the heritage of an ancient vision and practice.[29] As *smṛti* or re-expression of an ancient revelation, the *Gītā* gives a syncretic schemata to a culture that expresses a dialectical movement and concrete historical life.[30] And for an inquiry into the nature of this movement philology and the historical disciplines are "instrumental factors in understanding both the archaic language medium in which the *Gītā* was transmitted and also in recreating the intellectual milieu in which it was composed".[31] Thus, an integrated approach is promising for bringing out the integral factors that constitute a religious text like the *Gītā*. While emphasising the need of an historical approach to the Hindu religious tradition, we acknowledge the limitations of ancient Indian history. There have been many models, ideologies and perspectives in selecting the sources and interpreting the development of Indian history since the eighteenth century, first by British writers and followed by Indian and other historians.[32] Recently, the field has greatly improved by integrating different disciplines into a more comprehensive history of ancient India. Despite his tendency of reductionism, Kosambi is noted for his pioneering experiments with "an integrated approach combining the mytho-poetic literature, and interpretative methods of social anthropology, dialectical materialism and archaeological material".[33] Studies in the development of religious ideas certainly can contribute to these experiments.

One of the limitations of the study of the ancient history of India is posed by the absence of a precise chronology. Majumdar writes:

> The greatest handicap in the treatment of the history of ancient India, both political and cultural, is the absence of a definite chronology. The dates of political events and of the vast mass of literature which forms the basis of cultural study are but imperfectly known, and the farther back we recede, even the close approximations of these dates become more and more difficult and uncertain. This gives scope for endless discussions and wide differences of opinion.[34]

Another reason for the minimal use of early religious texts for historical information is that they contain material not only of different nature such as myths and legends but also of different historical periods, without giving any clear references to concrete events.

At the same time it is noteworthy that rituals and their development may provide insights for understanding history. N.N. Bhattacharyya goes so far as to say that "the study of any cult or ritual *in itself* is of no value unless it is used as a means to understand the vast and enormously complicated problems of Indian social history".[35] Scholars like Heesterman try to reconstruct ancient Indian history on the basis of certain elements found in Vedic ritual. Then it should be easier to understand historical situations from new insights provided by studies on changes in the understanding of ritual. For example, in the *Mahābhārata* we read about conflicts between ritual sacrifice and world affirmation on the one hand and interiorisation and world denial on the other; and also there is a question regarding poor people who cannot afford the performance of grand sacrifices. As we have already noted, new forms of affirming sacrifice and new types of questions concerning its practice found in the *Gītā* may give clues to the historical context of the text.

Having described the importance, prospects and limitations of a historical perspective to understand changes in Indian religious thought, it is necessary to present the important aspects that undergird such a perspective and an appropriate procedure. The following definition may give some important insights:

> The historical approach consists in the attempt to understand expressions by relating them to their historical context and to understand the whole

context by moving from expression to expression. The process of understanding expressions in their context and the process of understanding the context itself through these expressions are interdependent. The connections between the contents of expressions are themselves experienced and this experience has to be recaptured by understanding. In order to understand this experience we place expressions into different contexts, other than the ones in which they occur. We see that they are of a certain type and can place them into a classificatory context.[36]

As far as changes in the understanding of *yajña* are concerned the process is very complex; extra care is required to identify contexts and the sequence of expressions. For example, expressions for the quest of reality beyond the *yajña*-oriented Vedic world-view, allegorical interpretations of ritual and development of the sacrifice of knowledge and self, found in the *Upaniṣads,* seem to show a new phase in the history of brāhmaṇism when it encountered the earliest groups of the *śramaṇa* movement. Further moments of this encounter are more clearly evident in Buddhist and Jaina literature. The implications of this encounter for understanding socio-economic-political upheavals of 600 B.C. as pointed out by historians cannot be ignored because they make a pointed reference to sacrifice. Further, reaffirmation of Vedic sacrifice with new expressions, arguments for exempting killing of animals in sacrifice from the ban on killing in general, incorporation of new ideas and practices like *mokṣa, ahiṃsā* and *saṃnyāsa* found especially in the *Mahābhārata, Mānavadharma Śāstra* and *Bhagavad Gītā* cannot be understood clearly unless these texts are taken as addressing a new situation in the post-Vedic period, even though their chronology and inter-relationship may not be determined. Despite their distinctive characteristics these texts seem to share many things in common concerning the meaning and practice of sacrifice.

In this connection we need to point out that formulations like *puruṣārtha* and *āśrama dharma* were developed in the later phases of the post-Vedic period in the face of new challenges for the Vedic system centred around sacrifice. That they were yet in a fluid stage could be seen from the difference of opinions about their components and order of precedence. Thus the kind of synthesis attempted in this period was marked by tension and lack of coherence. These are examples of expressions that we have to understand in their context. The nature of the context will be discerned through these expressions in our inquiry into the historical process.

In the development of a religious idea the historical process is also a hermeneutical process, in which we not only arrive at the most authentic possible understanding of a tradition in its context but also study the particular nature of interpretation in the process. This has certain inevitable problems. One is a kind of tension between the interpretation of a particular religious community and the interpretation of the inquirer in the scholarly study of religion.[37] Though we are aware of this problem it need not restrict our concerns here because we are dealing with a hermeneutical process of the past without criticising that of the present. Yet we take the view that in order to understand the nature and problems of the hermeneutical process in present-day Hindu traditions, we need to identify similar processes in the past. This we try to do together with the Hindu scholars though we may be able to point out factors that have slipped their attention. The second problem is to read exactly the minds of the authors we deal with. The hermeneutical theories developed in the West in terms of different criteria for determining the correct meaning of a text[38] are hardly applicable here. We deal with different types of authors, formulations and interpretations of a religious category without questioning different meanings derived from it by the people of its tradition. This may indicate the natural limitation of an inquiry made by an outsider of the tradition studied, although this inquiry can greatly help his/her dialogic relationship with the people of the tradition concerned.

The nature of hermeneutical perspectives operative in Indian religious studies are not always clear and there is hardly any attempt to articulate them. A recent attempt in this connection is, however, remarkable though it does not represent the view of people in Hindu religious tradition. While setting an ideological background for his own interpretation of some of the fundamental aspects of the Vedic vision, R. Panikkar defines hermeneutics as " the art and science of interpretation, of bringing forth significance, of conveying meaning, of restoring symbols to life and eventually of letting new symbols emerge".[39] Further, he enumerates three types of hermeneutics. The first he calls "morphological hermeneutics" which entails the transmission of tradition and explanation by a parent or teacher. The third, "diatopical hermeneutics", is concerned with inter-cultural thematic understanding, which he himself takes up for his interpretation. The second is the most significant for our consideration. Panikkar calls it "diachronical hermeneutics" which, he says, refers to the knowledge of the context necessary in order to understand a text, because the temporal gap between the understander and that which is to be understood has obscured or even changed the meaning of the original datum. Diachronical hermeneutics also implies the problems of ideology and time. It takes the temporal factor as an intrinsic element in the process of understanding. Its method is fundamentally historical. It implies going out from my own 'stand' in order to understand another worldview. This is the proper place for dialectics: The movement here is from present to past in order to incorporate, subsume or delete it. Diachronical hermeneutics is not the youngster learning about the past from contemporaries. It is the adult firmly based in his present degree of awareness trying to enrich himself by understanding the past.[40]

This definition reaffirms some of the assumptions and procedures of an inquiry into an historical-hermeneutical process we have already outlined. But one of the problems in Panikkar's approach is that he does not provide a perspective equally acceptable to both the practitioners of Hindu religious tradition and the interpreters. He seems to combine different ideas without distinguishing their frameworks and historical background. Particularly, one may question whether an authentic "diatopical hermeneutics" can emerge without making use of the fruits of a "diachronical hermeneutics". In Panikkar's interpretations of Vedic sacrifice that is minimal if not absent. Or it may be more appropriate to say that these fruits are not adequately gained because of a lack of laborious cultivation in the field of historical studies in Indian thought. And without an historical perspective, changes in fundamental ideas like sacrifice and their influence in the present-day life of a religious tradition cannot be convincingly explained. This may call for a reppraisal of the tradition and also caution us about the confluence and coalescence of fundamentally distinctive visions, traditions and interactions.

The hermeneutical process of a particular religious tradition may have unique features even if the classical texts we deal with do not provide access to these. The post-Vedic period however seems to have experienced not only new interpretations but also reaffirmations, incorporation of new ideas and formulation of new schemes. This process seems to have lacked logical connections and serious analysis. Some new ideas may well have fitted into the old framework but not others. The idea of *ahiṃsā*, for example, is taken as an ethical principle, while killing in sacrifice and *dharmic* war is justified. More fundamentally, ritual *yajña*, *jñāna yajña*, and *bhakti yajña* are affirmed side by side though some unsuccessful attempts at connecting them may be identified. But it is clear that they carry different world-views, ideals and practices. What are put together are not different shades of meaning of a single idea or practice but essentially distinctive frameworks. This may be explained by the use of "paradigms" borrowed from science.

Thomas Kuhn talks about paradigms in relation to the structure of science. By paradigms he means to suggest that "some accepted examples of actual scientific practice—examples which include law, theory, application and instrumentation together—provide models from which spring particular coherent traditions of scientific research".[41] When a paradigm faces the crisis of social pressure, anomaly or new discovery, it may transform itself by broadening its framework. But when scientists are confronted with even severe and prolonged anomalies and are convinced by the coherence of an alternative paradigm, a shift takes place. On the part of the scientist, Kuhn calls this a conversion experience; but some may resist such shift, thinking their paradigm will finally prove to be valid. There may be overlaps between the problems of the old and the new but there will be decisive difference in the mode of solution which would demand new methods and new goals. If carefully used, Kuhn's paradigm thesis may contribute to the understanding of a religious tradition which contains a set of beliefs and practices.[42] For example, apparently ritual *yajña*, *jñāna yajña* and *bhakti* were originally undergirded by distinctive frameworks, methods and goals despite some intersection. But when the ritual *yajña* faced crisis by challenges coming from other traditions, the brāhmaṇic tradition seems to have resisted loss of an ancient vision and practice and also incorporated new ideas, and later accommodated new frameworks, as evident in the *Gītā*. We need to be aware of this distinctive position which is characteristic of Hinduism as a composite tradition when we analyse the interaction of different traditions in the question of sacrifice and the response of the *Gītā*.

Scope and Structure

Fully aware of the need to cover a long period of history and a wide range of material. I have had to set a limit to consideration of historical factors and consultation of Vedic and other texts. While focusing on the idea of sacrifice many related ideas coming from historical discussions and texts, though important otherwise, are either omitted or mentioned very briefly. Similarly, references to various sources are very selective though representative.

This book starts with the recognition of the fundamental aspects of the Vedic sacrifice and its development. Special attention is paid to the basic ideas of the authority of the *Veda, karman, brahman, tapas* and *dharma,* which have undergone a long process of acquiring new meanings. Our special task will be to see these concepts as originally arising from the context of ritual *yajña.* After a discussion on the meaning of Vedic ritual, the transcendental experience and expressed intentions are pointed out. Further, the stratification of Vedic society is mentioned in relation to sacrifice. As points to transition, certain clues for allegorical and interiorised understanding of sacrifice form the final part of the first section. This section is far from exhaustive, referring to only representative materials of the *saṃhitās, brāhmaṇas* and the ritual *sūtras* and relying more on the observation of scholars.

In the second section the *Principal Upaniṣads* (as presented by S. Radhakrishnan) are studied from the viewpoint of Vedic sacrifice. Attention is focused on the persistence of ritual, categories like *karman, brahman* and *tapas* as given a new meaning, and the nature of introspection and allegorical interpretation. A kind of stress between ritual *yajña* and *ātma yajña* is pointed out in relation to the growing prominence of the renouncer-tradition. There is, however, no treatment of philosophical views originating in the *Upaniṣads.*

The third section tries to identify major trends in the socio-economic-political history of our period and also in the development of the *śramaṇa* movement. Our focus will be on the impact on sacrificial religion. The challenges of the *śramaṇa* movement in general and that of the Buddhists, Jainas and *Ājīvikas* in particular for Vedic religion need more extensive study than we have done. The attention paid, for example, to the metaphysical positions of these groups in comparison with the Vedic world-view is deliberately minimal. Nevertheless, the reasons for the weakening of the *śramaṇa* voice at the same time that its influence on the socio-religious situation of the subsequent period grew, are sufficiently highlighted. This is followed by the *brāhmaṇic* reaction and revival which is studied with reference to the epics, in particular the *Mahābhārata,* and the *Dharmaśāstras* with particular reference to Manu. The reaction incorporated reaffirming the Vedic *yajña,* assimilating the *śramaṇa* ideals and formulating new schemes like *puruṣārtha* and *āśrama* and *dharma*. An extension of this revival, the amalgamation of *bhāgavatism* and brāhmaṇism, is given rather detailed treatment so that its significance for the study of sacrifice may become clear. This sets a background for viewing the response to the challenges indicated above in the *Gītā*.

The interpretation of *yajña* in the *Gītā* is taken up in the fourth section. After a brief discussion on the setting of the text, its *yajña* passages are presented for systematic classification and study. The affirmation by the *Gītā* of Vedic *yajña* in novel ways, accommodation of new practices and ideas, and interpretation of sacrifice through the *triguṇa* scheme of *Sāṃkhya* are dealt with in detail. Then the understanding of action *(karman)* in the *Gītā* in relation to sacrifice is taken for discussion. New ways of understanding the ideal of *niṣkāma karman* are suggested in the context of the *Gītā* and its affirmation of Vedic sacrifice. This is followed by an analysis of *jñāna yajña* in the *Gītā* and in the *Upaniṣads*. Further, different ways of relating sacrifice to *bhakti* and integrating various types of sacrifice with the supreme power of God are identified. There will be a discussion on the interconnections between various types of sacrifices and powers and on the nature of synthesis attempted in the *Gītā*.

Finally, in the conclusion, a summary of our procedure and findings is given which is followed by the mention of certain salient features of the hermeneutical process we have inquired into.

NOTES

1. Throughout this book 'sacrifice' translates '*yajña*' unless otherwise specified.
2. *Numen*, XIX/1 (1972), pp. 52-67.
3. *JOIUB*, XXVI/1 (1976), pp. 11-17.
4. *ABORI*, LXVI (1985), pp. 47-61.
5. *Le Sacrifice Dans l'Inde Ancienne*, Paris, 1976.
6. For a review of Biardeau's approach, see James Laine, "Hinduism and Mahābhārata—A Review", *WZKSAIP*, XXX (1986), pp. 73-81.
7. *Bhagavad Gītānuvāda, A Study in Transcultural Tradition*, Ranchi, 1983.
8. George Feuerstein, *Introduction to the Bhagavad Gītā: Its Philosophy and Cultural Setting*, London, 1974, p.16.
9. "Religion und Riten Die Opferlehre der *Bhagavad Gītā*", *ZKT*, 73 (1951), pp.170-213.
10. *AS*, 2 (1965), pp. 283-92.

11. E.J. Lott, *Vision, Tradition, Interpretation—Theology, Religion and the Study of Religion*, Berlin, 1988, p. 31.
12. M. Eliade, *Yoga: Immortality and Freedom*, London, 1958, p.113.
13. B.K. Smith, "Exorcising the Transcendent: Strategies for Defining Hinduism and Religion", *HR*, 27/1 (1987), p.40.
14. For different classifications of various types of phenomenology, see Ninian Smart, *Science of Religion and Sociology of Knowledge*, Princeton, 1973, p. 20ff; J. Wardenburg, *Reflections on the Study of Religion*, The Hague, 1978, p.105f,119f; Ursula King, "Historical and Phenomenological Approaches to the Study of Religion" in *Contemporary Approaches to the Study of Religion*, ed. F. Whaling, vol.1: Humanities, Berlin, 1984, pp. 29-164.
15. Julius Lipner, "Theology and Religious Studies" in *The Threshold of Theology*, ed. Paul Avis, Hants, 1988, p. 155.
16. B.G. Tilak, *Śrīmad Bhagavad Gītā Rahasya or Karma-Yoga-Śāstra*, Bombay, 1935, p. xxivf.
17. Ugo Bianchi, "History of Religions", in *ER*, 6, p. 400.
18. For the attempt of R. Pettozoni to develop such complementarity, see M. Dhavamony, *Phenomenology of Religion*, Rome, 1973, p.10f.
19. N. Smart, *Science of Religion*, p.156f.
20. For such an emphasis, remarkably by Indian scholars, see Harbans Singh ed., *Approaches to the Study of Religion*, Patiala, 1971.
21. For Gandhi's claim for reason combined with prayerful study and experience, see Callewaert and Hemraj, *Bhagavad Gītānuvāda*, p. 50.
22. Nataraja Guru, *The Bhagavad Gītā*, Bombay, 1961, p. 4.
23. See Gallewaert and Hemraj, *op.cit.*, p. 49f.
24. K. Bolle, "Sat and Asat in the BhG", *JSBhG*, IV (1984), p. 5.
25. F. Edgerton, "Dominant Ideas in the Formation of Indian Culture", *JAOS*, 62 (1942), p.155.
26. See D.D. Kosambi, *The Culture and Civilization of Ancient India in Historical Outline*, New Delhi, 1976, p. 209.
27. Lott, *op. cit.*, p.161.
28. G.C. Pande, *Studies in the Origins of Buddhism*, Delhi, 1983, p. 311.
29. A.L. Herman, *The Bhagavad Gītā—A Translation and Critical Commentary*, Springfield, 1973, p. ix.
30. For an enlightening discussion on the hermeneutical role of the *Gītā*, see P. Bilmoria and J.V. D'Cruz, "The *Bhagavad Gītā*: A Perspective of Text, Tradition and Transformation", *JSBhG*, V-VII (1985-87), pp. 51-81.
31. Callewaert and Hemraj, *BhG ānuvada*, p. 53.
32. See Romila Thapar, *Ancient Indian Social History, Some Interpretations*, New Delhi, 1978, pp.1-25.
33. M.J. Shendge, "The Inter-Disciplinary Approach in Indian Studies", *ABORI*, LXIII (1982), p. 93; also see Kosambi, "Combined Methods

in Indology". *IIJ*, VI (1962-63), pp.177-202.

34. R.C. Majumdar, ed., *The History and Culture of Indian People*, 1. Vedic Age, London, 1951, p. 43.
35. N.N. Bhattacharyya, *Ancient Indian Rituals and their Social Contents*, London, 1975, p. 25.
36. M. Dhavamony, *Phenomenology of Religion*, 1973, p. 21.
37. See Harvey, "Hermeneutics", *ER*, 6, p. 280.
38. For a useful summary of the theories of Schliermacher, Dilthey, Heidegger and Gadamar, see *ibid.*, p. 284f.
39. R. Panikkar, *Myth, Faith and Hermeneutics*, New York, 1979, p. 8.
40. *ibid.*, p. 8f.
41. T.S. Kuhn, *The Structure of Scientific Revolution*, Chicago, 1970, p.10.
42. For the shortcomings of this thesis if applied, for example, to theology, see Cordell Strug, "Kuhn's Paradigm Thesis: A Two-edged Sword for the Philosophy of Religion", *RS*, 20 (1984), pp. 269-79.

I

Vedic *Yajña*: Its Form, Power and Meaning

1. Introduction

Sacrifice (*yajña*) is so central to Vedic religion that the Vedic Aryans may be called "people of sacrifice".[1] It is the "ruling image of the Vedic texts and Vedic life".[2] Life in the Vedic home and society centred around the performance of sacrifice. Significantly, the seeds of the fundamental ideas of the Indian religious tradition like *dharma, karman, brahman,* and *tapas* lie in the sacrificial ritual of the Vedic cult.

As "the celebration of existence itself in its various powers, transformations and mysteries"[3] or "the fundamental law that regulates absolutely everything",[4] Vedic sacrifice is very distinctive. Therefore, it cannot be simply categorised by any one of the phenomenological theories of sacrifice like communion meal, gift-offering, exchange of the means of life, expiation for sin, totemic union, and diversion of violence, though some discussions on these refer selectively to certain elements of Vedic sacrifice.[5] Nor can it be identified with a particular type of ritual such as mythic and iconographic enactment, life-ennobling ritual, rites of passage, crisis remover or purificatory rites, although elements of some of these may be found in some forms of the Vedic ritual.[6] Recognition of the unique nature of the Vedic sacrifice is important for understanding its transformation in post-Vedic times.

Sacrifice is presented in a complex way in the *saṃhitā* and *brāhmaṇa* parts of the *Vedas* and ritual *sūtras.* Mythical stories, formulas and various descriptions of riual procedures make a comprehensive understanding of Vedic sacrifice very difficult. As far as the notions underlying different types of sacrifice are concerned, however, there is a "unity".[7] The purpose of this section is to identify these notions without reproducing the details of the different types of ritual and procedures of their performance. A development of complicated Vedic ritual from simple forms is noticeable. We shall, first, recognise such forms and the major components of their development. Second, we shall attempt to identify in the performance of Vedic sacrifice the fundamental sources regarded as generating sacred or magical power. Next we will try to present the manifold meaning of sacrifice along with a brief discussion on the nature of these meanings, and then show how sacrifice is important for understanding the stratification of Vedic society. Finally, we refer to early glimpses of the process of interiorisation of ritual and opinions about their sources. A recognition of the major aspects of Vedic sacrifice in this way would provide a basis for understanding the post-Vedic developments of sacrifice.

2. Development of Vedic Sacrifice

Theories about the original form of Vedic sacrifice are highly conjectural. The *Vedas* seem to preserve a mystery around the development of sacrifice. Particularly, the *Brāhmaṇas*, in which the development culminates, speak of sacrifice almost in terms of a primal revelation. Devasthali notes: "The *Brāhmaṇas* say nothing about its origin as such. They speak only of its discovery, recovery, re-establishment, or replenishment by gods generally or by some individual deities... or even by *ṛṣis*."[8] There are, however, dim glimpses which have led scholars to make different suggestions about the original form of Vedic sacrifice. Let us consider a few.

There are those who find the origin of Vedic sacrifice in fire-worship because of the importance given to fire in its performance which resembles the fire-worship prevalent among Iranians or Zoroastrians.[9] Another reference is with the Vedic horse sacrifice as borrowed by Babylonians from the Indo-Iranians.[10] Besides, connections are made between the Vedic fire-altar and the platforms of fire-altar found in the Indus Valley.[11] The evidence for explaining the original form from which the complex Vedic ritual developed is, however, too faint for serious consideration.

Another theory is that the Vedic sacrifices were originally inseparable aspects of the "primitive productive technique" related to agriculture and fertility. N.N. Bhattacharyya who has proposed this theory points out references to the importance of food in the Vedic texts.[12] Again there is no conclusive evidence for this theory.

More provokingly, J.C. Heesterman has suggested that the preclassical form of sacrifice was structured by the struggle of the

Aryan settlers. Accordingly, the consecrated sacrificer (*dīkṣita)* was originally a consecrated warrior who ventured out in the lean season to recoup his wealth by raids, contests and battles. The pivot of this violent struggle was an animal sacrifice in which guests were entertained and gifts distributed. This was equated with the cyclical rebirth of the sacrificer in which he shed on to his guests and rivals the impurity accruing from his engagement in violence and killing. There were such contests for the goods of life (agonistic festivals) sponsored and arranged in a ceremonial way. Thus this was a life-giving ritual but marred by death and destruction. But in the course of changes in the social and economic structures, Heesterman thinks, a radical reformation, "an axial breakthrough", took place which replaced the sacrificial contest that had involved violence and dependence by a system of ritual in which the opposites were absorbed and death overcome. He points out survivals of the above battle contest in the forms of rivalry, races, cattle raids, games of dice and verbal contests which are included in royal sacrifices. The process of ritualisation in which independence and individualisation become increasingly prominent has, for Heesterman, its logical conclusion in renunciation. On this assumption he attempts an explanation of renunciation emerging within the ritual tradition. So his rereading of Indian history.[13] Heesterman's theory, however, is criticised as an imaginative construct which lacks objective literary evidence and perspective.[14] We shall have occasion in this study to refer to some useful insights of Heesterman with an awareness of his ambiguous theory of ritual.

Coming to the Vedic texts, as evident in the earliest *saṃhitās*, the essential form of the sacrifice seems to be very simple: food and drink were offered to gods who were invited with praise and prayer to partake of them.[15] Thomas Hopkins calls this a "hospitality rite to the gods" which was probably the simplest and earliest form of Indo-Iranian sacrifice.[16] This hospitality was later extended to other beings also like humans, ancestors, the expression of which may be found in the five great sacrifices (*pañcamahāyajñas*). The earlier form required simple items like the establishment of fire, arrangement of grass seats and the oblations of milk, ghee, grains, cakes and the flesh of certain animals. Mostly the performance took place in the home.

But this simplicity disappeared in the course of further developments in the history of Aryans. The following verse seems to reflect this development: "Sacrifice was manifest among us; it sprang to life and then in time grew stronger. Then it became the deities' lord and ruler."[17] A passage gives an account of the discovery of the great fire-altar, layer by layer, done by gods and seers.[18] There are references to the "running away and returning" of the sacrifice that suggest fluctuations in the development of sacrificial religion.[19] The climax of this development was a complicated and elaborate system of ritual sacrifice which was considered to be "the creative first principle" and the "action *par excellence*".[20] The well-ordered sacrifice was conceived as a kind of machinery and an organism like the human body in which every part must tally with other parts. M. Haug writes:

> The term for beginning the sacrificial operations is "to spread the sacrifice"; this means that the invisible thing, representing the ideal sacrifice which was lying dormant, as it were, is set into motion, in consequence of which its several parts or limbs are unfolding themselves, and thus the whole becomes extended.[21]

This may have some connection with the socio-economic development of the Vedic Aryans. R.N. Dandekar observes:

> Towards the end of the *saṃhitā* period, Vedic Aryans had, by and large, become politically stable, economically secure, and socially organized. The transition from a toilsome, adventurous, nomadic life to a life of household comfort and leisure did not fail to influence their religion—more particularly their religious practices.[22]

We do not, however, have clear evidence to determine the nature of this change. It is difficult to discern its sequences since there is no chronology traceable in the *saṃhitā* and *brāhmaṇa* texts and the *śrauta* and *gṛhya sūtras.*[23] It stands to reason, however, that in the course of the mobility and migration of the Aryan tribes there was continual assimilation of local and popular cultic elements into the sacrifice cult.[24] Particularly, ambiguous practices like abusive language and sexual union, which certain forms of sacrifice involved, are attributed to the influence of the non-Aryan cults.[25] Moreover, when different rites were assimilated in different communities they were unified by the *Brāhmaṇas*; consequently sacrificial ritual became even more complicated. Gonda writes:

> Some traditional rites were in brahmanic circles, adapted, enlarged, combined, legalized, systematized and subjected to a theoretical interpretation, while other practices being rejected by the same authorities were to survive and develop in other milieus.[26]

Without going into the details of such developments, we shall identify the major components of the Vedic ritual in its developed form.

1. The most fundamental characteristic in the form of a sacrifice is its ritual law or order—the order of its performance. The *Ṛgveda* speaks about the "order" of movements and "furnishing" of sacrifice.[27] Extreme care needs to be exercised in handling the vessels and implements. "Thus it is that even the ropes, the brooms, and their numbers have been carefully recorded, the materials of which they were made, their size and their functions prescribed with the same thoroughness as the crushing of the *soma*-juice or the coronation of the king".[28] Although divergent views are presented pertaining to certain procedural matters,[29] once a particular authority's or group's opinion is accepted it has to be followed strictly. The *śrauta sūtras* try to avoid the controversies of the *Brāhmaṇas* and give a concise and systematic description of the rituals, apparently with partial success.[30] The repeated concern is that there should neither be anything in excess nor deficient in the performance. Error in the order, however small, would spoil the effect of the sacrifice. As Basu notes, "Sacrifice is a dreaded god and spares none if a serious flaw or breach of propriety occurs".[31]

The remedy for unavoidable faults in a performance of ritual is atonement (*prāyascitta*), a counter-ritual to be performed by the physician and superintendent of the ritual, i.e. the brahmin priest.[32] By atonement wrong is not only set right, "It is as good as not committed at all".[33] The significance of order in ritual lies in the notion that it is closely connected with the order of the universe, as we shall see later. The concern for the ritual order made the ritual extremely complex and a costly affair which was possible for wealthy patrons alone.

2. Unlike the simple oblations used in the earlier forms, large numbers of animals were required for grand sacrifices. Their numbers would vary according to the capacity of the sacrificer (*yajamāna*).[34] The killing of the animal was usually represented euphemistically as "quieting" or "strangulating" the animal.[35] Moreover, traces of human sacrifice tell of its existence in Vedic sacrifice at one stage.[36] There are indications, however, about its gradual disappearance from the ritual scene. According to a *Brāhmaṇa* text the sacrificial essence was transferred from a human sacrifice to vegetables and grains passing through animals. But the text mentions this

account not for the abolition of animal sacrifice but to suggest animal substitutes for human victims.[37] Further, undue destruction of animals affected the economy of a pastoral community. This was realised with greater force at a later stage.[38]

3. Priesthood was another important development. In earlier forms the sacrificer or the householder (*yajamāna*) performed the sacrifice on his own. His wife or the first one in case of many wives played an important role in the performance.[39] Though this practice continued in certain domestic ceremonies, the elaborate rituals required many skilled professionals. In the *soma* sacrifices, for example, seventeen priests were attendant.[40] Though the wives or queens had to take part, they did so under the direct guidance of the priests. Further, in due course a wide variety of popular religious practices were added to the priestly rituals, while domestic ceremonies were altered to conform to priestly standards. And also priestly training was more specialised along with the development of different priestly traditions.[41]

Dakṣiṇā (sacrificial fee) was the main income and benefit of the priests. The efficacy of the sacrificial performance was regarded as dependent on generous fee for the priests. Besides, *dāna* (gift) was given to the priests in various kinds like cattle, gold and clothes. The *dānaśtuti* hymns praise the liberal donors and these and other praises were recited by the priests to please them.[42] There are prescriptions of eligibility, procedures etc. to give and receive *dāna*. *Dakṣiṇā* and *dāna* were part of the gift-exchange system of the Vedic Aryans.[43]

4. There are mythical episodes which describe the heavenly origin of sacrifice.[44] They try to show how the ancient seers and gods found the sacrifice and how they sacrificed. Many rituals are said to follow what happened in ancient times and in heaven. Gonda observes: "They explain how a rite originated, why a ritual act is to be performed in a definite way, what is its effect, why a definite utensil should be used, what is the significance and result of definite practices and so on."[45] Renou asserts that the explanations in myths and the connections they try to make are unintelligible; they are fabricated by the priestly minds.[46] A repeated scene in the mythological episodes is the battles of *devas* and *asuras* (demons) over sacrifice at Kurukṣetra which was originally a central sacrificial ground.[47] Further, some texts give different accounts of the same mythological story.

5. Formulas, *mantras* and other utterances play an important role in the structure of ritual performance. Weber notes: "The more sacred the sacrificial performance grew, and the more fixed the form of worship gradually became, the greater became the importance of the prayers belonging to it, and the stronger their claim to the utmost possible purity and safety".[48]

Ritual speech (*vāc*) is different from ordinary speech; it is identical with order (*ṛta*) and truth (*satya*) and only the priests, by the power of *māyā* can use it.[49] In Gonda's words,

> Especially when they combined into formulae, into phrases definite in the sound, rhythm and order of their terms, words possessed might and effect whether dangerous or beneficent. Hence the ancient Indian belief that *mantras*, including not only the verses of the *Saṃhitās* but also the formulae of the *Yajur Veda*, are flash-lights of eternal truth (cf. ŚB. 7,1,1,5), seen and formulated by the *ṛṣis* of yore; that they are sacred and inherently powerful.[50]

Different types of utterances are used: utterances of the *adhvaryu* to establish potent identities, of the *hotri*, praising and inviting gods for feast, or the *yajamāna's* prayers for fulfilling his desires.[51] Also, in the recitation of *mantras* particular tones and pauses are significant.[52] Besides, there are particular utterances to keep the *asuras* away from the ritual and to atone for errors in performance.

6. The ultimate authority of the *Veda* is accepted in relation to the value of its verses for sacrifice. The *Vedas* were regarded coexistent with the sacrifice.[53] The *śruti* texts, i.e., the *Vedas*, are considered as timeless (*sāśvata*), non-personal (*apauruṣeya*) and transcendental (*parādvidyā*). They are the container of all truth and are omniscient. The stimulus to perform sacrifice comes from the commands of the *Vedas*, however unintelligible certain rules may be. Dasgupta says: "Instead of God we find here a body of commands which demand our obedience and reverence; but the source of their power and the secret of their omniscient character and uncreatedness cannot be determined by us through reason or experience".[54] Further, with reference to the mysterious omnipotence of sacrifice performed by following the authoritative injunctions of the *Vedas* independently of reason, he says: "There is nothing here of feeling or even of intellect, but a blind submission, not to a person but to an impersonal authority which holds within it an unalterable and inscrutable law, the secret of all powers which we may want to wield in our

favour".[55] It is interesting to note that according to the ritual exponents the *Vedas* are exclusively *mantras* and *Brāhmaṇas* which give guidelines to the performance of sacrifice and form the liturgy involved in it.[56]

7. In close relation to the notion of the eternal authority of the *Veda*, we need to acknowledge the idea of Vedic knowledge about correspondence established by sacrifice. As we have already noted, the Vedic ritual was conceived to have equivalents with cosmic potencies. Hence the need for skilled professionals who know the minute details corresponding to the universal elements. "Thus one of the outstanding characteristics of ancient Indian thought was a persistent adherence to the quest for knowledge of the mutual connection of all reality, power, for knowledge of the inherent causality of things".[57] Further, Gonda says:

> "Knowledge" (*vidyā*) itself had a practical aim; it was a means of attaining aims and realizing wishes, a key to difficulties and mysteries, a way to accomplishment of difficult tasks or to successful completion of extraordinary performances. The importance of instructions and study of the sacred texts is therefore repeatedly insisted upon...[58]

Thus Vedic knowledge is primarily sacrificial or ritual knowledge, and *ācāryas*, in ancient India, because of their mastery of *Veda* and expertise in ritual, attracted *brahmacārins*, students, for rigorous learning of the *Vedas* and rituals.[59] It was this learning that prepared a twice-born member of the Vedic society for fruitful household life.

8. The introduction of austere practices into ritual was apparently a significant moment in the development of Vedic sacrifice. About the probable source of these practices we shall see later. Hopkins points to the assimilation of ascetic techniques such as fasting, silence and isolated stay to increase the effectiveness of the ritual. In this light alone we can understand clearly the *tapas* of the *dīkṣita*, the consecrated sacrificer, his breath-control etc. which are attached to gods as well.[60] Besides the recognition of the fact that ascetic techniques and practices were increasingly introduced into the sacrificial cult, Kaelber also demonstrates "in the career of the *brahmacārin*, an assimilation, indeed a homology", "effected between ascetic practice and the orthodox conception of sacrifice".[61] He points out many ascetic parallels in the initiatory rite (*upanayana*) and the hermitage life of the *brahmacārin*. He also finds in the

brahmacārin, the forerunner of later *saṃnyāsa āśrama*. The problems related to this aspect we shall consider when we discuss the source of interiorisation and the system of four *āśramas*.

Before we conclude this section, three more points must be mentioned. In the foregoing passages we have identified only the most significant components in the development of an elaborate form of Vedic sacrifice. Many auxiliary developments may be identified if one looks into the details of the process. As regards notions about gods or God, they are taken up for discussion later. Second, it must be acknowledged that there was a constant struggle to summarise the complex components of Vedic sacrifice and render them intelligible. A *Sūtra* verse, for example, says that a sacrifice is constituted by material (*dravya*), deity (*devata*) and a renunciation (*tyāga*) of the former in favour of the latter.[62] It is not difficult to see that this simple definition omits important components like *mantras* and priesthood. Third, one distinctive characteristic of Vedic sacrifice is that it is predominantly the performance of an individual, not of a community, although there are clues that it developed from early forms of collective sacrifices. As Heesterman observes,

> communal or collective rituals are absent from the Vedic *corpus rituale*. They are even rejected. The *yajamāna*, assisted only by his brahmin experts, performs the ritual alone, at his own cost and for his own benefit. There is clearly an unresolved tension here between universal order and individual enterprise.[63]

So also the communion meal is absent in Vedic sacrifice. Although certain domestic ceremonies include sharing of food with others, and royal sacrifices include giving of gifts as an important item, within the sacrifice itself there is no communion meal with gods and fellow humans. The sacrificer and priest consume a part of the offering but, as Uma Vesci points out, "this act of theirs remains marginal with respect to the very essence of sacrifice, which precisely consists in the offering of the victim in almost its entirety. The part which is destined for them, in any case, is the remnant (*ucchiṣṭa*) and not a "portion" in the same sense as that destined to the Divinity".[64] This *ucchiṣṭa* or leavings of sacrifice was later considered a personified force in which rest all powers like name, form, heaven, earth and gods. Also there is a warning for those who are tempted not to wait for it lest they should lose all effects of the sacrifice.[65]

The development of Vedic sacrifice seems to be a complex process. It is not possible to identify a particular development in relation to an historical moment. It is reasonable to assume, however, that this development took place in the course of the mobility and settlement of the Vedic Aryans and their interaction with other ethnic groups and cults.

3. Power and its Generators in Sacrifice

The power of sacrifice is closely related to its form. We have already seen some element of power connected with orderly ritual and sacred utterance. In this section we shall examine the nature of power in sacrifice and the generators of power in the performance of sacrifice.

The *Yajur Veda* declares that all power to our life and to the vital organs like lungs, eyes, ears, and other parts is through sacrifice.[66] It is a conquering power bestowed on gods and human beings in the performance of sacrifice. It is creative power that permeates the whole universe. Its functions are mysterious. Though this power is understood as sacral, scholars of Vedic studies like A.B. Keith find elements of magic in the notion of power in sacrifice.[67] Hopkins points out that the mimetic or imitative magic relies on the establishment of identities between the ritual order and the phenomenal order. He says, "This is magic indeed on the largest possible scale, only for highly skilled practitioners".[68]

As we have seen, he also thinks that this idea was the result of the gradual synthesis of popular religious practice and sacrificial cult that may be seen most clearly in the *Atharva Veda*. It is to be noticed that this power is attached to all the implements in the performance of a sacrifice. The effect of the power remains even in the preparatory acts and post-sacrificial rites of the sacrificer. Although sacred or magical power springs from the whole of sacrificial performance we may identify three vital centres from which it emanates, *karman*, *brahman*[69] and *tapas*. In certain ritual texts these and related terms occur together.[70] We shall take them one by one for a brief discussion.

(i) Karman

The origin of the idea of *karman* lies in Vedic ritual. It denotes a careful act with knowledge of the minute connections it makes in sacrifice. Panikkar calls this sacred and creative action and Heesterman calls it a definite act, and the prototypical act.[71] The *Śatapatha Brāhmaṇa* calls *yajña* the greatest of all actions.[72] In one of its cosmogonic myths, with reference to the power of *karman* in *agnicayana,* it is described as one of the primordial vital elements that evolved from mind, speech, breath, eye and ear:

This *karman,* when created, wished to become manifest,—more defined, more substantial: it sought after a self. It practised *tapas.* It acquired consistency. It beheld thirty-six thousand Arka-fires of its own self, composed of *karman,* built up of (or by) *karman:* by *karman* they were established, and by *karman* built up; by *karman* the cups were drawn there at; by *karman* they chanted and recited hymns on them,—whatever rite is performed at the sacrifice, whatever sacrificial rite there is, that was performed by *karman* alone, as a *karman*-performance, on those (fires) composed of *karman,* and built up of *karman* ... so great is *karman.*[73]

According to the *Atharva Veda,* in primordial times *karman* and *tapas* were existent in the depths of the great billowy sea; *tapas* sprang up from *karman.* The gods worshipped and served *karman* as supreme.[74] As a personification of "all actions" one of the Vedic gods is Viśvakarman.

The effect of *karman* lies, as we have noted earlier, in the perfect performance of sacrifice. There are four elements distinguished, but not separated, in a ritual action: *kriya* (the act), *karman* (the action), *kartṛ* (the actor) and *kārya* (the acted). There is an inner power that connects them together so that the single act becomes the sum of all.[75] Thus it came to be regarded as the most excellent and productive act.[76] Ritual *karman* was believed to generate power independently; and there was a tendency, among those who understood the labyrinth of sacrifice, to misuse and manipulate it. We shall see later how the term *karman* carried wider and general meanings of action.

(ii) Brahman

The original meaning of the word *brahman* is much disputed. Gonda in his *Notes on Brahman* has made an extensive study of the various meanings of *brahman.* With reference to the occurrences of this term in the *Ṛgveda,* he notes that

The term generally applies to power or powerful objects or concepts connected with the ritual, the priests and the gods. But it is also obvious that its meanings represent only facets or manifestations of an idea which is more general than "sacred word", stanza, hymn or rite, ritual, potency etc., which is even more comprehensive than these objects added together, and that these objects are designated by the same name because they all participate in or partake of that important and central concept.[77]

Of all manifestations of this overall power, however, Gonda admits, words or sacred utterances which have connotations of charm and prayer were the most prominent as evident in the Vedic texts of ritual. Relatedly, he incorporates into this concept what Renou called the "ritual-cosmic enigma", the mysterious power created in ritual to control the cosmic forces, as one manifestation of the sacred power.[78] It is this aspect, namely, the sacred word or prayer (*brahman*) with which we are concerned.

Van Buitenen also identifies the central meaning of *brahman* as the sacred word which he calls solemn utterance, the creative word *par excellence*, the epitome of all speech and the verbal counterpart of the substance of the universe which was used by consecrated persons at appropriate rites.[79] For the brāhmaṇic ritualists *brahman* as sacred utterance meant cosmic power of the first magnitude and omnipotence. It is "the mystic power inherent in the holy word".[80] The priests who knew *brahman* in fact knew how to control the whole universe. As "the soul of sacrifice, a hidden or magical energy"[81] *brahman* became one of their main instruments of cosmic control.

A few references to *brahman* in the Vedic texts are in order. *Brahman* sprang from the loftiest point of the universe and its power was unmatched, plentiful and auspicious.[82] It exalts and pleases the gods: the gods (especially Indra) are not pleased with prayerless sacrifice because they are strengthened, along with oblations, by *brahman*.[83] Since the word or speech, once it has been uttered, has an existence and a power of its own, "It can be offered in sacrifice, and can strengthen a god, just as an offering of food strengthens him".[84] By accompanying *karman* and *tapas*, *brahman* upholds the earth.[85] As holy power it is equated with gods, the *Vedas*, sacred syllables and the vital airs.[86] *Brahman* as a formula is a slayer of evil powers and it renders the air free from danger and injury.[87] Thus *brahman*, the sacred utterance, generates sacred power in Vedic ritual.

Related to *brahman* as holy utterance or prayer, there are some important notions that draw our attention. One such notion concerns the power of speech (*vāc*) about which mention has already been made. Here it is important to recognise the notion of the innate power of words pronounced by priests at the performance of the sacrifice which can be directed for either construction or destruction.[88] Vācaspati, the Lord of speech "was granted priestly status along with Agni. Even speech itself was deified as the goddess *vāc* and took its place among the great divine powers of the developed Vedic system".[89] The *mantras* established the basic identities and correspondences and "examining the speech used in the sacrificial ritual would reveal the underlying structure of reality".[90] The *Aitareya Brāhmaṇa* calls *vāc* "life seed"; it also mentions the creation of the *praṇava oṃ (aum)* by the brooding of Prajāpati over the pure sounds of the *Vedas*.[91] Killingley thinks that *oṃ* may have been first expressed in ritual as a form of suppressed speech by priests.[92] Later, *oṃ* came to be regarded as the repository of power and the seed of all *mantras*.

Another notion is the power of sound. "Distinctions between both gods and powers were related to variations in the metres and sounds of *mantras*; the sound form was all important, since from it everything else could be produced."[93] The sound forms include loud utterance, muttering of formulas and silent rehearsal of most esoteric connections.[94] In this connection another term needs to be mentioned. It is *japa*, a form of recitation which has an affinity with low and silent sound forms. It points out the mysterious inner essence of sacred reality, the mystery of silence, which is parallel to the mystery of the origins of life.[95] *Japa* or the muttering of a formula is said to be a hidden sacrifice just as the oblation is the manifest sacrifice.[96] The gods love the mysterious and dislike the unsubtle.[97] *Japa* is one form of *brahman* that silently generates mysterious power in sacrifice.

Besides, the term *brahman* is extended to or identical with the *Brāhmaṇas*, the ritual manuals of the *Vedas*; with brahmin priests who possess the power of ritual; with the brahmin as guardian and superintendent of sacrifice; with *brahmacārin*, the Vedic student who is filled with holy power and knowledge; with Bṛhaspati or Brahmaṇaspati, the Vedic god of holy utterance or prayer, and with *Brahmā*, who represents the personal aspect of reality. Finally, there are traces in the *Vedas* of *brahman* as the basic cosmic principle or self-existent reality, which was developed further in the Upaniṣads.[98] The meaning of *brahman* as holy power and holy utterance, however, continued.

(iii) Tapas

The original meaning of *tapas* as heat comes from the context of Vedic sacrifice. It starts from the importance given to fire (*agni*) in rituals. There is no sacrifice without fire. The three sacred fires, established in three directions for use in ritual, are contradistinct from the ordinary or profane fire of the home.[99] Fire purifies and transforms the sacrificer and conveys his oblations to gods. The god Agni, the personification of fire, is the first to be invoked in every sacrifice because he is the heavenly high priest (*purohita*) and the mediator. As Hopkins points out,

> Agni on the three altars is present in his three forms as the terrestrial, celestial and aerial fires, bringing the three worlds together in the sacred sacrificial plot ... present in all the worlds and identified with all the gods. Agni as the unifying physical power in the sacrifice was supreme.[100]

In particular the *agnihotra, darsapūrṇamāsa* and *agnicayana* glorify Agni by giving him the most prominent place in their rituals.[101]

Another form of creative heat lies in the cooking of offerings. Vesci identifies calorific heat (*tapas*) as the central and the most dynamic element in Vedic sacrifice. The preparation and cooking of offerings "produces so much energy, the means of the heat innate in the act itself".[102] The power of calorific heat is the sacrifice in the sacrifice or the end of the sacrifice.[103] Relatedly, there is the idea in the cosmogonic myths that the primordial generative principle was *tapas* which created desire (*kāma*), another primordial principle.[104] The *tapas* in the ritual was believed to have correspondence with the activities of gods, the heat of the sun which draws water from the earth and produces rain just as heated vessels produce boiling liquid, and so on. It also has parallels in mental concentration, devotional fervour and physical activity, the combination of which is evident in the sweat of the priests in the sacrificial enclosures.

> The priest who toiled and sweated in the sacrificial performance thus manifested in his own person the same heat, the same *tapas*, that is the effective power of both the sacrifice and the sun, in which he participated ritually by his actions in the sacrifice and physically by his self-generated *tapas*.[105]

We shall have opportunity later to mention the increasing emphasis given to self-generated heat or interior *tapas*. It suffices to note here that *tapas* in the sacrifice, produced by fires and cooking, is one of the fundamental generators of power. It transforms the participants in sacrifice, taking them to a transcendent plane. To symbolise their return to normal condition, as David Knipe describes, there were cooling objects placed on the hearth of sacrifice and special baths prescribed for the participants at the end of its performance.[106] The dialectic of heating and cooling kept the cycle of the *yajña*-oriented life in balance.

Thus the fundamental notion of the Vedic sacrifice is that its performance produces sacred power which could be manipulated for right or wrong uses. Of all the components of the ritual of sacrifice the generators of power, were *karman, brahman* and *tapas,* perfect ritual act, sacred utterance or prayer, and ritual heat produced by fire and cooking. They indicate and reinforce the identity of means and ends and of form and conception in Vedic sacrifice.

4. The Meaning of Vedic Sacrifice: Experiences and Motives

We have already noted some of the notions centred around the performance of Vedic sacrifice. Here we shall focus our attention on the meanings derived from sacrifice by the Vedic Aryans. But how to interpret the "meaning" of the acts involved in the performance of elaborate rituals is a problem. Let us take up a recent discussion on the meaning of Vedic ritual before we proceed to see the derived meanings for life as expressed in the *Vedas.*

Although the Vedic term *yajña* is commonly used in the sense of offering something—an oblation or worship—there are different explanations about its origins.[107] And in fact if we apply this term to all Vedic rituals we cannot develop a single theory of its meanings. Does each part and act of a Vedic ritual have meaning? Fritz Staal speaks of "the meaninglessness of ritual".[108] He explains this statement with a sole reference to *Agnicayana,* and the building of a fire-altar for which he did field-work in Kerala in 1975.[109]

Staal first reviews the known theories of ritual as transitional medium from the realm of the profane to that of the sacred, as re-enactment of myth, as transmitter of cultural and social values for forthcoming generations, as rites of passage, paradigm structures or expression of neurotic obsessions.[110] Although these apply in a limited way to Vedic ritual, on the whole, for him these theories have neglected Vedic ritual and are reductionist. He holds that the widespread assumption that ritual consists of symbolic activities referring to some external meaning, is erroneous. The characteristics of a ritual performance are that it is self-contained and self-absorbed. Staal writes:

> The performers are totally immersed in the proper execution of their complex tasks. Isolated in their sacred enclosure, they concentrate on correctness of act, recitation and chant. Their primary concern, if not obsession, is with rules. There are no symbolic meanings going through their minds when they are engaged in performing ritual.[111]

He criticises the imposition of philosophical and religious ideas by those who do not know Vedic ritual. The only basis for the ritual performers, he asserts, is that it is their tradition (*parampara*). The only solution for the contradictory theories and puzzles about ritual, Staal proposes, is the hypothesis that ritual has no meaning, goal or aim. In his words: "Ritual is pure activity, without meaning or goal ... ritual is for its own sake...that is meaningless, without function, aim or goal, or also that it constitutes its own aim or goal. It does not follow that it has no value: but whatever value it has is intrinsic value".[112] He points to the formula of renouncing the fruits of action (*karma-phala-tyāga*) pronounced in certain rituals and emphasised in the *Bhagavad Gītā* in support of his view. Finally, he attempts a linguistic analysis to anchor his position. He demonstrates that syntax has a ritual origin and is older than semantics. His reference is to animals which also have rituals. As in language, there is a syntax in ritual, therefore, "the fire-altar is language, because it is constructed with language".[113] No specific desire or goal can be attached to a specific rite like *agnicayana*.

At the same time Staal does acknowledge certain side-effects of a ritual like the bond it creates, the solidarity it reinforces and the morale it boosts among the sacrificers and the link it constitutes between the sacrificers and the ancestors. But "the side-effects cannot be used to explain its preservation.... These side-effects fail to explain the most curious fact about ritual preservation: rituals are always guarded jealously and with extreme conservatism. This is directly explained by the theory that ritual has no meaning".[114] Then a ritual is constituted by traditionally prescribed rules and *mantras* which are unintelligible. They never change in form or pattern.

Staal's theory of Vedic ritual is provocative. It poses many questions. The fundamental problem concerns how one understands "the meaning of meaning". We cannot deal with this issue in detail, but a few comments on his theory from the Vedic context are in order. Staal is quite right that theories of ritual developed elsewhere, from anthropological or sociological perspectives, such as enactment of myth and rites of passage, cannot be directly applied to Vedic ritual as we have noted earlier. He is also right that there is no "meaning" available for the minute rules in a ritual or for silent utterances to be made. Nevertheless, the following concerns cannot be ignored:

1. Can we confine "meaning" only to the intellectual grasp of the

goal of a ritual? What makes one follow a family tradition regularly? The feeling for the need of an action and its connection with traditions should be sympathetically considered.

2. While Staal is critical of reductionism, he himself is not far from it. For instance, *agnicayana*, the basis of his argument, is an ancillary rite performed only by kings and chiefs. It is not typical of Vedic sacrifice. It is a composite ritual including other rites like *soma, pravargya, upasad,* and the establishment of *garhapatyāgni,* with in-built goals and desires.[115]
3. *Agnicayana* is in fact not independent of myth and symbol. The reference to the self-immolation and reconstruction of Prajāpati makes this clear. Besides, on the base of the fire-altar there is a design of the universe that symbolises its reintegration. And the shape of the altar is that of a bird facing the east, the symbol of heaven's gate.[116] Moreover, Prajāpati is identified with the sun or *agni,* and the sacrificer with the golden head placed on one of the layers of the fire-altar.

The idea of regeneration and the practice of *vrata* by the sacrificer cannot be stripped from the *agnicayana.*[117] There are symbolic actions and referential meanings involved in other rituals like the *agnistoma.*[118] With reference to the significance of sides, colours etc., Gonda notes:

> The ancients did not conceive symbols as signifying yet separate from, the concepts and power with which they are connected. They allowed the symbol and what it signifies to coalesce so that the one may stand for the other. This explains why they were convinced of the possibility of comprehending, arranging, regulating and influencing the facts and provinces of reality by means of the symbols representing these. Examples of this coalescence are not only the treating of a name as an essential part of the bearer, and the value attached and the functions allotted to kinds of woods and other requisites but also their use of and being influenced by anything relating to numbers, colours, movements, outward forms etc. Numbers, for instance, provide the key for controlling all entities united in a complex.[119]

4. While Staal emphasises the unchangeable structure of ritual, he does not acknowledge the process of its dynamic development through interaction and expansion, which we have already noted. What of modifications, or finding new substitutes for old practices, as evident in the history of brāhmaṇism?
5. The chanting in Vedic ritual includes not only "unintelligible"

mantras, but other types of utterances which are translatable, as we have pointed out.

6. The concept of *karma-phala-tyāga* is problematic. As far as the Vedic ritual is concerned there is no act without intention, and the result will come through irrespective of whether or not there are clear expressions about it in the ritual. By renouncing the fruit through a formula one in fact regained it abundantly.

If the above factors are taken seriously, Staal's theory of the meaninglessness of Vedic ritual needs more clarification. It is marked by sweeping generalisation. This is not only because the specific ritual of *agnicayana*, to a great extent, is untypical of Vedic sacrifice but also because it itself cannot be stripped of all "meanings" attached to it. We shall have more to say about this later.

Further, Staal's theory of ritual and language is not beyond dispute. In response to his provocative assertions, Hans H. Penner observes that they "are difficult to understand because we are not given further explanation concerning precisely what Staal means by "meaning", "pure activity" and "ritual for its own sake".[120] Penner acknowledges the inadequacy of a referential theory of meaning in the light of Staal's assertion that rituals have no reference. He points out that the meaning lies mainly in relations. Taking Staal's analysis of linguistics, he says that the articles "and", "the", "of", though meaningless in isolation, have their meaning constituted by the relations which define them in a sentence. Likewise, he holds, individual rituals can be meaningful if viewed in their role in a sacrificial performance.[121]

Moreover, Penner demonstrates clearly how the notion of "ritual for ritual's sake" indicates the power of romantic thought. And he picks upon Staal's statement that "syntax comes from ritual. A simple consideration in support of this idea is that animals have ritual, but not language" and underlines the fact that through rituals animals have the capacity to communicate with each other.[122] With reference to the importance of the necessary relation between thought and sound as well as between the signifier and the signified in a linguistic sign, Penner affirms that "if ritual is defined as a sign system in the context of semiotics then meaning is inherent in the system".[123] Further, viewing the extreme complexity of the *agnicayana* ritual as described by Staal himself Penner observes:

The context it is clear includes a specific time and place, numbers, forms, myths and cosmology. This should suffice as evidence that the ritual is more than a purely syntactic structure lacking significance. Moreover, the fact that all of this is done with precise rules which are not explained does not entail that the ritual is meaningless. Although the performers of the ritual may not be able to explain the rules, they do *know* when they are broken and they also *know* what is to be done when the rules are broken. The parallel between ritual and language at this point is quite striking. Language is based upon precise rules and most of us, since we are not linguists, cannot explain them. Furthermore, when the rules are broken we know how to correct the mistake without being able to explain the rules of syntax and semantics.[124]

This observation includes some of the comments we have made earlier on Staal's assertions. Moreover, it should be noted that explanation of minute details is not so essential as the rituals were believed to be of heavenly origin and related to the universal order. In the final analysis, what matters is not the explanation of rules in the ritual but the power it creates. And as in the kinship system—Penner's final illustration to show how Staal is mistaken—the participants enjoy the relationship though they do not know its rules.[125] Thus in terms of relationship, communication and signification, Vedic ritual may be taken to be full of meaning.

For Heesterman Vedic ritual is meaningless in the sense that it is highly individualised, extra-social, based on the transcendent authority of the *Vedas* and having the "insoluble problem of relating the ultramundane order of *Veda* and purity with the worldly realities of power and dominance".[126] In a response to Heesterman, Staal and others who hold the idea of "meaninglessness of ritual", Brian Smith points out the impossibility of idealisation and performance of sacrifice and the long history of giving new meanings to old ritual acts and modification in their procedure. He identifies the meaning of sacrifice in the very fact that human beings do an act with their designation for it and according to the meanings attached.

In the first place, to designate a set of actions as *"yajña"*, "sacrifice", "ritual" or anything else, is to give them meaning they otherwise do not have. Of course these actions have no intrinsic meaning—*nothing* has intrinsic meaning. This much is obvious.... Meaning is always imposed on "naturally" meaningless phenomena—this is what human beings do and must do or face chaos and insanity.[127]

Further, Smith points out that "*yajña*", for example, can signify the cosmos, and individual activities within the ritual can signify various cosmic phenomena".[128] As we shall see, there are infinite possibilities for meanings of sacrifice as evident in the new interpretation of sacrifice in post-Vedic brāhmaṇic Hinduism. Actually even in Vedic sacrifice a single act can fulfil a great variety of functions simultaneously, as we shall notice later.

Moreover, it is important to seek the meaning of Vedic sacrifice not in the explanation of every ritual act but in the "message" or a set of beliefs conveyed by the overall structure. It has a "message" to communicate in the formation of the cosmological and theological vision of the Vedic culture. Elsewhere Smith writes:

> In Vedism ritual activity at all levels does not merely "interpret", "symbolize" or "dramatize"; it constitutes, constructs and integrates. Ritual *forms* the naturally formless; it connects the inherently disconnected; and it heals the "sickness" of excess which is the state towards which all things and beings perpetually tend.[129]

Staal ridicules the so called correspondence between the ritual order and cosmic order which is for him the product of the priestly mind. But he does not recognise the notions of form and power which cannot be separated from the idea of correspondence. Further, the Vedic terms *sampad, nidāna* and *bandhu* signify not only correlation, connection and correspondence but also bond.[130] Whatever may be the problem in understanding the coherence of this bond, we need not doubt the fact that sacrificers sought to find meaning in this way.

(i) Transcendental Experience in Vedic Sacrifice

We understand transcendence not in the sense of an exclusive and inexplicable ritual performed outside the normal life situation, as noted by Heesterman,[131] but in the sense of a feeling and transformation that a sacrificer (*yajamāna*) undergoes in a ritual performance. Gonda chides those scholars who have failed to understand the important psychological and soteriological aspects of the Vedic ritual and miss the community of aims, intentions and interests of the sacrificer.[132] Here we are concerned with psychological and some sociological dimensions, leaving the rest for a separate treatment later.

The *Ṛgveda* says that *agni* is the sacrificial bond (*yajña bandhu*) with human beings.[133] Thus the Aryans were bound with *yajña* which led them to have mysterious experiences through *agni* or its heat. Knipe holds that brāhmaṇism declares its response to life revealed as *myterium tremendum...* but a mysterium with verbal handles. Existence is decidedly mysterious, for the gods as well as for men and the religious reply to the holy that is manifest in the sacred utterance (*brahman*) or in cosmic breath (*prāṇa*) or in cosmic heat (*tapas*) is no less than the awe and fascination rendered unto the numinous in Otto's classic definition.[134]

This experience is general, of course, in terms of the attitude of the sacrificer towards the transcendent reality. But there are particular experiences created in the process of ritual performance, that is, the transformation of the sacrificer's personality.

In the consecration (*dīkṣa*) the sacrificer is to undergo an experience of intensive self-awareness and regeneration. The *Śatapatha Brāhmaṇa* calls this a second birth, the first birth being emergence from the mother's womb and the third, transition into immortality at the funeral pyre.[135] Elsewhere it says that a human being is born again and again by the performance of *Agnihotra* and other sacrifices.[136] More significantly, the sacrificer becomes god himself in order to be capable of acting upon the gods.[137] With reference to various preparations of a *dīkṣita* for *soma yajñas* (secluded life in a hut for a long time, purificatory bath, restricted food etc.) Hubert and Mauss explain:

> This is the solemn moment when the new creature stirs within him. He has become a foetus... Then he unclenches his fists, he unveils himself, he is born on to a divine existence, he is god... And this existence lasts for many long months until his body has become translucent. Then, having as it were sacrificed his formal body and attained the highest degree of nervous excitement, he is fit to sacrifice, and the ceremonies begin.[138]

Thus the sacrificer passes from the world of men to the world of gods.[139] Now he has the right and duties of a god. But it is dangerous to remain in the consecrated state because it is not the normal human condition. In a way "the purpose of the sacrifice has indeed been the expulsion of a divine element".[140] At the end of sacrifice the sacrificer returns to his normal state by saying "Now I am he who I really am".[141] But significantly, the meaning of the above divine state has to be seen as the reward of sacrifice: though temporarily, the sacrificer has gained a pure condition.[142]

Another important aspect of the experience in sacrifice is that the sacrificer gradually comes to identify himself with the sacrifice in a mystical sense. It is in lieu of his own self he makes his offering. Perhaps the substitutes for old human sacrifice represent him in *yajña.* Following the model shown by the gods and Prajāpati, the supreme god, he expresses his readiness to sacrifice himself not only for his own regeneration but also for participation in the cosmic operation.

Aguilar writes: "It is this self-sacrifice which gives the right to the attainment of the supreme sacrifice and to the identification with it. ... who sacrifices himself here on earth does so with the intention of uniting himself with the sacrifice in the highest heaven".[143] There is an enigmatic phrase in this connection, "sacrificing sacrifice in sacrifice". Heesterman suggests that "The phrase implies that sacrificer and victim are amalgamated into a single identity, namely 'sacrifice'. Only then can one imagine sacrifice being sacrificed with sacrifice".[144] Again the sacrificer returns to his normal state by purchasing himself with the substitutes that represented him. Moreover, there are attempts, from the perspective of later developments in the tradition, to find the elements of *bhakti* and mysticism in Vedic sacrifice. Thus A. Coomaraswamy identifies giving to gods in sacrifice with loving them.[145] Dasgupta describes Vedic experience in sacrifice as ritualistic mysticism.[146] Finally, it should be noted that whatever may be the nature of transcendental experience in sacrifice, it is not ultimate but instrumental to achieve other ends, as we shall see.

We have already seen the power of sacrifice in connection with creation, relation, signification, integration, communication and personal transformation. We also noted that the meaning of sacrifice lies in the community of aims and intentions regarding the rewards of sacrifice. Let us now examine the implications of this meaning in relation to the universe, the gods and human beings. It is declared that *yajña* is the principle of the life and soul of all gods and all beings.[147] The triadic reality is central in the Vedic vision. It is in view of this triadic reality that Panikkar calls *yajña* a "cosmotheandric action".[148] We now consider each element individually in its connection with sacrifice.

(ii) Yajña *and the Cosmos*

According to the *Ṛgveda,* sacrifice is the navel (*nābi*) of the universe.[149] We have already pointed out the meaning of *yajña* in terms of its cosmic significance. It is the altar (*vedi*) which signifies the shape and extreme limits of the universe. The building of the fire-altar in *agnicayana* is a repetition of creation and reintegration. More significantly, the macrocosm is homologous to the ritual sacrifice or microcosm. Each level in the above construction is the form (*rūpa*) of its cosmic equivalent and the image (*pratimā*) of its cosmic correspondent.[150] In the words of Knipe:

> The universe itself, as a result of the primordial sacrifice, is nothing other than the total number of sacrificial components projected on to space and time. Not only does the entire projection have its cosmogonic counterpart in the unity of the sacrifice, but so too is each cosmic phenomenon "bound" essentially to one of the ingredients or dimensions of sacrifice. Knowledge of the rite is thus an all-powerful knowledge of the cosmos since it is literally the capacity to make connections, to see not only the overall homology of sacrifice and cosmos, but all of the distributive elements in universal concord.[151]

We need not examine the connections in detail. It is abundantly clear that the structure of *yajña* is the projection of the universe. Therefore, *yajña* may be said to be a celebration of the universe, and of life and its functioning.

In several passages the *Vedas* mention *śṛṣṭi* as a close ally of *yajña*. Thus it is said, creation was the outcome of primordial sacrifice or sacrifice was one of the first principles that sprang from creation.[152] Creation involves the sacrifice of gods and the self-sacrifice of the supreme God, as we shall see later. But sacrifice not only affects creation, it also sustains the cosmic order and remakes the world.

Sacrifice is undergirded by the important Vedic symbol *ṛta*, meaning order. "The participation in ritual is regarded as participating in the reality or conforming to the social world-view. *Ṛta* is the concept of reality for Aryans. The sacerdotal system of Aryans is one of the chief manifestations of *ṛta*".[153] The *Ṛgveda* says that cosmic *ṛta* is maintained by the sacrificial *ṛta*. In other words, *ṛta* is upheld by *ṛta*.[154] As Panikkar describes:

> *Ṛta* is the very energy of the sacrifice; it is what triggers the sacrifice. We may remember that ardor, truth, and *ṛta* share an intimate relationship. Truth without *ṛta* would not be true. All the powers of ardor, concentration, energy, and the like are connected with *ṛta*. Indeed, the whole order of the universe comes from and is maintained by the dynamism of *ṛta*.[155]

Gods and human beings are supposed to maintain the cosmic *ṛta* through perpetual *yajña*. It creates an autonomic mechanism that sheds power. This power has close links with the internal dynamism of the universal *ṛta*. Gonda calls this "a system of liturgio-cosmical equivalences".[156]

Bergaigne's study of Vedic religion shows clearly the significance of the link between the celestial world and the terrestrial world, in maintaining *ṛta*. He describes, for example, how the Vedic *yajña*, regulated by the hours of the day and by the seasons of the year, affects both the solar and meteorological phenomena resulting in light and rain. Thus the offering of the *agnihotra* early in the morning generates the luminous energy of the sun rise and its *tejas* is maintained by the offering of oblations "three times" a day.[157] Another correspondence is between the rite of taking the sacrificial fire around the sacrificial place and the circular movement of the sun.[158] Such correspondence may be extended to all the functions of *yajña* and the natural elements.

Finally the concept of *ṛta* as a cosmic principle faded away perhaps because of the emergence of new ideas along with the fall into the background of its guardian, Varuṇa. In course of time the meaning of *ṛta* was related to all aspects of life, moral, ethical, social and so on.[159] Later the more comprehensive term *dharma* became prominent and encompassed all these aspects.

(iii) Yajña *and* Devas

Every Vedic god is connected with sacrifice, but as presented to us, the function of particular gods in connection with sacrifice, is complex. According to several passages the gods spring from sacrifice, receive sacrifice, perform sacrifice and become themselves the sacrifice.[160] Thus it is said: Viṣṇu is the sacrifice,[161] Prajāpti is the sacrifice,[162] Agni is the sacrifice[163] and Rudra is the Lord of the sacrifice.[164] Rather than elaborate the meaning of such statements, we may explore how the ancients understood the association of gods with sacrifice.

In the early forms of sacrifice, as we have already seen, the gods depended on sacrificial food and drink. They were anxious to be invited to sacrifice so that they could satisfy their hunger. We read, for example, about Indra who is hungry and goes and asks for a gift.[165] Strengthened by food and drink the gods reciprocate by bestowing blessings upon the *yajamāna*. Here scholars discern the doctrine of *do ut des* (I give so that you may give).[166] But Gonda corrects this view by suggesting *do ut possis dare*, which means, "I give so that you may be able to give".[167] Since the gods' strength is essential for the proper functioning of the cosmos, refusal to give to them is regarded as a token of contempt.[168] Coomaraswamy finds an element of love and intimacy in this giving which goes beyond any quid pro quo.[169] The praise of gods and their heroic activities that found expression in hymns indicates their friendship with human beings. More prominent, however, is the idea that the gods fulfil the desires of the sacrificers and cooperate with them in sustaining the universe.

When *yajña* came to be regarded as an autonomous power generator, the gods were seen as nominal, standing equal with human beings in the *karman* of *yajña* in order to uphold the cosmic *ṛta*.[170]

> It is not without reason that the *devas* are less and less referred to as the passive recipients of the offering and more and more as those who offer it. As they too have to offer sacrifice, they begin to be seen by man more and more as models to imitate than as bestowers of favours in return for gratifications received.[171]

Now their supremacy, and immortality depend on their performance of *yajña*.[172] In the words of Dandekar "sacrifice itself is believed to bestow godhead on gods".[173] But perfection is their attribute while the sacrifices of human beings are imperfect.[174]

Another class of celestial beings mentioned in the *Vedas* in connection with sacrifice are the *asuras* (demons). The *asuras*, though born from the same father Prajāpati along with the *devas*, are depicted as representing a defect in *yajña*—untruth and selfishness.[175] More significantly, the *asuras* fight with the *devas* for the "acquisition of the sacrificial benefits and the appropriation for the correct performance of sacrifice", because their success depends on the secrets of the sacrifice.[176] As we have seen, the purpose of the silent utterance in sacrifice is to guard it from the *asuras*. Further, though *asuras* did not directly affect human beings, people needed to boost up the *devas* in their fight with the *asuras* so that the order and source of abundance should not be obstructed.

As we have seen, the notion of the impersonal power of *yajña* brought both gods and human beings to a state of struggle and anxiety. To counter such a notion, Vesci holds, the need arose for a personal first principle or a primordial supreme Being. The appearance of a Puruṣa in the *Ṛgveda* or Prajāpati in the *Brāhmaṇas* was a result of this exigency. Vesci notes: "Prajāpati is somehow a creation of the Brāhmaṇic speculation, still on the borderline between myth and philosophy, whose role is to 'save' the Cosmic Action from its inherent tendency to become impersonal".[177] We should note, however, that this development did not minimise the power of that cosmic action. In this light alone we can understand why Puruṣa or Prajāpati is introduced as the sacrifice *par excellence*: he was at the same time the self-immolating priest, the dismembered victim and the supreme receiver of the offering. Thus by the sacrifice of one-fourth of the Puruṣa, the world, beings and natural elements were created.[178] And Prajāpati, animated by *kāma* and *tapas*, emitted from himself the whole of creation. In consequence of this sacrificial action of his he became weak and dismembered. Hence the need for the *agnicayana*, the fire-altar, to reconstitute his body. Also he created sacrifice as a counterpart of himself, gave himself to the gods as an offering and thus became the Lord of sacrifice.[179] Thus the ownership of sacrifice depended on one's readiness for a perpetual self-sacrifice by which one can redeem oneself and others. A point of further departure in the Vedic understanding of gods in connection with sacrifice may be identified in the interrogative pronoun *kaḥ* (who?) which is one of the epithets attached to Prajāpati in the later parts of the *Brāhmaṇas.*[180] Vesci identifies in this a transition to an idea of an all-absorbing supreme Being and interior self-sacrifice.[181] But there is a problem in this linkage, as we shall see later. What seems more reasonable is that by questioning the supremacy of Prajāpati the ritual authorities tried to save the mechanism of sacrifice from a tendency to attach supreme position to a particular god. He was, for them, a model for sacrifice but nothing more.

Before we close this section, mention may be made about seers (*ṛṣis*), who were co-participants in seeing, creating and performing sacrifice along with the gods. To the *ṛṣis* was revealed the Vedic vision of reality. Particularly there is a tradition of seven ancient *ṛṣis* who were the models for the human sacrificers, having attained divine status and immortality through sacrifice alone. They are identical with gods.[182] The power of *tapas* available to them produced *mantras,* formulas and hymns; they saw the truth and the structure of sacrifice. Along with them ancestors were also remembered. In the *śrāddha* sacrifice food was offered to them. They seem to complete the scope of cosmic life as a broad living organism or totality.[183]

(iv) Yajña *and the* Yajamāna's Kāma

We have already pointed out certain aspects of the meaning of sacrifice for the sacrificer. He undergoes a transcendental experience in the performance of sacrifice. He also participates in the maintenance of the cosmic order by feeding gods and cooperating with them. As far as the individual is concerned, however, the most recurring expression is with reference to the mental attitude of the sacrificer.

The fundamental source of all his aspirations is the element of desire (*kāma*) in his inner core. In the *Vedas kāma* has a positive meaning of love and passion marking an authentic selfhood. In sacrifice, however, it always seems to denote an attachment to the abundance of temporal life. The fulfilment of *kāma* is the basic motive in sacrifice. The original model is again Prajāpati, who fulfilled all his desires and achieved all his goals by performing *soma yajñas* and *aśvamedha*.[184] *Kāma* became personified in the mythological episodes of especially the *Atharva Veda* which says,

> Thereafter rose *kāma* in the beginning, *kāma* the primal seed and germ of spirit; O *kāma*, dwelling in the lofty. *Kāma*, give growth of riches to the sacrificer. Thou, *kāma*, art victorious, famous, potent, splendid...O *kāma*, with whatever wish we make this offering to thee, may it all be fulfilled to us.[185]

With reference to the giver (*yajamāna*) and receiver (*deva*) it is stated: "*Kāma* gives gifts to *kāma*".[186] There is a glorification of the *kāmadhuk*, the cow (or bull) of desire which provides plenty.[187] All these aspects may be summed up in temporal fulfilment of desires. Apart from his part played in the maintenance of the world, the sacrificer is the single beneficiary of the sacrifice though, particularly for offspring, the presence of his wife is necessary.[188] The notion of community benefit seems to be alien to the sacrificial cult of the *Vedas*. Prosperity, victory, offspring, or protection from evil spirits recur as individual motives in both *śrauta* rituals and domestic ceremonies.

Two other important aspects of the sacrificer's attitude are *satya* and *śraddhā*. Human beings are said to belong in their normal state of life to untruth; and performing sacrifice, they are for a while transformed into truth. Thus they become gods as the *devas* represent *satya*. As Brian Smith observes, "In several passages we read that *satya*, here in the sense of ritual exactitude, is a quality of gods while *anṛtra* or error is the ... distinguishing quality of things human".[190] It is the aspiration of the sacrificers to follow the model of the gods and become like them. Allied to *satya* is *śraddhā* which means trust or faith. It is called ritual faith in terms of the full confidence of the sacrificer in the efficacy of the rite, competence of the priests, power of the *mantras* and in the might of the gods. It also implies trustful surrender to the *Veda* and the verse of the teacher.[191] *Śraddhā* is a most important element for the success of *yajña* by which *agni* is kindled, oblations offered and *ṛta* manitained.[192] Sometimes *satya* and *śraddhā* are combined for maximum effect in sacrifice. All such virtues, in fact, were understood in relation to ritual. As Gonda observes:

> A recommendation of virtues such as hospitality, generosity, faith and loyalty, may, to a certain extent, be found in various other tales; its first purpose is not to moralise but to explain rites and to justify ritual rules and prescriptions. The application of austerity, self-control, endurance and restraint of speech, a chaste life devoted to the study of the *Veda* must be seen against the same ritual background, as is perfectly clear from the passages in which it is expressed; these 'virtues' or meritorious works are first and foremost prerequisites to the success of a task or enterprise undertaken on thoroughly ritual lines.[193]

Sometimes *kāma* is directed to the attainment of the heavenly world (*svarga*) and immortality (*amṛtatva*). It means not only the optimisation of a perfect span of hundred years living in this world but also its continuation in a life after death.[194] Thus the vitalising power of sacrifice is extended to a trans-empirical future life. As we mentioned earlier, the bird-shaped fire-altar of the *agnicayana* faces east, the gate of heaven. The sacrificial post (*yupa*) also signifies the gate of heaven. Further, sacrifice is said to be a 'safe boat' to cross over to *svarga*.[195] There are 'exit' rites symbolising ascendance to heaven. Although the true voyage to heaven is not accomplished until after death, a foretaste or resemblance can be achieved in the sacrifice on earth. Brian Smith writes:

> The realization of the heavenly world and divinity within the sacrifices of humans transformed temporarily into "gods" is, again, a kind of counterpart or resembling form of the realization of *svarga loka* and *daiva ātman* on completion of life on earth.[196]

The heavenly world (*svarga loka*) is thus the corresponding form of this world in which there is "the anticipated image, or the real base of the other world and of the immortality in the beyond".[197] For the temporary enjoyment of this world by the sacrificer, the priests construct or prepare a perfect self or *daiva ātman* in him which he has to renounce at the end of the ritual. On his death, it is said, a splendid body is constructed by the sacrificer to enjoy the treasury of *yajña* accumulated in *svarga*.[198] The oblation of *yajña* becomes his *ātman* and calls him to the eternal home.[199] The sacrifices cause the sacrificer to attain the same region (*sāyūjya*), form (*sārūpya*) and union (*sālokya*) with the gods.[200] Although desire for immortality is expressed, it seems, the duration in the next world depends on the particular type of sacrifice.[201] It must, however, be noted that there is no consistent idea of *ātman* and *amṛtatva* in the *saṃhitā* and *brāhmaṇa* texts.

As an analogue of this world, *svarga* is conceived as a place for enjoying material abundance in the company of the celestial hosts of gods and seers. As Panikkar points out clearly, the traditional meaning of *svarga* was happiness, the further intensification of worldly pleasure. He says,

> Now happiness may be sought in different values: material, offspring, a wife, power, triumph and the like. We detect here a peculiar process of secularization; sacrifice is utilised for secular purposes because in secular "values" men see their relative or temporal heaven.[202]

Though there are scanty references in the Vedic texts to the motives of thanksgiving, vow-fulfilling, expiation and self-redemption (from the gods through an animal sacrifice in order to return to the normal state), life with its material fullness here and hereafter is the primary aim of Vedic sacrifice.

It is also noteworthy that the animals killed in sacrifice too are directed to immortality so that they could join the host of animals of gods in heaven. Thite is of the opinion that the term "quieting" or "strangulating" used for killing the animal, and purificatory ceremonies performed on the victims, indicate a kind of euphemistic sophistication in the attitude towards animal slaughter attempted by the ritualists.[203] We shall notice later the controversy over the killing of animals in sacrifice.

The meaning of Vedic sacrifice, thus, lies not in its perfection or intelligibility of every act and utterance, but the significatio . it points to, the reference it makes, the communication it achieves and the relation it establishes. Of the multiple intentions expressed and meanings derived the ideas of the feeding of gods, sustaining the cosmic function and order in cooperation with the gods and fulfilling the desire for material abundance here and hereafter are the most fundamental and prominent. The transcendental experience attained in ritual and the virtues like truth and faith, all stand only to this effect. Whenever Vedic sacrifice has been reaffirmed we can identify these fundamental elements.

5. Sacrifice and Stratification of Vedic Society

The idea of sacrifice is inextricably related to the structure of Vedic society because the ritual order in sacrifice has correlations not only with the cosmic order but with the social order as well. The order and totality of life in its entirety is embodied in *dharma*, which is inseparable from *yajña*. The combat of gods and demons over sacrifice in the Vedic mythology signifies the conflict between *dharma* and *adharma*. Any act to suppress sacrifice and brahmins is violence against *dharma*.[204] The social order of the Aryans was constituted by the interdependent organism of four *varnas*, the prototype of later castes. The earliest reference to this organism is found in the Ṛgvedic myth of the primordial sacrifice of Ādipuruṣa. When the gods and seers sacrificed Puruṣa, brahmins, kṣatriyas, vaiśyas and śūdras sprang from his head, shoulders, thighs and feet respectively. Thus the *varṇas* were "literally born of sacrifice".[205] It is interesting to note that following the above account the *Ṛgveda* declares: these were the first *dharmas*.[206] Already in the same *Veda* the term *dharma* occurs with special reference to the institution of sacrifice and the order of its performance.[207] Thus the social order of *varṇas* forms part of the overall order of the universe. Hopkins writes:

> The cosmos, the world of nature, human society, and the sacrifice are seen as parallel orders of reality of equal antiquity and performance. The four classes of society, listed for the first time ... are as much a part of the structure of things as earth, atmosphere, and heaven or the gods. The sacrifice of the Puruṣa is a common reference point for all things; it explains their unity and diversity and their relationship to each other and provides a means of moving from one order of reality to another.[208]

Coomaraswamy speaks of this social order of Vedic society as a "sacramental order" in which there is a need and place for all people's work just like the coordinating work of Viśvakarman in sacrifice. Every function from that of the highest rank to the lowest, he says, is literally a priesthood, and every operation a rite. Mutual loyalties and duties keep up the maintenance of heredity and a total confusion of the *varṇas* is the death of society.[209] Of course, this gloriously romantic picture contradicts the actuality maintained by discriminations, which crept in with time, if they were not there from the beginning.

The projection of hierarchy and different grades may be seen in Vedic ritual because the whole of *varṇa* and rank revolved around Vedic *yajña* which is the attribute often referred to as the relative degree of purity.[210] The brahmins were regarded as having inherent purity and constant consecration in their possession, which gave them the right to function as priests. Nevertheless, apparently the kṣatriyas always had conflict with the brahmins over this point. For example, it is said in the *Śatapatha Brāhmaṇa* that a brahmin could function without a king but not a king without a brahmin.[211] It is not without reason that only the first two groups were in the forefront of the power conflicts. The brahmins represented the sacred or priestly power (*brahman*) and the kṣatriyas the lordly or secular power (*kṣatra*). In its introduction to *Rājasūya* the *Aitareya Brāhmaṇa* has the following description that indicates the origin of these two powers and conflict:

> Prajāpati created the sacrifice; after the creation of the sacrifice the holy power and the lordly power were created; after the holy power and the lordly power both kinds of offspring were created, those who eat the oblations and those who do not eat the oblations; after the holy power those that eat the oblations, after the lordly power those that do not eat the oblations. The brahmans are the offspring that eat the oblations; the rājaṇya, vaiśya and śūdras are those that do not eat the oblations. From them the sacrifice departed; it the holy power and the lordly power pursued; the holy power pursued with the weapons of the holy power; the lordly power with those of the lordly power. The weapons of the holy power are the weapons of the sacrifice; the weapons of the lordly power are the horse chariot, corselet, the bow and arrow. The lordly power returned without attaining it; from its weapons it turns away trembling. The holy power followed it and obtained it ... therefore even now the sacrifice finds support in the holy power and in the brahmans.[212]

Further, although all other Vedic deities faded away Agni and Indra remained especially in their identification with brahmins and kṣatriyas respectively. Agni is now the priest or Bṛahspati on the earth. Indra is the warrior *par excellence* and related to the heavenly hosts (*āditya*). Hence the identification of two prominent powers in society with the two great divine powers.[213]

When the ritual became more and more complicated, priestly training was emphasised and the situation required the strict distribution of the sacerdotal function among several distinct classes of priests.[214] The fact that the brahmins were regarded as having in their possession the power of *yajña* brought to them considerable respect and reverence from the masses. In this capacity the chiefs of clans and kings had to depend on the brahmins for their own success. Consequently, they were considered to be equal with gods. The *Śatapatha Brāhmaṇa* repeatedly declares: "Verily there are two kinds of gods; for, indeed, the gods are the gods; and the brahmans who have studied and teach sacred lore are the human gods".[215]

Further, because of their purity the brahmins alone were allowed to partake of sacrificial oblations.[216] As they appeared to drive away the evil and impurity of people by ritual, to pronounce auspicious words and honours on people and to teach good conduct and knowledge of the *Vedas*, the brahmins were respected by the people as teachers (*guru* or *ācārya*) and masters.[217] Moreover, the monopoly of the sacred power in the hands of the priests who "grasped finally the handles of the holy"[218] brought to them abundant wealth. This was operated through the method of *dakṣiṇā* and *dāna* which was indispensable in the performance of sacrifice. It included gold, garments and cattle. References abound about the notion that the efficacy of a sacrifice depended heavily on the worth of *dakṣiṇā* and *dāna* given generously.[219] The brahmins had to struggle to keep their superiority over the kṣatriyas, especially the rulers. Indicative of this are the repeated assertions about the importance of brahmins for the prosperity of a ruler and his kingdom.[220]

Next in importance to the brahims came the kṣatriyas. They monopolised the ruling power. Perhaps, after a struggle they acquired the right to become brahmins temporarily in their own grand *yajñas* such as the *rājsūya* and *aśvamedha*.[221] It is clear that the kings are identified not only with the mighty gods like Indra, but also with the supreme God Prajāpati himself. It is said: "The *rājanya* is most manifestly of Prajāpati, while being one who rules over many. He is the representative of Prajāpati".[222]

The identification of the king with Prajāpati strikingly reveals the fact that the term *prajāpati* was deliberately preferred to the Ṛgvedic term *puruṣa* for Supreme Being. Expressing his surprise over the discarding of the term *puruṣa* and the choice of the term *prajāpati*, Eggeling suggests a reason for this. He points out that the term *prajāpati* is singularly convenient for those who could afford to have great and costly sacrificial performances. It is most appropriate for the "rulers of men and possessors of cattle, whether they were mighty kings, or petty rulers, or landed proprietors or chiefs of clans" to whom the creatures (*prajāḥ*) are subordinate.[223] Gonda notes:

> As one of the aims of gifts to men and to gods is that of buying peace, it may be observed that the term *bali* used for 'tax' or 'royal revenue' is also very often applied to any offering or propitiatory oblation to gods and semi divine beings, household divinities, spirits and various creatures including even lifeless objects.[224]

At the same time, the Vedic terms *rājan* or *rājya* should not be confused with later monarchies. The *rājan* in the early Vedic period was identical with a war-chief or a tribal chief.[225] Further, one may see in this process the sacrality attached to kingship later.

The vaiśyas and śūdras were kept in the background. While the brahmins despised them, as distant from their purity, sacred power and sacred knowledge, the kṣatriyas suppressed them with their ruling power. Even the reward of sacrifice for a king is expressed in terms of his subjugation of vaiśyas and exploitation of their labour.[226] In a sacrificial procession, a brahmin may go behind a kṣatriya, and in recession, a kṣatriya behind a brahmin, but

> inasmuch as the ass does not go first either in going from, or in coming back from there, therefore the *brāhmaṇa* and kṣatriya never go behind the vaiśya and śūdra: hence they walk thus in order to avoid a confusion between good and bad. And, moreover, he thus encloses those two castes (the vaiśya and śūdra) on both sides by the priesthood and by the nobility, and makes them submissive.[227]

The vaiśyas were placed in an ambiguous position, sometimes identified with the two upper classes and other times with the lower one.[228] The plight of the śūdras was even more subordinate when they were singled out. They were not allowed to perform sacrifice, to milk the cow for sacrificial purposes, to enter into sacrificial halls or to sit with brahmins.[229] In the *pravargya* cermony, for instance, while the priest is bringing the pot he should not come into contact with a group of beings—śūdra, woman, dog and black bird—which are untruth, sin and darkness in contrast with the sacred heat (*garma*) which is excellence, truth and light.[230] And although the śūdras were later allowed to perform a few domestic rites they were prohibited from studying the *Vedas*, instituting a sacrifice and uttering a *mantra*. These instances suffice to show the power of the sacred *yajña* and its impact on the power structure in society.

From the above discussion one may argue that the caste system was a social category developed by gradual exploitation of the powerful with the legitimising force of religion. But we should not lose sight of an important factor, namely the fundamental link between the notion about scripture and structure of society. Brian Smith's observation is in this regard is that

> The caste system or at least caste *in nuce* can thus be presented as canonical: The authority of the caste derives from the authority of *Veda*, but more than that caste is made to appear as a social transformation or reduplication of canon. The legitimacy, or even indisputability, of the distinctive social scheme of historical and contemporary India rides piggyback on the

unquestionable truth of the *Veda*, and both are part of the eternal cosmic order of things. Any challenge to either the sociological or scriptural structure can be debunked as obviously "unnatural and false".[231]

Thus vedic *dharma* signifies a comprehensive and integral order including ritual order, cosmic order, social order and scriptural order. Challenge to one of them is challenge to all, as we shall notice in due course.

6. Glimpses of Interiorisation in the Early Period

Despite a preoccupation with ritual performance and excess of worldly *kāma*, as evident in Vedic sacrifice, there seem to be glimpses of another level of sacrificial concept found in the *Saṃhitās* and the *Brāhmaṇas*. We pointed out, when we discussed the development of Vedic ritual, that ascetic elements were increasingly introduced into the sacrificial system. We need to examine the nature of this tendency in some detail because its impact on future developments in the understanding of sacrifice is remarkable. In this section, first, we shall point out some references to the idea of interiorisation, sacrifice of knowledge, and self-sacrifice before we take up a discussion on the source of these dimensions which stand external to the mainstream of the Vedic cult of ritual sacrifice.

Most affected in the process of interiorisation was *tapas*, which distinguished inner heat from the ritual heat produced by fire and cooking. *Tapas* is creative heat that exists for ever. Some texts note that *tapas* was a primordial principle and the first-born in creation.[232] It was the essence of gods and *ṛṣis* who gained victory over *asuras* and attained immortality.[233] *Tapas* is also the inner power in a *brahmacārin* by which he fills his *guru* and the whole world; it is also that by which a king protects his kingdom.[234] A devotee of Agni can 'heat' his head with devotion and brahmins 'heat' themselves before they go to kindle the fire.[235] References to *tapas* as inner heat are many.

Sceptical notes and indications of new forms of *yajña* distinct from ritual are also found. Barth points out a few references which mention people who denied the existence of Indra.[236] Other speculations and doubts about creation may also be attributed to such people. It is said that men are possessed with unbelief; those who do not sacrifice become sinners and those who sacrifice become righteous.[237] For example, *yajña* could be performed either through knowledge (*jñāna*) or through action (*karman*).[238] Through knowledge the wise go upwards, and get their desire quenched. No sacrifice or ignorant penance can reach there; immortality is for the sacrificer who makes mental offerings.[239] The self-offerer is better than the god-offerer;[240] mental sacrifice is possible for securing spiritual power in which the senses (*indriya*) and the breath (*prāṇa*) are to be offered with the help of gods in sacrifice of mind (*manas*).[241] One can perform an interior *agnihotra* for a life time.[242] The study of the *Veda* (*svādhyāya*) is a sacrifice to *brahman*, the cosmic spirit, with the tools of speech (*vāc*), mind, truth and the oblation of Vedic formulas which would lead to an imperishable heaven.[243] The quest for an imperishable heaven is remarkable because in the later *brāhmaṇas* a fear of re-death arose which of course did not involve rebirth and a return to earthly struggles.[244] There are also a few references to allegorical identification of the ritual with the inner organs. In addition, where there is no kind of oblation available, it is said, one can offer the truth in faith.[245] Even though there is no consistency or well worked out concept, in such observations we see glimpses of the *Upaniṣads* in which interior sacrifice and allegorical interpretation are more prominent.

The question arises, is interior sacrifice compatible with ritual sacrifice? If so, how is it possible to develop a coherent picture of both ritual and non-ritual or anti-ritual concerns in a single system? And if not, where lies the source for injecting these ideals into the ritual texts? Finding clear answers to these questions is difficult because the glimpses of interiorisation are scattered, unrelated to ritual. There is no reference in the texts to the problem of combining ritual and interior dimensions in one system. Most references to interiorisation occur in the later texts of the *Brāhmaṇas* and in the *Atharva Veda*, but the chronology of its development is not known.

We saw earlier that ascetic techniques were increasingly introduced in developing elaborate forms of Vedic sacrifice. This is evident in references to the ascetic activity of gods and seers in the mythical episodes and to the preparatory ceremonies (*dīkṣa*) for sacrifice and Vedic learning. In tracing the source of the ascetic practices, however, scholars differ. David Knipe, for example, though admitting its existence in non-Aryan circles, asserts that "the central ideology and expression of *tapas* is no midstream importation from an alien system".[246] One may then even suggest that those ascetic practices were adopted from the practices in sacrifice. After a discussion on this issue Kaelber concludes that "it is more plausible... that the sacrificer borrowed his asceticism from ascetics than that ascetics borrowed their asceticism from sacrificers".[247] If this conclusion is accepted then it is reasonable to think that the attachment to gods and seers in myths was a later development in the brāhmaṇic tradition. What is more remarkable is that the ritualists were open to accepting new elements and incorporating them into their system, which is typical of the entire history of brāhmaṇic tradition. Their ingenuity may be recognised in that they used ascetic practices not to push ritual sacrifice into the background but, instead, to enrich their complex system.

Next comes the question of the source of ascetic techniques and interiorisation injected into the ritual system. It is now widely acknowledged that a group of ascetics or spiritual circles were operative outside the brāhmaṇic fold but always in conflict with it. In *ṚV.* X. 136 we read of a *muni* with long hair and extraordinary powers to fly through the air and so on. This is the only hymn in the entire *Veda* which is fully dedicated to the description of such a strange figure, apparently unrelated to the ritual tradition. Scholars have various suggestions for identifying the figure, for example, as fore-runner of the later *śramaṇas*, member of a specific orgiastic cult led by Rudra, representative of early *yogic* spirituality outside the ritual tradition, or earliest dissenter from the orthodox religion.[248] K. Werner, reviewing different opinions, says:

> The *Vedas* are representative of one type of spiritual tradition ... The *keśin* hymn gives evidence of the existence of another ancient type of spiritual tradition which expressed itself in what we can call, using a term invented later, the Yogic way of life. This consisted of renunciation ... meditative approach ... which, according to the evidence given by the followers of this tradition, gave them access to a higher kind of knowledge of themselves, of the hidden reality and of other men and beings. As a result they were friends and helpers of others, possibly even assisting them spiritually by way of some kind of self-sacrifice...The authorship of this hymn is clearly to be ascribed to someone belonging to the Vedic tradition who reported sympathetically and perhaps even with admiration about the *keśins*, using of course the current mythological and symbolical images of the idiom of the later Vedic time.[249]

Relatedly, this *muni* or *keśin* is identified with the groups of *vrātyas* and *yatis* mentioned in the *Ṛgveda* and with the *yogis* of the pre-Vedic Indus civilisation.[250] Again opinions are sharply divided as to the nature of *vrātyas* and their place in Vedic society.[251] At one extreme, they are identified with the groups of mendicants or *munis* who were operative outside the Aryan fold, and at the other, with a group of Aryan warriors who were involved in raiding expeditions.

The central point of reference is the special rites called *vrātyastomas* in which certain ambiguous practices like abusive language take place. In between these extreme views, there are a few attempts to place them within the Aryan fold but as distinctive from the brāhmaṇic tradition. Heesterman considers the *vrātyas* as raiding warriors. This goes well with his theory that Vedic ritual originated in the context of agonistic battles. He explains the *vrātyastomas* as purificatory ceremónies and in the process of shedding the impure condition of the warriors on the brahmin priests, the impure language they use becomes a kind of ritual utterance.[252] For Gonda, the *vrātya* "in all probability was an Aryan, who having neglected the rites and becoming impure by visiting foreign countries, was deprived of the membership of the Aryan community".[253] Eliade supposes that "the *vrātyas* represented a mysterious brotherhood belonging to the advance guard of the Aryan invaders. But they were not entirely distinct from the *keśins* of the *Ṛgveda*".[254] Jaini identifies the *vrātyas* with a group of Aryans living outside that community and fallen from pure Aryanhood. For him the *vrātyastomas* were intended for their readmission into the brāhmaṇic community. They are the "dissident or the renegade Aryans", he thinks, who had non-Vedic practices and close association with the kṣatriyas along with the *yatis*. Though they called themselves Aryan they persistently refused to conform to the Vedic scriptures and sacrifices.[255] It is interesting to note that Rudra who is identified with the *mahāyogi* of the Indus Valley, is called Vrātyapati.[256] Dandekar relates *vrātyas* along with the *munis* and *yogis* to Rudra, the proto-historic Śiva.[257] These opinions seem to suggest on the whole that there were groups constantly identifying themselves with those gods and men who were known for their supernatural activities, with a belief in interior power analogous with cosmic power. They were basically non-Vedic and anti-brāhmaṇic even though they were converted or assimilated into the brāhmaṇic fold.[258]

Although the ascetic groups were living outside the brāhmaṇic fold, apparently they visited the Aryan homes and were held in high respect in society. The brahmins, however, loathed them because of their anti-ritual attitude. This is evident in some references to the *yatis*, who are identical with the group mentioned above. There is a story in the *Atharva Veda*, for example, in which Indra, the enjoyer of sacrifice, kills the *yatis*. It is fitting that Sāyana, in his reference to this account, explains them as people belonging to *asuras*, the opponents of Vedic sacrifice.[259] In other accounts it is said, when a *vrātya* arrives in a home as a teacher and guest, the host must take his permission to make an oblation if an *agnihotra* was going on.[260] We shall see later further developments of these groups as a powerful *śramaṇa* movement and their attitude towards the sacrificial religion and their influence in the *Upaniṣads*. Suffice it here to note that it is most appropriate to attribute the glimpses of interiorisation interwoven in the texts on ritual sacrifice to a group or groups of ascetics who lived outside the brāhmaṇic fold but with constant interaction with the latter.

7. Conclusion

Sacrifice is the quintessence of the Vedic religion. The Vedic world-view is based on a notion of power produced in the sacrifice and its correspondence with the forces of the cosmos. The earliest Vedic sacrifice, as entertainment of celestial guests (the gods), developed into an elaborate and complex system of rituals incorporating many external elements in the process. Hospitality to gods and elaborate rituals sustaining the orderly function of the universe existed seperately though in some sacrifices they are combined.

Prominent Hindu ideas seem to have originated in the ritual context of the Vedic sacrifice. Particularly, the ideas of *karman, dharma, brahman* and *tapas* originated in the Vedic ritual before they underwent a process of acquiring new meanings. *Karman* in the ritual context meant deliberate and exact ritual action. *Brahman* meant holy power in general, the special manifestation of which could be found in the sacred utterance or prayer at the performance of the sacrifice. *Tapas* was ritual heat produced by the established fires and cooking of sacrificial oblations. It was then related to cosmic principles and the interior fervour in gods and sacrificers. The original occurrence of *dharma* is in the sense of the *varṇa* division of Vedic society which was inextricably connected with ritual order, cosmic order and scriptural authority. It is only proper, therefore, to study the mainstream development of the pan-mythic religious tradition of India from the perspective of Vedic sacrifice.

The nature of meaning derived from the performance of sacrifice is highly disputed. We have noted discussions in this regard. The Vedic ritual seems to have been "meaningless" in the view of some scholars on the basis of which they have attempted new theories of ritual and social relations. For them the ritual order and formulas and the assumed correlations they make with the cosmos and society are unintelligible. But in the view of others Vedic sacrifice is meaningful in the sense of the relationships it makes, signification it points to and communication it carries. More remarkably, for the sacrifices the meaning of sacrifice lies in transcendental experience and the intentions of sacrifice. The "divine" experience created by ritual procedure and ascetic activities, however, is temporary. And the ultimate *kāma*-bound motive in sacrifice is to sustain the function and order of the cosmos by strengthening the gods and cooperating with them, the net outcome of which should be material abundance and happiness in this world and in heaven as well. All these constitute the sacrifice-centred Vedic religion, which has its own distinctive methods and goals. In other words, the Vedic religion with sacrifice at its heart presents a paradigm, despite its complexity and glimpses of certain elements apparently remaining "outside" its core.

Glimpses of a trend towards interiorising sacrifice mixed with anti-ritual speculations and sceptical notes seem to have affected the sacrificial system even in early times although they were accommodated without getting reconciled with the ritual sacrifice. This disturbance seems to have become further intensified in the *Upaniṣads*. We shall see this in the next chapter and point out its enormous influence in the subsequent development of religious thought in ancient India.

NOTES

1. H. Aguilar, *The Sacrifice in the Ṛgveda*, Delhi, 1976, p.111.
2. J. Koller, *The Indian Way*, New York, 1982, p. 38.
3. *ibid.*, p. 39.
4. R. Panikkar, *Myth, Faith and Hermeneutics*, New York, 1979, p.125.
5. For certain definitions, types and theories of sacrifice, see H. Hubert and M, Mauss, *Sacrifice: Its Nature and Function*, London, 1968, pp.1-13, 97ff; E.O. James, "Sacrifice (Introductory and Primitive)", in *ERE*, 11, pp.1-7; J. Henninger, "Sacrifice", in *ER*, 12, pp. 550-4; N. Drury, *The Sacrificial Ritual in the Śatapatha Brāhmaṇa*, Delhi, 1981, pp.2ff; Van der Leeuw, *Religion: Its Essence and Manifestation*, Princeton, 1986, pp. 350-60; G. Ashby, *Sacrifice: Its Nature and Purpose*, London, 1988, pp.11-20.
6. See E.J. Lott, *Vision, Tradition, Interpretation—Theology, Religion and the Study of Religion*, Berlin, 1988, pp. 16ff.
7. See B.K. Smith, "The Unity of Ritual—The Place of the Domestic Sacrifice in Vedic Ritualism", *IIJ*, XXIX/2 (1986), pp. 79-96.
8. G.V. Devasthali, *Religion and Mythology of the Brāhmaṇas with Particular*

Reference to the Śatapatha Brāhmaṇa, Poona, 1965, p. 141; see alo G.V. Thite, *Sacrifice in the Brāhmaṇa Texts,* Poona, 1975, pp. 7-15.

9. Kane points to the *agnistoma* and the *homa* ceremony of the Parsees and words like *atharvan, ahuti, uktha, barhis, mantra, yajña, soma* etc. which are common in Vedic and Parsee religions; see *HDhs,* II, p. 978; see H.D. Griswold, *The Religion of the Ṛgveda,* London, 1923, p.20; E.O. James, *Origins of Sacrifice: A Study of Comparative Religion,* London, 1933, p. 279f.
10. See W.F. Albright and P.E. Dumont, "A Parallel between Indic and Babylonian Sacrificial Ritual", *JAOS,* 54 (1934), pp. 107-28.
11. See A.L. Basham (ed.), *A Cultural History of India,* Oxford, 1975, p. 14.
12. N. N. Bhattacharyya, *Ancient Indian Rituals and their Social Contents,* London, 1975, p. 61f.
13. See articles on this topic compiled; J.C. Heesterman, *The Inner Conflict of a Tradition, Essays in Indian Ritual, Kingship, and Society.* Delhi, 1985.
14. See B. Smith's review of Heesterman's theory, *RSR,* 14/1 (1988), p. 7f.
15. See A.B. Keith, *The Religion and Philosophy of the Veda and Upaniṣads,* Cambridge, 1925, p. 258.
16. Thomas Hopkins, *The Hindu Religious Tradition,* Belmont, 1971, p.14.
17. *AV,* VII 5.2. All the references of *AV* are taken from Griffith's translation: *The Hymns of the Atharvaveda,* Benares, 1916.
18. *ŚB,* VI. 2.3.10. (All references to *ŚB* come from J. Eggeling's translation: *The Śatapatha Brāhmaṇa, SBE,* XII (1882), XVI (1885), XLI (1894), XLIII (1897), XLVI (1900), Oxford.
19. See J. Thachil, *The Vedic and Christian Concept of Sacrifice,* Alwaye, 1985, p.30f.
20. See Uma Vesci, *Heat and Sacrifice in the Vedas,* Delhi, 1985, p.79.
21. Martin Haug, *The Aitareya Brāhmaṇam of the Ṛgveda,* Bombay, 1863, I, p.74 (All references to *AB* are taken from this translation unless otherwise indicated).
22. Dandekar, "Hinduism" in *Historia Religionum,* ed. J. Bleeker and G. Widengren, Leiden, 1971, II, p. 259f.
23. For an introduction to the nature of this material and its interrelationship, see L. Renou, *Religions in Ancient India,* London, 1955, pp. 5ff; *HDhs,* II, p. 980.
24. See J. Thachil, *op. cit.,* pp. 40ff; T. J.Hopkins, *op. cit.,* p.17.
25. J. Basu, *India of the Age of the Brāhmaṇas,* Calcutta, 1969, pp. 207ff.
26. J. Gonda, *Change and Continuity in Indian Religion,* New Delhi, 1985, p.336.
27. *ṚV,* I. 162. 4, 5. (Ref. *The Hymns of the Ṛgveda,* tr. Griffith).
28. Raghu Vira, "Implements and Vessels used in Vedic Sacrifice", *JRAS,* 1934, p. 283; regarding location of sites etc., see Eggeling, *ŚB,* II, pp. 152-171.

29. See Devasthali, *op. cit.*, pp. 136ff.
30. See S.C. Chakrabarti, "On the Transition of Vedic Ritual Lore", *IIJ*, XXI/3 (1979), pp. 181-8.
31. J. Basu, *op. cit.*, p. 147.
32. For the kind of mistakes, bad effects and the remedies, see Gonda, "Prajāpati and Prāyaścitta", *JRAS*, 1983, pp. 32-54.
33. Devasthali, *op. cit.*, p. 133.
34. For the number of animals required ranging from 17 to 260 depending on the nature of the ritual, see Eggeling, *ŚB*, V, p. 311; G.U. Thite, "Animal Sacrifice in the Brāhmaṇa Texts", *Numen*, XVII/2 (1970), p. 26; G.S. Ghurye, *Vedic India*, Bombay, 1979, p. 54.
35. This may be taken as an attempt to gloss over the reality of human sacrifice. See Drury, *op. cit.*, p. 17
36. For difference of opinions, see J. Eggeling, *ŚB*, V, p. xxxiiif; G.V. Thite, "Animal Sacrifice", p. 153 and *Sacrifice in the Brāhmaṇas - Texts*, Poona, 1975, pp. 24ff.
37. *ŚB*, I.2.3.5-7.
38. See N.N. Bhattacharyya, *op. cit.*, p. 15.
39. J.B. Chaudhuri, "The Wife in the Vedic Ritual", *IHQ*, XVI (1940), pp. 70-98; N.N. Bhattacharyya, *op. cit.*, p. 66.
40. Renou, *op. cit.*, p. 33; *HDhs*, II, p. 979; Heesterman, "Vrātya and Sacrifice", *IIJ*, VI (1962-63), p. 31.
41. See T.J. Hopkins, *op. cit.*, p. 15f.
42. For a detailed discussion on the early forms of *dāna* with Vedic references, see Gonda, *op. cit.*, pp. 208ff.
43. See Heesterman, "Reflections on the Significance of Dakṣiṇā", *IIJ*, III (1959), pp. 241-58; Basu, *op. cit.*, pp. 172-80.
44. See Thachil, *op. cit.*, p. 122f; *ṚV*, VII. 2.3; VII. 52. 1-2; X. 63. 7; *AV*, VII. 51ff.
45. Gonda, 1. *Vedic Literature, HIL*, p. 341; see also Devasthali, *op. cit.*, p. 145.
46. Renou, *op. cit.*, p. 16.
47. See Heesterman, *op. cit.*, p. 48: *DH*, p.157.
48. Albrecht Weber, *The History of Indian Literature*, Varanasi, 1961, p. 21.
49. See W.H. Whillier, "Vision and Authority", *JSBhG*, V-VII (1985- 87), p.155.
50. Gonda, *Vedic Ritual—The Non-Solemn Rites*, Leiden, 1980, p. 231.
51. Wade Wheelock, "A Taxonomy of the *Mantras* in the New and Full-Moon Sacrifice", *HR*, 19/4 (1980), pp. 349-69.
52. For a general discussion of the significance of tone in Vedic liturgy, see Renou, "La valeur du silence dans le culte Vedique", *JAOS*, 69 (1949), pp. 11-18.
53. See Thachil, *op. cit.*, p.13.
54. S.N. Dasgupta, *Hindu Mysticism*, Delhi, 1976, p.10.
55. *ibid.*, p. 18; see also Gonda, *Vedic Ritual*, pp. 5ff.

56. For warnings against those who fail to sacrifice by obeying the commands of these texts, see B. Smith, "Gods and Men in Vedic Ritualism", *HR*, 24/4 (1985), p. 302. See also Thomas Coburn, "Scripture in India: Towards a Theology of Word in Hindu Life", *JAAR*, LII/3 (1984), pp. 439ff.
57. J. Gonda, *Notes on Brahman*, Utrecht, 1950, p. 9.
58. Gonda, *Change and Continuity*, p. 229.
59. For the characteristics of Vedic learning, see *ibid.*, pp. 229ff.
60. See T. J. Hopkins, *op. cit.*, p. 49.
61. See Walter O. Kaelber, "The Brahmacārin: Homology and Continuity in Brahmanic Religion", *HR*, 21/1 (1981), pp. 77-99.
62. See Gispert-Sauch, "Sacrifice in Hinduism" in *The Eucharistic Mystery*, ed. J. Dupuis, Darjeeling, 1968, p. 136 (unpublished).
63. Heesterman, *op. cit.*, p. 88.
64. Vesci, *op. cit.*, p. 17; as Vesci points out, this practice has great impact on the social behaviour of Hindus entertaining guests. The host waits till his guest is served to his/her satisfaction; waits for the left-over.
65. See *AV*, XI. 7; IX. 6.
66. *YV*, IX. 21.
67. See Keith, *op. cit.*, pp. 259ff, 379ff; see also S. Levi, *La Doctrine du Sacrifice Dans Les Brāhmaṇas*, Paris, 1898, p.20.
68. T. J. Hopkins, *op. cit.*, p. 27.
69. J. Gonda suggests that the suffix *man* in terms like *karman*, *brahman* and *dharman* "is evidently especially fit to express the idea of powers manifesting themselves either in action and processes or in beings or objects or at the same time in actions and beings or objects", Gonda, *Notes on Brahman*, p. 73.
70. e.g. *ŚB*, I.1.2 mentions *karman*, *yagyas* (offertory prayer) and *anuvākya* (initiatory prayer). *AV*, XII.1.1 speaks of *tapas* and *brahman*; *AV*, XI.8.2.6 mentions *tapas* and *karman*.
71. See Heesterman, "Self-Sacrifice in Vedic Ritual", in *Gilgul: Essays on Transformation, Revolution and Permanence in the History of Religions*, eds. S. Shaked and others, Leiden, 1987, p. 92; R. Panikkar, "The Law of Karman and the Historical Dimension of Man", *PEW*, XII/1 (1972), p. 27. For reference, see *ṚV*, I.22.19; II.21.1; III.33.7; IV. 37.2; VII.21.23; IX.46.3; X.28.7.
72. *ŚB*, I.7.1.5; also see *TB*, III.2.1.4.
73. *ŚB*, X.5.3.9ff,
74. *AV*, XI.8.2,6.
75. See R. Panikkar, *The Vedic Experience*, London, 1977, p. 348f.
76. For details, see Louis Maliekal, *Yajña* and *Eucharist*, Bangalore, 1989, pp. 32-46.
77. Gonda, *Notes on Brahman*, p.14. For a survey of various attempts of etymology and suggestions of the meaning of *brahman*, see further pp. 18ff.

78. *ibid*., p. 58.
79. See J.A.B. van Buitenen, "Vedic and Upaniṣadic Bases of Indian Civilization", in *Chapters in Indian Civilization*, I: Classical and Medieval India, ed. Joseph W. Elder, Iowa, 1970, p. 14f.
80. F. Edgerton, *The Beginnings of Indian Philosophy*, London, 1965, p. 24.
81. A. Barth, *The Religions of India*, London, 1891, p. 38.
82. *SV*, IV.1.3.9, 10.
83. ṚV, I.70.1, 9; 93.6; II.12.14; VII.61.2, 71.65, 103.8; X.105.8.
84. D. Killingley, "OṂ: The Sacred Syllable in the *Veda*", in *A Net Cast Wide: Investigations into Indian Thought in Memory of David Friedman*, ed. J. Lipner, Newcastle upon Tyne, 1987, p. 15.
85. *AV*, XI.5.10, 22; XII.1.1; XIX.72, 19.7.
86. *ŚB*, V.1.1.11, 4.14; VI.1.9.8, 10; VII.3.1.42; VIII.4.1.3; IX.1.2.16, 2.3.3; X.2.4.6, 3.5.10, 11, 6.3.2; XI.2.3.1ff.
87. *ŚB*, VI.1.1.20.
88. See Haug, *AB*, p.75.
89. T.J. Hopkins, *op. cit.*, p.19f.
90. *ibid.*, p.20.
91. *AiB*, II.38: V.32.
92. Killingley, *op. cit.*, p.16f.
93. T.J. Hopkins, *op. cit.*, p.12.
94. See Wheelock, "Mantras", p.358. For the significance of particular metres, number of syllables and instructions for silent utterance, see *AV*, VI.114; *AiB*, II.31.
95. *AiB*, II.38; *ŚB*, VI.2.2.22.
96. *ŚB*, III.1.4.1.
97. *ŚB*, III.1.3.25.
98. See T.J. Hopkins, *op.cit.*, p.37; Gonda, *Notes on Brahman*, pp. 58ff.
99. *Gārgapatya* fire belongs to the house. Established in the northwest corner, it is used to prepare food for the sacrifice. *Āhavanya* fire, established to the east of the above, is used to cook the prepared offerings. The *dakṣiṇa* or southern fire has the dual function of warding off the hostile spirits and receiving special offerings to departed ancestors. See T.J. Hopkins, *op. cit.*, p.19.
100. *ibid.*
101. See Keith, *op. cit.*, p. 287f.
102. Vesci, *op. cit.*, p. 43.
103. *ŚB*, I.7.3.26. For more references see Maliekal, *op. cit.*, pp. 52ff.
104. *ṚV*. X.129.1-4. According to *ṚV*, X.190.1-3 order (*ṛta*) and truth (*satya*) were born of kindled *tapas* from which were born night, year etc.
105. T.J. Hopkins, *op. cit.*, p. 26.
106. See D.M. Knipe, *In the Image of Fire*, Delhi, 1975, p.136f.
107. Usually *yajña* is attributed to the root *yaj*, meaning 'to give'. U. Rustagi gives an account of various other etymological meanings of *yajña.*

Accordingly, (i) it has connections with *ajnas*, skins of black antelopes; (ii) *yaju* signifying sacred power; (iii) worship offered to gods and having union with them; (iv) giving away or renunciation. See Rustagi, *Darṣapūrṇamāsa,* Delhi, 1981, p.1; Keith points out another etymology, '*yan-ja*' meaning a movement of perpetual series of deaths and rebirths with reference to *ŚB.* III. 9.4.23. See Keith, *op. cit.*, p. 460.

108. See Staal, "The Meaninglessness of Ritual", *Numen,* XXVI/1 (1979), pp. 2-22.
109. The outcome of field-work is Staal's (ed.) two volumes of *AGNI*, Delhi, 1983.
110. See *ibid.*, pp.9ff.
111. Staal, "Meaninglessness", p.3.
112. *ibid.*, p. 9.
113. *ibid.*, p.18.
114. *ibid.*, p.11.
115. cf. *ŚB,* IX.2.1.18ff.
116. For various references for the bird-symbol, see Eggeling, *ŚB*, IV, p. xxiff.
117. See Eggeling, *ŚB,* IV, p. xxiii.
118. For various acts in the process of crushing the *soma* plant and the idea of transubstantiation attached to *soma* juice, see Ananda Coomaraswamy, *Hinduism and Buddhism,* New York, n.d., p.38f.
119. Gonda, *Vedic Ritual,* p. 28f.
120. Hans H. Penner, "Language, Ritual and Meaning", *Numen,* 32/1 (1983), p. 2.
121. With reference to certain scholars, Penner says, "Referential theories of meaning continue to have a powerful hold on scholars interested in the study of religion and culture." Nevertheless, he continues, "Given the modern developments in linguistics we can no longer assume the meaning of something as its reference"; *ibid.*, p. 4.
122. *ibid.*, p. 7.
123. *ibid,* p.11.
124. *ibid,* p.13.
125. *ibid,* p.13f.
126. Heesterman, *op. cit.*, p.189. For a similar view see N.N. Bhattacharyya, *op. cit.*, p. 69.
127. B.K. Smith, "Review of *Inner Conflict*", RSR, 14/1 (1988), p. 8.
128. *ibid.*
129. B. K. Smith, "Sacrifice and Being—Prajāpati's Cosmic Emission and Its Consequences", *Numen,* XXXII/1 (1985), p. 72.
130. D. M. Knipe, *op. cit.*, p. 42f.
131. See Heesterman, *op. cit.*, p.189f.
132. Gonda, *Change and Continuity,* p.17f.
133. *ṚV,* IV.1.9.

134. Knipe, *op. cit.*, p.31f.
135. *ŚB*, XI.2.1.1.
136. *ŚB*, II.2.4.8; III.6.2.16; cf. Keith, *op. cit.*, p. 46.
137. See Basu, *op. cit.*, p.183.
138. Hubert and Mauss, *op. cit.*, p. 20f.
139. *ŚB*, I.1.1.4.
140. Hubert and Mauss, *op. cit.*, p. 55.
141. *ŚB* I.1.1.4ff.
142. For a discussion on the exchange of purity and impurity between priests, gods and the sacrificer, see Heesterman, "Vrātya", p. 29.
143. Aguilar, *op. cit.*, p. 49.
144. Heesterman, "Self-Sacrifice", p. 92; see also, A. Coomaraswamy, "Ātmayajña: Self Sacrifice". *HJAS*, 6 (1941), p. 359ff.
145. See Coomaraswamy, *Hinduism and Buddhism*, *op. cit.*, p. 36.
146. Dasgupta, *op. cit.*, p.10.
147. *ŚB*, VIII.6.1.10.
148. R. Panikkar, *The Vedic Experience*, p. 355.
149. *ṚV.* I.164.35.
150. See Knipe, *op. cit.*, p. 45.
151. *ibid.*, p.38f; also see Heesterman, *Inner Conflict*, p. 45.
152. e.g. see *ṚV*, X.15.88, 90, 130; *ŚB*, XI.2.8.1ff; *AV*. XII.1.6ff; Hopkins notes, "the primary act of creation is the creation of the sacrifice; that being created, all else is formed from it", Hopkins, *op. cit.*, p. 22; Hubert and Mauss note, "In India the continual creation of things by means of the rite eventually becomes an absolute-*creatio ex nihilio*", *op. cit.*, p. 93.
153. D.D. Rupwate, "A Versatile Significance of *Ṛta*", *ABORI*, LXII (1982), p. 8.
154. *ṚV*, I.23.5; V.68.4.
155. Panikkar, *Vedic Experience*, p. 350; also see Maliekal, *op. cit.*, p. 48ff.
156. Gonda, *A History of Indian Literature*, 1 Vedic, p. 340.
157. See Abel Bergaigne, *Vedic Religion*, Delhi, 1978. pp. xiiiff. cf. *ṚV*, V.69.3, 76.3; VII.41.4; VIII.1.29, 27.19, 21; X.15.15. For the connection between seasonal rites and distance of times, see Van Buitenen, "Vedic and Upaniṣadic Bases of Indian Civilization" in *Chapters in Indian Civilization*, Vol. 1, ed. by Joseph W Elder, Iowa, 1970, p. 25f.
158. *ibid.*, p.32.cf. *ṚV*, IV, 6.4, 5, 9.3, 15: 1-3.
159. See D.D. Rupwate, "A Versatile Significance of Ṛta", *ABORI*, LX III (1982), p.13.
160. The relation of the important gods Prajāpati, Varuṇa, Viṣṇu, Agni and Indra to sacrifice is extensively described by J. Gonda in his essay, "Vedic Gods and the Sacrifice", *Numen*, XXX/1 (1983), pp.1-34.
161. e.g. *ŚB*, I.1.3.1, 2.5.9ff, 7.4.20, 9.3.9.
162. e.g. *ŚB*, I.1.1.13, 2.5.12, 13.
163. e.g. *ŚB*, III.2.2.9.

164. e.g. *ṚV*, I.43.4, 5, 64.2ff.
165. *ŚB*, III.4.2.6.7.
166. E.g. See Keith, *op. cit.*, p. 259.
167. Gonda, *Change and Continuity*, p. 214.
168. *ṚV*, I.170.3; X.117, 36.
169. Coomaraswamy, *Hinduism and Buddhism*, p. 36.
170. See Lott, *op. cit.*, p.19.
171. Vesci, *op. cit.*, p. 274.
172. For an account of Viṣṇu's supremacy by encompassing first the end of the sacrifice, see *ŚB*, XIV.1.1.4-6; Coomaraswamy, "Self-Sacrifice", p. 360.
173. Dandekar, "Hinduism", in *Historia Relegionum*, eds. C. Jouco Bleaker and Geo Eindengren, Leiden, 1971, Vol II, p. 289; for details of gods' performance of sacrifice in Kurukṣetra, see Gonda, *HIL*, I. *Vedic*, p. 325.
174. For the difference between the ontological conditions of gods and humans in connection with sacrifice, see B. Smith, "Gods and Men in Vedic Ritualism: Towards a Hierarchy of Resemblance", *HR*, 24/4 (1985), p. 294f.
175. Panikkar, *Vedic Experience*, p. 380f; cf. *ŚB*, V.1.1.1-2.
176. See Vesci, *op. cit.*, p. 274.
177. *ibid.*, p. 276; for Prajāpati's identification with Puruṣa and Agni see T.J. Hopkins, *op. cit.*, p. 32.
178. See the *Puruṣaśukta* hymn in *ṚV*, X.90; cf.XIX.6.
179. *ŚB*, XI.2.8.2, 3; cf. Eggeling, *ŚB*, IV, p. xiiiff. For further details of Prajāpati and his connection with sacrifice as well as different faces of this deity, see J. Gonda, "The Popular Prajāpati", *HR*, XII/2 (1982), pp.129-49; *Prajāpati's Rise to Higher Rank*, Leiden, 1986.
180. *Prajāpati vai kāh*, *ŚB*, IV.5.6.4.
181. See Vesci, *op. cit.*, p. 277f.
182. See J.E. Mitchiner, *Tradition of the Seven Ṛsis*, Delhi, 1982, pp.193, 250, 280ff, 295ff.
183. See Biardeau and Malamoud, *Le Sacrifice dans l'Inde Anciene*, Paris, 1976, p. 24.
184. *ŚB*, XIII.4.1.1.
185. *AV*, XIX.52.1, 2, 4.
186. *AV*, III.29.3, 21.4.
187. *AV*, XI.2.1ff.
188. See Gonda, *HIL*, 1-Vedic, p. 376.
189. E.G. *ṚV*. I.9.5ff; *AV*. VI.39.1,2; A.B., I.9; *ŚB*, XIII.3.7.1ff; Gonda, *Vedic Ritual*, p. 4.
190. Smith, "Gods and Men in Vedic Ritualism", *HR*, 24/4 (1985), p. 295.
191. See Gonda, *Change and Continuity*, p. 218; R. Desmet, "Highlights of the Life of Faith (*śraddhā*) in India", in *God's Word among Men*, ed. G. Gispert-Sauch, Delhi, 1973, p. 40f; Panikkar, *Vedic Experience*, p.49.

192. *AV*, XV.2.16; ṚV, X.151; TB, III.12.3.2.
193. Gonda, *HIL*, 1. *Vedic*, p. 364.
194. *ibid*, p. 367.
195. E.g. *ŚB*, C.3.3.8; IX.1.2.43: X.10.1.5,2.6.7; *AiB*, III.2.29; *ṚV*, X.44.5, 6, 101.2. The rise of oblation and fire are identified with the rise of the sacrificer to heaven. See B. Smith, "Gods and Men", *op. cit.*, p. 293f; *AiB*,II,14; and for identification with bodily forms of the gods, see *ŚB*, XII.9. 1.8, 9.
196. Smith, *ibid.*, p. 298.
197. Hubert and Mauss, quoted, in *ibid*, p. 300.
198. *ṚV*, X.14.8; see *ibid.*, p.303f.
199. *ŚB*, XI.2.2.5.
200. *AB*, II.8.6.
201. *ŚB*, X.1.5.4.
202. Panikkar, *Vedic Experience*, p. 395.
203. See Thite, "Animal Sacrifice", p.156f; see also Ghurye, *Vedic India*, p. 51.
204. See Biardeau and Malamoud, *op. cit.*, p. 25.
205. Coomaraswamy, *Hinduism and Buddhism*, p.46.
206. *ṚV*, X.90.16.
207. *ṚV*, III.21.2; V.26.26; IX.64.1.
208. T.J. Hopkins, *op. cit.*, p. 25.
209. Coomaraswamy, *Hinduism and Buddhism*, p. 46ff.
210. See Heesterman, *Inner Conflict*, p.188.
211. *ŚB*, IV.1.4.5f.
212. *AiB*, VII.19. tr. A.B. Keith, *Rigveda Brāhmaṇas: The Aitareya and Kauṣitāki Brāhmaṇas of the Rigveda*, Cambridge, 1920, p.308f. For further reference to such conflicts, see Heesterman, *Inner Conflict*, p.112, 152.
213. *AV*, XV.10.1-11.
214. Among these, four classes of priests were at the core: the *adhvaryu* was the performer of the material part of sacrifice; the *udgātṛ* was the chanter of hymns; the *hotṛ* was the reciter of solemn sacrificial prayers; the *Brahman* was the superintendent and physician of sacrifice. The precise function of the various classes and the exact number of priests required in a sacrifice is, however, not clear. See Eggeling, *ŚB*, I, p.xxf.
215. *ŚB*, II.2.2.6; IV.3.4.4. cf. *ṚV*, III.7.7; see Gonda, *Vedic Ritual, op. cit.*, p. 196.
216. See Basu, *op. cit.*, p.17.
217. Gonda, *Vedic Ritual*, p.197.
218. Knipe, *op.cit.*, p.32.
219. E.g. see *ŚB*, I.2.3.4; II.2.2.2f; *AiB*, V.34; *AV*, IX.4.19.
220. See Gonda, *Ancient Indian Kingship from the Religious Point of View*, Leiden, 1969, p.63f; for the significance of the priestly chaplain to the

king (*purohita*) for the well-being of the king, see p.198.

221. *ŚB*, XIII.4.1.2ff; III.2.9.1, 5.6.67; see Heesterman, *Inner Conflict*, p.29f.
222. *ŚB*, V.1.5.14; see also Gonda, *Vedic Ritual, op.cit.*, p.52f.
223. Eggeling, *ŚB*, IV, p. xvi.
224. J. Gonda, *Ancient Indian Kingship from the Religious Point of View*, Leiden, 1969, p.11.
225. See N. N. Bhattacharyya, *op.cit.*, p. 29f; they were elected by people and assisted by administrative council. See Ghurye, *op.cit.*, p.292ff; Majumdar and others, *An Advanced History of Ancient India*, London, 1950, p.28f.
226. *ŚB*, I.3.2.15; see also II.5.2.7; I.3.4.15; III.9.3.7; Ghurye, *op. cit.*, p. 300.
227. *ŚB*, VI.4.4.13.
228. See Griswold, *op.cit.*, p. 51.
229. See Basu, *op.cit.*, p.12f.
230. *ŚB* XIV.1.1.31; Ghurye, *op.cit.*, p.301.
231. B.K. Smith, "Canonical Authority and Social Classification: Veda and *Varṇa* in Ancient Indian Texts", *HR*, 32/2 (1992), p.124.
232. *ŚB*, II.2.2.9; *ṚV*, X.129.1ff; *AV*, XII.1.39. It was an animating force in Prajāpati for his creation; *Ṛta* and *Satya* come from *tapas*, *ṚV*, X.190.1.
233. See Eggeling, *ŚB*, I. pp.18ff; *ṚV*, I.55.1; TB, III.12.3.
234. *AV*, XI.5.1ff.
235. *AV*, XIX.64.1-2; *ŚB*, II.3,4.21,
236. See A. Barth, *The Religions of India*, London, 189, p.85; e.g. *ṚV*, X.129.
237. *ŚB*, I.2.5.24.
238. *ŚB*, X.4.3.9; for further details and references see Coomaraswamy, *Hinduism and Buddhism*, p.37f.
239. *ŚB*, X.5.4.15; *AiB*, II.7.4.
240. *ŚB*, XI.2.6.13.
241. *AV*, XIX.58.1, 4-6; *YV*, VI.1.4.4: *ṚV*, IV. 2.6.
242. *ŚB*. II.2.4.7, 8.
243. *ŚB*, XI.5.6.3ff
244. *ŚB*, X.4.3.10; see T.J. Hopkins, *op.cit.*, p. 34.
245. *ŚB*, XI.3.1.1-3.
246. Knipe, *op.cit.*, p.118.
247. Kaelber, "The Brahmacārin", p. 98f.
248. See Karel Werner, "Yoga and the Ṛgveda: An Interpretation of the *Keśin* Hymn (ṚV, X, 136)", *RS*, 13 (1977), pp.289-302.
249. *ibid.*, p. 297.
250. See Hopkins, *Hindu*, p.49; Ghurye, *Indian Sadhus*, Bombay, 1964, p.14; J.C. Omen, *The Mystics, Ascetics and Saints of India*, London, 1903, pp.1ff; M.G. Bhagat, *Ancient Indian Asceticism*, New Delhi, 1976, pp.63ff; Thapar, *Ancient Indian Social History*, p. 67f.
251. For a discussion on different opinions, see P. Misra, *Evolution of the Brahman Class*, Varanasi, 1978, pp.72ff.
252. Heesterman, "Vrātya and Sacrifice", pp.1ff.

253. Gonda, "Ascetics and Courtesans", *ALB,* XXV/1-4 (1961), p. 85.
254. M. Eliade, *Yoga,* p.105.
255. P.S. Jaini, "Śramaṇas: Their Conflict with Brāhmaṇical Society" in *Chapters in Indian Civilization,* 1, p.46f.
256. Eliade, *op.cit.*
257. Dandekar, "Hinduism", p. 257.
258. P. Misra, *Brahman Class,* p.77.
259. See Jaini, "Śramaṇas", p.45.
260. See *ibid.*, p. 46.

II

Development of *Jñāna Yajña* and *Ātma Yajña*: The Tension between Ritual and Interiorisation in the *Upaniṣads*

1. Introduction

We have seen that glimpses of interiorisation accommodated in the framework of Vedic sacrifice are found in the *Saṃhitā* and *Brāhmaṇa* texts. A fuller development of interiorisation with a new framework, with emphasis on the sacrifice of knowledge and self (*jñāna* and *ātma yajña*), is found in the *Upaniṣads*. The complex literary structure of the *Upaniṣads*, however, makes a distinction between those two frameworks difficult. This chapter attempts to understand sacrifice in the *Upaniṣads*. We shall argue for a major paradigm shift seen from the perspective of Vedic *yajña*, which had a decisive impact in the post-Vedic period.

The *Upaniṣads* are usually studied from a philosophical perspective, within the metaphysical framework of *brahman-ātman-jñāna-mokṣa*. An explanation of the fluid thought of the *Upaniṣads* that gives way to a number of metaphysical positions (as evident, for instance, in the different interpretations of the schools of *Vedānta*) need not detain us here. We are concerned only with arguing that the main teachings of the *Upaniṣads* become clear if only viewed from the perspective of sacrifice, the central dimension of Vedic religion. Therefore, with a brief recognition of the problem in understanding sacrifice as found in the *Upaniṣads*, we shall focus on the tension between ritual sacrifice and self-sacrifice, giving further attention to the patterns of interpretation in order to emphasise the latter.

Even though the *Upaniṣads* have not generally been studied from the perspective of Vedic sacrifice, the persistence of ritual in the process of new departures has not gone unnoticed. The complex nature of the *Upaniṣadic* texts has however led scholars to arrive at different conclusions. For example, R.E. Hume finds in the *Upaniṣads* "intimations" of the futility of an empty ceremonialism. He holds further, "The development of a monistic philosophy removed altogether the necessity of believing in the various Vedic and brāhmaṇic gods".[1] For Paul Deussen, although the *Upaniṣads* teach and expound allegorically the ritual of sacrifice, they are "radically opposed to the entire Vedic sacrificial cult and the older they are the more markedly does this opposition declare itself".[2] P.M. Modi in the introduction to his study of the *Gītā* notes: "*Vedas* teach sacrifices, rites and ceremonies promising rewards for their performance. *Upaniṣads* protested against such a religion of actions done for the sake of the rewards, and they taught the religion of asceticism, retirement to forest, and realization of Brahman through meditation".[3] Dasgupta, while acknowledging that the *Upaniṣads* are inseparable from the preceding portions of the *Vedas,* seems to agree with the tradition which "looked upon the *Upaniṣads* as being of an entirely different type from the rest of the Vedic literature dictating the path of knowledge (*jñāna mārga*) as opposed to the path of works (*karma mārga*)".[4] This opinion appears in many studies of Indian thought in general.

There are also those who emphasise the persistence of Vedic sacrifice in the *Upaniṣads,* although some of them try to reconcile the ritual religion with the new path of spirituality. Keith refutes the opinion that Vedic sacrifice is totally rejected in the *Upaniṣads.* Though ritual sacrifice is brought to an inferior position, he argues, there are sufficient references to indicate that it was restored to honour after the élite had attempted to remove it.[5] Renou also refutes the anti-sacrifice opinion and adds that the *Upaniṣads* were intended for advanced people who wanted something beyond the formal course of instruction.[6] Radhakrishnan finds in the *Upaniṣads* a criticism only of empty and barren ritualistic religion.[7] But on occasions he is more blunt in pointing out the "uselessness of ritual and the futility of sacrifice" as brought out in the *Upaniṣads.*[8] Radhakrishnan seems to be more concerned that a new spiritual path was obscured by the mixture of the lower religion of sacrifice. Nevertheless, he tries to reconcile the two by explaining that the lower religion was a means to improve the soul and prepare the mind to attain the higher, and that the latter accommodated and refined the former.[9] Hiriyanna's explanation, too, is on similar lines. He holds that though Vedic sacrifice is indispensable for knowledge of the self, it has as at a higher stage to be transcended and relegated to an inferior position as done in the *Upaniṣads*[10]

One reason why a clear view of this issue is not available is that the *Upaniṣads* have not been studied from the perspective of sacrifice, the heart of Vedic religion. The few studies that have been made in this direction and their conclusions are, however, remarkable. Goman and Laura appear to have recognised the problem involved in understanding sacrifice in the *Upaniṣads.*[11] In a rather brief treatment of it they hold that *jñāna* and *tapas* are superior to *yajña;* also, it is not *yajña* but *tapas* that leads to *jñāna.* They also point out some references to sacrifice that are connected with internal organs, purification of self, the structure of the universe and ethical life, though they do not explain the nature of the connection. Further, with Keith they affirm that though there is a revolt against the established ritual order, nothing in the earlier texts could be interpreted as an injunction to do away with sacrifice altogether. On his part Mainkar contends that the "*Upaniṣads* contain nothing that departs from earlier Vedic Literature and tradition".[12] And for Thite,

> although there are a few anti-ritualistic thoughts in the *Upaniṣads,* the *Upaniṣadic* literature as a whole is not anti-ritualistic. It often uses the terminology of ritual and contains many thoughts having close similarity with ritualistic speculations also.... The magico-religious rites described in the *Upaniṣads* are essentially similar to those described in other ritual texts.[13]

Giving more weight to the anti-ritualistic ideas, Wadhwani-Shah[14] suggests that an imperceptible revolution against sacrificial ritual or a gradual replacement of the external ritual by mental meditation or a fusion of old and new ideas can be found in the *Upaniṣads.* R. Panikkar identifies three phases in the *Upaniṣadic* treatment of sacrifice: (i) anthropocosmic sacrifice in which the ancient-style sacrifices still predominate; (ii) anthropocentric sacrifice, which stresses less the traditional sacrifice but underlines the meaning of sacrifice for human life, almost identifying one sacrifice with another; (iii) and *mānasya yajña,* "the internal sacrifice of an undisturbed and perfect mind re-enacting within itself the whole dynamism of the outer world, whose existence, if not always denied or doubted, is certainly minimised. We are present here at the birth of another ritual".[15] These observations, while recognising the major aspects of sacrifice in the *Upaniṣads,* fail to clarify the absence of easy compatibility between ritual sacrifice and interior sacrifice.

To have a clear view with proper perspective of sacrifice in the *Upaniṣads* is also difficult because of their complex structure, in continuation of the preceding Vedic texts. Dandekar observes:

The *Upanishads* cannot be regarded as presenting a consistent or unified philosophical system, though there are certain doctrines held in common. Divergences of method, opinion, and conclusion are everywhere apparent even within a single *Upanishad*. It is for this reason that the *Upanishads* are considered speculative treatises. Another significant feature of the *Upanishads*, particularly the older ones, is that practically every basic idea expounded has its antecedent in earlier Vedic texts. What distinguishes the *Upanishads* is not so much their originality as their probing for new interpretations of the earlier Vedic concepts to obtain a more coherent view of the universe and man.[16]

New tendencies or new directions about the question of sacrifice can, however, be identified in the *Upaniṣads* as we attempt to view them from the Vedic perspective.

To understand the new direction of the *Upaniṣads* it is important to recognise its relation to the part of the *Vedas*, preceding the *Upaniṣads*, particularly the *Brāhmaṇas* and the *Āraṇyakas*. As far as the main themes are concerned, as Radhakrishnan observes, "The Āraṇyakas shade off imperceptibly into the *Upaniṣads* even as the *Brāhmaṇas* shade off into the *Āraṇyakas*".[17] Then it is understandable that some of the oldest *Upaniṣads* are included in the *Āraṇyakas* and according to tradition they form together part of the *Brāhmaṇas*.[18] Nevertheless, new trends are noticeable in the portions called *Upaniṣads* that are incipient in the *Āraṇyakas* in which we see a movement from ritual to meditation, community to solitude and home to forest. As Gonda notes, although the *Āraṇyakas* do not replace ritual, they came to be imparted to and studied by advanced students in the solitude of the forest because their contents were too "sacred", too secret and esoteric, too uncanny and dangerous to be communicated and learned in the villages. Their main subject was, indeed, not only the explanation of the sacrificial rites, but the relevant texts and their mystic and allegorical, "symbolical" and "philosophical" significance.[19]

Gonda notes further that in course of time the tendency was for the explanation contained in definite portions of the *Brāhmaṇas*

to develop into expositions of meta-ritualism, and then [they] grew independent of the ritual until the stage was reached where the name *āraṇyaka* was no longer applicable, because the subject matter had passed into that of an *Upaniṣad*. At that stage the growth of speculation, as leading to the highest goal, had gradually resulted in the suppression of ritualism. As a result of this development these texts came also to be studied by ascetics.[20]

Such attempts to make logical connections between these texts do not, however, take into account the tension involved between ritual and interiorisation as found particularly in the *Upaniṣads*. The texts as they are presented to us may suggest that originally two different methods and goals existed before they came into conflict and intermingled. We need to go further than this approach.

It is difficult to frame a satisfactory chronology of the *Upaniṣads* although the earliest principal *Upaniṣads* are fairly recognisable.[21] They are said to belong to the eighth and seventh centuries B.C.[22] The main focus of this chapter is the emergence of the sacrifice of the self (*ātma yajña*). It includes a recognition of the continued presence of Vedic sacrifice and points of departure into new ways of understanding; the significance of the allegorical interpretation with a rich use of symbols and imagery; the nature of *ātma yajña* and its means; and finally the emergence of a new group of sacrificers, the *śramaṇas,* who dominate the scene of the post-Vedic developments in the idea of sacrifice.

2. Persistence of Ritual Sacrifice and New Directions

In this section we shall note the continuation of the Vedic *yajña* in the *Upaniṣads* and the ideas related thereto and how new directions are initiated for a fresh understanding. We shall maintain a link between the earlier ideas of *yajña* and their continued persistence despite radical changes in understanding them with a new framework.

(i) Continuation of Vedic Sacrifice

The *Aitareya Āraṇyaka* describes in detail sacrifices and their fruits in the same terms as they are understood in the Ṛgveda. The second *Āraṇyaka* begins with the following words, which support the Vedic sacrifice and identify it with *brahman,* the holy power or prayer.

> This is the path; this is sacrifice; this is *brahman*; this is truth. Therefore let no man diverge from it, let no man transgress it. For they did not transgress it; of old, those who did transgress it were overcome.[23]

The same *Āraṇyaka* says further that the brahmin priest, who is full of *brahman,* the holy power of ritual utterance, is the essence of the

Vedas. It describes in deatil the *mahāvrata* ceremony, which is one form of *agnistoma,* holding it to be of high rank.[24] The *Kauṣitakī Upaniṣad,* which speaks about meditation (*dhyāna*) and other spiritual practices, speaks at the same time of worship of the sun three times accompanied by the sprinkling of water for the removal of sin, and worship of the moon from which issues forth prosperity.[25] Almost in the syle of the *Śatapatha Brāhmaṇa,* but with a different order, the *Bṛhadāraṇyaka Upaniṣad,* in parts one of the earliest *Upaniṣads,* mentions that Prajāpati produced sacrifice along with the *Vedas,* humans and cattle.[26] It also has the following description: Yama, the deity of the southern quarter, is supported by the offerings of the priests, the offerings being supported by *śraddhā* and *śraddhā* by the heart.[27] A *ṛtvij* priest is said to be desired by people for his good tone, which is the gold and wealth of *sāman.* He who knows this wealth attains gold and wealth.[28] And a departing father says to his son, 'You are *brahman,* you are sacrifice and you are the world'. This is repeated by the son through whose breaths the father enters into him and stands firm.[29] There is also an affirmation that sacrifices, oblations, *Vedas* etc. issue forth from the Supreme Self.[30] In the *Chāndogya Upaniṣad* the knowledge of sacrifice means to know the deity and the rewards of a particular rite, the silence of the brahmin priest in appropriate moments and the correct utterance of *mantras* to save the sacrifice from injury.[31] The rite called *mantha,* in which offering is made to the vital elements of nature, fulfils desires, the sign of its success is said to be the sight of a woman in a vision.[32] The *Taittirīya Upaniṣad* attaches the sacred syllable *OṂ,* which is identical with the Supreme Being, to the utterance of priests in a ritual performance.[33] For the *Śvetāsvatara Upaniṣad,* the *Vedas,* sacrifices and rituals are sent forth by God, the creator.[34] In the context of what has been said, there seems no need to explain how all these references echo the elements of Vedic *yajña.*

(ii) Towards a Search for Reality Beyond Sacrifice

It is significant to note that questions about ultimate Reality are raised mostly at sacrificial ceremonies.[35] The famous prayer—"from the unreal lead me to the real, from darkness lead me to light and from death lead me to immortality"—is recited by a *yajamāna* in the midst of the rituals and recitations of the priests with the "world-conquering" *kāma.*[36] The terms real, truth and immortality seem to have denoted in this context ritual perfection and worldly well-being.[37] Even after awareness of the Supreme Self, it is said, he who recites it secretly before an assembly of brahmins during ceremonies for the dead will prepare for eternal life.[38] It is striking that those who, intent on the *brahman*, the Supreme Self, approach the *gurus* for the explanation of truth are said to go with sacrificial fuel in their hands.[39] The *Muṇḍaka Upaniṣad* reaffirms that the *Vedas*, *yajñas* and *yajamānas* come from the *brahman* or *ātman*. More strikingly, even after minimising the importance of *yajña* certain texts struggle to preserve its ritual sense. This *Upaniṣad* concludes with its central affirmation that the liberation of the self by the realisation of *brahman* should be taught only to those who have performed rites and studied the *Vedas*. Its final words are: "let none who has not performed the rite read this".[40] Thus it becomes clear that, as presented in the *Upaniṣads*, there is an attempt to show the Vedic ritual *yajña* as preparing the ground for a setting out on the search for a deeper or new meaning of *yajña*.

Just the same, amidst the untiring attempts to find some room for ritual *yajña* in the new path, the search for the ultimate meaning of life and the transcendent being in this transient world increasingly comes to the fore. This movement involves even the total rejection of the old ritual *yajña* and its related notions. The sense of the perpetual thrust of the human being to transcendence is stated succinctly in the following words: "This man is the sea; he is above all the world. Whatever he reaches he desires to be beyond it. If he gains the sky world he desires to be beyond it. If he were to gain the yonder world, he would desire to be beyond it".[41] This transcendental attitude is considered as the animating factor for a radical departure from the *kāma*-bound, material pleasure-oriented Vedic *yajña*. The latter has no ultimate value even if it is allowed to be performed for lower ends. At times, this movement leads to the rejection of ritual sacrifice.

The *Muṇḍaka Upaniṣad*, for example, after describing eighteen forms of sacrifice, declares that they are "unsafe boats" to cross the world and inferior actions (*karman*) because the delight they produce is evanescent. Therefore, it says, to remain in sacrifice is to be ignorant like a blind person being led by another blind person; for the sacrificers sink down again with attachment when their fruits are exhausted in *svarga*. For attaining the imperishable world this *Upaniṣad* suggests the alternative of *tapas*, *śraddhā*, solitary and wandering life, non-attachment, learning and getting established in the supreme Brahman.[42] The idea of re-death in *svarga* as developed in the later *Brahmaṇa* texts is further emphasised; all material boons are of lesser value in comparison with re-death (*punar mṛtyu*) in heaven. Thus permanence and imperishability become the focus of further search.

The new activities generated by this search and the new ideas that emerged in this process we shall consider later. At this juncture it may be useful to describe certain new forms of this departure as against the ritual forms. There are new myths about gods, the supreme god Prajāpati, creation and so on. The prominence of the Vedic priests is now transferred to the teachers of knowledge. For a learned student, not the Vedic gods or the brahmins but his father, mother, teacher (*guru*) and guest become his gods.[43] The term *brāhmaṇa* is now defined as the one who meditates on the *brahman* and not as the controller of *brahman,* the holy power.[44] The *dakṣiṇās* of cows, gold etc. are now to be given for instruction in truth.[45] Thus the place of the priests is now taken by teachers (*gurus*) of the new truth. The role of the *guru* is important to lead one from the empirical or lower knowledge (*apara-jñāna*) which includes the study of the *Vedas,* performance of sacrifice to the supreme and the knowledge (*prajñāna*), by which the imperishable is directly perceived.

The relationship between the old *ācāryas,* the priests skilled in Vedic knowledge, and the new *gurus* is not clear. Originally it seems to have denoted teachers of the *Vedas* and sacrifice.[46] The term *guru* occurs for the first time in the *Chāndogya Upaniṣad.*[47] Gonda observes, "The term guru in itself is an illustration of the widespread belief that mighty, divine, or holy persons are held to be characterized by an uncommon weight".[48]

Probably their weight was given for their special knowledge of the functioning of the cosmos and of the human personality. It stands to reason that the new circle of teachers was a new formation affected by the ascetic tradition even though some teachers of the old type tried to combine the new knowledge with their knowledge of ritual and its cosmic significance. No hierarchical structure was needed for the new teachers. There are references to certain fathers who taught the idea of an Imperishable Reality to their sons who had no knowledge of it even after having spent several years in the study of the *Vedas* under teachers qualified in Vedic lore.[49] This shows that the new *guru*-ship was not confined to a particular caste as was the priesthood.

In the new shift from priesthood to *guru*-ship the old gods of sacrifice become the students of knowledge (*jñāna*). Prajāpati, for example, is no more the Lord of sacrifice from whom knowledge had to be shared by gods and *asuras* in competition, but the *guru* who taught them about the Imperishable Self.[50] The *guru* Prajāpati instructs his three offspring: to *devas* he says, "control yourself"; to *manuṣas,* "give" and to *asuras,* "have compassion". Therefore, it is said, one should practise the triad of self-control, giving and compassion.[51] Then the *brahmacārin* comes to be regarded not for his skill in performing sacrifice but for his disciplined life. The *Chāndogya Upaniṣad* declares: "Now, what people call *yajña* is really the disciplined life of a *brahmacārin.* Only by the *brahmacārin* one knows and attains the *ātman*".[52]

It should be noted again that despite the shift in emphasis (for a new paradigm) from ritual to knowledge, priesthood to *guru*-ship, the ritual elements persist. Thus in the discipline of a *brahmacārin* protracted sacrifice of mainly *agnihotra,* a vow of silence, and a course of fasting are included. Study of the *Vedas* is also emphasised but for their essential meaning. The essential meaning is the meaning of the *Upaniṣads* and for this reason some *Upaniṣads* claim that the very reading of them is equal to all sacrifices and all purificatory ceremonies.[53] Elsewhere, it is stated that praising gods and ritual may be a preparation for *ātma darśana.*[54] Thus the mixture of a persistence of old ritual and introduction of new substitutes is characteristic of the *Upaniṣads.*

In a dialectical process of a new paradigm interacting with an old one tension or incertitude occurs. This will become more obvious when we point out old terms given new meanings.

(iii) Old Terms and New Meanings

In the ritual context *karman* was one of the generators of power resting in the exactitude of ritual act. In the *Upaniṣads karman* becomes general and ethical. Another significant development is *saṃsāra,* which is associated with *karman.* As Basham points out, "one of the greatest unresolved problems of Indian history is the origin of this doctrine and the reason for its rapid spread."[55] Deussen notes how the doctrine of the *ātman* stood in "sharp contrast to all the principles of the Vedic ritual".[56] Some hold that the seeds of the idea of *karma-saṃsāra* may be found in the earlier sections of the *Vedas;* but obviously the references they cite to this effect are ambiguous and their interpretation appears forced.[57] There are different opinions about the source of the ideas of soul and transmigration. One suggestion is that it came from the animistic view of the aborigines. It may have been introduced into brāhmaṇism by early mendicants or shamans. In any case the idea took a clear shape only in the *Upaniṣads.*[58] It is presented as a new secret. Thus Jāratkārava Ārtabāga questions Yājñavalkya:"when a person dies, what is it that does not leave him?" The answer given is "name" (*nāma*). But when pressed further, Yājñavalkya takes him aside and they discuss the issue in secret (*rahasya*): "The two went away and deliberated. What they said was *karma* and what they praised was *karma.* Verily one becomes good by good *karma* and bad by bad *karma".*[59]

The process of rotation and the animating power of *kāma* are described subsequently.[60] We need not explain the repercussion of the idea of *karma-saṃsāra* on some other notions. It provides, for instance, a means of relegating Vedic gods to rebirth in lower forms and elevating śūdras to the higher status of brahmins and kṣatriyas. We shall see later how this tool was handled by critics of the brāhmaṇic tradition.

In the ritual context *brahman* meant the holy power which rested especially in prayer or sacred utterance in the performance of sacrifice. But now it has come to mean the universal self or ultimate reality. Gonda writes: "Brahman, indeed, is more and more regarded as the potency or principle from which all things are derived, as the ultimate basis of the world, as one with the true immortality and eternal reality".[61]

Though *brahman* is presented in personal terms as creator in a few pasages, the Upaniṣadic emphasis is that *brahman* is a super-personal, eternal, self-existent, unifying principle. It is the imperishable source of all beings and all things. It is a macrocosmic reality whose microcosmic form may be identified with the individual soul (*ātman*). As we shall see later *brahman* is the ultimate goal towards which all *ātmans* move through the path of knowledge.

In the ritual context *tapas* was another generator of power which lay with the established sacred fires and with the cooking of oblations. We have seen a glimpse of interiorisation of *tapas* as the inner heat. In the mythical accounts *tapas* as described as a cosmic principle, a creative warmth glowing like a kind of incubation.[62] It is in the *Upaniṣads,* however, that *tapas* becomes fully interiorised. First, we see in the *Upaniṣads* a shift from ritual fire to meditative fire.[63] *Tapas* as cosmic heat comes to be identified with *brahman, jñāna, vidya, ātman* and contemplative power and meditation.[64] It is more and more associated with ascetic life as well.[65] The most significant in this shift is the development of techniques "to kindle the inner flame" or to actualise the interior forces of the self. The growing popularity of yogic techniques in the *Upaniṣads* needs to be seen in this light.

(iv) Allegorical Interpretation

The method of allegorical interpretation of the ritual sacrifice plays a significant role in the new shift from ritual sacrifice to self- sacrifice as found in the *Upaniṣads.* There is no fixed rule or consistent method followed in these interpretations. Since they are considered to be the most secret *(rahasya)* explanations of the ritual they are accepted without question, at least in the *Upaniṣads* concerned. Symbolic meditations are found in the *Āraṇyakas* also. As Dasgupta points out,

> these symbols were not only chosen from the external world as the sun, the wind etc., from the body of man, his various vital functions and the senses, but even arbitrary alphabets [sic] were taken up and it was believed that the meditation of these as the highest and greatest was productive of beneficial results.[66]

This pattern of symbolic meditation develops into finding new substitutes for old correspondence or equivalence between ritual elements and cosmic forces.

Renou points out the first occurrence of the term "*Upaniṣad*" in the *Brāhmaṇas,* which means only equivalence and formulation.[67] The equivalence established in the *Upaniṣads* between the physiological functions and the life of the cosmos is of deep significance contributing to the understanding of self-sacrifice. "This homologising the physiological organs and functions with the cosmic regions and rhythms", Eliade notes, "is pan-Indian". "It is only in tantrism", he says, "that it will acquire the coherence of a system".[68]

We have a few references to allegorical interpretations of new equivalence in the *Brāhmaṇas.* The *Śatapatha Brāhmaṇa,* for example, describes the *agnihotrī* cow as the *vāc* of the *agnihotra* and her calf as the *manas;* the calf and its mother are tied with one and the same rope; the fire is *śraddhā* and the ghee is *satya.*[69] Elsewhere in the same *brāhmaṇa* the study of the *Veda* is symbolically interpreted as one of the *pañca-mahāyajñas.* Accordingly, the recipient of the offering is *brahman;* the *juhu* spoon is *vāc, upabhrit* is *manas, dhurva* is eye, *sruva* is mental power, purificatory bath is *satya,* conclusion is *svarga* and the reward is an imperishable world; the *Ṛg* texts are the milk offerings, *Yajur* texts the ghee offerings, *Sāma* texts the *soma* offerings, *Atharvangiras* the fat offerings, precepts, dialogue, *itihāsa*, *purāṇa* etc. the honey offerings to gods. The reward is wealth, *prāṇa* and all auspicious blessings.[70]

The *Bṛhādaraṇyaka Upaniṣad* starts with a cosmic interpretation of the *aśvamedha*. The symbolical meanings of the parts of a horse are described as follows: dawn–head, sun–eye, wind–breath, open mouth–*vaisvānara* fire, year–body, sky–back, atmosphere–belly, earth–hoof, quarters–sides, intermediate quarters–ribs, seasons–limbs, months and half months–joints, days and nights–feet, stars–bones, clouds–flesh, sand–stomach, rivers–blood vessels, mountains–liver and lungs, herbs and trees–hair, sunrise–forepart, sunset–hind part, lightning– yawning, thunder–shaking, rain–urine.[71] In the same manner the *Chāndogya Upaniṣad* describes the sacrificial form of the universal self: head– good light, eye–the universal form (*viśvarūpa*), breath–air of varied courses, body–fullness, bladder–wealth, feet–earth, chest–sacrificial area, hair–sacrificial grass, heart–*gārhapatya* fire, mind–*anvāhārya pacana* fire, mouth–*āhavaniya* fire;[72] and the thirty three Vedic gods are identified with the natural elements, seasons and the non-material elements of the human body.[73] Almost in the same way are described the four Vedic priests.[74] In order to represent the whole world as the self the natural elements are identified with the organs of the human body. And following the interpretation, it is said that "He who knows thus the union obtains children, cattle, fame, glory and the world of heaven. He lives all his days".[75] Further, the *Bṛahādaraṇyaka Upaniṣad* notes that the cosmic self desired a wife in order to produce offspring and wealth; these were needed to perform rites, without which one is incomplete. But now, it adds,

> mind truly is his self, speech his wife, breath is his offspring, the eye is his human wealth, for he finds it with the eye, the ear is his divine wealth, for he hears it with his ear. The body, indeed, is his work, for with his body he performs work. So this sacrifice is fivefold, fivefold is the animal, fivefold is the person, fivefold is all this world, whatever there is. He who knows this as such obtains all this.[76]

The same *Upaniṣad*, elsewhere, says that the universal fire is within a person and identical with his fivefold structure.[77] In addition, it identifies the household fire with the wife; her organs are correlated with sacrificial implements and sexual intercourse is treated as a kind of *soma yajña*.[78] In the *Chāndogya Upaniṣad* V.4.1-8.1 there is complex and elaborate allegory, involving a number of images, symbols regarding the function of fire in the universe, and the birth and death of man. There we also find the whole life-span of man described symbolically as a sacrifice.[79] The *Praśna Upaniṣad* identifies different fires and offerings with speech, mind and breath and their functions.[80] He who is seen within his eye is compared to chants and formulae of sacrifice.[81] These references will suffice to show the extent and complexity of allegorical interpretations given to sacrifice.

Such interpretations presuppose the existence of the actual sacrifice, the parts of which are taken for new explanations. These explanations are said to be the knowledge of sacrifice, especially of its meaning. As we have noticed, all the important aspects of Vedic sacrifice such as gods, priests, fires, *mantras* and the sacrificer are covered in this interpretation. Apart from the indication of the cosmos and the different worlds, the *pañcabhūtas* find considerable expression in this attempt. The dispositions of the human body, the external organs (eye, ear) and three internal elements (speech, mind, breath) are repeatedly mentioned. The seven archetypal *ṛṣis*, the models for the ritualist, are now said to be seated on the head as breath.[82] Such symbolic identifications are ample in the *Upaniṣads*. But from the perspective of change and continuity of Vedic sacrifice in the *Upaniṣads*, it is difficult to determine the function of these allegorical interpretations. Deussen notes:

> in many of the instances enumerated it remains doubtful whether it is intended merely to interpret allegorically the still existing sacrificial cult, or to set it aside and replaced by physical and psychical conditions. The latter is distinctly the case with the last and most important phenomenon that we have to notice, where the *agnihotram* is replaced by *prāṇa-agnihotram*.[83]

Dandekar holds that "Here the link between man and the cosmos is ... no longer the ritual act, but a knowledge of the forces symbolically represented in the ritual".[84] Now we turn to see how this knowledge is associated with a quest for links between interior forces and cosmic elements.

3. Ātma Yajña: Its Nature and Means

Thus far we have seen certain background elements that have made for the development of *ātma yajña*, the central concern of this chapter. From the point of departure from external sacrifice to internal sacrifice, from objective to subjective perception, and from ritual elements to new meanings and allegorical interpretation, we may now proceed to the Upaniṣadic "depths" involving a new kind of sacrifice. After a brief discussion on the new understanding of power and meaning, we shall follow "the path of inner ascent, the inward journey by which the individual soul gets at the Ultimate Reality".[85] We may not tarry here to discuss at length the nature of the *Atman-Brahman* reality; many have done this. Instead, we shall point out the basic presuppositions and different layers of the *ātma yajña.*

(i) A New Understanding of Power and Meaning

The creative and sustaining power of the cosmos and the body is no more the Vedic sacrifice but wind, fire, water, earth, speech, mind, eye and ear, i.e. the vital elements of nature and body which are at various levels identical with the Supreme Reality.[86] Further, *prāṇa* is the quintessence of all these elements which dwells in the core of the body and functions as different breaths. It is the centre of all rites and gods. Moreover, in the *Vedas,* creation was attached to the creative principle of sacrifice. But now although there are a few references to the brāhmaṇic Prajāpati bringing out the creation[87] (or to *brahman* as person), in most cases, it is said that creation is the emanation or expansion of the primordial 'I' (*aham*), like thread coming out of the spider, or sparks from the fire or hair from the head. So also there is a new way of controlling the forces in the universe by identifying their connections, not in ritual, but in the internal forces within one's self. Edgerton writes:

> By 'knowing' the one I may 'know'—and *control*—the other. And surely there is nothing which I control more obviously and perfectly than my own 'self'. If now I 'know' that the *brahman,* which is the *ātman* of the universe, is my own *ātman,* then not only do I control the fundamental principle of the universe, because knowledge is magic power; but even more than that I *am* the fundamental principle of the universe, by mystic identification. For this double reason, there is nothing beyond grasp.[88]

Thus both the creative power and sustaining power are operative independent of any ritual support.

In Vedic sacrifice, *dīkṣa* meant a temporary transcendental experience. Now there is an alternative, a permanent transcendental consciousness. The universal self is not only the recipient of all forms of sacrifice but also the ultimate goal to be achieved by knowledge and self-realisation. About the process of this experience we shall see soon. And according to the new *jñānāgnihotra,* an offering to a poor, low-born *caṇḍāla* etc. is in fact an offering to the universal self; a mere *agnihotra* is an offering on dead ashes.[89] Such is the *vijñāna* (understanding) which gives a new direction to ritual sacrifices and all actions.[90] People now praise *jñāna* because that alone leads to the world of the gods, the best of all worlds.[91] Its goal of imperishable nature is superior to the perishable goal of ritual sacrifice. Yājñavalkya says

> Whosoever ... in this world, without knowing the imperishable, performs sacrifices, worships, performs austerities for a thousand years, his work will have an end; whoever... without knowing this imperishable departs from this world is pitiable. But ... he who knowing the imperishable departs from this world is *Brāhmaṇa* (a knower of Brahman).[92]

Thus the supreme goal of life transcends the material *svarga* and lies in the attainment of the imperishable. And the way to it is not ritual sacrifice but knowledge.

In the performance of Vedic sacrifice the fundamental concern is to fulfil the many-faced *kāma* of the sacrificer. In the *Upaniṣads* this *kāma* is viewed with contempt. It is asked, what is the good of the enjoyment of desire in this 'foul smelling, unsubstantial body?"[93] *Kāma* is self-binding. It covers the mundane life with falsehood. The antidote is, however, not absence of desire (*niṣkāma*) but authentic forms of desire, *satya kāma, jñāna kāma and ātma kāma.*[94] The operating power of *karma samsāra* is *kāma* and as is the *kāma* of the sacrificer, so is his will, so is his *karman* and so is his *saṃsāra.* Once free of *kāma* a person never dies again and being *brahman* goes to *brahman.*[95] The primary goal must be freedom from *kāma* and thereby from *saṃsāra.*

Yajña, dāna, tapas etc. cause only the rotation of births, though in some places, it is said that *yajña* could be one way to cross the sea of *saṃsāra* or at least reach its shore.[96] The only way out is somehow to tackle the power of *kāma.* It is significant that the temporary value of *yajña,* temporary stay in *svarga,* and the power of *kāma* that underlies the act of ritual sacrifice form a link with the new idea of *karma-saṃsāra.* This development is crucial because it generalises *karman,* giving it a remaining potency which causes the chain of births; it also redefines *kāma* and intensifies the search for a permanent and perfect state of life. In fact world denial and disdain of material blessings are not necessary characteristics in the progressive path of *jñāna* towards the ultimate goal of the supreme *brahman.* For example, a *guru* who combines the knowledge of Self and of the *Veda* prays not only for intelligence, sacred knowledge and good students, but also for the increase of cloth and cattle, food and drink, prosperity, fame and wealth. The same he wishes for his departing pupils as well.[97] And following the description of *brahman* as intelligence (*vijñānam*) and joy (*ānanda*), it is said, "he who knows this becomes established. He becomes possessor of food and eater of food. He becomes great in offspring and cattle and in the splendour of sacred wisdom; great in fame".[98]

Even the *brahmavādin* is said to attain all his desires. If he worships the knower of the Self his desire for prosperity is fulfilled.[99] Likewise, the *brahmaloka* is described in terms of *svarga*, as situated beyond the *devalokas*, having the fulness of material blessings.[100] And it is always difficult to reconcile the ultimate goal of self-realisation here and now with the idea of a *brahmaloka* yonder to be reached after death.[101] We have every reason, however, to believe that there was a persistent struggle to preserve somehow the old ritual tradition and its related notions in the face of new departures. And it is possible to see the distinctive nature of this departure.

(ii) Inward Journey to Self-Sacrifice

In the *Chāndogya Upaniṣad*, Nārada tells Sonatkumāra that though he knows all *Vedas* and all science (of ritual), he wants to know the knower of the Self so that he may cross over from the realm of sorrow. Then a list of internal elements is given in the order of an inner ascent. Though each one is *ātman* at one level, one is greater than another in the process, *prāṇa* being the innermost limit. The list includes in its own order name, speech, mind, will, thought, contemplation, understanding, strength, food, water, heat, ether, memory, hope and life-breath (*prāṇa*).[102] Elsewhere the list is reduced to include only five: eye, ear, speech, mind and breath.[103] The eye and the ear are the representatives of all the gross elements and the senses (*indriyas*). But the number of vital powers or elements are further reduced to three: speech, mind and breath. Each of these is identified with *brahman* at one level until the breath is singled out for sole identification with *brahman* or *ātman*.[104] Thus speech and mind are pushed aside because not only do they subside first as in the process of sleep and death but also because they provide the seat and function for doing whatever one pleases, the major hurdle in the interior way.[105] It is by the sacrifice of all the above coverings that one reaches *prāṇa,* the most essential and the innermost point in a person.

Prāṇa is said to move about in the body, binding the inner unity of the self; it is the oldest and greatest element of life which alone is beyond the reach of evil; it is the life force, or itself the great self or the primordial *aham,* the source and highest form of all.[106] But in some places the ultimate reality is said to lie beyond this form. The *Kaṭhopaniṣad,* for instance, says, "Beyond the great self is the unmanifest; beyond the unmanifest is the Spirit. Beyond the Spirit there is nothing.... This is the final goal".[107]

The function of speech, mind and breath is also described as a perpetual *yajña.* For example, speech is identified with *Ṛg* and breath with *Sāman*; breath is also the divinity in a *yajña;* the *Gāyatrī* chant is woven with speech, mind and breath which is Bṛahspatī, the Lord of *brahman,* the prayer.[108] They are also allegorically identified with the *Vedas,* worlds, *bhūtas,* etc.[109] The highest form of *yajña,* however, is *prāṇa yajña,* the conscious control of the different courses of breath. This can be superseded only by *ātma yajña,* the sacrifice of one's self to the Universal Self. This is the supreme sacrifice. Then, in the words of Panikkar, "the true sacrifice is the sacrifice of *brahman* (in the double meaning of both subjective and objective genitive). The sacrifice of *brahman* is both performed by Reality *in toto* and that which men offer to brahman".[110] The *ātman* now finds its authentic identification. The end is an ontological silence; as a sacrificial animal is quietened or strangulated the *ātman* is freed from the clutches of all senses and desires. But this *brahma yajña* or *ātma yajña* is not easy to perform because there are many obstacles in its way which are to be removed or sacrificed first.

The means to achieve the supreme *ātma yajña* are described in both general and particular terms. Vision *(darśana)* and knowledge (*jñāna)* are examples of the general terms. Thus, it is said, the way to *brahman* is "seeing" the self in all and all in self.[111] Seeing, hearing, perceiving and understanding are, however, only names of knowing. Hence the primacy of *jñāna,* the knowledge of an interior sacrifice. "All that is guided by knowledge rests on knowledge. This world is guided by knowledge. Knowledge is its foundation. Knowledge is *brahman.* He by his knowing self having left this world and having obtained all delights in the world of heaven became immortal".[112]

Jñāna is superior to *yajña* and *puṇya karma.* It could be called the *agni* which is essential in *yajña.* He who makes his own body the lower fire-stick and the syllable *OṂ* the upper fire-stick, by the effort of kindling the flame of *jñāna,* becomes the knower. He burns the bond of ignorance.[113]

We must also note the fundamental aspects of the path of *jñāna. Śraddhā,* formerly the faith in the power and efficacy of the ritual, is now taken to mean a unified concentration in the inward sacrifice to *brahman.*[114] We have already pointed out the inner heat (*tapas)* which has to be kindled by certain techniques. At this juncture we have to acknowledge the role of *yoga* in actualising the inner forces for the realisation of *brahman.* Though Patañjali systematised the *yoga* philosophy, as Eliade points out, "in fact yogic practices were known in the esoteric circles of Indian ascetics and mystics long before Patañjali".[115] Eliade also notes the bold homologisation of Vedic sacrifice with the techniques of ecstasy which is already forecast in the *tapas* of the sacrifricer.[116] *Yoga* in the path of knowledge has, however, many new dimensions, although the components of *yoga* are mostly sacttered in the *Upaniṣads* without a coherent formation.[117]

The *Kaṭhopaniṣad* asserts that the form of the Supreme Self does not stand within the field of sense vision. Even the senses (*indriya*), *manas* and *buddhi* must cease to operate in the inner ascent and they must be "sacrificed" by *yoga.*[118] The *Maitrī Upaniṣad* introduces a sixfold *yoga,* the final end of which is the realisation of *brahman.* A higher form, it says, is concentration which is pressing the tip of the tongue down the palate, restraining speech, mind and breath till one attains *darśana* of the self. Another form is a *dhyāna* on *oṃ,* which is considered to be the quintessence of all sacrifices, *mantras* and beings. The *Upaniṣad* concludes its description of *yoga* by saying that by yogic practice one gains contentment, endurance of the dualities and tranquillity but it warns that this most secret doctrine should not be declared to anyone who is not a son, not a pupil and not a prepared mind.[119] Thus the preparatory stages are important in the path of knowledge. We need not go further to see the development of *yoga* and its various forms as found in the *Yoga Upaniṣads* and the *Yoga Sūtras.*

4. Towards a Flexibility of Social Stratification

Finally, in terms of new departures we have to acknowledge the change found in the understanding of the four-*varṇa* stratification of the Vedic society. As we saw in the previous chapter, the original *dharma* was associated with the organic structure of the *varṇa* system that sprang from the primordial sacrifice of Ādipuruṣa. The ritual order was closely connected with the social order. Like their view of *yajña* the *Upaniṣads* at certain points seem to subscribe to the idea of *varṇa* based on social stratification while also denouncing the system.

Regarding *karma-saṃsāra,* it is declared that there are various forms of birth, the highest being that of a brahmin, then kṣatriya, vaiśya and then the lower, evil births of a dog, a hog or a *caṇḍāla.*[120] The *Bṛhadāraṇyaka Upaniṣad* has the following creation account confirming that any superiority for *kṣatriya*-hood is only temporary, or confined to a limited period of ritual. The passage is also indicative of some tension existing between the two higher castes.

> Verily, in the beginning this (world) was Brahman, one only. He created further an excellent form the *kṣatra* power, even those who are *kṣatras* (rulers) among the gods... Therefore there is nothing higher than *kṣatras.* Therefore at the *Rājasūya* sacrifice the Brahmin sits below the *kṣatriya.* On Kṣatrahood alone does he confer this honour. But the Brahmin is nevertheless the source of the *kṣatra.* Therefore even if the king attains supremacy, at the end of it, he resorts to the Brahmin as his source. Therefore he who injures the Brahmin strikes at his very source. He becomes more evil as he injures one who is superior.[121]

The verses that follow speak about the creation of the vaiśya and śūdra. Even then the creator did not flourish. Then he created an excellent form, *dharma,* the guardian of which was again the *kṣatriya. Dharma* is said to be identical with *satya.* Speaking of class relations the *Kauṣitāki Upaniṣad* calls the brahmins the eaters of kings and the kings the eaters of the people.[122] The *Kaṭhopaniṣad* exhorts hospitable treatment of a brahmin guest who enters into a house. It says, "Hope and expectation, friendship and joy, sacrifice and good works, sons, cattle and all are taken away from a person of little understanding in whose house a brahmin remains unfed".[123] Such verses seem to reflect the sacrifice-oriented values that continue to persist in the process of new directions for a different set of values.

The earlier rigidity in the exclusion of certain segments of society from sacrifice, however, gets relaxed in the process of the shift from *yajña* to *jñāna.* We have already noted a reference to *dāna* to *caṇḍāla* being considered as *brahma yajña.* Moreover, in the story of Satyakāma Jabāla, though he was unable to give the name of his father, he was called a brahmin and initiated into spiritual discipline because of his *satyakāma,* desire for truth.[124] And unlike in the context of *yajña* some women appear to ask questions about the ultimate reality. Gārgī's questions, for instance are compared to the foe-piercing arrows which make the teacher nervous.[125] These are examples of a flexibility in social structure and values.

5. The Tension between Ritualists and Ascetics

Who were the people responsible for the new shift found in the *Upaniṣads* which had both religious and social implications? We have already mentioned a group of people who operated outside the brāhmaṇic fold and who were challenging it socially and as religion. The glimpses of interiorisation found in certain parts of the Vedic texts could be attributed to them. The presence of such a group becomes more prominent in the *Upaniṣads*. As Deussen observes,

> By the time of the oldest Upaniṣad texts the ascetic life has already been elevated into a special 'calling', which assumes equal rank by the side of the position of householder. Men abandon household goods and family, as Yājñavalkya does in Brih..2.4, and depart into the solitude of the forest in order to practise *tapas* and by gradually increasing privations and penances to destroy in themselves the last remains of dependence on earthly existence.[126]

In continuation of the ideals of *munis, keśins* and *vrātyas,* mentioned in the early parts of the *Vedas,* the *śramaṇa* circle seems to be more popular in the *Upaniṣads* which further strengthened the *śramaṇa* movement as we shall see in the next chapter.

The name *śramaṇa* occurs only once in the early *Upaniṣads.*[127] This term comes from the root '*śram*' meaning to toil and exhaust oneself. In the *Upaniṣads* this root occurs in relation to *yajña, tapas* and *yoga.* Such a meaning would apply mainly to those ascetics who were involved in severe forms of austere practices.[128] In a new sense theirs was also a sacrificial experience. The stress, effort, exertion, the labour and exhaustion involved in the creation of Prajāpati and the ritual action of the Vedic priests in the enclosures of *yajña,* were paralleled by the austere practices of the ascetics.[129] But the goals of the practices of the latter were different from those of the former.

The term *saṃnyāsa* occurs only once in the early *Upaniṣads.*[130] It means renouncing the world. Those identified with this name are said to be liberated. The glory of the *saṃnyāsa* ideal is described in the later *Saṃnyāsa Upaniṣads.*[131]

Becuase the terms *śramaṇa* and *saṃnyāsa* occur in the *Upaniṣads* they are often viewed as the ascetics either belonging to one of the two human types found in the Vedic tradition or representing the highest stage in life in continuation of the earlier stages in which ritual sacrifice played the central religious role. The final stage of *saṃnyāsa* in the later fourfold *āsrama* system should not be confused with the life-style of early ascetics who, in our view, originally represented an alien tradition operative outside the brāhmaṇic fold before they were incorporated into it. Some *Upaniṣads* probably betray early incorporation without defining the exact relationship and logical connection between the two.

The tension between the ritual tradition and renouncers' movement is noticeable in certain passages. For example, the *Muṇḍaka Upaniṣad* refers in its very title to shaven-headed ascetics (*muṇḍakas*) who reviled the *Vedas* and undermined the Vedic ritual. They are the *ātma yajamānas*, free from *kāma* that bound the ritual *yajamāna.*[132] The self-transcendence of the ritual *yajamāna* was temporary but that of the *ātma yajamāna* permanent. But as early as the time of the *Maitrī Upaniṣad* there was reaction to the growing movement of ascetics from the brāhmaṇic side. Thus it is said:

> Now there are some who are always hilarious, always abroad, always begging, always making a living by handicraft. And others there are who are beggars in town, who perform sacrifices for the unworthy, who are the disciples of śūdras and who, though śūdras, are learned in the scriptures. And others there are who are wicked, who wear their hair in twisted knot who are dancers, who are mercenaries, travelling mendicants, actors, those who have degraded in the king's service... And others there are who, under false pretexts, wear the red robe, earrings and skulls. And others there are who love to distract the believers in the *Veda* by the jugglery of false arguments, comparisons and paralogisms, with these one should not associate ...[133]

Further, they are identified with the *asuras*, who confuse auspiciousness with inauspiciousness, *dharma* with *adharma* and knowledge with ignorance.[134] This is one of the earliest references to not only the types of mendicants and their activities but also brāhmaṇic reaction to them. The mendicants, however, increased and developed into a great movement with more definite identities and groups as we shall see later.

At the same time we have to acknowledge that a number of scholars minimise, bypass or ignore the incompatibility between the two traditions we have noted above. Now a number of questions arise: can we find a linear development from the ritual sacrifice to self-sacrifice? Does the act of ritual sacrifice provide necessary insights for yogic activities? Who are the authors of the *Upaniṣads* in which there is a tension between ritual sacrifice and self-sacrifice, between their respective world-views? If the ideas of *karma saṃsāra,* supreme *brahman* and interior *tapas* are external to the sacrificial religion where does their source lie? We shall have a brief discussion about these issues.

It is not an exaggeration when Hopkins says that although "legend, parable, ritualistic absurdities, belief in gods, denial of gods, belief in heaven, denial of heaven, are all mingled and for a purpose", "it is a new religion that the *Upaniṣads* offer. This is no religion of rites and ceremonies, although the cult is retained as helpful in discipline and teaching; it is a religion for sorrowing humanity."[135] He also observes: "One cannot read the *Upaniṣads* without feeling that he is already facing an intellectual revolt.... The close and stifling air of intellectualism has been charged with an electrical current of thought that must soon produce a storm".[136] Hopkins finds this storm reaching a climax in Buddhism and Jainism. Studies in Indian religions usually do not give adequate attention to the interaction of two traditions found in the *Upaniṣads.*

The greatest confusion in the study of the pan-mythic religious traditions of India is about placing the *saṃnyāsa* ideal in a logical development of Vedic religion, the essence of which is *yajña.* Likewise, the inner conflict between the ritual *yajña* of the *Vedas* and the *ātma-yajña* of the *Upaniṣads* seem to slip the attention of the scholars of Indian religions. The reason for somehow finding connections between Vedic sacrifice and the new teachings of the *Upaniṣads* is twofold. First, the *Upaniṣads* were later called *Vedanta,* the goal or essence of the *Vedas,* but undoubtedly this label carries different interpretations about the Vedic thought as done by the Vedāntic schools.[136] Second, in the *Upaniṣads* the negation of ritual religion and the voice for interior vision are mixed with the persistent continuation of the former. We may take this as the result of the earliest brāhmaṇic struggle to preserve the ritual from challenges. This struggle continued in later times as well, as we shall see in the next chapter. Some have tried to reconcile ritual sacrifice and sacrifice of the self by fixing levels and degrees. Thus, as we have noted, for Radhakrishnan ritual sacrifice stands at a lower stage which should necessarily move to the higher stage of self-sacrifice. With reference to a few Upaniṣadic verses A. Coomaraswamy says that if rituals are performed in right knowledge and attitude, they are not obstacles but means of enlightenment or sublimation.[138] But those who hold such views do not explain how this happens.

Even those who admit the external impact of the ascetic ideals on the development of Upaniṣadic thought hesitate to accept the difficulty in reconciling two traditions with distinctive methods and goals but somehow try to see an internal development of thought. K.N. Upadhyaya, for example, while setting the *Upaniṣads* in the background of early Buddhism and the *Gītā*, says that "the rituals and the sacrifices of the *brāhmaṇas* had passed their spring-time and had started dwindling *partly due to their own inner evolution of thought* and partly due to the external impact of the ascetic ideals (italics added)."[139] But a person who takes this position seems to acknowledge sufficiently the tension between ritual *yajña* and *ātma yajña*, between the material *kāma* of the Vedic *yajamāna* and the spiritual *kāma* of the *yogis* who moved away from the ritual system.

It should be acknowledged at this juncture that those who recognise the contradictions in the *Upaniṣads* have expended effort in finding out the *varṇa*, brahmin or kṣatriya, of the authors of the *Upaniṣads*. According to one view it was the kṣatriyas who were the sceptics and thinkers who challenged the ritual system by interiorised and symbolical interpretations and depersonalising the Vedic gods. Repeated instances of kings instructing the brahmins and householders are cited in support of this view.[140] On the contrary, those who argue for brahmin authorship of the *Upaniṣads* point out the existence of the Upaniṣadic ideas in germ in the *Brāhmaṇas*, the limiting duty of kṣātriyas to wield the weapons of war and their equal interest in sacrifice, the possibility of brahmin livelihood depending on sources other than *dakṣiṇā*, the continued use of the term *brahman* for the supreme and so on.[141] Yet there are others who take a middle view that Upaniṣadic thought emerged either out of the interaction between the brahmins and the kṣatriyas or that they were the final formulation by the former of what was initiated by the latter.[142] Kosambi suggests that "Our *Upaniṣads* represent a long process of assimilation and adoption of foreign ritual as well as philosophy by the indigenous brāhmaṇas, who could not all have been associated with kṣatriyas from the earliest times".[143] In any case, the brahmins later claimed that all the new doctrines were their heritage; it is also likely that the glimpses of these doctrines found in the *brāhmaṇas* were later additions in order to establish a connection.[144]

There have been other attempts to find the connecting links

between ritual sacrifice and interiorisation. We shall mention a few of them and point out the problems involved in their approach. Kaelber attempts to demonstrate that the *brahmacārin's* career is in large measure a forerunner and legitimising model for initially heterodox practices and *saṃnyāsin.*[145] We have already noted his opinion that ascetic practices were borrowed and assimilated in the ritual procedures. Kaelber finds the assimilation of asceticism and sacrifice in the career of the Vedic pupil but fails to see the difference between temporary practices of ascetic activities in order to qualify for the household life, as in the case of the *brahmacārin,* and the determination of the *saṃnyāsin* to renounce ritual and home for ever. It is remarkable further that the *ācāryas* of the *Vedas* and the *gurus* of the *Upaniṣads* do not adopt celibacy, and despite the emphasis on self-control the *Upaniṣads* often mention the most treacherous sin of a *brahmacārin* as sleeping with his *guru's* wife. Moreover, Kaelber calls *brahmacārya* the first *āśrama.* In fact, however, though only the two stages of studentship and householder-life were known in the Vedic period, these were never called *āśramas.* The four-*āśrama* ideal was a later development when the brāhmaṇic tradition tried to contain the development of the *śramaṇa* movement by assimilating some of its ideals. P. Olivelle observes:

> Although the historical development of the Vedic religion may explain certain of its aspects, renunciation erupted into the religio-cultural tradition of India as a totally new and unique phenomenon. It represented an anti-structure to the society of that time, a total rejection and the reversal of the value system of the world. Precisely for this reason, it was never totally assimilated into the structures of orthodox society nor integrated into the framework of the orthodox doctrine of Society.[146]

We shall consider later attempts at integration and the related problem.

Thomas Hopkins attempts to link ritual knowledge with interior knowledge, "based on the belief that ritual sounds and actions could be internalised, converted into thought, without a loss of potency".[147] He holds that the meaning of the rituals could be possessed by private mental ritual performance without assuming any physical or external performance. Hopkins refers, for example, to the older meanings of *brahman* as the Vedic *mantras* or as the power of the sacrifice which have been replaced by a more comprehensive understanding of *brahman* as the ultimate reality. For him "This is a logical development from the ritual tradition: sacrifice is the universe;

brahman is the sustaining power of the sacrifice; therefore *brahman*, or *Brahman*, is the sustaining power or reality behind the universe".[148] He acknowledges, however, that in order to know the nature of *brahman* ritual knowledge is not enough; an introspective search or interior vision is necessary. Besides, Hopkins admits that

> Full-scale asceticism within the Vedic framework came only gradually with the trend toward detached forest life ... This trend made ascetic life more acceptable and at the same time gave it a new rationale as the concept of mental performance of sacrifices brought about an integration of the personal and ritual aspects of *tapas*.[149]

The completion of this development, of course, is self-sacrifice, sacrificing the individual self in the Supreme Self.

Obviously Hopkins also fails to recognise the different world-views and different goals of two paths between which he tries to establish a logical development. There is no clue in the *Upaniṣads* that knowledge of ritual leads to knowledge of the mental process and its internal vitalities. The latter is called *parajñāna*, before which ritual has no value. As Killingley points out,

> The knowledge is not knowledge of many things, but of the one, often called Brahman; the contrast between this knowledge and the knowledge displayed by the ritual functionaries is stated more than once ... and dramatized in several Upaniṣadic narratives ... The syllable *OṂ* is mentioned several times as a means to this knowledge, or as a symbol of the ultimate reality."[150]

Likewise in the older idea of *brahman* as sacred utterance, the power it created was directed to the attainment of material abundance. The idea of Supreme Brahman on the other hand sets a new goal and new path, although two paths are presented in a mixture at certain places. This comment is applicable to A. Çoomaraswamy who tries to identify ritual knowledge with interior knowledge.[151]

Heesterman notes a connection between ritual sacrifice and the Upaniṣadic interiorisation. The contest between ideology and agonistic cooperation of the pre-classical age develops into individualisation as evident in the idea of *karma saṃsāra*.[152] The opposites were first fused into the single unit of ritual. "It had to advance to its logical conclusion, that is, the interiorisation of the ritual".[153] The brahmin who is already outside the world in a transcendental plane is not diferent from the renouncer, the true brahmin.[154] With reference to the opinion that the institution of renunciation emerged from non-brāhmaṇic or non-Aryan circles to protest against the brāhmaṇic orthodoxy which was then legitimised in the tradition, Heesterman says:

> But the important point is that these influences do not seem to have made a decisive eruption in the development of religious thought. They seem rather to have fitted themselves into the orthogenetic, internal development of Vedic thought. Or one might say that these extraneous beliefs and practices were not in principle dissimilar from those that obtained among the adherents of the pre-classical ritual.[155]

Especially in the mythical Prajāpati, both the sacrificer and the sacrifice, Heesterman finds fusion of the dualistic view of ritual sacrifice and the monistic view of self-sacrifice.[156] More convincingly, he points out that in *tyāga*, abandoning, renouncing, sometimes abandoning all for gods, lies the prototype of *saṃnyāsa*.[157] Further, he identifies the elements—trekking, drowning etc.—of certain sacrifices as foreshadowing the ideal of wandering mendicants.[158] Thus in a great effort to find connections and identical elements between ritual sacrifice and self-sacrifice, between the Vedic *yajamāna* and *saṃnyāsin*, Heesterman tries to establish a logical continuation of Vedic *yajña* in the Upaniṣadic thought and *śramaṇa* movement.

We have already noted in the previous chapter the inner conflict in Heesterman's approach, especially in his hypothesis that ritual *yajña* originated in the sacrificial contests in the pre-classical age. Most of his assertions, as mentioned above, seem to be generalisations to fit into his ritual theory. The fundamental problem in his connections between ritual sacrifice and self-sacrifice is that he is concerned only with those activities which resemble each other. But he fails to take note of the other aspects of these two, especially the world-views on which they are based and the intentionality in which they differ widely. We may remember that the self-sacrifice of Prajāpati and sacrificers in the *Brāhmaṇas* were taken not to move towards new paths but to recommend ritual sacrifice with the attitude of material *kāma* which is reversed in the path of self-sacrifice and the ideal of *saṃnyāsa*. Even the *karma-phala-tyāga* formula in certain rituals cannot be taken to mean that there is no reward for them: the intention is to multiply the reward.

Uma Vesci speaks of sacrificial action which is transformed into interior action because the need for it arises as a logical continuation; and the latter level cannot be separated from the former just as the *Āraṇyakas* and *Upaniṣads* cannot be separated from the *Brāhmaṇas*. She says

This spiritual transformation of sacrifice ... has had profound repercussions not only on man and on his newly born reflective consciousness, but also on the philosophy and cosmology of the divine ... the sacrifice performed on the earth is raised by the means of the divinization of the offering and of the ritual implements, to a divine cosmic action containing with its ritual centre the entire universe and being the centre of attraction where the two poles of global reality find their complementarity in a mutual assimilation.[159]

Moreover, she holds that the transcendental experience of the *dīkṣa* and interior *tapas* are the beginnings of self- transformation in which the need arose to seek a permanent state of the divine. In this connection she points out that the Upaniṣadic great mystical personalities are the same great ritual masters of the *Brāhmaṇas*.[160] We need not repeat our earlier agrument that like Heesterman and others Vesci also fails to recognise the tension between the preservation of ritual *yajña* and the radical departure for *ātma yajña* as found in the *Upaniṣads*. No scholar gives us the reason why the *saṃnyāsins*, the *ātma yajamānas*, would look down upon ritual *yajña* if it were truly a preparatory ground or stepping-stone for their spiritual transformation.

Vesci draws the line from yet another perspective. For her, Prajāpati was first introduced to save the ritual sacrifice when in the *Brāhmaṇas* it came to be regarded as an impersonal potence which could turn very dangerous. But subsequently Prajāpati was brought down by a question: who is Prajāpati? The transformation of his very name into its substitute—an interrogative pronoun—is significant, she feels, before philosophical doubt becomes "conscious of itself" and "reflection cracks out" in the minds of thinkers the names of whom are the same in the *Brāhmaṇas* and the *Upaniṣads*.[161] But Vesci fails to recognise that it is not uncommon to find the same names in different places and periods throughout the history of Indian religious literature. Also, she misses the point concerning what happened to Prajāpati and his children of sacrifice afterwards. As we noted, in the *Upaniṣads*, Prajāpati became a teacher of the new truth to his pupils, *devas, asuras* and *manuṣyas*. And the assertions of "consciousness itself" and "cracking out of reflections" are untenable unless we acknowledge certain external forces which challenged the ritual system and helped to raise new questions for alternative frameworks; no matter whether these forces were contained in the reworking of the Upaniṣadic material in order to give the picture that the *ātma yajña* and *saṃnyāsa* ideal are part of the evolution of the brāhmaṇic ritual tradition.

We have already noted the tradition of *munis, keśins, yatis,* etc. who lived outside the brāhmaṇic fold but had interaction with it. Presumably their influence gradually became so powerful that no thinking mind could evade a response to it. As Gonda says, the spiritual circles or other professions which were more exposed to foreign influences "consisted of people who from the brahmin point of view were outsiders, though they might have made Aryan proselytes and influenced the way of life of Aryan ascetics".[162] Unless we accept this possibility we cannot understand and logically treat "some Upaniṣadic puzzles and changing conceptions of sacrifice", as partially tried by Goman and Laura as well as by others.

6. Conclusion

Vedic sacrifice and its related ideas continue in the *Upaniṣads.* The direction for a new world-view and meanings of the old terms found in the *Upaniṣads* are, however, remarkable. In place of elaborate ritual performance and priesthood a new pattern of questioning and learning becomes more prominent. This questioning and learning is not limited to a structure of *gurus* and disciples who seem to represent a mixture of both old and new traditions but is carried out by a group of persons, mostly fathers of the families and wandering teachers. This shows the growing influence of a new tradition in the Vedic society. And in the transition of ideas, the power centres in the performance of Vedic *yajña,* viz., *brahman* as holy utterance, *karman* as careful ritual act and *tapas* as the sacrificial heat in fire and cooking, are now reconceived respectively as the supreme power or ultimate reality, action in general, and interior heat. Though there are clues about such an understanding in the earlier parts of the *Vedas* themselves, as pointed out in the previous chapter, the role of the *Upaniṣads* is of paramount significance for looking into the depths of things, identifying the hidden powers and bringing them out through introspection and interpretation on the basis of a new framework. For the creation and sustenance of the cosmos no more ritual power is needed but by its innate potency it operates itself. The power needed is to actualise the inner forces of the self for the realisation of the macrocosmic forces in the microcosmic unit, i.e., the soul. The unquenchable material *kāma* that prompted the ritual *yajña* is judged as transient and *saṃsāra*-bound. Instead, a spiritual *kāma* for knowing the ultimate reality of life and its meaning is emphasised.

The allegorical interpretation of sacrifice found in the *Upaniṣads* is a hallmark in the development of Hindu hermeneutics. Despite the inconsistency of connections, it attempts to introduce a new way of looking at the whole universe as an area of sacrificial operation which does not need ritual *yajña* but *jñāna yajña* to remove *avidyā* and attain *ātma yajña*. The allegorical interpretation facilitates this vision by homologising the cosmic forces with the internal forces of the human personality but using the ritual language of correspondences and equivalences.

Jñana yajña is described as the process of the peeling off of outer layers or crossing the coverings and reaching the core of the being. Particularly, the five senses and three internal forces (speech, mind and life-breath) have to be sacrificed in this process in order to reach the supreme self. Yogic techniques help in the process. Though yogic activity is as laborious as the ritual act, its goal is different. The goal of *jñāna yajña* and its yogic means is the vision (*darśana*) or realisation of the real self or the feeling of nothingness, which is irreconcilably different from the goal of ritual *yajña*, i.e., material abundance here in this world as well as in *svarga*. The outcome of the experience of *ātma yajña* through *jñāna yajña* is the appearance of newborn beings, *tyāgins, saṃnyāsins,* the living sacrifices. Their concerns go far beyond the "this worldly" religious concerns of ritual religion. Further, we have indicated the problems in reconciling Vedic sacrifice and interiorisation found in the *Upaniṣads*. They represent two distinctive methods and goals. In other words, they do not speak about two paths to a goal but two entirely different goals. As Wadhwani-Shah points out, in order to make the novel ideas palatable to people nurtured in the ritualist traditions, the Upaniṣadic seers explained them through the imagery and idiom of the sacrificial rituals. Here she sees the "tendency of serving new wine in old bottles" which is "peculiar to the Indian ethos".[163] Then it is appropriate to ascribe the inclusion of ritual *yajña* in Upaniṣadic thought and of *saṃnyāsa* ideal in the brāhmaṇic fold to the early process of brāhmaṇic reaction to ascetic influence. We shall examine the further development of this reaction and assimilation in the next chapter. As Pande points out,

> the *Upaniṣadic* point of view is thus a development of Vedicism and a half-turn towards Śramaṇism, or rather a position where further interaction

between Brāhmaṇism and Śramaṇism could take place, an interaction which did take place in the subsequent age and had the profoundest effects on the origin and development of Buddhism, *Sāṃkhya* and *Vedānta*.[164]

Before we close this chapter mention may be made of the need for a fresh look at the *Upaniṣads* in their relation to the *Vedas*. In what way do they form the final end, essence and goal of the *Vedas*? In the *Upaniṣads* allusions to the authority of *Veda* and the recitations of the *mantras* become very rare.[165] In fact the practice of calling the *Upaniṣads Vedanta* was a later development. Presumably, those who tried to propound different metaphysical views on the basis of the *Vedānta Sūtras* (earlier called *Brahma Sūtras*) and the *Upaniṣads* were not willing to diminish the authority of the *Veda*. But they do not attempt to reconcile the views that go against the *Vedas* with those enshrined in them. And from the perspective of the Vedic *yajña*, if one does not take the opinion that there is a paradigm-shift in the *Upaniṣads*, as we have maintained, it is very difficult to answer certain fundamental questions regarding differences and strain between the Vedic and Upaniṣadic emphases. What is required at this point is to recognise the peculiarity of the Indian mind in accommodating together different views, however contradictory they might be to each other, which is evident even in the early phases of Indian thought. This recognition of a double-paradigm scheme is essential as we turn to see further development of multi-paradigm schemes in the historical-hermeneutical process that we are investigating.

NOTES

1. R.E. Hume, *The Thirteen Principal Upaniṣads*, London, 1921, p. 52; see also pp. vii and 52ff.
2. P. Deussen, *The Philosophy of the Upaniṣads*, Edinburgh, 1906, p. 396.
3. P.M. Modi, *The Bhagavad Gītā, A Fresh Approach*, Bhavnagar, 1955, p.105.
4. S. Dasgupta, *A History of Indian Philosophy*, Delhi, 1875, I, p. 29.
5. A.B. Keith, *The Religion and Philosophy of the Veda and Upaniṣads*, 1925, p. 514.
6. L. Renou, *Religions of Ancient India*, London, 1953, p. 26f.
7. S. Radhakrishnan, *The Principal Upaniṣads*, London, 1953, p. 49f.
8. See S. Radhakrishnan, *The Philosophy of the Upaniṣads*, London, 1924, p. 24; *Indian Philosophy*, London, 1971, I, p. 147f.
9. See *ibid.*, *Indian Philosophy*, p. 147f; *Upaniṣads*, p.50; *Philosophy of the Upaniṣads*, p. 24f.

10. See M.A. Hiriyanna, *Outlines of Indian Philosophy,* London, 1968, p. 91.
11. See T.G. Goman and R.S. Laura, "A Logical Treatment of Some Upaniṣadic Puzzles and Changing Conceptions of Sacrifice", *Numen,* XIX/1, (1972), pp.54ff.
12. Wadhwani-Shah, "Sacrificial Ritual and the *Upaniṣads*", *ABORI,* LXVI (1985), p. 47.
13. G.U. Thite, "Magico-Religious Elements in the Principal *Upaniṣads*", *JOUIB,* XXVI/1 (1976), p.16f.
14. Wadhwani-Shah, *op.cit.*, p. 60.
15. R. Panikkar, *The Vedic Experience,* p. 402.
16. R.N. Dandekar, "Brahmanism", in *Sources of Indian Tradition,* compiled by Wm T. de Bary and others, New York, 1964, p. 26f.
17. Radhakrishnan, *The Principal Upaniṣads,* p. 48.
18. See *ibid.*, p.47; Keith, *op. cit.*, p. 491; M. Winternitz, *A History of Indian Literature,* Calcutta, 1927, p. 223ff; Renou, *op. cit.*, p. 27.
19. Gonda, *HIL,* 1. *Vedic,* p.423.
20. *Ibid.*
21. See Deussen, *op. cit.*, pp. 23ff, 398; Keith, *op. cit.*, pp. 498ff.
22. See Radhakrishnan, *Principal Upaniṣads,* p. 22; all the references to *Upaniṣads* are taken from Radhakrishnan's translation, *ibid.*
23. A.B. Keith, *The Aitareya Āraṇyaka,* Oxford, 1969, p.199; all references to *AiĀr.* are taken from Keith's translation.
24. *AiĀr,* III.2.3.
25. II.7.8.
26. 1.2.3ff.
27. *BṛU,* III.9.21.
28. *BṛU,* I.3.25, 26.
29. *BṛU,* I.5.17.
30. *BṛU,* IV.5.17.
31. See *ChU,* I.10.8ff; II.24.1-16; IV.6.1ff, 17ff.
32. *ChU,* V.2.4ff.
33. *TU,* I.8.1.
34. *SvU,* IV.9.
35. For instance, in Janaka, king of Videha, the desire arises to know the wisest of brahmins who might ask questions concerning truth, at the performance of a sacrifice, *BṛU,* III.1.1; elsewhere Janaka and Yājñavalkya discuss truth at a ceremony of *Agnihotra, BṛU,* IV.3.1.
36. *BṛU,* I.3.28.
37. Gispert-Sauch's study of the *sitz-im-Leben* of this prayer shows that originally the terms in this prayer meant rewards of the Vedic nature, such as wealth, victory in war and enjoyment in *svarga,* though it avoids the exclusively sacrificial terminology of earlier prayers. This gives way to new interpretations as in the Vedāntic tradition. See G. Gispert-Sauch, "An Inquiry into the Upaniṣadic prayer: From the Unreal Lead me to the Real... " in *Dialogue in Action,* Essays in Honour

of Johannes Aagard, ed. Lars Thunberg and others, New Delhi, 1988, pp.179-213.
38. *KU*, I.3.17.
39. *PrU*, I.2.
40. *MuU*, I.1.8; II.1.6, 7.
41. *AiĀr*, II.3.3; Keith notes that the 'sea' is typical of all unsatisfied desires. And this verse is followed by a strange description of the five-foldness of man, air and sacrifice. It is concluded with the words "He who knows one sacrifice above the other, one god above the gods, is clever. This great litany is the sacrifice above the other, the day above the other, the god above the others" Keith observes that this section is "unusually foolish".
42. *MuU*, I.2.1-12; also see *ChU*, V.10.1ff. which adds works of public utility and alms-giving to sacrifice the practicers of which reach heaven but return with the residues of their *karma.*
43. For the later brāhmaṇic belief in *punar-mṛtyu* and the Upanṣadic emphasis on the imperishability of the *ātman,* see Radhakrishnan, *The Principal Upaniṣads*, p.46f. For another description of boons as impermanent and the search for undecaying immortality, see *KU*, I.1.20ff.
44. *TU*, I.11.2.
45. See *BṛU*, III.1.1; IV.3.14-16, 33.
46. See Deussen, *op. cit.*, p.370f.
47. *ChU*, VIII.15.1.
48. J. Gonda, *Change and Continuity in Indian Religion*, Delhi, 1985, p.237.
49. Ref: the dialogue between Śvetaketu and his father, *ChU*, VI.1.1ff.
50. *ChU*, VIII.7.1, 11.3.
51. *BṛU*, V.2.1ff; *MuU*, III.5 mentions truth, austerity, knowledge and chastity.
52. *ChU*, VIII.5.1.
53. *KU*, IV.7ff
54. *ChU*, II.22.1ff.
55. A.L. Basham, "The Rise of Buddhism in its Historical Context", *AS*, IV/3 (1966), p. 399.
56. Deussen, *op. cit.*, p.19.
57. The references cited by Radhakrishnan (*The Principal Upaniṣads*, p.115), for example, in fact do not speak clearly of transmigration. For a refutation against a claim such as above, see Keith, *Religion and Philosophy of the Vedá and Upaniṣads*, p. 570f. The animistic origin of the idea of the soul as an entity is now widely accepted. The few Vedic references to the movement of souls after death (e.g. *ṚV*, X.58.1-2; 1.164.31; *AV*, XII.3.17) cannot be taken as referring to the idea of *karma saṃsāra* as developed in the *Upaniṣads.*
58. See Basham, "The Rise of Buddhism in its Historical Context", *AS*, IV/3 (1966), p.399f; Deussen, *op.cit.*, p.317ff; N.R. Reat, "Karma and

Rebirth in the *Upaniṣads* and Buddhism", *Numen*, XXIV/3 (1977), pp.163ff.

59. *BṛU*, III.2.12, 13.
60. *BṛU*, III.5.1.
61. J. Gonda, *Notes on Brahman*, Utrecht, 1950, p.10.
62. For details, see D.M. Knipe, *In the Image of Fire*, 1975, pp.107ff.
63. *KU*, I.1.18; *MaiU*, I.1.
64. *TU*, III.2.3; *MāU*, I.1.9; *MuU*, I.1.8, 9; III.5; *MaiU*, IV.4; also see Knipe, *op. cit.*, p.120f.
65. Deussen, *op. cit.*, p.69f.
66. Dasgupta, *op. cit.*, I, p.35.
67. See Renou, *op. cit.*, p.18; cf. *ŚB*, X.4.5.1.
68. M. Eliade, *Yoga: Immortality and Freedom*, London, 1958, p.112.
69. *ŚB*, XI.3.1.1.
70. *ŚB*, XI.5.6.3ff.
71. *BṛU*, I.1.1; this is the most important part of its *Brāhmaṇa* and the whole chapter is the third chapter of the *Āraṇyaka*.
72. *ChU*, V.18.2.
73. *BṛU*, III.9.1ff.
74. *BṛU*, III.1.1ff.
75. *AiĀr*, III.1.2.
76. *BṛU*, I.4.17.
77. *BṛU*, V.9.1; VI.2.12.
78. *BṛU*, VI.2.13, 4.3.
79. *ChU*, III.16.1-7, 17.1-6.
80. *PrU*, II,5; also see *KauU*, II.5.
81. *ChU*, I.7.5-9.
82. *BṛU*, II.2.3-4; cf, Mitchiner, *Ṛṣis*, p.284f.
83. Deussen, *op. cit.*, p.123f.
84. R.N. Dandekar, "Brahmanism" in *Sources of Indian Tradition*, compiled by Wm. T. de Bary and others, New York, 1964, p.27.
85. Radhakrishnan, *The Principal Upaniṣads*, p.49.
86. *PrU*, II.2.
87. *PrU*, 1.4.9ff; *MaiU*, II.26; *BṛU* I.2.1f; 5.1. Interestingly the animating power of *kāma* is substituted by *jñana* along with *tapas* for the creation of Prajāpati; *BṛU*, I.5.1; but in *TU*, II.6.1. *kāma* and *tapas* are attached to the creation of *brahman*.
88. F. Edgerton, *The Beginning of Indian Philosophy*, London, 1965, p. 27.
89. *ChU*, V.24,1-5.
90. *TU*, II.3.1.
91. *BṛU*, I.5.16. For a list of worlds and the means to attain them, see I.4.16.
92. *BṛU*, III,8.10.
93. *MaiU*, I.3; *KU*, I.2.3, 4.
94. *ChU*, VIII.1.4-6, 2.1ff, 3.1, 2.

95. *BṛU,* IV.4.6.
96. *KU,* I.3.2.
97. *TU,* I.4..1, 11.1.
98. *TU,* III.6.1.
99. *MuU,* III.1.10.
100. *KauU,* I.3ff.
101. For some interpretations to reconcile both, see Radhakrishnan, *The Principal Upaniṣads,* pp.125f, 130.
102. *ChU,* VII.1-15; also see *KeU,* I.2.
103. E.g. see *ChU,* III.18.1, 2; IV.3.3; V.1.1ff; *KauU,* II.1.
104. *BṛU,* I.2.1-5, 3.2-7, 5.3; IV.1-7; for the inter-connection between speech and breath, see *AiĀr,* III.1.6.
105. *BṛU,* II.1.17f; IV.3.12; VI.1.13; *AiĀr,* I.3.2.
106. *BṛU,* I.3.8, 12, 17, 4.1-9; II.1.17f, 5.5; IV.3.5, 12, 4.5, 19; VI.1.1, 13; *ChU,* IV.3.3; V.1.1f; *TU,* II.2.1; *ŚvU,* VI.1-11; *MaiU,* VI.11-13; see the story of *asuras* unsuccessfully trying to make the breath defective in BṛU, I.3.1.
107. *KU,* I.3.11.
108. *ChU,* I.1.5, 2.6, 7.1, 11.5; II.11.1; *AiU,* III.2.6; cf. *YV,* VI.1.4.4.
109. See *BṛU,* I.3.12-27, 5.3-23; *AiĀr,* I.1.1, 4.1, 5.1; cf.AV, IV.20; *ChU,* V.19.1-23.2.
110. Panikkar, *op. cit.,* p.418f.
111. *KaiU,* 9, 10.
112. *AiĀr,* II.6.
113. *BṛU,* I.4.15; *KaiU,* 11; this *jñāna* is *para jñāna* in contradistinction to *apara jñāna,* that includes the study of the *Veda,* performance of *yajña* etc. see *MuU,* 1.4,5.
114. For different spiritual senses in which the *Upaniṣads* use the term *śraddhā,* see R.V. De Smet, "Highlights of the Faith (*śraddhā*) in India", in *The Bhagavad Gita and the Bible,* ed. B.R. Kulkarni, Delhi, 1972, p.41f.
115. Eliade, *Yoga,* p.7.
116. See *ibid.,* p.108f.
117. See Deussen, *op. cit.,* pp.384ff; E.W. Hopkins, "Yoga Techniques in the Great Epic", *JAOS,* 22 (1901), p.333f; Ewing, "The Hindu Conception of the Functions of Breath", *JAOS,* 22 (1901), pp.261f.
118. *KU,* II.3.9ff.
119. *MaiU,* VI.18-22, 29. Note, the sacred syllable *oṃ* is said to have been created by the primordial sacrifice of Prajāpati according to *AiB,* V.32; *ChU,* I.1.1ff describes the nature and the power of *oṃ.*
120. *ChU,* V.10.7. Note, the beings listed in the lower births were excluded from the presence of a sacrificial performance.
121. *BṛU,* I.4.11; in *AiĀr,* III.1.3. We read that to a brahmin one must not say anything save what is auspicious; brahmins deserve honour always.

122. *KauU,* II.9.
123. *KU,* I.1.7.8.
124. *ChU,* III.6.1f.
125. *BṛU,* III.6.1f.
126. Deussen, *op. cit.*, p.67.
127. *BṛU,* IV.3.22.
128. See *Bṛu,* I.2.2, 5.2; IV.3.19.
129. For a discussion on this parallel, see Knipe, *op. cit.*, p.122f.
130. *MuU,* III.2.6.
131. Ref. A.A. Ramanathen, *The Saṃnyāsa Upaniṣads,* Madras, 1978.
132. *MaiU,* VI.30.
133. *MaiU,* VI.8.
134. See *MaiU,* VII.9.
135. E.W. Hopkins, *The Religions of India,* London, 1896, pp. 219, 239.
136. *Ibid.*, p.280.
137. For a discussion on the origin of the school which came to bear the name *Vedānta* and its development, see H. Nakamura, "*Upaniṣadic* Tradition and Early School of Vedānta as Noticed in Buddhist Scipture", *HJAS,* 18 (1955), p.74f.
138. See A.K. Coomarasawamy, *The Vedas–Essays in Translation and Exegesis,* Kent, 1976, p. 35.
139. K.N. Upadhyaya, *Early Buddhism and the Bhagavadgītā,* Delhi, 1983, p.79.
140. See M. Winternitz, *A History of Indian Literature,* Calcutta, 1927, I, p. 227f; Deussen, *Philosophy,* p.396f.
141. See Keith, *Āraṇyaka,* p. 257; *Religion,* pp.494ff.
142. See M. Winternitz, *op. cit.*, I, p. 232; Dasgupta, *op. cit.*, I, p.318f; U.C. Bhattacharya argues that the teachers of the *Upaniṣads* were the itinerant, liberal minded brahmins who were supported by certain princes. See Bhattacharya, "External Evidence about the Teachers of the *Upaniṣads*", *IA,* LV (1926), pp. 31-5 and "The Home of the *Upaniṣads*", *IA,* LVII (1928), p.189.
143. D.D. Kosambi, "Early Brahmins and Brahmanism", *JBBRAS,* 23 (1947), p. 44; for him there were pre-Aryan brahmins before they were assimilated in to the priesthood of the conquerors, and also the cult of Brahma was pre-Aryan,
144. See Deussen, *op. cit.*, p.397.
145. See W.O. Kaelber, "The Brahmacārin: Homology and Continuity in Brāhmaṇic Religion", *HR,* 21/1 (1981), p.78f.
146. P. Olivelle, "A Definition of World Renunciation", *WZKSIP,* XIX (1975), p. 83.
147. T.J. Hopkins, *The Hindu Religious Tradition,* Belmont, p. 36.
148. *ibid.*, p. 37.
149. *ibid.*, p. 50.
150. Killingley, "*OṂ:* The Sacred Syllable in the Veda", in *A Net Cast Wide,*

ed. J. Lipner, Newcastle upon Tyne, 1987, p. 25.

151. See A.K. Coomaraswamy, "*Ātma Yajña:* Self Sacrifice", *HJAS*, 6(1941), p. 385ff.

152. J.C. Heesterman, *The Inner Conflict*, p. 35.

153. *ibid.*, p.38f.

154. *ibid.*, p.104.

155. *ibid.*, p.40.

156. See J.C. Heesterman, "Self-Sacrifice in Vedic Ritual", in *Gilgul: Essays on Transformation, Revolution and Permanence in the History of Religion*, eds. S. Shaked and others, Leiden, 1987, p. 93.

157. See Heesterman, *Inner Conflict*, pp.40, 102.

158. See Heesterman, "Self-Sacrifice", p.94f; "Householder and Wanderer" in *Way of Life*, ed. T.N. Madan, New Delhi, 1982, pp. 253, 269.

159. U.M. Vesci, *Heat and Sacrifice*, p. 270f.

160. *ibid.*, p.287.

161. *ibid.*, p. 280f.

162. Gonda, *Change and Continuity*, p. 275.

163. Wadhwani-Shah, "Sacrificial Ritual and the *Upaniṣads*", p.60.

164. G.C. Pande, *Śramaṇa Tradition – Its History and Contribution to Indian Culture*, Ahmedabad, 1978, p. 4.

165. See L. Renou, *The Destiny of the Veda in India*, Delhi, 1965, p.19f.

III

New Challenges to the Cult of *Yajna* and the Brāhmaṇic Reaction: Some Considerations on the Influence of Changes in Socio-Economic-Religious Spheres

1. Introduction

The development of religious ideas cannot be separated from other developments in the history of a tradition. This is particularly true in the case of sacrifice. The period following the early *Upaniṣads*, especially from the sixth century B.C., saw enormous changes in the political, social and economic situation in and around the Ganges Valley which was the centre of Vedic religion. This situation compels our attention because it can help to elucidate the dynamics of change in religious perceptions. This is not to reduce religious vision to an outcome of socio-economic factors, but to recognise the mutual interaction of the two. It is not our aim to study in detail different perspectives of Indian history of this period, or to attempt a chronological account. Rather we shall identify key issues from the social history of ancient India as evidenced by scriptural and other sources.

In the cultural history of India, it is widely acknowledged, the period dating from the sixth century B.C. was significantly marked by the rise of *śramaṇa* movements. They seem to have played an important role if not in initiating certainly in furthering changes in the social and religious perspectives that have deeply affected the Vedic cult of sacrifice. With reference to the development of a number of schools, sects and ideas in this period, which extends up until the second century B.C. Charles Moore observes that it "is probably the most productive, the most creative, the most open minded and the richest period of Indian thought". And Radhakrishnan adds that it was "an age full of strange anomalies and contrasts".[1] This will become obvious when we study changes in the understanding of sacrifice in this period.

Disucssion of a unilinear development of ideas in the process of interaction between socio-economic forces and interpretation of religious views is difficult, for there are various complications on the way. The complexity seems to lie in the struggle to preserve the traditional views but without ignoring the possibilities of accommodation, assimilation and interpretation. The emergence of the system characterised by *āśrama dharma*, *puruṣārtha* etc. needs to be viewed in the light of this struggle on the part of the brāhmaṇic tradition.

Any attempt at synthesising the formulation of Bhāgavatism and its impact on the *Bhagavad Gītā* seems to present certain problems of coherence and consistency. A recognition of these problems would help us understand the nature of *samuccaya* or synthesis, which is one of the characteristics of Hinduism. Here we will consider a few crucial moments of change and attempts at synthesis.

2. Political-Social-Economic Upheavals

The history of India has been studied from different perspectives, the most common and traditional being a priestly perspective. Earlier scholars relied solely on brāhmaṇic literature for their understanding of ancient Indian history. This source seems to have a natural antipathy towards the free republics that existed in the seventh and sixth centuries B.C. The priestly records, especially the law books, emphasise monarchy and the monarchic order of society, ignoring the more empirically decisive factors. "They convey the impression that the only recognised, and in fact universally prevalent, form of government was that of kings under the tutelage of priests."[2]

In endeavouring to know the other side of this history, the history of republics and other forms of government, one cannot ignore the important sources which come from Jainism and Buddhism. Scholars like Rhys Davids at the turn of the present century highlighted an alternative way of reading the ancient history of India using these sources. This has been taken up further with additional sources from archaeology and other records. Analytical social histories of ancient India have recently been attempted fruitfully by scholars like D.D. Kosambi and Romila Thapar. They do not minimise the importance of the priestly records, but understand them mainly as records of reaction and interaction with forces that affected the orthodox religion and the social position of the priests. We shall also presuppose the need for recognising such political-social-economic interaction for understanding the religious history of north India during the period under consideration.

In Vedic society there were kings, but their power and dignity was little more than that of tribal chiefs, even though a few kings acquired supremacy over other kings. "The king was not, however, the owner of the land".[3] Nevertheless there was a growing tendency to have an emperor. The lineage of the Paurava dynasty, of which the most famous king was Janamejaya, is presented in the epics and the *Purāṇas* in a complex way. There are references to two Janamejayas. Therefore it is difficult to determine the date of this famous king. As an owner of horses and as a performer of an *aśvamedha* as recorded in the *Brāhmaṇas* he lived probably in the ninth century B.C.[4] As we saw earlier, the brāhmaṇic Prajāpati could well have inspired the idea of an all-embracing king since most probably the introduction of Prajāpati in place of Puruṣa was the work of the ruling class. The priestly class must have had no difficulty in accepting this because the great sacrifices were sponsored by rich rulers who gave liberal *dakṣiṇā* and *dāna* to the priests, and the Prajāpati myth was quoted in support of performing such great sacrifices. About the increasing favour of the brāhmaṇical tradition for great monarchy, A.K. Warder writes:

> Indeed we probably ought rather to say that under the trend towards monarchy of late times it was those Vedic schools which had been associated with the famous Paurava monarchy, not others, which might have flourished under republican governments, were favoured and have survived.[5]

From the eighth century B.C. the Paurava dynasty started to decline, especially with King Nicakṣu changing the capital from Hastinapura to Kausambi due to flooding. When the empire broke up, it caused the rise of numerous independent states with different types of government, with mostly republics and a few survivals of monarchy asserting their independence from the Paurava hegemony.[6]

In the seventh and sixth centuries B.C. there existed more or less powerful monarchies alongside independent republics. Magadha and Kosala were rapidly growing as empires. After the settlements and migrations due to political conflicts and natural calamities were over, by the end of the sixth century B.C. there was constant struggle between the monarchical and non-monarchical forms of government. "The contest plainly showed the decline of republics, the rise of absolutism, and the growing success of Magadhan imperialism. These manifold political changes naturally provoked much discussion".[7]

Changes were manifold not only in the political sphere but also in the social sphere. There was a transition from a pastoral to urban culture, from tribal ties to those of social responsibility in urban units. Commerce emerged as a major occupation along with agriculture. Territorial expansion effected a rapid change in social structures. The consolidation of small kingdoms and economic centralisation attained its peak in the Mauryan empire.[8]

Following a revolt against the Magadhan emperor Dhanananda, the Mauryan dynasty was established by its first king Chandragupta (322–298 B.C.). An ambitious ruler, he brought almost the whole of India under his control, invading the "hearts" of states and towns, and resisting the incursions of the Greeks.[9] All the three characteristics of a powerful empire, i.e. efficient bureaucracy, good communications and a strong ruler, existed under the Mauryas as is evident from the *Arthaśāstra*.[10] The culmination of Mauryan rule was the model government of the great Aśoka (272-233 B.C.) who was described as *cakravartin*, "the holder of the wheel of power".[11] We shall consider the significance of his rule later.

In the society of this period of monarchic ascendancy the brahmins held the highest position of respect as sacred priests and often as *ācāryas*, although many were involved in other activity as administrators and landlords.[12] In terms of ruling power the kṣatriyas, especially the nobles and princes, held the highest position. Their aristocratic status in society was maintained by heredity. The kings were engaged in hunting, erotic sexual life, warring and patronising the new vogue of philosophy. As Pande puts it, "The Kṣatriyas appear in this age as much the leaders of intellectual life as the Brāhmaṇas".[13]

Under the brahmins and kṣatriyas were the vaiśyas and śūdras. The vaiśyas were involved in trade and agriculture and the śūdras in occupations of servitude. Apart from these four traditional classes there were also "outcastes" like the *caṇḍālas*. Further, in the wake of rapid changes probably there was imperceptible fusion between Aryans, Dravidians and other ethnic groups.

In the economic realm, land was brought under control of the king, to be used at his discretion. Since there was a decline in pastoralism the form of *dāna* shifted from cattle to lands, especially given by the kings to the priests for their performance of royal sacrifices.[14] New economic forces were produced in society by the exploitation of natural resources and the development of industry and trade. A money economy developed in place of barter. When unprecedented wealth followed its own law of circulation the states tried to control it by legislation.[15] Consequently, some who were in the current of economic changes became poor while others became wealthy.

The above changes affected views and practices too. Pande writes: "In the atmosphere of town-life much of the symbolism of the older religion derived from natural phenomena and pastoral and agricultural functions, would become dim, the gods less convincing, and the ritual obscure and even pointless".[16]

Nevertheless Vedic ritualism and related beliefs held their sway. The leading kings were certainly not free from Vedic practices, mainly with a view to enhancing royal fame. They patronised grand sacrifices in times of war and victory, being constantly involved in petty warfare against tribes and other republics. Sacrifice also provided an occasion for the kings to receive tribute from defeated territories. The priests, who ensured the preservation of the rules and *mantras* of sacrificial performance, received royal gifts of land on a large scale. Both the priestly and princely classes had a natural right to enjoy public resources.

At the same time, the condition of the poor remained miserable. The lower classes were nevertheless compelled to give cattle for royal sacrifices. D.D. Kosambi observes: "Vivid descriptions remain of the misery and dismay of the peasantry when innumerable beasts were requisitioned—without payment, of course—for the royal fire sacrifices".[17]

The protest against this state of affairs and the decline in sacrificial religion will be noticed more clearly when we take up the *śramaṇa* movement for study. What is significant to note here is that changing economic conditions contributed to change of religious practices. Thus, for example, the *Mahābhārata* describes an interesting discussion. It is said that grand sacrifices are possible only for kings and wealthy merchants. Then what will the poor do? The reply is that for the poor are prescribed *tīrthas* (visiting sacred rivers, etc.), *vratas* (fasting, etc.) and *pūjās* to gods with simple offerings like water. These practices are said to be meritorious—or even more meritorious than—the grand sacrifice of *aśvamedha.*[18] Else where in the same epic fasting is said to be of special merit as ensuring sensuous delights in heaven. Indeed, it affords the poor similar opportunity of acquiring merit as sacrifice gives to the rich.[19] Such substitutes must have been borrowed from other cults and ascetic traditions because in their mobility for new settlements, and trade, the Aryans came in contact with many such traditions.[20] Moreover, such accommodation of new elements along with or in place of sacrifice took place when the brāhmaṇic tradition had to face new challenges.

In the climate of political and economic changes that produced a sense of social distress, an unprecedented awakening and the spirit of questioning also emerged. As Pande points out, "the political troubles of the age provided its more thoughtful and sensitive souls with incentive to withdraw from the world".[21] A.L. Basham writes:

> The craving for salvation, which seems to have possessed many of the best minds at the time of the Buddha, must have sprung from a deep-seated fear of change and a profound sense of insecurity. While material culture was advancing by leaps and bounds, while trade was expanding, and while the geographical horizons of Aryan India were rapidly being pushed forward at a time when one might expect positive and pragmatic world views to develop, thoughtful men were seeking for an end of change in something permanent, immutable and absolute.[22]

This reason, however, cannot be applied to all the *śramaṇas*: There could be various other individual reasons too, although those who spearheaded the movement appeared to provide an alternative in life.[23] Moreover, this was not an evasive resignation with a spiritual contentment. Particularly, persons like Gautama Buddha, who is said to have belonged originally to the Sākya clan of the Virāj republic, seem to have admired the ancient customs of the republics, their democratic governments, more egalitarian structure of economy and their respect for wise men. The sweeping force of the Magadhan empire, its economic exploitation and uncritical approval of grand Vedic *yajñas* created for such thinkers a hopeless situation. Although these thinkers looked outside political life for a solution abandoning their own wealth and power, thus contracting out of society to preserve inner freedom and happiness, they, did not in fact, withdraw for ever. In Warder's words, "Only from an independent vantage point could they hope—as they certainly did hope—to exercise any influence on the society they had left, to infuse into it better ideals than money and violence".[24]

Since the monarchic development and brāhmaṇic religion had mutual support the thinkers had to challenge both. In order to strengthen their protest they joined a movement having a great impact on society.

3. The *Śramaṇas* and their Challenge

We have already recognised the presence and influence of ascetic elements in the *Vedas* and *Upaniṣads*. In this section we examine the development of ascetism into a great movement that challenged the monarchic imperialism and the brahmāṇic ritualism together.

It is generally acknowledged, based on sufficient evidence, that in and around the sixth century B.C. Indian history is clearly marked by the presence of ascetics, mystics and thinkers wandering throughout the Ganges Valley. They represented not only the earlier ascetic groups but also the great spiritual and intellectual ferment of the day.[25] It is of utmost importance to recognise the significance of these wanderers if we are to understand not only the spiritual enlightenment of that time which affected the ritual sacrifice but also the rise of both heterodox and orthodox schools of Indian thought. Generally these wanderers were called *śramaṇas* though some of them do not exactly fit the etymology of the term (*śram*=to labour, exert, exhaust etc.).

It is difficult to identify the *śramaṇa* movement with a particular caste or class. As Pande points out, "The *śramaṇa* movement was a world-renouncing ascetic movement—classless and casteless. In its essential idea and spirit it has no specific affinity with the attitude of any particular social class".[26]

Obviously the movement became stronger when it was joined by those critical minds who had gone out of society due to the pressures, as we have already noted. Besides, apparently some brahmins who had similar feelings and who had been influenced by the novel ideas of the *Upaniṣads* also joined the movement, not all strictly as ascetics but wandering teachers involved in critical discussions. Although they had peculiar ideas, on the whole their life was not distinctive from that of other wanderers. Gonda notes:

> In customs and way of life the ascetics of "orthodox" brahmāṇic origin did not, as far as may be judged from appearances, stand out considerably from the heterodox recluses and wanderers, however much diversity of opinion

there might, among these ascetics, have existed with regard to view of life, soteriology and ascetic practices.[27]

It must be noted that there is no clear evidence for the contention of earlier scholars like Max Muller, Buhler, Kern and Jacobi that the heterodox groups borrowed their model from the brāhmaṇical ascetics. We shall see how reluctant the brāhmaṇic tradition was to accommodate renunciation as one stage of life. Therefore, probably, the borrowing was the other way round although it is fair to admit that different ascetic groups, both orthodox and heterodox, "all belonged to the same ancient stock of wandering religious mendicants".[28] The *śramaṇas* were very much attached to the forest. This may have reflected their dislike for the sweeping innovations of urbanization initiated by the monarchy. From a sociological point of view, it is argued that even the brahmins had a tradition of simple, non-killing food gathering life in the forest which was considered to be meritorious.[29] Perhaps this tradition can be identified with the *vrātyas* or with similar groups who were outsiders but converted to brāhmaṇism. Insights from this tradition were introduced later by the heterodox movement to challenge a food-producing urbanised society.

In those days there were meeting halls on the journey routes which were often used for discussion by the mendicants of different views. The intellectual ferment was so high that some were even engaged in betting on the disputations on spiritual matters.[30] Some groups came to form communities for shared living in which the teachers could develop and materialise their vision of life and build up schools of thought. Others were reluctant to become settled, and continued a vigorous *tapas* and *vairāgya* in isolation. Members of such groups spent their time in gathering fruits and roots in the forests and food as *dāna* from the people. But their main concern was to be engaged in *dhyāna* and *tapas*. Perhaps those who had come out from the brāhmaṇic fold continued to perform simple forms of Vedic sacrifice. Regular functions in the groups were teaching, listening and discussing.[31]

Some schools or movements of the *śramaṇas* succeeded in becoming fully organised communities, while the hermitages of others slowly disappeared due to the colonisation of invaders and reservations made for hunting kings. The break-up of clan-based tribal societies, oligarchies and republics with the emergence of urban centres sowed a nostalgia in the minds of many, a nostalgia for their original life-styles. This led to the monastic establishments. Particularly Jainas and Buddhists were enthusiastic about this. Thapar identifies such ecclesiastical terms as *sangha, kula,* and *gaṇa* which were used in relation to monastic communities as originating from the clan-based republics.[32] The monastic establishments posed a greater challenge to the brāhmaṇic society—its beliefs and supremacy—than individual mendicants.[33] Moreover, parallel structures between the monasteries and states made necessary a great deal of awareness among people about their authentic community life. In the words of Thapar, "The monasteries were seen ideally as egalitarian sanctuaries in an otherwise increasingly hierarchical society dominated by the monarchical state".[34]

Members of the monasteries in general took no part in the production of life-goods or in the control of production. Denial of ownership and family bonds, viewing all people as equal and dependence on the direct support of the people in the form of *dāna* were the chief marks of life in monasteries.

The political role of the *śramaṇas* is significant. On the whole they did not negate political power as such. They however established a counter-weight to temporal power so that *dharma* could be upheld with sacrificial effort. While royal power and priestly power uncritically supported each other, *śramaṇa* power implicitly challenged both. In later periods, the ascetic movement supported just kings but did not spare anyone who wielded power arbitrarily and capriciously. While they were able to protect the universe for the sake of dharmic rulers, the ascetics threatened to burn kings, their kingdoms and even the gods by the power of *tapas.*[35] Since the *śramaṇas* had the combined power of people's support and interior force no ruler could ignore their influence.

More significant for our study is the *śramaṇa* position in the matter of religion, especially in relation to the brāhmaṇic ritual cult. With the exception of a few orthodox schools, "We might loosely say that these *śramaṇas* were, in general, ascetic, atheistic, pluralistic and 'realistic'. The essential basis of this world-view seems to have been the idea of *saṃsāra*—of *karman* and transmigration".[36]

The *śramaṇa* mendicants developed new definitions of *karma saṃsāra* and theories of its functioning and thereby distinguished themselves from the brāhmaṇic teachers. Although the Upaniṣadic emphasis on *jñāna yajña* and *ātma yajña* had great impact on them, they moved beyond the *Upaniṣads* in the matter of metaphysics. Presumably, this was again to distinguish themselves from the orthodox schools since they somehow accommodated the new teachings of the *Upaniṣads* in their system.

The *śramaṇas* came in conflict with brahmin priests. They challenged the authority of the *Vedas* and ridiculed the power of ritual sacrifice. As they did not need to depend on any ruler or tradition they gained a moral status "far higher than that of even a sacrificing brahmin".[37] To the people in society the act of feeding and helping the mendicants was interpreted as producing greater merit *(puṇya)* for the giver. The *śramaṇas'* teaching, which discouraged *dakṣiṇā* and *dāna,* the sole income of the priests, produced a power-competition between the *śramaṇas* and the brahmin priests to win the confidence of the giver. It was this conflict that later led Patañjali to describe them as eternal opponents, cat and mouse, dog and fox and snake and mongoose.[38] The worst affected in this conflict were the common people who could not neglect either and hence tried to satisfy both by giving *dāna* apart from their tax to rulers. The main losers were the brahmins since the *śramaṇas'* views appeared to be progressive and more convincing.

There were numerous schools in the *śramaṇa* movement. According to one reference, probably a rather exaggerated one, there were 363 views stated to have been condemned by the Jainas as erroneous.[39] It is difficult to ascertain the exact number of views which existed as well-formulated schools of thought. The main organised schools of the heterodox sect were those of the Buddhists, Jainas, *Ājīvikas, Lokāyatas* and *Ajñānas* (agnostics). Of these, Buddhism was the most successful.[40] As far as the idea of sacrifice is concerned, in explicit references, only Jainism, Buddhism and Āji-vikism draw our attention, for these three in similar vein rejected the *yajña*-centred Vedic cult and formulated alternative world-views. We shall take each of them for separate consideration.

(i) The Jainas

The Jainas claimed a very ancient tradition. Tradition identifies Riṣabha, the founder of Jainism, with the *muni* of the *Ṛgveda.*[41] Pārṣva, the *tīrthaṅkara* before Mahāvīra, who flourished probably towards the end of the ninth century B.C., is said to have fought against the brāhmaṇic system of *varṇa* and the merciless slaughter of animals in the Vedic sacrifices. He emphasised *ahiṃsā* in his protest against the slaughter of animals in sacrifice.[42] After about 250 years the teaching of Mahāvīra, the last *tīrthaṅkara,* took place contemporaneously with early phases of the *śramaṇa* movement and the final production of the *Upaniṣads*. Although there is no explicit reference to them in the *Upaniṣads* some Jaina texts bear a resemblance with the teachings of the Upanisads on self-sacrifice.[43] According to the tradition of the *Śvetāmbaras*, the first audience of Mahāvīra after his enlightenment consisted only of gods, the lords of Vedic sacrifice, to whom he preached for a short time. After a while he preached in a sacrificial enclosure on *ahiṃsā* while the performance of *yajña* was in progress. There he converted three brahmin priests.[44] This pattern of mission was adopted by his followers.

It is typical that many Jaina mendicants visited houses where sacrifice was in progress. In many such events the initial experience was traumatic: they were despised, beaten up and denied *dāna;* but later they would win converts. We note one example in detail: the twenty-fifth lecture in the *Uttarādyāyana* contains a dialogue between Jeyaghosa, a great sage, and Vijayakosa, a sacrificing brahmin in Benares. The sage goes to the sacrificial hall for alms. But the brahmin says that the priests versed in the *Vedas* and sacrificial science, who can save themselves and others, are alone eligible to receive alms. The sage replies calmly that the most essential subject in the *Vedas* is the sacrifice of virtues; the priests pretend to know the sacrifice; but the true brahmin is the one who has no worldly attachment, who does not repent of having become a monk, who takes delight in noble words and in loving living beings and not injuring them. The binding of animals for sacrifice cannot save the sinner because the binding of *karman* is very powerful. One does become a brahmin through chastity and virtues as one becomes a *śramaṇa* by equanimity, a *muni* by knowledge and a *tapasa* by penance; by one's actions one becomes a brahmin, kṣatriya, vaiśya or *śūdra.* The Enlightened One has declared all good qualities. Those who possess these good qualities alone are able to save themselves and others. Then Vijayakosa says to the sage, "You are the sacrificer of sacrifices, you are the most learned of those who know the *Vedas*; you know perfectly the *dharma*; you are able to save yourself and others; so accept our alms". But denying the alms, the sage asks the brahmin to join the order at once so that he can save himself from the sea of *saṃsāra.* The brahmin obeys.[45]

In the same book a monk is said to preach to a sacrificing brahmin; he allegorises the ritual as follows:

the real fire was penance, the real fire-place was life, the real ladle (*sūvā*) was right exertion, the real cowdung was body, the real fire-wood was *karman*, the real oblation was self-control, right exertion and tranquillity, the sacred pond was law, and the real bathing-place was celibacy.[46]

Those who were reluctant to accept their teaching—mainly the brahmin priests—condemned the Jaina sages for their negative attitude to *yajña*. Hence the Jainas faced "the undying hostility of the brāhmaṇical community".[47]

To counter the *yajña*-centred world-view, denying creation and the existence of a creator, Jainism holds that the world is eternal, self-existent and composed of constituent substances and atomic particles. It propounded a doctrine of the fundamental universal force of *karman* composed of material particles that makes the soul (*jīva*) become entangled with matter (*ajīva*), thus creating a bondage. Liberation of the soul depends on a thorough knowledge of *karma*, eliminating accumulated *karma* by hard *tapas* and hindering the absorption of new *karma* by excellent conduct in the present life.[48] Jainas adopted extreme forms of *tapas*, both external and internal, to the extent of voluntary deaths of mendicants. It is remarkable, further, that women were accepted for monkhood.[49]

In view of animal killing in Vedic sacrifice, Jainas gave great importance to *ahiṃsā*. Their fundamental ethical principle is to restrain from killing even an insect. For them doing harm to others is doing harm to oneself because such behaviour inhibits the *jiva*'s ability to free itself from *saṃsāra* and attain *mokṣa*, the supreme consciousness and bliss.[50] A Jaina *sūtra* says: "Some kill animals for sacrifice, some for their skin, flesh, blood...some kill them intentionally and some unintentionally.... He who understands the nature of sin against animals is called a true sage who understands *karma*."[51]

Relatedly, it is noteworthy that "The widespread vegetarianism of the present day Hindus ... is very much due to the influence of the Jainas who not only made vegetarianism binding on their followers but even raised it to the hallmark of true Aryanhood".[52] Their extreme forms of *tapas* interpreted as self-sacrifice, however, appeared to contradict their own principle of *ahiṃsā*. For this reason Buddhism rejected the animal killing of the brahmin priests and the self-killing of Jainas alike.

(ii) The Buddhists

Buddhism was the most successful of all *śramaṇa* schools. It had the largest following from various sections including brahmins.[53] The Buddhists' attitude to ritual *yajña*, and their inattention to gods and priests are as among the Jainas. Buddhism, however, had no equivalent to the extreme forms of Jaina austerity. Thus in his address to his disciples in Benares after his enlightenment, for which he found the above two extremes useless, the Buddha denounces both. On the one hand, ritual sacrifice is passion-oriented, lowly, pagan, unworthy, unprofitable and worldly-minded. On the other hand, the extreme form of austere practice is painful, non-Aryan, egoistic, hysterical, anti-social, excessive and futile.[54] The middle path avoids these two extremes, opens the eyes, bestows understanding and leads to enlightenment.[55] With reference to the Buddha's departure from the ancient brāhmaṇic and *śramaṇa* tradition and his new middle path Jaini writes: "He now not only claimed to be a 'Jina' and 'omniscient' in the manner of Gosala and Mahāvīra, but even claimed to be a 'Master of the *Vedas*' and a 'Brahmavādin'. He was thus a true *śramaṇa* as well as being 'true brahmin".[56] It was from the point of view of the middle path that Buddhism was influential in religious and social reforms, as we shall soon see.

References to explicit opposition to sacrifice are not many in the early Buddhist literature. The reason may be that though Buddhism joined forces with other movements in attacking ritualism, brāhmaṇic influence inhibited outright rejection of ritual. The few available references may however be taken as representing the real position. The *Kūtadanta Sutta* describes an event in which the Buddha and his disciples went to a brahmin village in Magadha where hundreds of animals were ready for a grand sacrifice on behalf of Kūtadanta, a rich brahmin. A dialogue started between this sacrificer and the Buddha. The Buddha told him story of a king who performed an excellent sacrifice with ghee, oil, butter etc. using his own wealth and voluntary contributions of his people. He had not taxed the people for this purpose which was why they were spontaneously generous. The king was none else than the Buddha himself in a previous birth. He continued to teach the right sacrifice of knowledge, possibility of simple rituals without killing animals and the merit of *dāna* to virtuous recluses and support for their monasteries. This was the *dharma* of that king and his people. At last Kūtadanta was convinced, the *yajña* was stopped and a feast was served to the Buddha and his disciples at the sacrificial pit.[57] It is interesting to see in this story a criticism of the ritual relationship between kings and brahmin priests by which the latter sought wealth. Further, the implication of this story is much more than an attack on animal sacrifice. Trevor Ling writes:

The tale is, of course, entirely ludicrous and one can imagine the delight with which the Buddha's contemporaries would have responded to its humour. What emerges as the point of the story is a critique of brahminical sacrifice on the ground of economic wastefulness, cruelty to animals, forced labour, with harsh treatment of the labourers, and oppressive taxation of the people in order to pay for it all. It is clear, too that the supposed efficacy of the sacrifice is being quietly dismissed. By implication this heightens the objection to the lavish expenditure, cruelty and social oppression.[58]

In another instance, Kāsappa, a notable early convert to Buddhism, is asked by the Buddha to make a public confession to the question why he has left *agni* and *yajña*. He answers by saying that "sacrifices speak of things we know and hear, the desires of people. They bring rebirth. Therefore I will no more take delight in them."[59] Later, Kāsappa tells a prince:

> . . . where oxen are slain, or goats or fowls and pigs, or diverse creatures are put an end to; and those that take part in the sacrifice have wrong views, wrong intention, wrong speech, wrong action, wrong livelihood, wrong endeavour, wrong mindfulness, wrong rapture, such a sacrifice, Prince, is neither of great fruitfulness nor of great profit, nor of great renown, nor of widespread effect.[60]

The discourse continues to indicate that if one takes part in a sacrifice without killing animals but with the right intentions it is profitable. Immediately the prince institutes a gift to *śramaṇas* and brahmin wanderers.

In all these references it is important to note that Buddhism was not totally antagonistic to ritual *yajña* but to the killing of animals and wrong intentions. In the *Jātakas*, for instance, there is a poetic description of the horrible sight of an animal facing death in a sacrifice.[61] This specific concern, shared equally by the Jainas that animals should not be killed, goes well with the socio-economic context of the time, apart from the psychological side of such killing. Bhattacharyya points out that the significance of the concern of the Buddhists and Jainas for the protection of animals lies in its impact on the socio-economic structure:

> because they are the givers of food, beauty and happiness. This was certainly a teaching based upon the growing demands of the traders. In fact, this was the crying demand of the age; even the kṣatriya rulers desired to depend more upon the wealth of the traders than upon the magical powers of the brāhmaṇa priests.[62]

Thus in the development of urbanisation and trade, killing animals in large number for religious purpose affected the socio-economic life.

It is remarkable that the relationship between early Buddhists and brahmins was less hostile than that between Jainas and brahmins. With reference to the development of Buddhism within the brāhmaṇic fold and sharing many of its views, Monier-Williams goes so far as to say that the Buddha himself was a Hindu and he remained so to the end.[63] Rhys Davids points out that "There are many *Suttas*, roughly one hundred, telling of meetings between them. In almost every case the meeting is, in these *Suttas*, marked by courtesy on both sides".[64] She refers to interviews in which the Buddha was honoured by brahmins. But then she notes:

I do not wish to overestimate the respect here alleged as shown. The *Suttas* are the work of prejudiced compilers, and we have no brahman counterparts of these interviews. But it is evident that the Buddhist editors had retained no tradition of any chronic ill-feeling as existing between their founders and brahmans.[65]

With reference to the negative attitude, expressed in certain places, Rhys Davids finds it unclear whether it was the later or earlier position. She points out, however, that disagreement on matters like ritual sacrifice and *varṇa* is presented rather clearly. It is in this light, she suggests, that we should understand the earliest, chief disciples of the Buddha being converts from brāhmaṇism. This suggestion is helpful in understanding the cordiality and criticism between early Buddhism and brāhmaṇism.

As we have already noted, the view of the middle path and the toleration for simple forms of ritual with right intention in early Buddhism must have made easy for many brahmin mendicants to join the Buddhists, for they could not but perform certain rites as the brahmins of the orthodox schools and the teachers in the forest did. The development of rituals and ceremonies in later Buddhism is understandable in this light. Moreover, there was an attempt to interpret the death of the Buddha as a personal sacrifice. This must have been done by a brahmin who had the knowledge of the dialectics of heating and cooling in the Vedic sacrifice. Thus when all the disciples had finished homage to the body of the Buddha, the funeral pyre caught fire of itself. When all had been burnt away neither soot nor ash was seen and only the bones remained behind (as the leavings of sacrifice.) Immediately streams of water came from heaven and earth and extinguished the funeral pile.[66] Thus a blessed body went through the sacrificial process of heating and cooling.

A more explicit attack was made on the claims of the *yajña*-centred world-view of brāhmaṇism and of the priestly power of the brahmins. Against the Vedic world-view Buddhism presents a new scheme of what is called *bhāva cakra*,[67] the wheel of existence or becoming. It enumerates twelve independent links that represent a dependent origination (*pratītyasamutpāda*) of all that exists. *Karma saṃsāra* and *dukkha* (sorrow) issue forth from the operation. The doctrine of *anatta* (non-soul) which understands the apparent soul as formed by the conglomeration of five elements (*skandas*) and the idea of the inexorable and impersonal force of *karman* etc. negate the Vedic as well as the Upaniṣadic world-view, though Buddhism takes the notion of ethical *karman* from the *Upaniṣads*. The Buddhist enumeration of psychic or interior forces in the human personality also differs from that of the *Upaniṣads*.[68] The gods, the human gods (priests) and the supreme God, all are brought down as subject to the perpetual flux of the cosmos, *karman* and the soul.

Seen from the perspective of *kāma*, the fundamental element in Vedic *yajña*, for Buddhism the greatest enemy of a good becoming is desire (*tanhā* or *tṛṣṇa*) which is the immediate cause of *dukkha*.

> Desires can never be quenched through the fulfilment of desires as the mind is quick enough to cling to a new object and the objects themselves are of transitory character to last only for a short time. All desires are therefore undesirable; they are like flames of fire ... which burn and like "spears and javelins" "pierce and rend the mortal frame of us".[69]

According to the Buddha, conscious volition is a necessary condition for *karman*. Volition and intention prompted by the deep-lying desire, and not the act as such, make *karman* effective.[70] The freedom of existence lies in subduing, if not annihilating, the desire which leads to a state of transcendence or *nibbāna*. To use the sacrificial language,

> For the Buddhist, *existence itself is heat*—the fire of passion, greed, craving for sense experience. All this is fire and is burning. Thus the "disbecoming" that is *nirvāṇa* is a "blowing out" (as in the *Ṛgveda* 10.16.4 imagery) of the fire, and a return to the cooling that preceded this passionate mode of being.[71]

Unike the Jainas, the Buddha redefined the brahmin as one who has freed himself from all desire and craving for attachments.[72] The only way of achieving this freedom is a reflectively ascetic life which alone can facilitate the process.

The ascetic life is marked by the actualisation of inner forces like thought and memory by yogic techniques on the one hand and practice of the eightfold ethical path on the other.[73] Like Jainism, Buddhism also emphasised *ahimsā;* but whether *ahiṃsā* is commensurate with the doctrine of *amatta* and a world-view of creative process is open to question. Does killing an animal, for instance, obstruct the perpetual flux, or is destruction in some way not part of the process? And if kinship between various creatures is maintained, is it not leading to a passionate attachment to objects? Besides the total abandonment of animal sacrifice, *agnihotra* was given a new allegorical interpretation. Thus the Buddha exhorted a brahmin to consider honouring his son, womenfolk, slaves, messengers and workmen as the *agni* of the householder. The householder has to worship every day six quarters now represented by parents, teachers, wife, children, friends, servants, *śramaṇas* and brahmins.[74] Elsewhere he said that the kindling of fire in the inner altar to tame the self is the holy fire.[75] It was the responsibility of ascetic monks to teach these ethical ideals to householders.

The Buddha's teaching must have first disturbed the family system of Aryans. A legend describes how on the Buddha'a first preaching mission in Magadha, there was an outcry against him and propaganda that he intended to make families sonless and women widows and to cut off lines of succession.[76] But since the renouncers needed the support of the householders they would not have undermined household life. "The early Buddhist protest was cautiously directed at weaning the layman from brāhmaṇical ritualism and divine dependence, and to substitute for them a sober life in this world chastened by a morality of *dāna* and awakened intentionality."[77] Though mutual interaction between the monks and the householders is evident in Buddhist circles, in order to keep the path direct to *nibbāna*, an appropriate kind of ascetic life is encouraged in Buddhism. In many places the stories of the Buddha's previous births (*Jātakas*) mention kings becoming renouncers, ascetics challenging kings, and temptation of ascetics by women.

Once the Buddha had a discussion with a brahmin who favoured household life as more fruitful than the wandering life. The opinion of the Buddha was that one cannot be categorical about this but must make distinctions. One may succeed or fail in either way. He maintained, however, that the life of a wandering monk might be more conducive to fruitfullness because there are hindrances in the household life. The brahmin partner in dialogue agreed to this. Yet the Buddha concluded this discussion by saying that "the purpose of such virtue in one who has gone forth is to produce the kind of joy in the good life which enables him to develop thought which is without hatred or malevolence (which is a preliminary to his further training)".[78]

Relatedly, unlike the brāhmaṇic circles, the Jainas and the Buddhists encouraged the adoption of monkhood from youth. How this movement affected the brāhmaṇic religion we shall see later. It is notable that at the beginning, the youth movement of monks upset many. For example, once Pasenadi, the king of Kosala, had a discussion with the Buddha before he became an adherent of the new movement. The king asked the Buddha how he, being so young as compared with already well-known teachers, could claim an insight beyond theirs, the Buddha replied,

> no "religieux" should be despised because of his youth. Who would show disrespect to a prince, or to a venomous serpent, or to a fire, merely because it was young? It was the nature of the doctrine, not the personal peculiarities of the teacher, that was the test.[79]

Such a view encouraged many young people, both male and female, to join the Buddhist order. For their disciplined life and ethical qualities the householders respected them and gave them *dāna.* The monks did not ridicule the household life though ultimately renunciation was inevitable for *nibbāna.* For such a state a suitable birth could be gained by a good family life. The merit of the household life depended mainly on *dāna* to monks. Those who were niggardly in their *dāna* were threatened by rebirth in animal form or by torture of hell.[80] We need not explain how the growing movement of Buddhist monks would have affected the livelihood of the brahmin priests who once had the sole privilege of *dāna.*

Besides the monks, there were lay followers of the Buddha, both men (*upāsaka*) and women (*upāsikā*). They did not need to go out of their society but were required to observe certain ethical principles applicable to them. It was felt, however, that disadvantages were more than the advantages in this mode of life as far as the attainment of *nibbāna* was concerned. Therefore in the precise sense only the monks were Buddhists and they were also the Buddhist élite.[81] Buddhism is essentially a *bhikku*-oriented religion.

By organising the monks in the *saṅgha*, the Buddha wanted to develop an egalitarian society as a challenge to the centralised power of monarchy. Further, members of the *saṇgha* denounced *varṇa* amongst themselves. This had great appeal to those who were low *varṇas*. There was a constant appeal from the *saṅgha* not to waste wealth in rituals but to conserve it for the maintenance of the *saṅghas*. This was different from the brāhmaṇic schools which did not encourage conservation of wealth if it meant discouraging ritual. The Buddhists placed the ethical code as a substitute for ritual sacrifices. "The *yajña*, therefore, was replaced by an ethical code encouraging austerity and ensuing the conservation of wealth."[82]

Relatedly, formation of community and conservation of wealth were important components of the *dharma* that the Buddha preached. As Coomaraswamy observes, the Buddha nothing but the *dharma*. With reference to the symbol of the chariot in monarchic atmosphere and its meanings, he says,

> The eternal law (*dharma*) is, in fact, the charioteer; and while the king's chariots age, and just so the body ages, the Eternal Law of existences does not age. The Buddha identifies himself—that self he calls his refuge—with this Law, he calls himself the "best of charioteers".[83]

It must be pointed out, however, that the initial vision of *dharma* which had to be embodied in the *saṅgha* became obscured by certain ambiguous developments. The *saṅgha* came to be supported mainly by wealthy merchants and broad-minded kings. And although the Buddha originally favoured republican government, he seems, in view of the possibility of violence and the weakness of democracy, to have, in course of time, allowed monarchy.[84] Trevor Ling points out that the Buddha recognised social stability as a necessary condition for the success of social and moral reconstruction as well as of spreading the Buddhist ideal.[85]

The Buddha seems to have developed the idea that in the evolution of society, the first and foremost human being was the primordial king, "Great Elect", who was supposed to delight all with *dharma* following the "wheel gem" that appeared in the sky. According to this myth, before degeneration took place ancient society was perfect.[86] The Buddha envisaged *dharma* as conquering the whole world without force. He first placed the *saṅgha* as the agent to do this.[87] This ideal, however, materialised in a different form, a few centuries later, when Aśoka became the emperor. He was considered as the Great Elect, beloved of gods and the holder of *dharma cakra*.

The attachment to politics and interpretation of a new Law or *dharma* brought enormous support to Buddhism on the one hand, to improve the order and spread the docrine. On the other hand, it paved the way for monks to corrupt themselves with power and political alliance. And even though the challenge of Buddhism to brāhmaṇic religion and sacrifice created a permanent influence in history, because of its later development of "worldly" concerns and ritual it did not succeed in eliminating the *yajña* as it initially intended.

(iii) The Ājīvikas

The teachings of the *Ājīvikas* (the men of livelihood) are strictly deterministic, ascetic and atheistic. They seem to have existed earlier than the Buddhists, perhaps even the Jainas, though they reached their zenith in the sixth century B.C. The Buddhists and Jainas considered them opponents, although the three had certain views in common. *Ājīvikas* lived as an organised community and, like the other sects, later gained royal patronage. Aśoka was closely associated with the *Ājīvikas.*[88] Though the sect died out early, its impact on other sects and Hindu philosophy is considerable. Tantrism particularly inherited many values of the *Ājīvikas.*

Like the other *śramaṇas* the *Ājīvikas* condemned sacrifice. They held that the Vedic cosmology, which is oriented to the power of *yajña,* is confusing. They revived the concept of Vedic *ṛta* and incorporated into it an atheistic or impersonal first principle. As Basham points out, among the three great sectarian movements "ājīvikism stands out for its thoroughgoing recognition of order in the universe". The cosmos of Makkhali Gośāla, the earliest proponent of Ājīvikism, "is immense in space and time, and ordered in every detail".[89] According to him the universe is constituted by elemental atoms.

The working of *karma saṃsāra* is explained by the *Ājīvikas* on a grand scale. The transmigration of the soul is automatic. After having experienced every possible kind of life in millions of forms, at last the soul takes the life of an Ājīvika *śramaṇa.*[90] But the soul is passive and not affected by any action. *Pūraṇa,* the next exponent of these teachings, developed this doctrine known as *akriyavāda,* or the "way of non-action". Then why should one act? The answer is, because of *niyati,* the law or operation of a fatalistic order.[91] No one can change this order. Although fatalism was prevalent even before the Buddha and Mahāvīra who raised their voice against it, it is the *Ājīvikas* who gave it a conceptual framework. Basham writes: "The slogan of the *Ājīvika* sect, 'human effort is ineffectual', may have been a widespread and popular phrase in time of distress often on the lips of the ordinary people of the Ganges Valley."[92]

The only way out is to destroy the soul's embodiment by severe austerity. *Ājīvikas* were known for their nudity and hard austere practices including lying on beds of thorns, cutting their hands etc. They also performed mysterious secret rites.[93] Such rites later included tantric elements.

In relation to *Ājīvikas,* the fundamental view of another two sects is worth mentioning. As opposed to the *Ājīvikas,* the *Lokāyatas*

> asserted complete freedom, absolute free will, as the natural way of life and were also known as do-as-you-like school (*yadṛcchāvāda*). Everything happens through the spontaneous actions of nature. The school agreed with the *Ājīvikas* in rejecting moral causation but for opposite reasons: all acts and experiences are spontaneous, not determined by anything; moreover, there is no soul and no transmigration which could make the working out of moral causation possible.[94]

Hence the adoption of a hedonistic life-style, cherishing the view of highest happiness, but recognising the unavoidable transient nature of it which produces newness and relieves one from boring permanence. Difficulties have to be overcome in order to increase pleasure. The materialists, because they objected to ritual and sacrifice, were regarded with scorn by the orthodox. As Thapar points out, "references to materialist schools of thought were blurred in the priestly writings that have survived, and until recently it was generally thought that Indian philosophy had more or less bypassed materialism".[95]

The other sect, *Ajñānas* (agnostics), ridiculed any use of speculation on matters debated by philosophers as merely confusing. For them such speculation causes obstruction to a peaceful mind and friendly life.[96] The exact view of the *Lokāyatas* and *Ajñānas* on sacrifice is not known. Surely, however, their metaphysical framework did not allow any place for *yajña* and the sacred power that centres in it. Since the ritual *karman* of *yajña* was transposed to ethical *karman* and action in general, they expressed their opinion mainly in terms of ethical *karman.* Whether or not their views still continued to have impact by the time of the *Bhagavad Gītā,* undoubtedly the views on *akarman* (non-action) and *ajñāna* were so influential that the literature of the period following their existence could not ignore them.

(iv) The Overall Impact of the Śramaṇa *Movement*

In the foregoing sections we have outlined the development of the *śramaṇa* movement, its attack on ritual sacrifice, its social protest, the formulation of world-views opposed to Vedic religion and the fundamental ideas of the most important schools. On the one hand, in this historical situation, *yajña* was in a steady decline among the common people because of socio-economic pressures. On the other hand, more powerfully, the *śramaṇa* teachings conceptually ridiculed ritual sacrifice. These two challenging forces are very significant in effecting change in the understanding of *yajña*.[97]

There was a special focus on the cruel killing of animals which taxed the peasants and the poor and which was abhorrent to see. The *śramaṇas*, taking insights from the *Upaniṣads*, further ethicised the idea of *karman* but incorporated the idea of power entailed in every minute act as was believed in the ritual order. They reduced the amount of *dakṣiṇā* to priests and received *dāna* themselves from the people. They questioned the authority of both priests and *Vedas*. They emphasised empirical knowledge as opposed to the revealed knowledge of the *Vedas* as claimed by the brahmins.[98] The *śramaṇas*, however, took over the idea of *puṇya* from the brahmins and attached it to the hearing of their teachings. In addition, to convince the people, some claimed to have esoteric kinds of spiritual experience.[99] The dichotomy between householders and monks in various degrees, was originally the contribution of *śramaṇa* movements, especially the Buddhists.[100] We shall see in the next section how the brahmins tried to weaken this dichotomy and integrate both in a single life-cycle.

In the process of *śramaṇa*-brāhmaṇic interaction, although the *śrauta* ritual sacrifices were in steady decline, evidently the domestic sacramental rites (*saṃskāra*) continued to exist. These life-sacraments helped the brahmin priests to survive when the grand sacrifices were disappearing. Some, however, resorted to pseudo-religious forms of ritual, like black magic and sorcery, as is evident from the repeated warning against such mean practices in the literature of early Buddhism and Jainism.[101] On the other hand, it must be noted, even the Buddhists and Jainas were not completely free from ritual and ceremony in due course incorporating elements from the Vedic ritual.[102] Thus, the Buddhist cult adopted elements of theistic cults along with myths.[103] Gonda points out that the Buddhist ritual of ordination into monkhood has a considerable number of elements similar to those of the *dīkṣa* in *soma yajña*.[104] Complete deritualisation was never possible in mutual interaction and modification of different religious groups. Further, strict discipline in the *saṅgha* seemed to restrict the freedom enjoyed in the wandering life. Monier-Williams notes:

> In truth it might almost be said that to every movement and action, in waking and sleeping, in dressing and undressing, in standing and sitting, in going out and coming in, in fasting and eating, in speaking and non-speaking the Buddhist monk had to submit to the most stringent regulations.[105]

This situation must have appeared to have the element of rigid order similar to that followed in Vedic ritual. This fact made it possible for the brahmins to revive their *yajña* at an appropriate moment.

In the political-socio-economic sphere, we noticed how the individual wanderers challenged princely and priestly powers alike. Special emphasis was given to *ahiṃsā* because partly it had direct effect on the killing of animals which in turn affected the trade and the agricultural economy of ordinary people. All these challenges were posed directly to priestly religious life. Relatedly, the rejection of *varṇa* by the *śramaṇas* appeared to confuse the *varṇa dharma* based on *yajña*. Organised communities that attempted to develop an egalitarian society after the administrative pattern of original tribal republics also indirectly countered monarchic power. While the unorganised or less organised sects only had a passing social impact, the well-organised sects, particularly Buddhism, succeeded in effecting an interaction with society at large. But once they had become fully institutionalised, their adherents lost their original interest in protest. In Thapar's words, "The expression of dissent and protest was one element in renunciation but the joining of an order or sect could and did modify if not nullify the social content of the protest".[106] One important factor in this change is that the monasteries had to depend mainly on the wealthy merchants and middle class people.[107]

Just the same, the influence of the *śramana* movement was considerable. First, Buddhism, Ājīvikism and Jainism tried to effect a direct influence on the kingdoms through their rulers. According to the Jaina tradition Chandragupta Maurya was a follower of their doctrine and at the end of his reign became a Jaina monk. His son Bindusāra (293-268 B.C.) or at least his queen Dharmā, patronised the *Ājīvikas*. It was an *Ājīvika* mendicant who foretold that the queen would deliver a son who would become a great king. Aśoka was that son, who continued his family support for the *Ājīvikas*.

The first political science in India was developed during the Mauryan empire as contained in Kautilya's *Arthaśāstra*. It may be an interesting study to identify the values of *śramaṇas* in the *Arthaśāstra*. In any event, it gives ample evidence of the powerful force of the ascetic institutions within society and the king had to exercise careful check on their power. Some ascetics were used as agents of the government and even as spies.[108] With reference to the administrative depths in the arrangement of the book Heesterman observes: "Briefly then, whichever way we look, in practice the essence of the system remains diffusion of power and scattering of resources".[109] This may indicate *śramaṇa* influence on the Mauryan rulers to move towards the polity of the old republican states. Heesterman observes further that particularly Buddhism gave the Mauryan empire a new ethical legitimisation through its intimate connections with it. He writes:

> Buddhism owes to empire the realisation of its universalistic claim. Even though the Maurya empire lasted only for a relatively short time, the pattern for a new type of universalistic imperial order, based on the ultimate connection of the ruler and the monastic establishment, the *saṅgha*, was set.[110]

The universal appeal for a moral order (*dharma*) was most evident in the rule of Aśoka.[111] When Aśokā became emperor a special interest arose in Buddhist circles even though Aśoka's professing of a particular religion is not clear. According to Buddhist sources, in spite of his support for *Ājīvikas*, (perhaps because of obligations passed on to him from his family, at first) Aśoka was a harsh and ruthless ruler until he was convinced of his error by a Buddhist monk and became a lay Buddhist. The horrible sight in the battlefield of Kaliṅga, a victory at the cost of thousands of human lives, made him extremely remorseful and despondent. This was a great turning point in his life. Subsequently, he associated himself with the concerns and activities of the Buddhists. He not only supported the missionary movement of Buddhism but was significantly interpreted as the paradigm of *dharma*.[112] His wheel is an important Buddhist symbol. It reminds us of the first sermon of the Buddha by which he set the wheel of *dharma* and existence in motion. It also symbolises Aśoka's conquering efficacy and universal sovereignty in the name of *dharma.*[113] We have already pointed out the development in Buddhism of the idea of a "universal moral ruler". While the Jainas protested against imperialism and political violence, the Buddhists favoured a dharmic rule which in their sight was put into practice by the most famous emperor of ancient India.[114] Aśoka does not, however, seem to have done this as an avowed Buddhist. Although one of his inscriptions is taken to indicate the confession of his faith in the Buddha, *dhamma* and *saṅgha,* there is no evidence for his commitment to Buddhist ideas like *nirvāṇa.* His message has a twofold aspect: one is practical concerning interpersonal relationships; the other is doctrinal in a general sense that includes a special concern for the sanctity of animals, toleration of other faiths, discipline and moral progress. Interestingly the goal of his *dharma* is neither *mokṣa* nor *nirvāṇa,* but *paraloka* or *svarga.* He is said to be the beloved of gods.[115] Thapar notes, "Aśoka was careful to make a distinction between his personal belief in and support for Buddhism, and his duty as emperor to remain unattached and unbiased in favour of any religion".[116] For Pande, "Aśoka's *dhamma* represents the quintessence of Śramaṇism as applicable to the laity".[117] With reference to the *śramaṇa* emphasis on compassion and the Vedic virtue of liberality he says, "Aśoka's *dhamma* is so broadly conceived that even with a Śramaṇic background and the rejection of animal sacrifice and ritualism, it could well be the meeting point of the pure ethical traditions of Śramaṇism and Brahmanism".[118] This position led the brāhmaṇic orthodoxy to arise with a new awareness of the possibilities of orthodoxy (seen in the *Gītā,* for example) to combat the Buddhist strategy of attaining their ends with political support.

The edicts of Aśoka ban the killing of animals in the Mauryan empire,[119] but killing was not eliminated. A special list of animals and birds were exempted which had probably both totemic and economic value. Meat was still sold publicly though in a greatly reduced quantity.[120] Many diverse ceremonies were trivialised. Though Aśoka encouraged *dāna* he warned lest it degenerate into an automatic substitute for moral responsibility. *Dharma,* for him, is the foundation of religion. A rock edict says: "There is no gift that can equal the gifts of *dharma,* the establishment of human relations on *dharma,* the distribution of wealth through *dharma,* or kinship in *dharma".*[121]

The fundamental character of this *dharma* is to embrace all people irrespective of their class and religious identities. Thus there great concern is expressed regarding *śramaṇas* and brahmin priests alike. They should not suffer but deserve liberal *dāna*.[122] State officers were charged with special responsibilities for *dharma*, to help all people and all sects. A pillar edict reports Aśoka saying about his officers. "I have ordered some of them to look after the affairs of the *saṁkha* ... some to take care of the brahmin and *Ājīvika* ascetics, some to work among the *nirgranthas* [the Jaina monks], and some among the various other religious sects".[123]

The inclusive principle of Aśoka leaves no clue about his exact religious position. The edicts do not in any way project a particular religious point of view. By reason of his equal support for brahmins "some have even maintained that Aśoka was not a Buddhist but a brāhmaṇical Hindu".[124] For him *dharma* is a way of life, convenient to all, no matter where it comes from. For such an inclusive, broad mind, Aśoka may be compared to King Solomon and the Emperor Constantine. But history has proved that inclusive compromises do not last long; after Aśoka the Mauryan empire declined.

There is no need to discuss in detail the nature and effect of Aśokas' eclectic position. On the one hand it achieved the fusion of the great ethical principles implicit in various aspects of the *śramaṇa* movement. By this the Buddhist ideal of a dhārmic rule was partially fulfilled. On the other hand, the kings and their allies, the brahmin priests, were greatly relieved of the pressure forced upon them by the *śramaṇas*. It appeared to them that the *śramaṇa* movement was stripped of its power, its value already incorporated into their life. The more shrewd brahmins used this opportunity to revive Vedic religion. The consequence was a great revival in *yajña*. In the period that followed the Mauryan dynasty new political developments were conducive to the revival of the sacrificial religion. The nature of this situation and the revival of Vedic *yajña* will be the special focus of our discussion in the next part of this study.

4. Brāhmaṇic Reaction and the Revival of Sacrifice

At the turn of the second century B.C., Vedic religion with its basis in *yajña* enjoyed a great revival. This is crucial for understanding the further developments in the understanding of sacrifice. As we have already seen, the socio-economic pressures of the preceding centuries, the challenges of the *śramaṇa* movement and the philosophy of *ahiṃsā* almost wrecked the sacrificial religion. Apart from the survival of Vedic *yajña* in different forms and development of new ritual practices, however, the Aśokan reform provided room for the brāhmaṇic religion to regenerate although it banned killing animals in sacrifice. As R.N. Nandi demonstrates, in the wake of changes, the brahmins transplanted the traditional gift-exchange economy to a market-based economy by means of domestic rituals and new meritorious practices like *tīrthas*. This readjustment has been characteristic of the brahmins throughout their history.[125]

More remarkably, the political situation in this period was favourable for the revival of sacrifice. After the Mauryan dynasty (322-185 B.C.) the Suṅga dynasty came to power. The founder of this dynasty Puṣyamitra was a staunch brahmin who came to power by a revolt. He revived the great *yajñas* like *aśvamedha* in his celebration of victories and at royal ceremonies. Dandekar says that the performance of this sacrifice did not mark the revival of Vedic ritual in the right brāhmaṇic fashion. It was rather intended to assert political power, the decline of non-Vedic religions and the authority of the *Vedas*.[126] It should be pointed out, however, that although there was openness for new ideas and practices, as we shall see, the power and meaning of Vedic sacrifice was reaffirmed. This revival continued in the following centuries and spread to other parts of India also.[127] Persecution of *śramaṇas* by certain kings was part of this revival. In Buddhist literature Puṣyamitra figures as a prominent persecutor of the Buddhists.[128] The reason for such activities was that the Suṅgan rulers "became puppets in the hands of their Brāhman counsellors".[129] During this period an enormous amount of brāhmaṇic literature was also produced. Different types of this literature echo a brāhmaṇic reaction against a decline in sacrifice, and confusion of social order and Vedic ideas.[130] The nature of this reaction and the principles of reinterpretation will be studied in this section. Despite the rejection of *śramaṇas* the way in which certain *śramaṇa* values are incorporated in the process of new interpretation will be of great importance.

The revival was initiated and supported at three levels, philosophy, law code and epic stories. The orthodox schools of philosophy, particularly *Pūrvamīmāṃsā*, reaffirmed the authority of the *Veda* and the karmic power of ritualism. The legal codes, particularly the *Mānavadharmaśāstra*, provided rules for a reconstruction of society and religion. In this process they slightly modified the practice of *yajña* and incorporated relevant elements that came from the *śramaṇa* movement. The epics, particularly the *Mahābhārata* which is rightly called the fifth *Veda*, attach great importance to *yajña*, accommodate discourses on new meanings of it and incorporate material from the *Pūrvamīmāṃsā* and *Mānavadharmaśāstra*. We shall discuss the method of interpreting sacrifice adopted in these sources.

(i) The Orthodox Darśanas

We have already mentioned the development of the brāhmaṇic schools of thought as parallel to or part of the *śramaṇa* movement. They are distinguished as the orthodox (*āstika) darśanas* from the heterodox (*nāstika*) schools. They are *āstika* not because they emphasise the existence of God, or because they all approve the *yajña*-oriented world-view, but because they all accept in some way or other the authority of the *Veda* and take it as the primary source of knowledge (i.e., *sabda pramāṇa*).

As Dandekar points out, except the *pūrva* and *uttara mīmāṃsas*, the *āstika darśanas* were connected with the *Veda* "only in a forced, tenuous and essentially formal manner".[131]

Ideas on *ātman* and *karma saṃsāra* overlap between orthodox and some heterodox schools. But whose was original is difficult to assert because of lack of chronological precision. Jaini oberves:

> One of the outstanding distinctions between the brāhmaṇical and the *śramaṇa* doctrines is that whereas the former can be traced only to a body of literature of varying antiquity, the latter can be attributed to definite historical persons who flourished around the sixth century B.C. in the ancient kingdoms of Videha and Magadha.[132]

Nevertheless, it may not be totally untenable to view the brāhmaṇic schools as a counter-movement against the *śramaṇas*, formulating alternative world-views but affirming the Vedic authority along with the law givers and epic writers. Some of the *sūtras* of the *āstika darśanas* refer to Buddhist doctrines and refute them. These references have been found useful clues to the approximate dates of these *sūtras*.[133]

Since the aim of the brāhmaṇic schools was to propound metaphysical viewpoints they are not explicit regarding religious practices. *Dharma*, however, is regarded as basic to life in all systems. To be sure *yajña* should necessarily be the basis or part of this *dharma* but except for the *pūrvamīmāṃsa* school they do not give it a central place. Yet we have a few hints in the sources of the other schools about the place and meaning of sacrifice in their philosophical framework.

Gautama's *Nyāya Sūtras* refer to the debts of everyday life on the spiritual journey. The debts are due to the sages, gods and fathers. They also indicate that the performance of sacrifice must continue till death for there is no release without it.[134] One of the proofs for the existence of God they give is that various sects worship him in various ways and the sacrificial cults worship him as the sacrificer.[135] In another sense it is said that the power produced by the sacrificer is not to succour the departed spirits but to succour the sacrificer himself.[136] Further, the deterioration of the universe is related to the dwindling of the *Vedas* and *yajñas,* though the constituent elements of the universe are the ultimate atoms.[137] There are good effects of right sacrifices and bad effects of wrong ones.[138] The *Vaiśeṣika Sūtras* limit the references to mention of only the exaltation of life from merit which is produced by following Vedic precepts, entertaining pure brahmins, bathing, fasting, sacrifice, gift or sacred formula.[139] In the *sūtras* of the *nyāya-vaiśeṣika* schools, however, there is no mention of the structure and sacred power of sacrifice as understood in Vedic times. Moreover, there is no attempt to respond to the criticism of the heterodox movements on the question of *yajña* though their metaphysical views the subject of comment.

The classical forms of *sāṃkhya* and *yoga* developed later than the *Bhagavad Gītā*. Many thinkers including Śaṃkara regard *Sāṃkhya* as a non-Vedic or pre-Aryan concept of high antiquity which developed in different circles.[140] The fundamental categories of these schools may, however, be found in earlier literatures.[141] Apart from scattered ideas found in the *Vedas* and the *Upaniṣads,* particularly in the *Śvetāsvatara Upaniṣad,* the earliest record of *sāṃkhya* teaching is found in the *Mokṣa Dharma* of the *Mahābhārata*.[142] In this section there are no details about the place of sacrifice except the mention of two paths, *pravṛtti mārga* and *nivṛtti mārga;* the former perpetuates birth, pleasure, pain etc., but the latter gives imperishable emancipation by a discriminative knowledge between *puruṣa* and *prakṛti*. Therefore, probably *Sāṃkhya* viewed the ritual *karman* as inferior to knowledge. *Yoga* as personal discipline helped in the way of knowledge and realisation which required no *yajña*.

Uttara mīmāṃsa or *vedānta* in its classical form was also a later development, although its foundation is laid in the *Upaniṣads*. Like *Sāṃkhya, Vedanta* also emphasised *ātma yajña* and considered ritual *yajña* as inferior. Gaudapāda's *Kārikas* describe various fundamental categories of things including gods, sacrifices, enjoyers etc. which are not different from the Self, but are imagined to be so.[143] *Vedānta*

Sūtra III.1.12 says that only the performance of *yajña* will get one to the moon in order to assume new birth; III.1.25 justifies the killing of animals in sacrifice as it is done as a duty prescribed in the *Vedas*; IV.1.16 gives similar reasons for the performance of *agnihotra*; III.4.25, 26, 30 seems to suggest that *yajña* is indispensable till one attains *jñāna* to which the former is a means. The classical *vedāntins*, though concerned primarily with *jñāna* and the upaniṣadic section of the *Veda*, acknowledge the value of sacrifice for an ego-centred empirical life and consider it a stepping stone to its own transcending *jñāna*.[144] And *karma yoga* generally is seen as a means of purifying the mind in preparation for inner enlightenment. Thus while the *nāstika* schools completely rejected *yajña*, the *āstika* schools, following the upaniṣadic pattern, found some room for it, although, from the viewpoint of Vedic sacrifice, their world-views are different.

It is the *pūrvamīmāṃsa* school which attaches paramount significance to ritual sacrifice. The word '*mīmāṃsa*' is used in the *Yajurveda* and the *Brāhmaṇas* where it means a deliberation on some problem regarding ritual practice.[145] Many scholars think that the *pūrvamīmāṃsa* cannot properly be spoken of as a system of philosophy. It is a systematised code of principles in accordance with which the Vedic texts are to be interpreted for the purposes of sacrifice.[146] Apart from the reaffirmation of *yajña*-based Vedic *dharma*, eternal authority of *Veda*, karmic potency and the meaningfulness of sacrificial action at various levels, it provides guidance to *smṛti* literature for instructions for orderly performance of ritual reaffirmation of the power of sacrifice,[147] and to *vedānta* for a correct interpretation of the *Vedas*.

The *Jaimini Sūtras*, the earliest work of the *pūrvamīmāṃsa* school (*c.* 200 B.C.) "set out to show that the *Vedas* are eternal, self-existent and wholly authoritative and to defend their authority aganist all comers".[148] What the heterodox schools attributed to the universe, to its eternal self-existence and automatic operation, the *mīmāṃsakas* did to the *Vedas*. For them, their authority of the *Vedas* "was not derived from the authority of any trustworthy person or God. Their words are valid in themselves".[149]

The *mīmāṃsakas* rejected the claim of the *śramaṇas* that empirical knowledge is superior to the revealed knowledge of the *Vedas*. They based their system on the doctrine of the self-validity of knowledge (*svata-prāmaṇya*). For them self-validity need not be in agreement with the objective facts of experience as *Nyāya* and other schools hold. Further, they asserted that the essence of the *Vedas* are the *vidhis* or injunctive sentences for the performance of sacrifice. They classified these *vidhis,* and developed principles of their interpretation.[150] The overall guideline adopted in this exercise was to the effect that obedience to the Vedic *vidhis* for the performance of sacrifice should be uncompromising. This, essentially, is *dharma.*

Jaimini disallows privileged status for gods and maintains that *dharma* occurs "only through and *in* the privileged sacrificial event".[151] He does not allow any higher reality, particularly the ideas of *brahman* and *ātman,* to threaten the intrinsic importance of the sacrificial occurrence.

> Instead, in a fashion significantly reminiscent of early Buddhism, Jaimini relies on the word "dharma" to talk about the functioning of the sacrifice ... every element of the sacrifice has its functional identity marking out when it appears, what happens to it, who uses it for what purpose, when it is discarded and so on. The totality of these discrete functions and relationships is the complex whole, the *dharma* of the sacrifice and primary object of enquiry for the *mīmāṃsaka.* The sacrifice alone... is significant.[152]

In the complex event of sacrifice, Jaimini holds, everything exists as a *śeṣa* for the sake of something else, the primary element which is termed as *śeṣin,* "that which has a *śeṣa*"[153] There are different sets of *śeṣas* that include all the material, persons, activities and results involved in ritual performance. The injunctive force of the *Veda* impels the potential performer into action. The correct act produces a force or capacity which did not exist before. This is authenticated by the authority of scriptures. This capacity of force, generated either in the action or in the agent, is called *apūrva.* Such potency abides in the performer of sacrifice till the results spring forth automatically.[154] Thus the performance of sacrifice contains both the dharmic and karmic force.

The *mīmāṃsakas* classify *karma* as *nitya karma* that includes obligatory Vedic duties such as prayer; *naimittika karma* which denotes occasional obligatory ceremonies, the *saṃskāra;* and *kāmya karma* meaning desire-oriented sacrifices. All *karmans* have the power of automatic association with the doers. Later, Vedāntic schools took these ideas into their scheme. For example, it was held that to qualify for the study of *vedānta* one should have performed *nitya karma* and *naimittika karma* but avoided *kāmya karma* because that alone has the potency to defile the mind and generate new births.[155] But as far as the *mīmāṃsakas* are concerned, *kāma* and *karma phala* are natural and unavoidable and not in contradiction to *dharma* although the purpose of *yajña* should not be reduced to the achievement of personal rewards.

Jaimini uses *artha* or object in three compounds: *puruṣa-artha, kratu- artha* and *sabda artha.*[156] *Puruṣa-artha* indicates desire for *phala* in the Vedic sense. The desire of self-interest and happiness is inherent in potential performers. Different *karmans* have their result in varying degrees. Sacrifices for which no results are mentioned are presumed to result in *svarga,* a desirable pleasure. This should not be minimised by abstract considerations of human nature like ultimate goals and ethics. Both *yajamānas* and priests undertake the performance of sacrifice only with rewards in mind and their behaviour is blameless. But anthropocentricity must be transcended without renouncing it. The sacrificer has larger interests than himself. "When the performer undertakes the sacrifice it is because he desires sons or cows or heaven. Yet he soon discovers that his desire has implicated him in a system larger than himself that makes demands on him that are not reducible to his wants".[157] Hence *puruṣa-artha* is not more important than *kratu-artha.*

The "internal motivation or logic of the sacrifice not pertaining to the performer's view-point is the *kratu-artha.* It is the internal cohesion of the action as a whole and has to do with things and actions and the calculations undertaken in regard to them".[158] This is another legitimate perspective held as equally right and fundamentally meaningful. *Sabda-artha* denotes the meaningful referentiality of Vedic words.

For Jaimini the *mantras* used in the ritual are not only powerful but also understandable. For him words spoken at sacrifice are to be understandable for listeners and having inner coherence like the coherence of sacrifice. Besides, "Jaimini insists that the texts are intrinsically oriented to the performance of sacrifice, the *sabda- artha* is not a detached meaningfulness but a sacrificial purposefulness".[159] Words are important since they enjoin action but there should be preference of verbs over nouns and *mantras* over *brāhmaṇas* since the former is actualised in the performance while the latter describes it. Thus the *Veda* reflects the elaborate complexity of actions which are of meanings. Then, sacrifice expresses an "overall meaningfulness, necessarily plural and diverse, that functions on the levels of (human) intention, the integrity of action, and the intelligibility of words, among which only intention is dependent on a human contribution".[160] We find in Jaimini's contribution to the revival of

Vedic sacrifice elements of modification and interpretation, which are important aspects of the hermeneutical process.

Further, in response to the *śramaṇa* emphasis on *ahiṃsā* in the context of killing in sacrifice and its impact on Aśokan reformation, the *mīmāṃsakas* took special care to deny any independent, extra-scriptural authority to the ideal of *ahiṃsā*. This is more evident in the writings of later exponents like Kumarila.[161] Accordingly sacrificial killing and the suffering inflicted on the victims in ritual should not be confused with killing otherwise. This argument was carried on further by the law-givers and epic writers.

(ii) The Dharmaśāstras

Although Kautilya, was a brahmin, his *Arthaśāstra* lays no stress whatsoever on *yajña*. Apparently he was a liberal brahmin supporting the Mauryan dynasty on which the *śramaṇa* influence was powerful. But the *Dharmaśāstras* lay great stress on sacrifice and, on that basis, *dharma* as well. They reaffirm the power of Vedic sacrifice, the result of which not only fulfils the desire of the sacrificer but also sustains the cosmic process. They seem to respond to the challenges of the *śramaṇa* movement, clarifying certain intricacies of the sacrificial system and incorporating some new elements. As J.M. Derret observes, "religious principles helped the jurists to make a cogent, coherent and plausible corpus out of the many injunctions which the *śāstra* contains".[162]

There are diverse opinions about the exact date of the *Dharmaśāstras*. No opinion, however, seems to refute the view that the *Dharmasūtras*, and their versified and modified form in the *Dharmaśāstras*, emerged as the final stage or part of the *Kalpa Sūtra* at a time of revival in Vedic religion around the second century B.C.[163] The law codes of the *Dharmaśāstras* are said to be based on the *Vedas*, traditions *(smṛti)* and customs. There is mention in them of *mīmāṃsa* as well as the *Upaniṣads*. Certain ideas of the epics and *Purāṇas* may also be recognised in them.[164] All these sources, despite their distinctive features and emphases, are unanimous in reaffirming the practice and meaning of Vedic sacrifice. Our special reference in this study is to the *Mānavadharmaśāstra*.[165]

In the *Dharmaśāstras* there is an uncompromising insistence on the regular performance of *pañcamahāyajña*, ordained from the beginning of creation.[166] Manu tries to solve the problem of the intricacies of ritual sacrifice: if two acts are presented inconsistently in the *Vedas*, he recommends one does both.[167] For any deviation from the prescribed rules of the performance he suggests expiatory rites.[168] Presumably in response to the *śramaṇa* attack on animal killing and emphasis on *ahiṃsā* and also to the Aśokan ban on animal killing, the *śāstras* insist that animal slaughter in sacrifice must be exempted from killing in general. Manu, for example, quotes the support by ancient sages, priests and tribes for sacrifice of excellent animals and birds and for the sustenance of life. For Manu, one who kills for sacrifice is not a slaughterer; such, he says, attain exalted births in the next world; they convey the animals also to the summit of beatitude. Thus allowance is made for the annual performance of *aśvamedha.*[169] At the same time *ahiṃsā* is a virtue, yet outside sacrifice, as we shall see. Moreover, we noted earlier that the *Brāhmaṇas* define the experience of the *yajamāna* in *dīkṣa* as of a second birth and Manu adds that then the act of offering in sacrifice signifies a third birth.[170] By this he affirms the karmic power in ritual action.

As far as the intention and meaning of *yajña* are concerned, the *śāstra* writers affirm the fundamentals of the *Vedas.* Manu thus says that the gods need our offerings and he gives the hierarchical order of the gods to whom oblations must be offered, beginning with Agni.[171] The reward is automatic. Although Manu later adds other goals higher than reward, basically for him *kāma* for *phala* cannot be dispensed with. He declares that though desire for fruits is not laudable, there is no exemption from it in the world. On *kāma* is grounded the study of the scriptures and the performance of sacrifice. No single act in this world is done without the expectation of reward. Even should one discharge duties without expecting reward, the reward will be there in the next life, in the worlds of immortals, apart from an enjoyment in this world in all virtuous gratification.[172] Besides these personal benefits, there is also cosmic benefit from ritual action. Manu thus reaffirms with Jaimini the Vedic view that sacrifice upholds the functioning of the universe. By performing sacrifice to the gods one thus supports the whole animal and vegetable world. The following verse explains the operation: "The oblation duly cast into the flame ascends in smoke to the sun; from the sun it falls in rain; from rain comes vegetable food; and from such food animals derive their sustenance".[173] This verse, in sum, expresses the fundamental notion of Vedic sacrifice.

The *śāstra* writers also express their concern to save the *varṇa dharma* system from the disturbance and confusion created by the *śramaṇas*. With an acknowledgement of such a confusion, Manu, for example, gives strict instruction for the observance of *varṇa dharma* and the duties thereof. He describes the duties of the four *varṇas* in detail and adds that "it is better to do one's own duty badly than another's well".[174] This is one of the famous statements of the *Gītā* too.[175]

The superiority of the brahmins is repeatedly emphasised by Manu; they are indispensable in the performance of sacrifice; they deserve great honour; their weapon is speech in which rests the sacred power of the *Atharvans*; they must be given royal patronage and exemption from tax and hard punishments.[176] He notes:

> A brāhmaṇa, whether learned or ignorant, is a powerful divinity; even as a fire is a powerful divinity whether consecrated or popular.... From priority of birth, from superiority of origin, from a more exact knowledge of scriptures and from a distinction in the sacrificial thread, a brāhmaṇa is the Lord of all classes.[177]

As teachers and sacrificers, the order of the brahmins and their life-style is well instituted by Manu. As for the functions of *gurus, ācāryas* and *upādhyāyas* as described by Manu, there is "a terminological confusion".[178] It is interesting to note that the term *guru* is identified with the one who performs sacrifice and domestic rites. Again the procedures for *dakṣiṇā* and *dāna* due to the brahmins, described extensively by the *śāstra* writers, need to be viewed in the light of the *śramaṇas*' claim and competition for *dāna* that had affected the income of the brahmin priests and teachers.

Next to the brahmins, as in the *Vedas*, kṣatriyas are given prominence in the *Dharmaśāstras*. In order to avoid any temptation to ignore the brahmins, it is repeatedly stated that there can be no royal family without *purohitas*, the domestic priests.[179] Though the foremost duty of kings is to protect *dharma*, that is in fact beyond their grasp since it has to encompass new customs and usages. Therefore they need the cooperation of the brahmins who can define *dharma* and exercise authortiy over established customs and rights. As before, the *śāstras* call for the mutual cooperation of these two, reviving their position to uphold order and the life of all creatures. Manu says, "both classes by cordial union, are exalted in this world and in the next.... The Lord of creatures entrusted the whole human species to the brāhmaṇas and the kṣatriyas as he has given herds, trade and agriculture to the vaiśya".[180] It becomes clear that the vaiśyas are the producers, but it must be noted that the use of their production is not at their disposal. They are to work under the dominion of the priestly and princely powers. Further, all the law-givers suggest that if one caste group is in crisis it can do the work of the group just below it. No wonder then that the vaiśyas had to come to the level of the śūdras.

In the dharmaśāstric order of things the śūdras are expected to be content with servitude. But, if they carry out their duty in the prescribed manner they can attain the most eminent class in another birth.[181] The *śūdras* have no share in sacrifice or the study of the *Vedas*. Their status is like that of women who also are never independent and never allowed to perform the grand sacrifices or study the *Veda*. In order to protest against the freedom given by the *śramaṇas* for śūdras, women and even mixed *varṇas* to adopt the ascetic life, the *Dharmaśāstras* prescribe restrictions for their progress.[182] The following statement indicates succinctly the severity of such restrictions: "The ears of a śūdra who listens intentionally when the *Veda* is being recited are to be filled with molten lead. His tongue is to be cut out if he recites it. His body is to be split in twain if he preserves it in his memory".[183]

Thus, a major concern for the maintenance of the *varṇa dharma* was an important part of the revival in the sacrificial religion. On the whole the law-givers hold that the regular performance of rituals and maintenance of the order of society on the basis of *varṇa* constitute *dharma*, the totality of life including its customs and behaviour.

(iii) The Epics

It is not possible to discern a single idea of sacrifice in the epics because of their encyclopaedic nature. They seem to have gone through a long process of interpolation and redaction. There are indications, however, that lead one to believe that in their final redaction the epics share the concerns of the *Dharmaśāstras* to revive Vedic *yajña*. It is interesting to note that both the *Rāmāyaṇa* and the *Mahābhārata* start with sacrifice and end with sacrifice. This picture may permit one to view them as an allegorical representation of the "exile and return" of Vedic sacrifice. We shall see later certain further clues for the plausibility of this view.

Especially the *Mahābhārata*, the "fifth *Veda*" which contains the *Bhagavad Gītā*, "is the outcome of a long process of expansion, assimilation, revision and redaction".[184] Consequently, it contains elements of a reaffirmation of Vedic sacrifice but mixed with counter-affirmations. As Hiriyanna observes, "The attitude of the *Mahābhārata* towards Vedic ritual is quite indefinite. Passages can be cited from it which glorify sacrifice; but there are others in it whose general spirit is unfavourable or even antagonistic to ritualism".[185]

As the epic is of obscure origin and marked by inconsistency it is not easy to determine its original theme.[186] Many scholars, however, find in it a process of brāhmanisation. Thus Monier-Williams is of the opinion that the epics originally contained the heroic battles of tribes. At the time of a revival of brāhmaṇism the brahmins converted them "into instruments for moulding the popular mind in accordance with their own pattern. Possibly too, they may have hoped to turn them into important engines for arresting the progress of Buddhistic rationalism".[187] By remodelling the epics, Monier-Williams observes, there was an attempt to bring down the supremacy of the kṣatriya rulers under the counsel of the brahmins. J.A.S. van Buitenen also sees brāhmaṇisation as one of the phases in the growth of *the Mahābhārata*.[188] The affirmations of Vedic religion and sacrifice in this epic then need to be seen in the light of the process of brāhmaṇisation.

The *Mahābhārata* declares the authority of the *Veda* and the customs of the orthodox society as guiding principles over against the claim of empirical knowledge, perhaps made by the *śramaṇas.*[189] It calls for every householder to fulfil the duty of *pañcamahāyajña*, failure of which would incur sin.[190] It says *svarga* can be attained only by those who perform *aśvamedha* and make liberal *dāna* to brahmins.[191] There are many events in which sacrifice is performed in order to produce mysterious power which not only brings reward of the fulfilment of *kāma* and of natural gifts, but also can be directed against enemies.[192]

There are some interesting dialogues which seem to respond to the challenges of the *śramaṇas* who, in the view of brahmins, confused the order of Vedic religion and society. For example, there is a dialogue between a king and his queen who are in exile, having been robbed of their kingdom. The queen asks her husband to take vengeance on those who robbed them. The king, in reply, sings a song of forgiveness which he identifies with virtue, sacrifice and *Veda.* Irritated by this reply, the queen doubts God and his grace and supports the idea of predestination. But the king says that her argument is heterodox (*nāstikyam*). Describing this story, E.W.

Hopkins compares the queen to Gārgi who asked Yājñavalkya questions for which the latter warned her that her head would fall off.[193] For our reference, the most significant part of the above dialogue is as follows:

> I have sacrificed and practised virtue not for the sake of reward but because it was right. I give what I ought to give, and sacrifice as I should. That is my only idea in connection with religious observances... If religious observances were without fruit the universe would go to destruction. People would not have been good for so many ages if there had been no reward for it. This is a mystery of the gods. The gods are full of mystery and illusion.[194]

The *Anuśasan Parva* is full of such dialogues and discourses which affirm the power and reward of sacrifice and which react, sometimes subtly and other times openly, to the *śramaṇa* views.

Related to the affirmation of sacrifice, there is an emphasis on the kings not leaving war and rule. This also seems to be a response to the *śramaṇa* influence on kings for renouncing war and kingdom. For example, there is a dialogue between Yudhiṣṭhira on the one hand and his brothers, their wife Draupadī and friends on the other. Yudhiṣṭhira decides to abandon the kingdom and the world after the war. His brothers, Draupadī and friends bring forth arguments to persuade him not to give up the kingdom. Their arguments include the following points: the kingdom has been gained by violence and therefore it should not be given up; his brothers fought and they should not be denied their rewards; only eunuchs seek tranquillity and are afraid of violence; it is unnatural for a warrior to give up his duty to fight and rule; violence is unavoidable and even meritorious if exercised for the maintenance of order; the gods themselves employ violence against their enemies to achieve their right status.

Again, for our reference, the most significant part of the dialogue is what comes from the mouth of Arjuna:

> Finally, violence properly administered is compared to a king's sacrificial ritual. The bow is the king's sacrificial stake, the bowstring is the cord that ties the victim, the king's arrows and sword are his sacrificial ladles, and the blood he sheds is the sacrificial butter. His chariot is the altar and his wrath is battle, the consuming sacrificial fire. That is, to administer punishment and to fight in battle are sacred rites for a king and result in no sin or blame.[195]

Further, it is said by others that the whole world depends on the king's duty; many people, particularly brahmins, depend on the king's generosity which is meritorious; gods prosper by the king's sacrifices. This dialogue has a double significance for understanding sacrifice: it reaffirms the role of the kṣatriyas within the Vedic *dharma;* and also it interprets war as the sacrifice of kṣatriyas.

Side by side with the supremacy of brahmins, the supremacy of kings is repeatedly affirmed in the *Mahābhārata.* It is said, that the king is superhuman if he follows *dharma;* he is god; he is the guardian of the earth and protector of *dharma.*[196] Sacrifice is of course the most important part of this *dharma.* The epic affirms:

> For if the king does not observe the duty of protection, ruin would befall everything, no property would be safe, unrighteousness would prevail, everything would be destroyed untimely, the *Vedas* and morality would disappear, sacrifices would no longer be celebrated, in short, society would cease to exist.[197]

Thus there is a great concern for the restoration of *dharma* which is centred around sacrifice, the ritual sacrifice performed by the brahmins and the sacrifice of war by the kṣatriyas. Their "ritual relationship" by being revived guarantees mutual support.

Regarding the fourfold division of *varṇa,* it is remarkable that the *Mahābhārata* separates the vaiśyas from the two upper groups and puts them on a par with the śūdras. Calling the vaiśyas as the people-caste and indicating their plight as recorded in the epic, Hopkins writes:

> We see the reflex of an unacknowledged process of amalgamation between the people-caste and the un-Aryan population. This process has two phases. First, the inevitable tendency of the third estate to take up with new work, needful and profitable, but not sanctioned by usage; this was a natural drifting away from the Aryan aristocrats. Second, the long-continued priestly-castes, practically leading to an exclusion of the third estate from the inner and intenser Aryahood of the two more powerful orders. The people-caste was partially seduced and partially pushed out of the national ring. They stood on the edge between good blood and barbarous.[198]

It is in this light we have to understand the *Bhagavad Gītā* categorising vaiśyas as base-born along with śūdras and women.[199]

Having seen the clear expression of revival of Vedic *dharma* and *yajña* we turn to the main stories of the epics for their significance in terms of a brāhmaṇic revival. The epic stories have been viewed from different perspectives. The allegorical interpretation of war in the epics takes it as the conflict between good and evil. From a historical perspective it is held that it represents the war between Aryans and non-Aryan tribes.[200] More significantly, particularly the whole story of the *Mahābhārata,* is viewed from a ritual perspective. We consider the main ideas of the ritual theory of the epic.

Heesterman finds connection between the exile and return of the epic and the preclassical pattern of ritual in which reciprocating hospitality and contests were involved. He also notes that the sacrificial battle of the *Mahābhārata* indicates the end of this conflict.[201] For van Buitenen Yudhiṣṭhira's consecration and the dice match is modelled on the structure of the *rājasūya* sacrifice. Gehrts has pushed this notion to include the whole of the epic as an extended *rājasūya.* Biardeau and Hiltebeital hold that the battle itself is a sacrifice of weapons or sacrifice of battle. In this connection Biardeau interprets Arjuna's going to the exile as *dīkṣa,* preparing himself for the sacrifice of battle. These scholars point to passages describing certain aspects of the battle as modelled on sacrificial themes in support of their theories.[202] Although these theories give important insights, it should be noted that they are not grounded on the historical background which was marked by a brāhmaṇic revival, as we have pointed out earlier.

From a historical-mythical perspective we should not fail to notice the dual motif of *deva* and *asura, dharma* and *adharma,* that has penetrated the whole of the *Mahābhārata.* Scholars like Sukthankar point to the fact that the Pāṇḍavas and Kauravas are the incarnations of *devas* and *asuras* whose conflict over sacrifice was a prominent theme in the *Vedas.*[203] As we shall soon see, the *śramaṇas* were identified with the *asuras* by the brahmins. References to conflict between the two are ample in the epics. In this light we suggest hypothetically that the main stories of the epics may be taken as the symbolic representation of the decline and revival of Vedic *yajña* that took place in the post-Vedic period. We shall indicate very briefly certain clues from the epics for the plausibility of this explanation.

As noted, the epics start and end with sacrifice. Especially significant are certain identifications made at the victory of the Pāṇḍavas and their celebration of an *aśvamedha.* The actors in the story are interpreted as incarnations of celestial beings. Indra, the Vedic victor of sacrifice, comes again jubilantly with his companions; Draupadī, the wife of the five Pāṇḍava brothers, perhaps symbolising the *pañcamahāyajñas,* is said to be the incarnation of Śrī, the goddess of wealth, the main purpose of Vedic *yajña.* Then the Pāṇḍavas' exile is the decline of *yajña* for some centuries. This is due to the influence of wandering mendicants. It is interesting to note that when the

Pāṇḍavas set out for the forest, a brahmin, named Saunaka comforts them by discoursing on the nobility of a life of detachment from the world. This proved to be not a permanent detachment, however. Likewise, in the *Rāmāyaṇa* Sītā who was abducted by an *asura* incarnate in the disguise of a mendicant is explained as the daughter of the goddess of earth and the incarnation of Śrī. Remarkably her abduction took place during the exile of Rāma in the forest. Her return is of course his victory. Hence the revival of *yajña* and its ally *artha* (wealth).

The revival is, however, marked by interruptions which show the lone voices of some *śramaṇas*. Thus, while the *ásvamedha* of the Pāṇḍavas was in progress there appears a half-golden mongoose and in a loud voice proclaims that the merit of the sacrifice is not equal to that of a certain ascetic who has given a few handfuls of powdered barley to a guest. This is followed by a dialogue in which it is said that the merit of the sacrifice depends not on its costliness or the nature of its offerings, but on the mental attitude of the sacrificer and that even seeds have been approved as suitable offerings instead of animals by Agastya and other *ṛṣis*. It is also declared that the mongoose is *dharma* in the form of anger *(krodha)*. Besides, the *dakṣayajña* of *Sauptikaparvan* may be taken as symbolising a great battle and renaissance of brāhmanic sacrifice which again is disrupted by Śiva, the rough outsider, the *yogi*.[204] The same kind of protest may be recognised in the *aśvamedha* of the victorious Rāmā also. The twin sons of Rāmā, brought up by a *muni* without the knowledge of their father, fight with him and defeat him while the *ásvamedha* is on, although the story makes them reconciled finally. These examples suffice to indicate a brahmin-*śramaṇa* conflict which resulted in the decline of *yajña* and finally its victory. In fact even in the *Brāhmaṇas*, as we have noticed, occasional disappearance and appearance of *yajña* is indicated. But the distinctive aspect of the present revival is that it has brought with it new elements which are then assimilated into the sacrificial system. This assimilative process we must now examine.

(iv) The Process of Assimilation

In our study of the major aspects of Vedic sacrifice we identified the assimilation of ascetic techniques into the sacrificial system. In our discussion of the Upaniṣadic understanding of sacrifice also we pointed out new ideas as incorporated into Vedic religion. These attempts, however, seem to be implicit and imperceptible. But the assimilative process which is part of the revival of *yajña* that we have noted in the foregoing passages appears to be explicit and deliberate. Without changing its own *yajña*-oriented framework, brāhmaṇic orthodoxy has tried to absorb some of the compelling views of the *śramaṇa* movement. The chief characteristics of this assimilation are incorporation and reconstruction. We shall point out examples of this process in relation to the idea of sacrifice.

In the course of our discussion we noted the development of new practices like the study of the *Vedas (svādhyāya), vrata, tīrtha* etc. in the place of *yajña* in the wake of socio-economic-ideological pressure. These must be understood in the light of the revival of *yajña.* The study of the *Veda,* for example, by the twice born, intensively and repeatedly, is said to be meritorious and it can remove sins and consume guilt like fire. It is a form of sacrifice, *brahma yajña,* one of the five great sacrifices; and recitation of *ṛg, yajus* etc. are different oblations.[205] And *japa,* the uttering of Vedic *mantras,* is said to be very efficacious.[206] Particularly the triple *mantras oṃ, tad* and *gāyatrī* are the essence of the universe and the *Vedas.* They are even superior to *yajña* in terms of permanent merit.[207] *Tīrtha* is mentioned as equivalent to sacrifice and in some places it is interiorised.[208] Although various 'crossings' are mentioned in the *Vedas,* there *tīrtha* is not directly termed a sacrifice. But one can find that *tīrtha* shares the sacrificial paradigm of transcendence, and many ritual actions in the later tradition came to be described in terms of sacrificial equivalence.[209] *Dāna* as almsgiving is another practice considered equivalent to *yajña.* Going for it is the sacrifice of a *brahmacārin* and the alms received are equivalent to sacrificial food. Besides, *vratas, utsavas* and *yātras* are also said to be meritorious and some of them carry the weight and benefit of *aśvamedha* and other grand sacrifices.[210] This could be a comforting arrangement for the poor who were not able to be part of the revival in sacrifice. But though such practices had sacrificial elements they in fact cannot be reconciled with the uncompromising insistence on the performance of sacrifice. They are added to *yajña* but never replace it. The central place is still occupied by *yajña.* There is an ambiguity and paradox when new substitutes are suggested without replacing the old. As Heesterman says, "So whenever we look for confirmation of the central place of sacrifice, we end up with ambiguities and paradoxes."[211] Such ambiguities and paradoxes may be more in the case of the incorporation of some other elements which have specific meanings in their respective frameworks.

Ahiṃsā, the main emphasis of Jainism and Buddhism, is taken as one of the virtues by the *śastra* and epic writers. Though killing in sacrifice and in war, which is the sacrifice of the kṣatriyas, should be exempted, they say, outside that even hurting an animal is against the virtue of *ahiṃsā.*[212] As we shall notice later, there is a continued tension between the ideal of *ahiṃsā* and the allowance of *hiṃsā* in the name of sacrifice.

Jñāna is also taken into account and placed along with *yajña.*[213] In one place Manu admits that of those who do not perform the external great sacrifices *(pañcamahāyajña)*, some make continual offerings in their own organs of sensation and intellect; some sacrifice their *prāṇa* in their *vāc* and vice versa in silent meditation. But what they perceive in their *prāṇa* and *vāc* is *the imperishable fruit of a sacrificial offering.*[214] In the *Mahābhārata* there are a few occurrences of the Upaniṣadic pattern of allegorical interpretation with an emphasis on interiorisation.[215] Also the Upaniṣadic idea of identification with one eternal *ātman* finds mention in it.[216] We meet with many *yogis* and yogic practices in the epics.[217] Manu goes to the extent of saying that perceiving the *paramātman* equally in all beings, and all beings in the *paramātman,* is to sacrifice one's own spirit by fixing it on the Supreme Spirit and approach the nature of that sole divinity, who shines by his effulgence.[218] Even though these Upaniṣadic ideas are incorporated in the orthodoxy which affirms the power and meaning of Vedic sacrifices, the directions in the *Upaniṣads* for a new framework and world-view are ignored. Elements of the Upaniṣadic world-view are mixed up with the *yajña*-oriented world-view. As Gonda points out with reference to the Vedic *ṛta* and epic *dharma,* in the process of assimilation Vedic and non-Vedic principles are fused together, giving birth to Hinduism incorporating fundamentally distinctive principles.[219]

Moreover, sacrifice is combined with ethical qualities like patience, philanthropic action, truthfulness, discriminative knowledge and *yoga* for self-control.[220] The *sāṃkhya* category of three *guṇas* is related to *karman* and to each *guṇa* is ascribed a particular kind of *karman* and reward. *Bhakti* also is mentioned along with *yajña* and *jnana.*[221] This accommodation with minor adjustments led terms like *yāga, yoga, homa, dāna,* and *pūjā* to be used almost interchangeably. But it is said that the ethical virtues of truth, pure heart, self- control and detachment are worthier than a thousand horse sacrifices.[222] Thus the affirmation of sacrifice and counter-affirmations that occur side by side make it difficult to draw a clear synthesis of the process of the incorporation of additional elements into the sacrificial system.

Thus far we have seen isolated practices and ideals as incorporated into the sacrificial religion. But we need to acknowledge that certain schemes are also worked out, among which the most important ones are the fourfold *puruṣārtha* and *āśrama dharma*. The number "four" immediately reminds us of the four *varṇas* and the later formulation of four *yugas*, though to correlate all of them with clear correspondence is difficult.

Purṣārtha (four goals of human life) came to gain popularity only in the *śāstra* period although ideas of *artha, kāma* and *dharma* were prevalent in the *Vedas* and *mokṣa* in the *Upaniṣads* and *śramaṇa* teachings. It has been a constant problem for the interpreters of *puruṣārtha* to present its components in the right order and to see the precedence of one over the other.[223] The reason is that even in its formative stage the formulation was marked by divided opinions about its components and their order. The problem will become clear when we study them in the context of changing views of sacrifice.

Kāma as the animating force and *artha* as the expected reward emerged originally in the context of ritual sacrifice. *Dharma* was once identified with the primordial *karman* of *yajña*, but later it came to be used in an inclusive sense in different ways and viewed from different perspectives. *Mokṣa* was considered to be the supreme end, to be attained only by the *saṃnyāsins*. Obviously, there was a conscious attempt to set all these four goals in an acceptable scheme since the avoidance of any one of them was found to be undesirable in the process of revival and assimilation.

On the whole there seem to be different emphases in the varied understanding of the first three goals, especially *kāma* and *artha*, which were devalued by the *śramaṇas*. Even after the conceptual boost given to *kāma* by the *mīmāṃsakas* and *lokāyatas*, there was ambiguity in accepting it as a goal in life. The Upaniṣadic and Buddhist criticism of *kāma* as the root cause of evil and suffering continued to be influential. The general view of the *śāstras* is that *kāma* should not be eschewed but kept in such a way as not to conflict with the requirements of *artha* and *dharma*. For example, though Manu declares *kāma* as unavoidable for any act, at one point he says that *kāma* is never satisfied with sense objects and is ever contaminated by sensuality; even sacrifice cannot procure felicity. Then subduing *kāma* should be considered a virtue.[224] In this respect *kāma* is the lowest of all goals.

In one of the extensive discussions on the first three goals found in the *Mahābhārata* [225] Yudhiṣṭhira asks his brothers which is the most important goal and which the lowest. Vidura praises *dharma*, mentions *artha* as second and *kāma* as the lowest of these three. Arjuna declares *artha* to be the foremost while Nakula and Sahadeva acknowledge the importance of *artha* but modify it: "*Artha* when connected with *dharma* and *dharma* when combined with *artha* are like honey mixed with ambrosia... one should first attend to *dharma*, then to *artha* and last to *kāma*." [226] But Bhīmasena interrupts this sequence and declares that *kāma* is the main principle without which the other two cannot be attained. Despite these differences of opinion some *śāstras* take pains to accommodate all the three goals which of course retain the value of the performance of sacrifice. The *Arthaśāstra*, for example, says: "a man may enjoy in an equal degree the three goals of life that are dependent on each other, since any one of the three, if pursued to excess, harms not only the other two but also itself."[227]

There is no divided opinion about *mokṣa*, which is to be taken as the foremost of all goals. The duty of the king is said to enable people to attain the first three goals and prepare them for the final goal, *mokṣa*.[228] Its intrinsic connection with the preceding three is, however, not without tension.

The final goal appears to stand detached from the preceding ones. It is detached from life in society and its nature is understood in different ways. Kane observes that the *Dharmaśāstras* do not emphasise that each individual must actively pursue the good of society as a whole. As the final goal was *mokṣa*, he says, undue emphasis was laid on other-worldliness, on individual attainment, on detachment and on running away from ordinary worldly affairs, the realm of the first three goals.[229] This was not, however, the initial intention of the *śramaṇa* movement which emphasised *saṃnyāsa*. In this light the concern of some *śāstra* writers who hold that the *saṃnyāsins* must identify with the rest of society not only by setting a model and reminding them of the ultimate goal of life, but also by continuing to perform *yajña* for the good of all as well as for their own benefit of purifying the mind, is remarkable. The concern will become clear when we take up the discussion on *samnyāsins* and sacrifice.

Puruṣārtha cannot be applied neatly to the sequence in the *varṇas*.[230] Charles Malamoud in his discussion on the rhetoric and semantics of *puruṣārtha* argues that though *artha* is distributed and maintained by kṣatriyas, in fact *artha* is the speciality of vaiśyas, while *dharma* is upheld equally by brahmins and kṣatriyas.[231] *Kāma* both in its narrow sense of sensual pleasure and wider sense of the reward attached to any action is common to all. In classical brāhmaṇism, however, the fertility of man, his fields and cattle, and production of wealth that are the purview of vaiśyas are not related to ordinary *kāma*. An autonomous area of *kāma* seems to have been set up. As Malamoud points out, *kāma* in its specific sense is different from the ordinary desire for wealth and the desire to procreate.[232] The *Kāmasūtra*, for example, approves this and defines *kāma* in terms of intense passion between partners in love and sensual pleasure in arts, hunting etc. It is specifically excessive *kāma* against which there is a warning addressed mainly to courtesans and nobles of the kṣatriya class.[233] This reflects an implicit conflict between brahmins and kṣatriyas, the prime upholders of *dharma*. But while the brahmins chide the kṣatriyas for excessive *kāma* in terms of sensual pleasure, the latter cannot attack the former, since the *kāma* involved in *yajña* in terms of wealth and offspring applies to both. As we have seen both had to face the criticism of the *śramaṇas* that the motivation in *yajña* is always prone to excessive *kāma*.

Similarly, attempts to relate *puruṣārtha* to fourfold *āśrama*[234] may not succeed because like the former the latter also took shape under great diversity of opinion. As we have pointed out earlier, there is great confusion about the origin and development of *āśrama dharma*. The point of view that Jaina and Buddhist traditions borrowed the ideals of *vānaprastha* and *saṃnyāsa* from brāhmaṇism is misleading, as we have said. We have also pointed out that the resemblances of ascetic practices and life-style found in certain persons like *dīkṣita* and *brahmacārin* cannot be evidence for the existence of *saṃnyāsa* as a life-ideal in the post-Vedic period. So also, the early understanding of Vedic life having the stages of studentship and household life, was not understood in terms of *āśrama*. The references to different stages of life in a few texts of the early *Upaniṣads* may indicate increasing influence from the ascetic tradition that operated in conflict with the brāhmaṇic religion.[235] Therefore, though it is not possible to determine the exact period at which the graduated system of *āśramas* was constructed, there are reasons to believe that its construction was a response to the challenge of the *śramaṇa* movement and its new ideals of life. (*Āśrama* comes from the same root as *śramaṇa*). We have already seen examples of brāhmaṇic reaction to the influence of the *śramaṇas*. Particularly, references to reaction to renunciation are ample in the *Mahābhārata* and *Dharmasūtras*. Yudhiṣṭhira, for instance, wants to renounce his kingdom and retire to the forest in pursuit of liberation. Bhīma persuades him not to do so by saying that, if by *saṃnyāsa* one obtains liberation in the forest, then hills and trees would have attained it long ago.[236] Further, while brāhmaṇism denies such retirement from society and dharmic obligations including sacrifice, it tries to incorporate *saṃnyāsa* by assigning it a final stage in life.

The formulation of fourfold *āśrama* has rarely been understood in the correct perspective. There are, however, a few studies remarkable for their perception. Louis Dumont approached the formulation from a sociological point of view. In his famous essay on renunciation in Indian religions, he points out the artificiality of the theory of fourfold *āśrama*. He notes that the intention of the theory seems to accomodate *saṃnyāsa* merely as a moment in the life of a brahmin and to delay it until he accomplishes all his worldly obligations. He writes: "In short, over and above the habitual orthodox tendency to aggregate, there seems here an attempt to limit renunciation in its relation to worldly conditions and, finally, a subdued hostility to renunciation itself".[237]

More recently, Patrick Olivelle has done a profound study of *saṃnyāsa* and its incorporation into the orthodox *dharma*, from a historical perspective. His valuable contribution to the semantic history of *saṃnyāsa* shows that its classical meaning was finalised only after Manu. He points out:

> The motive for the construction of the theory of the four *āśramas* was the maintenance of the universality of the *dharma* by finding a place within it for the renouncer's way of life, thus neutralizing by assimilation a force that threatened the very fabric of orthodox society.[238]

Olivelle demonstrates clearly the development of the fourfold *āśrama* within a single life from the earlier theory of four modes of life that presented themselves to a Vedic student, as evident in the *Dharmasūtras*; so also the development of *saṃnyāsa* within the domestic life from the life of a mendicant as evident in the *Mānavadharmaśāstra*.[239] What is more important is to see how *saṃnyāsa* was incorporated with great reluctance and how uncertainties were unavoidable in the formation of the *āśrama* system.

As we have seen, *mokṣa* was applicable only to ascetics according to the *śramaṇas*, though the householders by their good life can attain future births as ascetics. But although the law-givers and epic writers incorporated unavoidably "the ascetic heresy and added its goals to those of the conventional life",[240] they praise household life in no uncertain terms as basic and supreme *dharma*.[241] There is no consensus among these writers about the exact number of *āśramas*. For some it is four and for others three. Even the attempts of commentators at compromise are not successful.[242] It is in this light that Basham says "the *āśrama dharma* is an idealization of facts and an artificial attempt to find room for the conflicting claims of study, family life, and asceticism in a single life time".[243]

For Rhys Davids, the formulation of this *dharma* was a "bold bid for supremacy" over the claims of the *śramaṇas*, which "remained a dead letter".[244] The evidence for the correctness of this assertion is that, despite glorifications of this system, the *āśrama dharma* never gained a consistent shape nor popular support.

Our main concern, however, is to understand how the assimilation of *saṃnyāsa* as the last stage in life saved Vedic sacrifice from decline. There are attempts to insist on *yajña* in all the four stages. Obviously, there is no problem about reinforcing the performance of sacrifice in the stages of *brahmacārya* and *gṛhastha*.[245] The third stage, *vānaprastha*, is a transition to *saṃnyāsa*. In this stage sacrifices must continue in a modified form along with self-control. Thereby the individual is still tied to the household life and removed from renunciation.[246] O'Flaherty observes that the third stage is the most complex and it is here that the traditions of asceticism and eroticism meet.[247] She identifies the exemplification of this combination in the *Purāṇas*.

More significant is the question whether at the stage of *saṃnyāsa* one has to give up sacrifices or continue them. It is interesting to note that when *saṃnyāsa* was formally defined later, it was in terms of the abandonment of all types of ritual and rite.[248] But earlier opinion is divided. According to some law-givers, certain sacrifices, especially *agnihotra*, should be performed even after the adoption of *saṃnyāsa*.[249] And as we find in the *Saṃnyāsa Upaniṣads*, elaborate ceremonies were held at the time of initiation into *saṃnyāsa-hood*.[250] Others of course allow giving up sacrifice at *saṃnyāsa*. According to Manu, though the *saṃnyāsin* can give up sacrificial fire etc., he must constantly study that part of the *Veda* which relates to sacrifice; that which treats subordinate deities; that which reveals the nature of the supreme God; and whatever is declared in the *Upaniṣads*.[251] Perhaps this view appeared to be an acceptable solution. The *Mahābhārata* contains spirited admonitions not to yield to an unmanly and premature desire for renunciation from not only the performance of *yajña* but also the *kṣatriya dharma* of war.[252]

Actually, even if one abandons *yajña* at *saṃnyāsa*, it may not be a great loss for the brahmins. There was, however, an ever present danger of following the *śramaṇa* practice, adopting *saṃnyāsa* without going through the prior stages. Manu gives a new definition of a *bhikṣu* who is a virtuous brahmin fulfilling all his duties, particularly the *yajña*, before he becomes a *saṃnyāsin*.[253] But such arrangements were upset by more liberal moves. The *Jābāla Upaniṣad* (verse 4), for example, offers the option of going through the prior stages or bypassing them.[254] It is in such a context we locate the disparaging comment of the *Baudhāyana Dharma Sūtra* that the *āśrama* scheme was brought by an *asura* called Kapila; his intention was that if no sacrifice was performed by *vānaprasthas* and *saṃnyāsins* the gods would become powerless. Therefore, it says, a wise man should pay no heed to it. The only real *āśrama* is *gṛhastha*.[255] Further, ascetics are also depicted in epic and purāṇic stories as producing magical powers to attain worldly enjoyments.[256]

Although the fourfold *āśrama* scheme was not successful, it must be noted that *saṃnyāsa* has been greatly valued in the religious tradition of India. Since, however, it was restricted to a particular *varṇa*, i.e., the brahmins, all people could not make use of it irrespective of their social status.[257] This is one reason that the fourfold *āśrama dharma* cannot easily be correlated with the fourfold *varṇa* and *puruṣārtha*. This is more so with the scheme of four *yugas*. Assigning sacrifice to a particular *yuga* would raise similar problems to those outlined above.[258] Thus brāhmaṇic reaction to the influence of the *śramaṇas* and assimilation of some of their values and ideals betray nervousness and unresolved tension.

5. A Great Form of Cultic Synthesis: The *Bhāgavata-Brāhmaṇa* Amalgamation

The development of *bhāgavata*-brāhmaṇic amalgamation as a distinctive part of the assimilative process is very significant in the background of the *Bhagavad Gītā*. The Bhāgavata cult is not recognised as a religion in any of the edicts of Aśoka. Therefore, it is proper to view that it became popular only after it was amalgamated with brāhmaṇism during the revival of the turn of the second century B.C.[259]

The development of *bhāgavata-brāhmaṇa* amalgamation seems to have been very complex and it is very difficult to trace a clear sequence of this development. We will only point out the salient features of this amalgamation and its significance for changing understandings of sacrifice. Originally a non-Vedic cult, bhāgavatism is associated with certain *śramaṇa* groups, *Upaniṣads* and tribal clans, even though the exact nature of this association is not clear. What is more obvious is that the *bhāgavata* cult existed among the Sātvatas, a warrior tribe, a branch of the pastoral clan of the Yadavas who settled in the Mathura region. Apparently they had a good relationship with the *śramaṇas* and the *sāṃkhya-yoga* thinkers.[260] Similarly there is another cult, namely *Pāśupata* which was assimilated by brāhmaṇism; so also many other minor groups.[261]

It is generally agreed that the astuteness and skill of brahmins can be clearly seen in drawing the unorthodox *bhāgavatas* and other groups into their fold.[262] The purpose of this attempt was to meet the challenges of the *śramaṇas,* particularly the Buddhists and Jainas. As a result, the heroic fidelity and popular figures who had gained super-human status from the *bhāgavata* cult provided new instruments for the brahmins to affirm their tradition. In turn, the *bhāgavatas* were given a higher status in the social scheme of the brāhmaṇic tradition.[263] It is beyond the scope of this section to describe in detail the process of this exchange in a decisive amalgamation.[264] Apart from the *Bhagavad Gītā,* the earliest literary source on bhāgavatism is the *Nārāyaṇīya* section of the *Mahābhārata.*[265] The pattern of discourse in this section includes curious metaphysical and practical questions and answers. The questions appear "like fleecy clouds before the wind" that confused many.[266] This shows that the situation was full of divergent, even contradictory, view-points. The authorities quoted in support of the answers are mostly the traditional *ṛṣis* as well as some visiting guests who appeared to be wandering teachers.

The accommodation of new figures and new views from bhāgavatism was marked by tension. Particularly, the introduction of Kṛṣṇa caused a conflict. Majumdar writes:

Whatever might be the reason, it must have cost the brāhmaṇas a bitter pang. The memorable scene in the *Mahābhārata* in which Śiśupāla poured forth the venom of his heart, against Bhīṣma for honouring Kṛṣṇa as the most "worshipful" seems to be a reminiscence of the spirit of the die-hards, who refused to acknowledge the divine character of one who was not a brāhmaṇa by birth.[267]

As we see in Vaiṣṇavism, however, the amalgamation enriched the brāhmaṇic tradition with new myths and cultic forms. Especially the concept of a supreme God, already attached to the figure Vāsudeva by Sātvatas, would develop a "new middle path" between heterodox atheism and orthodox polytheism, as well as between Vedic ritualism and the simple offerings of *bhāgavata* worship. The process by which was achieved identification of Vāsudeva with Nārāyaṇa, another figure representing the combination of Vedic and ascetic traditions, and with Viṣṇu, the Vedic god of sacrifice, is a complex one. As Mrinal Das Gupta points out, the different types of figures were equalised by a mysterious process of religious syncretism. "Mutual compromise may be suggested. But all these cannot be the whole explanation. The connecting links are unfortunately missing; only surmise but no definite solution of the problem is possible."[268]

There are some attempts to present the connecting links of identification. But no unanimous opinion is available. The chronological confusion continues.[269] For our purpose the most significant figure to focus on is Kṛṣṇa.

The identification of Kṛṣṇa, the leader of the Yādus and the kinsman of Sātvatas, with the manifestation of the supreme Lord, is the most significant development in the transition between Vedic brāhmaṇism and Vaiṣṇavism, though a chronology of this development is hardly possible. We have a few references to the name Kṛṣṇa in the *Vedas* and the *Upaniṣads*, such as an *asura* in conflict with Indra, a demi-god of the Yadus, and a son of Devaki, the disciple of a *ṛṣi* and later a herdsman, a playboy and the supreme Lord—thus a many-faceted God displaying great variety, supported with a number of myths.[270] Radhakrishnan observes:

The *Mahābhārata* contains several layers of thought superimposed one upon another in the course of ages representing Kṛṣṇa in all the grades, from a historical character to an *avatār* of Viṣṇu.

It is clear that the editors of the *Mahābhārata* felt that some popular hero must be made the rallying centre to counteract the mighty influence of the heretical sects. The figure of Kṛṣṇa was ready to hand.[271]

The most important clue in some of the mythical references to Kṛṣṇa is his victory over the sacerdotalism and sacrifice of Vedic religion. The defeat of Indra by Kṛṣṇa and the surrender of the former to the latter shows that Kṛṣṇa saved cattle, especially cows, from slaughter in sacrifice. Kṛṣṇa is said to have persuaded the cowherds to abandon the worship of Indra and suggested that they venerate cattle and mountain.[272] Thus Indra, the primary god of Vedic sacrifice, is replaced by Kṛṣṇa. Moreover, there were socio-economic reasons for Kṛṣṇa's growing popularity at a time when pastoral life was yielding to the agrarian, which affected the tribal societies. Jaiswal points out that "although the Sātvatas did not conform to the *varṇa* order, they had some affinity with the third *varṇa* which was assigned to the pursuit of agriculture and trade. Perhaps only at a later stage the tribe of Kṛṣṇa was assigned a kṣatriya status".[273] In this new status Kṛṣṇa came to be regarded as equal to Indra, friend of warriors and later the supreme God.

It stands to reason that the growing popularity of Kṛṣṇa has something to do with changing forms of sacrifice. We do not have reliable sources to know for certain the forms of sacrifice prevalent among the Sātvatas and other tribes. Pointing out the single reference in the *Mahābhārata* to Uparisaravas, an early devotee of Nārāyaṇa performing ritual according to the *sātvata vidhi*, Das Gupta points out that it has to be understood in the context of brāhmaṇic influence due to amalgamation with other cults.[274] Those who emphasise Kṛṣṇa's identification with the Upaniṣadic *Devakiputra*, son of Devaki, pupil of Ghora Āngirasa, associate him with the tradition that rejected the ritualistic interpretation of sacrifice. The influence of this tradition, they say. could be seen in the *Gītā*.[275] But this emphasis does not take into account Kṛṣṇa's later association with Vedic sacrifice. The observation of Kosambi in this regard is noteworthy:

> Kṛṣṇa was a protector of cattle, never invoked at a fire sacrifice where animals were offered up as ... Vedic deities were invoked. Whatever sacrifices the Yādus might have made to an ancestral founder-god, there was no reason for their continuance by other tribes. On the other hand, the pastoral tribes who were changing to agriculture would constantly prefer Kṛṣṇa to Indra; so would the pre-Aryans who had begun to learn from and intermarry with the headsmen, but still worshipping someone of the innumerable local goddesses conveniently made into wives for Kṛṣṇa.[276]

But Kṛṣṇa's popularity over Vedic gods among the tribes around him proved the fear of Śiśupāla and other brahmins to be true. Then, as usual the only choice left to brāhmaṇism was to absorb Kṛṣṇa into its fold and somehow save the sacrifice. Hence the identification of Kṛṣṇa with Viṣṇu, the saviour of Vedic *yajña.*[277]

In the *Mahābhārata* Viṣṇu is presented as not only having supreme qualities but also protecting the Vedic *dharma* and *yajña.*[278] More significantly, there he becomes the centre of famous heroes and teachers who are interpreted as the *avatāras* of Viṣṇu. As Renou points out,

> The *avatāras* were originally independent legends which came to centre on Viṣṇu, perhaps because from the beginning Viṣṇu was the symbol of the propagation of the divine; they are legends for prowess over demons, of the usual type, which portray a hero.[279]

The most important *avatāra* is of course Kṛṣṇa, the hero of the *Gītā* where he is portrayed as God and Man.

Once Kṛṣṇa was identified as one of the *avatāras* of Viṣṇu, the lord and saviour of Vedic sacrifice, he had to somehow adjust with the sacrifice of the brahmins. It is interesting to note that when Kṛṣṇa is introduced for the first time in the *Mahābhārata* as the incarnate Hari, he appears as a royal guest in a *rājasūya.* It is here that Śiśupāla objects to gifts being given to Kṛṣṇa, obstructs the sacrifice and finally is killed by Kṛṣṇa. Thus the sacrifice was completed in the presence of the leader of herdsmen and Lord of all.[280] This shows the initial stages of absorption of Kṛṣṇa into the brahmin fold. The influence of brāhmaṇism in this fusion with Bhāgavatism in turn may reflect the performance of *aśvamedha* by a *bhāgavata* king in honour of Saṃkarṣaṇa and Vāsudeva as found in an inscription belonging to the first century B.C.[281] At the same time, apparently this absorption, at least at the beginning, effected some change in the forms of Vedic sacrifice. Thus because of the inclusion of Kṛṣṇa into the sacrificial religion, along with the influence of the *śramaṇa* movement, Vedic sacrifice was stripped of the killing of animals. Mrinal Das Gupta finds this development which has influenced all Vaiṣṇava sects significant.[282] Thus in the description of an *aśvamedha,* it is said that the king performed it without animals and God accepted it and smelled the scent of the cereal offerings.[283] This may provide a clue that the original *bhāgavata* cult had only simple forms of offering. As far as brahmins are concerned, however, their supremacy is affirmed as they are the first-born of creation, supporting the universe and human life by strengthening the gods and performing *tapas.*[284] Due to the interaction with the *śramaṇa* movement, the brahmins came to be considered sustainers of the cosmos as *tapasvins* and advocates of *ahiṃsā.*[285] Now their supremacy stands not only on their power of *tapas* but also in their relation to a supreme God who is an integrating force of various traditions.

Bhāgavatism was a religion of activism. It had a tradition of great heroes. Its commitment to duty seemed to excel the brāhmaṇic commitment to the *sanātana dharma.* Many kinds of duties find place in an elaborate dharmic whole, but the question is, what is the foremost duty for emancipation? The reply follows:

> The duties ordained in respect of every mode of life are capable, if well performed, of leading to heaven and the high fruit of truth. Duties have many doors, and none of the practices inculcated by them are futile in respect of consequences. Whoever adopts whichever duties with steady and firm faith, praises the duties adopted by him to the exclusion of the rest.... [286]

Further, it is declared that "Heaven has a thousand doors of duty all standing wide open".[287] The list of duties here include sacrifice, war, study of scriptural texts along with ascetic life, self-control and compassion. Interestingly the goal is *svarga* and not *mokṣa.*

Bhakti is given great prominence. Although the supreme Lord is able to synthesise all modes of action, he cannot be seen by the performance of sacrifice, rites or *tapas* but only by intensive devotion. He shows himself to the devout ones out of his grace. This is the greatest privilege, which was denied to the archetypal *ṛṣis.*[288] Further, to this potent effect of intensive *bhakti, jñāna* is accepted, though their exact relationship is not clarified. *Jñāna* is praised in the following way: "Bow unto Him who is unrevealed, who is capable of being apprehended by knowledge only... who can be known with the aid of the eye of knowing alone."[289] Perhaps *jñāna* helps in developing full concentration on the Supreme Lord in loving devotion.

Within the triple ideals of *karman, jñāna* and *bhakti* focused on God, the synthesis accommodates innovative views to the extent of incorporating Buddhist terms (e.g. *bhagavat*), identifying with Rudra and even the supreme Brahman; and Nārāyaṇa is nevertheless the supreme Lord of all.[290] And being aware of the criticism of inconsistency in such absorption even in the early period, the *Nārāyaṇīya* declares itself as the great *Upaniṣad* which is perfectly consistent with the four *Vedas* and *Purāṇas,* is in harmony with *sāṃkhya-yoga* and is called by God by the name of *Pāñcarātra* scriptures. Although the *pāñcarātra* literature of later Vaiṣṇavism is distinctive in many respects it is interesting to note that even at its earlier stage its close connection with the Vedic religion was asserted. All systems and all religions are simultaneously valid provided, it is noted, they acknowledge Nārāyaṇa as the self and end of all.[291]

Before we close this section it may be useful to highlight the fact that the *sāṃkhya-yoga* categories attached to Nārāyaṇa-Kṛṣṇa indicate that even in the early period Bhāgavatism had close connections with the school of *Sāṃkhya-Yoga*. Perhaps both originally emerged side by side in two related clans. In any case later all the epithets of a supreme God and all the *tattvas* of *Sāṃkhya-Yoga* were assimilated in the all-comprising figure of Kṛṣṇa, the hero of the *Bhagavad Gītā*.

6. Conclusion

In this chapter we have surveyed the development of the idea and form of Vedic sacrifice in the historical process leading up to the Bhagavad Gītā. The period we have covered in this survey, the sixth to second centuries B.C., is a most creative period effecting changes in the idea of sacrifice. Socio-economic-political forces have undoubtedly contributed to change in the understanding of sacrifice. Being sensitive to these forces the great visionaries, the *śramaṇas*, challenged the system of sacrifice and monarchy which supported it. They formulated alternative world-views that had no place for grand sacrifices, upset the social order of *varṇa*, and established model communities. But those who got well established, especially the Buddhists, had to make in due course many compromises. Thus Buddhism supported monarchy provided it promoted *dharma*. It allowed a certain amount of ritual but stripped it of the Vedic meaning. Even so, with an ethical ideal like *ahiṃsā* there was no compromise.

The monarchic system of centralised economy left many people unable to afford elaborate forms of sacrifice. The *saṃnyāsa* ideal of the *śramaṇa* movement won many converts from brāhmaṇism. The competition of *śramaṇas* for *dāna* and their attack on Vedic sacrifice made the brāhmaṇic religion of sacrifice decline. All these created a crisis for that system. It should be underlined that this crisis occurred not in the cumulative process of brāhmaṇism but in its interaction with new ideas. Many adherents to brāhmaṇism resisted any change infused from outside and were firm about the validity of the *yajña*-oriented world-view.

There were developments, however, in favour of brāhmaṇism. Aśokan reform introduced a spirit of tolerance which could accommodate brāhmaṇism without sacrificing the *śramaṇa* ideals. The Suṅgan dynasty founded by a staunch brahmin, Puṣyamitra, at the turn of the second century B.C. fostered a revival of brāhmaṇic ritual. The force of the *śramaṇa* movement was contained but its ideals could not be ignored.

In the process of revival the orthodox *darśanas* reaffirmed the authority of the *Vedas*, though Vedic *yajña* was not central in their thought. Their main concern was to formulate new metaphysics in the style of *śramaṇa* world-views. But *purvamīmāṃsa*, without worrying about alternative metaphysics, affirmed the validity of Vedic sacrifice, its power and its meaning. To this effect it developed principles of interpretation of the Vedic texts.

As revivalist literature in the truest sense, and the most potent, we have the *dharmaśāstras* and *itihāsas*. They reaffirm the fundamental views of sacrifice, namely, that in performing Vedic sacrifice in its entirety one fulfils the demands of a primordial *dharma*, strengthens the gods and sustains the cosmic order. Relatedly, they stress the maintenance of the *varṇa* system for the order of society.

The difficulty in taking these as revivalist literature, especially the *itihāsa*, lies in the fact that they are of encyclopaedic nature containing divergent views without any discussion about their interconnections. They seem to indicate, however, the characteristics of a historical-hermeneutical process in which brāhmaṇism actively participated. These characteristics include not only a reaffirmation of an ancient vision of reality and traditional customs but, more significantly, assimilation and reconstruction. Thus, new practices like *svādhyāya, dāna, pūjā, tīrtha* and *vrata* are taken to be of equal merit as *yajña*. But in what way these new practices can be adjusted with *yajña* in its Vedic sense is a question which is not given any serious attention. Moreover, the formulation of *puruṣārtha* and *āśrama dharma* attempts a conceptual and practical framework which can accommodate all the salient features of the *śramaṇa* movement without in any way diluting the original meaning of ritual *yajña*. But, as we have pointed out, this formulation created diverse opinions. The same kind of development could be noticed in a cultic synthesis which represents an amalgamation of brāhmaṇic religion with the *bhāgavata* cult. The conception or perception of a supreme God seems to promise a harmony of divergent views developed around the idea of sacrifice. But it is not clear whether the simple offerings in the worship of this God reduced the meaning of sacrifice to instrumental value, depriving it of intrinsic value. This problem will be discussed in our next chapter.

It may be an interesting and important exercise to compare the *yajña*-based Vedic world-view with the world views of *śramaṇas*, and orthodox *darśanas*. In what way does the difference between these world-views address the question of the changed meaning of sacrifice if any such fundamental change took place at all? One may notice, for example, that the ideal of *ahiṃsā* developed by the *śramaṇas* originally in protest against sacrificial slaughter and war, was not consistent with the ideas of, for instance, self-torture and *anatta*. Yet the *śramaṇas* themselves propagated, in their rule of *dharma*, at least minimum violence on self, without which there is no discipline. Probably this was an advantage for the brāhmaṇic revivalists to exempt killing in sacrifice from killing or harming in general. But more than such accommodation and readjustment we may not find clearly the impact of differing world-views developed by the *śramaṇas* or the brahmin visionaries.

The paradigm shift in science is helpful to understand the change of religious frameworks. On the part of brahmins, one may expect that their authentic response should be either the stubborn persistence of the *yajña*-based world-view or to undergo a conversion experience in adopting a new one. But the brāhmaṇic tradition seems to be unique in the preservation of the old paradigm while incorporating into it elements of other paradigms. Or any number of paradigms within the tradition are allowed without giving up the fundamental practice attached to an ancient vision. As far as brāhmaṇism is concerned this practice is the performance of Vedic *yajña*. Despite crises created by historical and ideological challenges, the door is kept open for any number of new ideas as long as they do not question the continuation of a sacred act, i.e. the sacrifice, however simplified its form may be. But if we take the underlying ideas of this practice seriously, it is not easy to develop a consistent framework of assimilation. Authorities like ancient *ṛṣis* give contrary views conjointly. And a kind of uneasiness and artificiality is evident in counter-questions that follow. We noted this when we studied the Upaniṣadic understanding of sacrifice. In some passages the *ātma yajña* is presented in such a way that it is part of a cumulative process and transition from ritual *yajña*. But the underlying ideas of the former seem to be radically different from that of the latter. Likewise, a ritual sacrifice cannot have cosmic significance before a supreme God who is creator and sustainer. But ritual, interiorisation and supreme God all appear as powers existing side by side. We can already see a tendency towards a poly-paradigmatic position which is characteristic of Hinduism. The Kṛṣṇa-Arjuna dialogue in the *Bhagavad Gītā,* especially on *yajña* and *dharma,* seems to be a supreme example of this position.

NOTES

1. Charles Moore (ed.), *The Indian Mind,* Honolulu, 1967, p. 6.
2. T.W. Rhys Davids, *Buddhist India,* London, 1903, p. 2.
3. R.C. Majumdar, *Ancient India,* Delhi, 1982, p. 45.
4. See *DH,* p.126; A.K. Warder, *Indian Buddhism,* Delhi, 1970, p. 24.
5. Warder, *ibid.*, p. 29.
6. See *ibid.*, p. 28f.
7. G.C. Pande, *Studies in the Origins of Buddhism,* Delhi, 1983, p. 312.
8. Romila Thapar, *Aśoka and the Decline of Mauryas*, Delhi, p.149ff. This culmination was also marked by the development of political science that gained shape in Kautilya's *Arthaśāstra.*
9. See Warder, *op. cit.*, p. 239; Rhys Davids, *op. cit.*, p. 269.
10. Romila Thapar, *op. cit.*, p.144.
11. *ibid.*, p.146.
12. G.C. Pande, *op. cit.*, p. 315f; cf. A.L. Basham, *The Wonder that Was India,* London, 1956, p.140ff.
13. Pande, *op. cit.*, p. 313.
14. The gifts of lands and villages to the priests later came to form brāhmaṇic colonies called *agrahāra.* See Romila Thapar, *Ancient Indian Social History, Some Interpretations*, New Delhi, 1978, p.118; also see Rhys Davids, *op. cit.*, p.48. In the period under consideration, however, Majumdar notes, "'Grants' of land only implied transfer of privileges regarding revenue but no ownership", see R.C. Majumdar ed., *The History and Culture of Indian People,* 1. *Vedic Age,* London, 1951, p. 436; see also N.N. Bhattacharyya, *Ancient Indian Rituals and their Social Contents,* London, 1975, p.16.
15. See A.K. Warder, *op. cit.*, p.30.
16. G.C. Pande, *op. cit.*, p. 314f.
17. D.D. Kosambi, *The Culture and Civilization of Ancient India,* Delhi,

1972, p.128. The misery further included the depletion of herds, heavy tax and obstruction of trade and agriculture particularly affecting the vaiśya class. See also, D.D. Kosambi, *An Introduction to the Study of Indian History*, Bombay, 1975, p.166f.

18. *Śānti Parvan,* section 82; Ref. P.C. Roy, The *Mahābhārata,* (tr.) Calcutta, 1928, II, pp.174-81. All references to *Mbh.* are taken from Roy's translation unless otherwise indicated.
19. See, *Mbh,* XIII 106, 107.
20. See D.D. Kosambi, *The Culture and Civilization,* p.118f.
21. G.C. Pande, *op. cit.*, p.313.
22. A.L. Basham, "The Rise of Buddhism", p. 400; Trevor Ling calls the mood created by monarchy "a psychological malaise", a heightened sense of dissatisfaction with life as it had to be lived, " or called *dhukka,* by the Buddha, see Ling, *The Buddha—Buddhist Civilization in India and Ceylon,* London, 1985, p. 62.
23. For different possible reasons, see J.C. Jain, *Life in Ancient India as Depicted in the Jaina Canons,* Bombay, 1947, p. 192ff.
24. A.K. Warder, *op. cit.*, p. 31.
25. For identification of the *śramaṇas* with *munis* and *yatis* of the *Veda,* see H.D. Sharma, *Contributions to the History of Brāhmaṇic Asceticism (Saṃnyāsa),* Poona, 1939, p.19f.
26. G.C. Pande, *op. cit.*, p. 327.
27. J. Gonda, *Change and Continuity in Indian Religion,* Delhi, 1985, p. 377.
28. S. Dutt, *Early Buddhist Monachism,* Bombay, 1960, p.40; with reference to the pair *śramaṇa* and *tapasa* in *BṛU,* IV. 3.22 and *śramaṇa* and *brāhmaṇa* in the Pali canon P.S. Jaini clarifies that while *śramaṇa* denotes all kinds of mendicants including the Buddhists, *brāhmaṇa* and *tapasa* indicate the brahmin mendicants. See Jaini, "*Śramaṇas:* Their conflict with Brahmanical Society" in *Chapters in Indian Civilization,* p. 42.
29. See D.D. Kosambi, *An introduction to the Study of Indian History,* p.166.
30. See Romila Thapar, *Aśoka and the Decline of the Mauryas,* p.247.
31. For a vivid picture of the life-style of hermits, see T.W. Rhys Davids, *Buddhist India,* p.140f.
32. See Romila Thapar, "The Householder and the Renouncer in the Brahmanical and Buddhist Traditions", in *Way of Life,* ed. T. N. Madan, New Delhi, 1982, p. 278f; D.D. Kosambi, *op.cit.*, p.168; S. Dutt, *op.cit.*, Bombay, 1960, pp.113-45.
33. See S.J. Tambiah, "The Renouncer: his Individuality and Community", in *Way of Life, ibid.*, 1982, p. 317.
34. Romila Thapar, *op.cit.*, p. 279.
35. *ibid,* p. 294; A.L. Basham, *The Wonder that Was India,* p. 246f.
36. G.C. Pande, *op.cit.*, p. 260.
37. Romila Thapar, *A Histroy of India (Vol. I),* p. 49.
38. See G.C. Pande, *op.cit.*, p. 260; P.S. Jaini, "*Śramaṇas*", p. 42.

39. See K.N. Upadhyaya, *Early Buddhism and the Bhagavadgita,* Delhi, 1983, p. 87f ; J.C. Jain, *op.cit.*, pp. 201- 11; These may include a group of brāhmaṇic ascetics also. A Jaina *Sūtra* mentions a group of *tapasvins* living on the bank of the Ganges; they performed sacrifice and ate the flesh of elephant. See K.C. Jain, *Lord Mahāvīra and His Times,* Delhi, 1974, p.176ff.
40. See A.K. Warder, *op.cit.*, p.37ff.
41. K.C. Jain, *op.cit.*, p. 6.
42. J.C. Jain, *op.cit.*, p. 22f.
43. See H. Nakamura, "Yajñavalkya and other Upaniṣadic Thinkers in a Jain Tradition", *ALB,* 31-32 (1967-68), pp. 216-28.
44. See P.S. P.S. Jaini, *The Jaina Path of Purification*, Delhi, 1979, p. 36.
45. See H. Jacobi, *Gaina Sūtras,* SBE, XLV, pp. 135-41.
46. Quoted in J.C. Jain, *op.cit.*, p.141.
47. P.S. Jaini, *op.cit.*, p.76.
48. For an introduction to the fundamentals of Jainism, see C. Eliot, *Hinduism and Buddhism,* New York, 1957, I, p.106; K.N. Upadhyaya *op.cit.*, p. 89.
49. J.C. Jain, *op.cit.*, p.166f.
50. See P.S. Jaini, *op.cit.*, p.167.
51. A.L. Basham, "Jainism and Buddhism", in *Sources of Indian Tradition,* compiled by Wm. Theodore de Barg and others, New York, 1964, p. 63.
52. P.S. Jaini, "Śramaṇas", p. 61f.
53. For example, it is said, three Jātila teachers including the famous Kāsappa joined the Buddha with their followers. See G.S. Misra, *Development of Buddhist Ethics,* New Delhi, 1984, p. 33f.
54. For references to the Buddha's opposition to extreme forms of asceticism, see U. Dhammaratana, "Buddha and Asceticism", *IHQ,* XXXIII (1957), p.129ff.
55. See T.W. Rhys Davids, *Buddhist Suttas, SBE,* XI, Oxford, 1900, p.146f; M.G. Bhagat, *Ancient Indian Asceticism,* New Delhi, 1976, p.165; T.W. Rhys Davids, "*Asceticism* (Buddhism)", in *ERE,* 2, p.70.
56. P.S. Jaini, *op.cit.*, p. 63.
57. See T.W. Rhys Davids, *Dilogues of the Buddha,* London, 1894, I, pp.173-85.
58. T. Ling, *The Buddha - Buddhist Civilization in India and Ceylon,* London, 1985, p. 68.
59. See T.W. Rhys Davids, "Sacrifice in Buddhism", *ERE,* 11, p. 8.
60. T.W. Rhys Davids, *Dialogues of the Buddha,* II, p.371.
61. *Jātaka* no. 543, quoted in T.W. Rhys Davids, "Sacrifice in Buddhism", p. 8.
62. N.N. Bhattacharyya, *op.cit.*, p.16; see also D.D. Kosambi, "Early Stages of the Caste System in Northern India", *JBBRAS,* 22 (1946), p. 45.
63. See M. Monier-Williams, *Buddhism in its Connection with Brahmanism*

and in Contrast with Christianity, Varanasi, 1964, p.131.

64. C.I.F. Rhys Davids, "The Relations Between Early Buddhism and Brahmanism", *IHQ,* X (1934), p.278.
65. *ibid.,* p. 279.
66. T.W. Rhys Davids, *Buddhist Suttas,* p.129f.
67. For the background and significance of the symbol of the wheel in Buddhism, see T.W. Rhys Davids, *ibid.,* p.153f; C.I.F. Rhys Davids, *A Manual of Buddhism,* London, 1932, p.175.
68. For details of the Buddhist scheme of understanding the operation of the world, *karman,* soul etc. see S.N. Dasgupta, *A Histroy of Indian Philosophy,* Delhi, 1975, I, p.64ff; G.S.P. Misra, *Development of Buddhist Ethics,* New Delhi, 1984, p. 22f; Edward Conze, *Buddhism, Its Essence and Development,* Oxford, 1974, pp. 50ff; K.N. Jeyatilleke, *The Message of the Buddha,* London, 1975, p.152f.
69. G.S.P. Misra, *op.cit.,* p. 24f.
70. See K.N. Jayatilleke, *op.cit.,* p.141.
71. D.M. Knipe, *In the Image of Fire - Vedic Experience of Heat,* Delhi, 1975, p.136f.
72. See M.G. Bhagat, *op.cit.,* p. 35.
73. For a description of fundamental points in the spiritual jouney, see G.S.P. Misra, *op.cit.,* p. 26, 59f; A.K. Warder, *op.cit.,* p. 88ff.
74. See G.S.P. Misra, *ibid.,* p.104.
75. T.W. Rhys Davids, "Sacrifice in Buddhism", p. 8; A.K. Coomaraswamy, "*Ātma Yajña:* Self-Sacrifice", *HJAS,* 6(1941), p. 384.
76. *Mahāparinirvāṇa Sutta,* I.24.5; cf. M.G. Bhagat, *op.cit.,* p. 58.
77. S.J. Tambiah, *op.cit.,* p. 318.
78. A.K. Warder, *op.cit.,* p. 200; see also T.W. Rhys Davids, *Buddhist Suttas,* p.188.
79. T.W. Rhys Davids, *Buddhist India,* p. 8f.
80. See Romila Thapar, "The Householder and the Renouncer", p. 284f; for details of the rules about *dāna* as presented in the *Suttas,* see D.N. de Young, "The Sangha in Buddhist History", *RS,* VI (1970), p.247f.
81. See E. Conze, *op.cit.,* p. 53f; A.K. Warder, *op.cit.,* pp. 187ff.
82. Romila Thapar, "The Householder and The Renouncer", p. 284.
83. A. K. Coomaraswamy, *Hinduism and Buddhism,* n.d., p.100.
84. See A.K. Warder, *op.cit.,* p.172f.
85. T. Ling, *op.cit.,* p.140f.
86. See A.K. Warder, *op.cit.,* p.161ff.
87. See *ibid.,* p.174f.
88. See T.W. Rhys Davids, *Buddhist India,* p.143; Romila Thapar, *Aśoka and the Decline of the Mauryas,* p.154; A.L. Basham, *History and Doctrines of the Ājīvikas,* Delhi, 1981, pp.146ff.
89. *ibid.,* p. 285.
90. See A.K. Warder, *op.cit.,* p. 40.
91. See A.L. Basham, *op.cit.,* p. 284.

92. *ibid.*, p. 9.
93. A.L. Basham, *ibid.*, pp. 107ff.
94. A.K. Warder, *op.cit.*, p. 41.
95. Romila Thapar, *A History of India,* I, p. 64.
96. *ibid.*, p. 42.
97. For historical references to the decline of *yajña,* see T.W. Rhys Davids, *Buddhist India,* p.151.
98. L. Renou, *The Destiny of the Veda in India,* Delhi, 1965, p. 27f.
99. The Buddha came to be regarded as to have possessed a supernatural power (*siddhi*) in his spiritual experience. He accepted the possibility of others getting it, it is said, in the spiritual journey, though he discouraged anyone from indulging in it and displaying it publicly. See G.S.P. Misra, *op.cit.*, p. 96f. It stands to reason, however, that on occasions in conflict with the brahmins the *bhikkus* would have made claims over such experience in order to convince the people on whose *dāna* they depended.
100. See Young, *op.cit.*, p. 248.
101. See J.C. Jain, *op.cit.*, p. 226ff.
102. See Young, *op.cit.*, p. 246ff.
103. See P.S. Jaini, "Śramaṇas", p.75ff.
104. J. Gonda, *Change and Continuity*, p. 386ff.
105. M. Monier-Williams, *Buddhism in its Contrast* with Christainity, p. 83.
106. Romila Thapar, "The Householder and the Renouncer", p. 279.
107. See A.L. Basham, "The Rise of Buddhism in its Historical Context", *AS*, IV/3 (1966), p. 404; N.N. Bhattacharyya points out that Buddhism "gave moral support to all the demands of the trading class. Money-lending, usury and slave-keeping are not condemned in the Buddhist texts", Bhattacharyya, *op.cit.*, p.16.
108. See P. Olivelle, "King and Ascetic—State Control of Asceticism in the Arthaśāstra", *ALB,* 51 (1987), pp. 39-59.
109. J.C. Heesterman, *The Inner Conflict*, p.140.
110. *ibid.*, p. 96.
111. See R.C. Majumdar and others, *An Advanced History of India,* London, 1950, p.104.
112. A.K. Warder, *op.cit.*, p. 242ff.
113. See H.C. Raychaudhuri, "The Aśoka Chakra - Its Symbolism", *IC,* 15 (1948-49) pp.179-83.
114. See G.C. Pande, *op.cit.*, p. 312. This view was originally advocated by the brahmins and is reflected in the ritual of some of the sacrifices.
115. See R.C. Majumdar and others, *op.cit.*, p.107; R. Mookerji, *Aśoka,* London, 1928, p.62, 68ff.
116. Romila Thapar, *A History of India,* I, p. 73.
117. G.C. Pande, *Śramaṇa Tradition - Its History and Contribution to Indian Culture,* Ahmedabad, 1978, p. 50.
118. *ibid.*, p. 51.

119. See N.A. Nikam and Richard Mekeon, (ed. tr.), *The Edicts of Aśoka*, Chicago, 1959, p. 41, 55ff.
120. See D.D. Kosambi, *The Culture and Civilization*, p.162; R. Mookerji, *op.cit.*, p. 62.
121. Nikam and Mekeon, *op.cit.*, p. 44.
122. *ibid.*, pp. 28ff.
123. *ibid.*, p.34; See also Mookerji, *op.cit.*, p. 64f.
124. Romila Thapar, *Aśoka and the Decline of Mauryas*, p.148.
125. See R.N. Nandi, "Client, Ritual and Conflict in Brahmanical Order", *IHR*, VI/1-2 (1979-80), pp. 64-118.
126. R.N. Dandekar, "Hinduism", p. 268.
127. See R.C. Majumdar, *Ancient India*, Delhi, 1992, p.116f; A.L. Basham, *The Wonder that Was India*, p.58; J.E. Mitchiner, *Traditions of the Seven Ṛṣis*, Delhi, 1982, p.134.
128. See E.J. Rapson (ed), *The Cambridge Histroy of India, 1. Ancient India*, Cambridge, 1922, p. 520.
129. *ibid.*, p. 522.
130. See A.L. Basham, *op.cit.*, p.147; the use of Vedic terms with new meanings by the *śramaṇas* was apparently part of the confusion.
131. R.N. Dandekar, *op.cit.*, p. 272.
132. P.S. Jaini, "*Śramaṇas*", p. 49.
133. See H. Jacobi, "The Dates of the Philosophical Sūtras of the Brahmans". *JAOS*, XXXI (1911), pp.1-29.
134. See Karl Potter (ed.), *The Encyclopaedia of Indian Philosophies*, II, Delhi, 1977, p. 265.
135. See *ibid.*, p. 558.
136. See *ibid.*, p. 565.
137. See *ibid.*, p. 573.
138. See *ibid.*, p. 589.
139. See *ibid.*, pp. 217, 452.
140. See S.N. Dasgupta, "Is Sāṃkhya Non-Vedic?", *IC*, I/1-4 (1934-35), p. 79f.
141. For details about the development of *Sāṃkhya-Yoga* in different periods, see G.J. Larson, *Classical Sāṃkhya*, Delhi 1979, pp.71ff; E. Harzer, "SĀṂKHYA', *ER*, 13, pp. 47-51.
142. *Mbh*, XII. 174ff.
143. See Karl Potter, *The Encyclopaedia of Indian Philosophies*, III, p.108.
144. See Julius Lipner, *The Face of Truth*, London, 1986, p.10f.
145. See S.C. Chakrabarti, "On the Transition of Vedic Ritual Lore", *IIJ*, XXI/3 (1979), p.186.
146. S.N. Dasguta, *A History of Indian Philosophy*, I, Delhi, 1975, p. 68.
147. For details of instruction and resemblance of the *Mīmāṃsa Sūtras* with the law givers, see P.V. Kane, "The Pūrva Mīmāṃsa System", *ABORI*, V/1(1924), p.9.
148. A.L. Basham, *The Wonder that Was India*, p. 330.

149. S.N. Dasgupta, *op.cit.*, p. 394.
150. For details of the classification of *viddhis* and principles of interpretation, see *ibid.*, p.404f.
151. Francis Clooney, "Jaimini's Contribution to the Theory of Sacrifice as the Experience of Transcendence", *HR*, 25/3 (1986), p.200.
152. *ibid.*, p. 204.
153. Francis Clooney, "Sacrifice and its Spiritualisation in the Christian and Hindu Traditions: A Study of Comprehensive Theology", *Harvard Theological Review*, 78/3-4 (1985), p. 369; the *śeṣa-śeṣin* relationship served as a tool for Rāmānuja later to interpret human-divine relationships.
154. See A.B. Keith, *The Karma Mīmāṃsa*, Calcutta: 1921, p.74f; S.N. Dasgupta, *op. cit.*, p. 405.
155. See S.N. Dasgupta, *ibid.*, p.489.
156. See Francis Clooney, "Jaimini's Contribution", *op.cit.*, pp. 205ff.
157. *ibid.*, p. 210.
158. *ibid.*, p. 206.
159. *ibid.*, p. 207.
160. *ibid.*, p. 210; see also Clooney, "Sacrifice and its Spiritualisation", p. 368.
161. See Wilhelm Halbfass, *Tradition and Reflection—Explorations in Indian Thought*, New York, 1991, p. 90f.
162. J.D.M. Derrett, *Dharmaśāstra and Juridical Literature*, HIL, IV, p. 21.
163. See A.L. Basham, *op.cit.*, p.113; *HDhś*, I, pp.13f, 335. The inclusion of *dharmaśāstras* in the denotation of the term *kalpasūtra* must be a later practice; see S.C. Chakrabarti, *op.cit.*, p.186.
164. *HDhś*, I, p.14; *Manu*, XII, 109-11.
165. References to *Manu* are taken from G.C. Haughton, *The Institutes of Manu*, New Delhi, 1982, translation, 3, 4.
166. See e.g. *Manu*, I.22, 23; III; 370; cf,IV, 21.
167. *Manu*, II. 14, 15.
168. *Manu*, XI, 27, 41.
169. *Manu*, V. 22, 23, 39-56.
170. *Manu*, II. 169.
171. *Manu*, III. 84ff..
172. See *Manu*, II. 2-5; cf. C. Malamoud, "On the Rhetoric and Semantics of Puruśārtha", in *Way of Life*, p.45.
173. *Manu*, III. 75-77.
174. *Manu*, I. 88ff; X.97: see also *HDhs'*, II, pp.105ff.
175. *BhG*, 3.35.
176. See *Manu*, II.128; IV,57, 81, 205, 206; XI. 32-4, 380.
177. See *Manu*, IX.317-319; X.3.
178. J. Gonda, *Change and Continuity in Indian Religion*, p. 241; cf. *Manu*, II.140-145; VIII. 206-11.
179. E.g. *Manu*, VII.78, 79; VII.9, 10.

180. *Manu,* IX. 322, 327.
181. *Manu,* XI, 335.
182. See *HDhś,* II, p. 945; *Manu,* V.155; A.L. Basham, *op.cit.,* p.179.
183. Quoted by T.W. Rhys Davids, *Buddhist India,* p.118; cf. *Gautama's Dharmasūtra,* XII.4- 6; *Manu* VIII. 270-272.
184. R.N. Dandekar, "Hinduism", p. 269.
185. M.A. Hiriyaṇna, *op.cit.,* p. 92.
186. As E.W. Hopkins notes, "In the same heroes we discover different characters. Oppoisite tendencies seem at work. The highest god is at the same time a tricky mortal. The chief knights are depicted now as good and now as simple men", E.W. Hopkins, "The Social and Military Position of the Ruling Caste in Ancient India as Represented by the Sanskrit Epic", *JAOS,* XIII(1889), p. 58.
187. M. Monier-Williams, *Indian Wisdom,* London, 1893, p. 314.
188. See J.A.B. van Buitenen (tr.), *The Mahābhārata,* Chicago, I, p. xxiii.
189. See *Mbh,* XIII.162.
190. See *Mbh,* XIII, 97.
191. See *Mbh,* XII, 129.
192. See relevant portions in *Mbh,* III.183, 186, 190, 191, 195, 195; XII.76, 132, 136, 165; XIII.8, 9, 27, 30, 50, 101.
193. E.W. Hopkins, *The Religions of India,* London, 1896, p. 386.
194. *ibid.,* cf. *Mbh,* III. 29.3.
195. Quoted by D.R. Kinsley, *Hinduism —A Cultural Perspective,* New Jersey, 1982, p. 35; cf. *Mbh,* XII. 161.
196. See J. Gonda, *Ancient Indian Kingship from the Religious Point of View,* Leiden, 1969, p. 1ff, E.W. Hopkins, *op.cit.,* pp. 72ff. 157f.
197. J. Gonda, *ibid.,* p. 3; cf. *Mbh,* XII.68.10ff.
198. *Op.cit.,* p. 93.
199. *BhG,* 9.32.
200. See M. Monier-Williams, *op.cit.,* p. 308ff.
201. See J.C. Heesterman, *Inner Conflict of a Tradition,* p. 41, 86f.
202. See Alf Hiltebeital, "Kṛṣṇa and the Mahābhārata", *ABORI,* LX (1979), pp.67-104 "Mahābhārata". *ADLR,* p.449; M. Birdeau and C. Malamoud, *Le Sacrifice dans l'inde Ancienne,* Paris, 1976, p.117ff.
203. See G. Johnsen, "Varuṇa and Dhṛtarāṣṭra," *IIJ,* IX(1965-66), p.247ff; V.S. Sukthankar, *On the Meaning of the Mahābhārata,* Bombay, 1957, p. 68f; but Sukthankar tends to generalise *dharma* as a universal principle and does not emphasise further the importance of this fight for the understanding of sacrifice.
204. See Alf Hiltebeital, "The Mahābāṛata and Hindu Eschatology", *HR,* 12/2 (1972) p.133ff.
205. See *HDhś,* IV, p.47ff; *Manu,* II.166; IV.100, 148f; XI.263.
206. *HDhś,* IV. pp.44ff; J. Gonda, "The Indian Mantra", *Oriens,* 16(1963), p. 259; *Vedic Ritual,* Leiden, p. 228.
207. *Manu,* II.76-79, 84-86; XI.265f.

208. *Mbh*, III.80-85 enumerates three hundred *tīrthas* for the Pāṇḍavas to visit as a substitute for sacrifices when they are in exile; XII.108 notes that the greatest one is *mānasa tīrtha* of the heart.
209. See Diana Eck, "India's Tīrthas: 'Crossings' in Sacred Geography", *HR*, 20/4 (1981), p. 329ff.
210. See *HDhś*, IV, pp. 49ff; V, pp. 81ff.
211. J.C. Heesterman, "*Veda* and Dharma" in *Concept of Duty in South Asia*, ed. O'Flaherty and D. Derret, New Delhi, 1978, p. 87.
212. See *Manu*, V.22, 23, 39-56; *Mbh*, XIII.32, 114-116, 130, 197; XII.261ff; III.207, 208; XII.97-99; cf. D.D. Kosambi, *An Introduction to the Study of Indian History*, p.167.
213. Manu enumerates seven worlds and assigns to them different merits (IV.181-183); he places *jñāna* in the second of four *yugas* (I.86).
214. *Manu*, IV.21-23.
215. E.g. *Mbh*, IV.20-25, 28, 34.
216. *Mbh*, XII. 176ff.
217. See E.W. Hopkins, "Yoga-techniques in the Great Epic", *JAOS*, 22(1901), pp. 333-79.
218. *Manu*, XII.89-91, 122, 125; cf, IV.120.
219. See J. Gonda, "The Vedic Mantra and the Epic Dharma", *JRAS* (1971), p.129.
220. See *Manu*, IV.226ff; Mbh, XIV.29, 30; M.A. Hiriyanna, *op.cit.*, p.108f.
221. See *Manu*, XII, 34ff, 87.
222. *Mbh*, XII.162f.
223. A. Sharma in his booklet *The Puruṣārthas: A Study in Hindu Axiology* (Michigan, 1982) brings together the attempts of Hindu scholars to give a coherent explanation of the formulation of *puruṣārtha* without in any way trying to solve the problem.
224. See *Manu*, II.94ff; IV, 246.
225. *Mbh*, XII.161; see also Fredrich Wilhelm, "The Concept of Dharma". in *Concept of Duty in South Asia*, ed. O'Flaherty and Derret, p.67f.
226. *ibid.*, p. 68.
227. *HDhś*, III, p.241; *Kāmasūtra* also expresses a similar view. See Wilhelm, *op.cit.*, p. 71.
228. *HDhś*, II, p. 8; III, p. 240f.
229. *HDhś*, III, p. 240.
230. See A Sharma, *op.cit.*, p.16f.
231. See C. Malamoud, "On the Rhetoric and Semantic of Puruṣārtha" in *Way of Life*, 1982, p. 49f.
232. *ibid.*, p. 51.
233. *ibid.*
234. For an unsuccessful attempt, see Pandharinath Prabhu, *Hindu Social Organization, A Study in Socio-Psychological and Ideological Foundations*, Bombay, 1979, p. 96f; Prabhu does not acknowledge the problem involved in the formative stage of the scheme.

235. See W.O. Kaelber, "The Brahmacārin: Homology and Continuity in Brahmanic Religion", *HR*, 21/1 (1981), p. 87f; P. Deussen, *The Philosophy of the Upanisads*, (tr. A.S. Geden), Edinburgh, 906, p. 367f.
236. *Mbh*, XII.10.24.
237. L. Dumont, *Religion, Politics and History in India*, The Hague, 1970, p. 44f.
238. P. Olivelle, "The Notion of Āśrama in the Dharmasūtras", WZKSIP, XVIII(1974), p. 27f.
239. See *ibid.* and "Contributions to the Semantic History of Samnyasa", *JAOS*, 101/3 (1981), p. 270f.
240. W.D. O'Flaherty, *Śiva, the Erotic Ascetic*, Oxford, 1973, p. 78.
241. See M.G. Bhagat, *op.cit.*, pp. 221ff, 276f, 299f.
242. See *HDhś*, II, p. 424ff.
243. A.L. Basham, *The Wonder that was India*, p.160; see also J.N. Farquhar, "The Organization of the Sannyasis of *Vedanta*", *JRAS*(1925), p. 479f; Romila Thapar, "The Householder and the Renouncer", p. 276f.
244. T.W. Rhys Davids, *Buddhist India*, p. 250; see also T.W. Rhys Davids, *Dialogues of the Buddha*, I, pp. 212-19.
245. *Manu*, II.183 says that a *brahmacārin* must never be deficient in performing the sacrifice which the *Veda* ordains; and for him the main duty of *gṛhasta* life is the performance of *pañcamahāyña* and support for priests.
246. See *Manu*, VI.4, 8-9, 25-9; *HDhś*, II, p.920; G.C. Pande, *Studies in the Origins of Buddhism*, p. 330.
247. O'Flaherty, *op.cit.*, p. 79.
248. W.D. Olivelle, (tr.) *Vāsudevāśrama Yatidharmaprakāśa: A Teatise on World Renunciation*, II, Vienna, 1977, p.30, 55f.
249. See *HDhś*, III, p. 425; D.D. Ramanathan, *The Saṃnyāsa Upaniṣads*, Madras, 1978, p.15; for Vasistha, ascetics can do away with sacrifice but not with the *Veda* which can make them śūdras, see E.W. Hopkins, *The Religions of India*, p. 256.
250. See D.D. Ramanathan, *ibid.*, p. 69f; there are *saṃskāras* and *yajñas* prescribed in the way to qualify for *saṃnyāsa*, see *HDhś*, II, p. 931f; W.D. Kaelber, "The Brahmacārin", p. 93f.
251. *Manu*, VI.83.
252. See P.S. Jaini, "Śramaṇas: Their Conflict with Brahmanical Society", p.72.
253. *Manu*, II. 1ff.
254. See also D.D. Ramanathan, *op.cit.*, p. 58.
255. Romila Thapar, "The Householder and the Renouncer", p. 280f.
256. See H.F. Holck, "Some Observations on the Motives and Purposes of Asceticism in Ancient India", *AS/EA*, XXIII/1-2(1969), pp. 45-57.
257. According to some authorities kṣatriyas can also be included for *saṃnyāsa*hood. For reference to discussions on this issue, see *HDhś*, II, p.943f; Romila Thapar *op.cit.*, p. 277.

258. For the development of four *yugas*, see *ADLR*, p. 818f. On the chief meritorious acts of each *yuga* see *Manu*, I.85-86; *Mhb*, XII.232.31-2. According to one view *yajña* belongs to a fallen age; see J.C. Heesterman, *The Inner Conflict of a Tradition*, p.102.
259. See E.J. Rapson, *op.cit.*, p. 259.
260. See R.C. Majumdar, *Ancient India*, p.171; Majumdar and others, *Advanced History*, op. 95; see also M.R. Hiriyanna, *op.cit.*, p. 99f.
261. For an introduction to such various groups, see R.G. Bhandarkar, *Vaiṣṇavism, Śaivism and Minor Religious Systems*, Strassburg, 1913; S.N. Dasgupta, *A History of Indian Philosophy*, II, p. 539f.
262. See G.A. Grierson, "The Nārāyaṇīya and the Bhāgavatas", *IA*, XXXVII (1908), p. 253; R. Raghavan and R.N. Dandekar, "Hinduism", p. 279.
263. See S.N. Dasgupta, *op.cit.*, p. 542ff; Majumdar adds that political reasons were also involved here, see Majumdar, *Ancient India*, p.174.
264. For different stages in the process of amalgamation, see G.A. Grierson, "Bhakti-Marga", *ERE*, 2, pp. 539-51.
265. *Śānti Parvan*, sections 334-51.
266. See Roy, *Mbh*, VI, p. o15.
267. R.C. Majumdar, *op.cit.*, p.174; Biardeau sees in this act the absorption of ascetic tradition into sacrificial tradition and a justification of violence in sacrifice; see Biardeau and Malamoud, *Le Sacrifice dans L'Inde Ancienne*, p.142f.
268. M. Das Gupta, "Early Viṣṇuism and Nārāyaṇīya Worship", *IHQ*, VII (1931), p.110.
269. E.g. Ref. S. Chattopadhyaya, *Evolution of Hindu Sects—upto the time of Śaṃkarācārya*, New Delhi, 1970; S. Jaiswal, *The Origin and Development of Vaisnavism*, Delhi, 1967.
270. See D.D. Kosambi, *The Culture and Civilization of Ancient India*, p.114f; R.C. Majumdar, *op.cit.*, p.172; *HDhś*, V, pp.129ff; particularly for Kṛṣṇa's identification with the *ṛṣi* tradition, see J.E. Mitchiner, *Traditions of the Seven Ṛṣis*, pp. 51ff, 126, 225; for different sources see A. Ray, "Sri Kṛṣṇa and the source of the BhG". *IHQ*, IX (1933), pp.188-96; for a terminological confusion see B. Majumdar, *Kṛṣṇa in History and Legend*, Calcutta, 1969, pp.1-25.
271. S. Radhkrishnan, *The Philosophy of the Upanisads*, London, 1924, p. 494f.
272. See S. Radhakrishnan, *BhG*, p.29; J. Gonda, *Aspects of Early Vaiṣṇavism*, Utrecht, 1954, p.155f; R. Raghavan and R.N. Dandekar, "Hinduism", p. 279f.
273. S. Jaiswal, *op.cit.*, p.151.
274. See Mrinal Das Gupta, "Early Visnuism and Narayaniya Worship", IHQ VII (1931), p. 662.
275. E.g. see H. Raychaudhuri, *Materials for the Study of the Early History of the Vaishnava Sect*, Calcutta, 1936, p.80; B. Majumdar, *Kṛṣṇa in History*

and Legend, Calcutta, 1969, pp.266-278.

276. D.D. Kosambi, *The Culture and Civilization of Ancient India,* p.117f.
277. See J. Gonda, *Aspects of Early Viṣṇuism,* pp.77-84; G.S. Ghurye, *Vedic India,* 1979, p.107f.
278. See *Śānti Parvan,* section 208; Roy, *Mbh,* V, p.87ff; *Nārāyaṇīya,* 351, 352; there is a remarkable mention of the revival of sacrifice. Besides the reappearance of Prajāpati, Hari-Nārāyaṇa is said to be the creator, the enjoyer and the Lord of sacrifices. There is, however, tension and readjustment. See *Nārāyaṇīya,* 340.
279. L. Renou, *Religions of Ancient India,* p. 66.
280. See *Mbh,* II.33-45.
281. See L. Renou, *The Destiny of Veda in India,* Delhi, 1965, p.113.
282. M. Das Gupta, *IHQ,* VIII (1932), p. 80.
283. *Nārāyaṇīya,* 337; in section 338 animal sacrifice is denied and seeds are prescribed as substitutes. This is because the ancient *ṛṣis* used only seeds. It was the gods who sacrificed animals and for this reason there was conflict between *ṛṣis* and *devas.*
284. See *Nārāyaṇīya,* 341f.
285. See Biardeau and Malamoud, *op.cit.,* p. 84f.
286. Roy, Mbh, VI, p. 612.
287. *ibid.,* p. 615f.
288. See Mbh, p. 531ff.
289. *ibid.,* p. 558.
290. *ibid.,* p. 561; cf. D.D. Kosambi, *Indian History,* p. 262.
291. See Roy, *Mbh,* p. 549f, 602f.

IV

Yajña in the *Bhagavad Gītā*: Affirmation, Accommodation and New Interpretation

1. Introduction

Sacrifice is one of the recurring themes in the *Bhagavad Gītā*. In this chapter we take up for discussion the understanding of sacrifice in the *Gītā*. We have proposed that a historical-hermeneutical perspective may lead to the clearest understanding of this aspect. The background of the *Gītā* set in the last chapter should be conducive to this understanding.

The treatment of *yajña* in the *Gītā* is a difficult one, as many interpreters of this famous text have recognised. William Judge, a theosophist leader, in his interpretation was reluctant to tackle the meaning of sacrifice on the ground that he would only expose himself to "a charge of madness, superstition or ignorance", though he tackled it somehow by giving an allegorical explanation.[1] There is no consistent view in the *Gītā* regarding the Vedic religion, the quintessence of which is sacrifice. Franklin Edgerton observes: "The curious manysidedness, tolerance or inconsistency—whichever one may choose to call it—of the *Bhagavad Gītā* ... is shown nowhere more strikingly than in its attitude towards what we may call orthodox established religion."[2]

One may take the same view regarding the attitude of the *Gītā* to the *Vedas* and sacrifice. The *Gītā* speaks about not only the ritual sacrifice of the brahmins but also war, the sacrifice of the kṣatriyas. It uses many terms like *yoga, karman, dharma* and *jñāna* for sacrifice. In terms of ideas and terminology, it presents a many-sided view-point. This in our opinion can be understood only in the light of the post-Vedic understanding of sacrifice. But first, we need to acknowledge the variety of perspectives and conclusions that have coloured the concept of sacrifice in the *Gītā*. In the vedāntic approaches, it is particular metaphysical positions that colour the interpretation. Śaṃkara, for example, interprets these verses from an advaitic point of view. Although he holds that Viṣṇu the creator God assumed the form of Kṛṣṇa to restore the brāhmaṇic *dharma*, as far as ritual sacrifice is concerned one should transcend it by performing the superior form of *jñāna yajña* in order to attain Brahman, the supreme reality. Then for the sake of consistency he interprets in his own way certain key texts, some of which will be referred to in the course of this study. Similarly, for Rāmānuja and Madhva, ritual *yajña* may be taken as one form of worship of the supreme Lord. Later interpreters of the *Vedānta* take one of the above views though some would try to combine all of them.

The literary critics dissect the *Gītā* into many portions which in their view existed independently before they were compiled together. But they do not agree with each other as to the exact number of such portions. Particularly, their classification of different sections does not provide the key to the exact position of the *Gītā* on sacrifice.[3] Such theories have been refuted as highly conjectural. Further, there are a few discussions about slight variations between different manuscripts of the *Gītā*. But these do not suggest any insights about variation of the *yajña* verses.[4]

In the modern period covering the last two centuries, the position of the *Bhagavad Gītā* as a *smṛti* has been *de facto* elevated to that of a *śruti*.[5] This has led modern thinkers of Hinduism to believe that in a variety of ways they are in touch with the revealed truth which provides an esoteric understanding of the text, more authentic than that discovered by Indologists. After a survey of modern Indian interpretations of the *Gītā*, Robert Minor points out that they "differ at times considerably from the author of the *Gītā*, even to the extent of affirming another *Weltanschauung* altogether".[6] Here hermeneutics has tended to pass beyond the question 'What does this text mean?'[7] Allegorical interpretation seems to be dominant in modern interpretations. The theosophists started it and have also greatly influenced many interpreters of the *Gītā*. Thus for Tilak *yajña* means all duties and for Gandhi dedicated service by body-labour.[8] Vinoba talks about *bhoodan yajña* while Swami Bhaktivedanta calls for *saṅkīrtana yajña*.[9] Such interpreters are not concerned with the original meaning or meanings of *yajña* in the *Gītā*.

But those who have in different ways attempted to find the original position of the *Gītā* on *yajña* differ among themselves. For Charles Wilkins, the first translator of the *Gītā* into English, the purpose of the *Gītā* appeared to be to set the doctrine of the Godhead "in opposition to idolatrous sacrifices, and the worship of images to undermine the tenets inculcated by the *Vedas*".[10] In the view of Dasgupta, however, "The *Gītā* admitted that the sacrifices produced the good of the world, but its whole outlook was different; for the *Gītā* looked upon the sacrifices as being bonds of union between gods and men".[11] After some discussion, however, the same scholar writes that "the attitude of the *Gītā* towards Vedic performances is merely one of toleration and not one of encouragement."[12] Panikkar holds that the *Gītā* "offers an extraordinarily well integrated conception of sacrifice. It maintains, though a little in the background, the ancient Vedic vision; it accepts the Upaniṣadic interiorization and it adds the element of love, of *bhakti*, of personal involvement".[13] He adds further, "The new path does not reject tradition; it conserves, rather, its essential values while at the same time deepening and purifying them: it brings them within the grasp of the ordinary Man".[14] It is an integral sacrifice, for Panikkar, combining cosmic, anthropomorphic and theistic elements. Upadhyaya sees the elements of rejection, purification and acceptance of Vedic sacrifice. In his words, "the sacrifice is taken in three different senses, rejected in the first sense, undermined in the second and accepted in the third sense".[15] Kosambi finds that since different views are claimed to come from the one God there is no polemic in the *Gītā*, "though Vedic *yajña* and ritual in general are slighted with a passing sneer".[16] Belvalkar points to the universalisation and purification of Vedic *yajña* in the *Gītā*.[17] D.S. Sarma writes:

> Rituals, sacrifices, popular forms of worship, severe penances, ascetic ways of life and cast-iron rules of traditional ethics are criticised in a spirit of sympathy and love and replaced by a purer and more inward and living religion. It is pointed out that rituals may be observed, but that they should serve to purify the heart. Sacrifices may be offered, but they should be the sacrifices of the spirit and not merely of material objects.[18]

For S.C. Roy, "the author of the *Gītā* maintains a conservative attitude and enjoins that sacrifice should be performed in the right spirit and in the right manner as enjoined by the scriptures and should not be renounced".[19] Many more examples could be given to show how diverse the scholarly opinion is about the attitude of the *Gītā* to Vedic sacrifice.

The large number of translations and commentaries do not give serious attention to a systematic understanding of sacrifice in the *Bhagavad Gītā*. Kees Bolle points out how the subject of sacrifice is generally among the most neglected subjects in translations. He says,

> Over and over the text speaks of the tradition, the age-old customs (*dharma*) that should be followed, practised. Ritual work, cult (*karma*) is to be performed and specific sacrifices (*yajña*) are to be brought, all in accordance with the established liturgy (*vidhi*). It is quite obvious from the existing translations that most scholars had a hard time evaluating all those references positively.[20]

Commentaries which follow the pattern of giving cross references and a verse-by-verse treatment depending on earlier interpretations are not of great use to clarify the actual position. Zaehner, for example, in his introduction to the main themes of the *Gītā*, describes almost all the elements of the teaching of the text on sacrifice but does not attempt a comprehensive treatment discussing the meanings and interconnections of these various elements.[21] More recently, Robert Minor's commentary on the *Bhagavad Gītā*, though it provides insights for interaction with many scholarly interpretations, takes an unhealthy bias in the understanding of sacrifice. Minor seems to suggest that the mention of Vedic *yajña* in the *Gītā* is provisional, setting a platform to suggesting higher forms of sacrifice. With reference to verse 6.1, for instance, he says, "Though the *Gītā* has not rejected Vedic rites, it has reinterpreted the idea of sacrifice so as to make Vedic ritual unnecessary and insignificant".[22] Had Minor given close attention to those passages of the *Gītā* that reaffirm the power and cosmic significance of Vedic *yajña* (e.g. 3.8–16) and the passages that press for the revival of the Vedic *dharma* directly and indirectly, he would not have come to this conclusion.

As we have noted earlier, Josep Neuner's essay on religion and rite in the *Gītā* recognises major aspects of *yajña* in the *Gītā*; but since his is a comparative study he does not discuss topic in detail. Jordens' response to the question how the *Gītā* reacts to the important religious heritage of *yajña* is: "Its reaction is one of progressive assumption and integration of *yajña* into an entirely new world-view and new ethic. This integration is naturally accompanied by a process of purification".[23] He also holds that there is deritualisation and profound ethical significance in this process which has the character of new wine contained in an old wine-sack.[24] These observations lack exactitude and perspective mainly because Jordens' study has no interest in seeing the post-Vedic developments in the concept of sacrifice and its related ideas to which the *Bhagavad Gītā* responds. All these different opinions and observations show the need for a more systematic study of sacrifice in the *Gītā* in the light of its original context.

2. Some Notes on the Setting of the *Gītā*

The range of the different scholarly opinions about when exactly the *Gītā* was produced covers a period of at least one thousand years, from 500 B.C. to A.D. 500.[25] Few of the opinions are based on detailed reasoning. Robert Minor is one of the few who has taken pains to discuss the probable period of the *Gītā* at length. Without stating his arguments, we may accept his conclusion that the *Gītā* probably dates around 150 B.C.; this stands, as he says, "without much evidence, but recognising this low probability conclusion may be the highest probability one can attain".[26] This conclusion is in agreement with the opinion of the majority of scholars.

What is remarkable is that the *Gītā* emerged in the post-Buddha period. K.N. Upadhyaya's study of early Buddhism and *Gītā* points out many ideas, words and expressions in the latter which appear to counter the Buddhist views. At the same time, he places the *Gītā* some time between the fifth and fourth centuries B.C. following immediately the period of the Buddha.[27] It stands to reason, however, that the influence of Buddhism found in the *Gītā* is of a later period. Further, we need to take into account the reformations of Aśoka as well. Richard De Smet seems to be right when he situates the *Gītā* during the first post-Aśokan century (i.e. also the second century B.C.); he shows "the intrinsic consistency which accrues to *Gītā*-hermeneutics within the historical perspective opened up by it".[28] The reference to Aśoka is very important for our discussion. We have seen in the last chapter the revival of Vedic religion and sacrifice at the turn of the second century B.C., following the decline of the Mauryan empire when Puṣyamitra established the Suṅgan dynasty. We also noted brāhmaṇic assimilation of *śramaṇa* ideals and amalgamation with other cults, particularly the *bhāgavata* cult. Further, with reference to the reaffirmation of Vedic *dharma* and *yajña* in a new way in the *Gītā*, we can take Kṛṣṇa and Arjuna as counter-figures to the Buddha and Aśoka. We shall discuss this reaffirmation later. In the light of all these observations the middle part of the second century B.C. is the most probable period of the emergence of the *Gītā*.

Coming to the scriptural context, we see that the *Gītā* shares some of the concerns of the *sūtra* and *śāstra* writers regarding new practices added to *yajña* as equally meritorious. We shall make special reference to the *Mānavadharmaśāstra* when we explain certain *yajña* verses of the *Gītā*. Further, while the *Gītā* refers to *Brahmasūtras* (13.4), Bādarāyana quotes the *Gītā* twice; then the *Brahmasūtra* in the *Gītā* is likely to have been some collection antedating Bādarāyana.[29] With reference to the definition of the knowledge of *dharma* noted in the first two *sūtras*, the basic text of the *Mīmāmsa Sūtras* ascribed to Jaimini may be taken to belong to the pre-*Gītā* period.[30] More significantly, the *Gītā* now stands as part of the *Mahābhārata* even if its relationship with the latter is greatly disputed.[31] While many consider the *Gītā* as a later interpolation, Sukthankar, for example, states, "The *Gītā* is in fact the heart's heart of the *Mahābhārata*, and the *Mahābhārata* is a sort of necessary commentary on the *Gītā*".[32] In any case, as far as the idea of sacrifice is concerned, in terms of expression, style, and didactic nature the *Gītā* shares the general trends of the *Mahābhārata*. As we have seen, the process of brāhmaṇic synthesis is amply evident in the *Mahābhārata*. The same may be said of the *Gītā*.

The nature of the synthesis in the *Gītā* will become clear when we examine its position on sacrifice. It should be noted again that the situation that necessitated the emergence of the *Gītā* seems to have been marked by an interaction between many traditions and viewpoints. As Belvalkar notes, in the *Gītā* we see "a synthesis undertaken by a master-thinker who felt the urge for it in order to meet certain social, philosophical, and religious situations that had threatened to become explosive."[33] A recognition of this peculiar situation is essential for a comprehension of the struggle of the *Gītā* to harmonise various meanings of sacrifice. That various meanings were combined in a complex way will become obvious if one presents the *yajña* verses in the order of the text.

We classify those verses which have the verb *yaj* or the noun *yajña* as well as a few cases of *prayacchati* and *arpaṇam* (offering). Many more may be referred to, which are related to ideas of sacrifice. We are aware that translators are not consistent in rendering certain terms in certain places. Kees Bolle, for example, in a number of places translates *karma* as ritual or cultic acts (2, 48; 3.8, 20, 25; 4.12, 18; 6.3, 4; 12.6, 10; 16.24; 18.2, 7, 9, 10; 18.23, 24, 41). But viewed in the context this appears far-fetched. The following discussion on the attitude of the *Gītā* to sacrifice in the context of different interpretations is based mainly on the *yajña* verses although the overall messages of the text is kept in mind.

3. An Affirmation of Vedic Sacrifice

We can tell that the verses of the *Gītā* that reaffirm the validity of Vedic sacrifice appear rather abruptly. No systematic and detailed description is given. It is remarkable, however, that, though briefly, the *Gītā* recognises the major aspects of sacrifice. It refers to old sayings, adds new meanings and provides new expressions.

(i) Sacrifice as Primeval Creation

The *Gītā* declares that in ancient times, or in the beginning (*purā*), Prajāpati, the Lord of all creatures, created *yajña* along with the creatures or humans (*prajā*). He said to them, "by sacrifice you propagate or multiply and may the sacrifice be your cow of desire" (*kāmadhuk*, 3.10). As we have seen, according to the *Brāhmaṇas* Prajāpati is the creator god *par excellence.* From him were born the gods, *asuras* and all other creatures. He also emitted the *yajña* as his own counterpart. The primeval creation of *yajña* was later reaffirmed by the brāhmaṇic writers.[34] But at one point Prajāpati's supremacy was questioned; and he was brought to a lower position as teacher, as we noticed in the *Upaniṣads.* Nevertheless the *Gītā* acknowledges him as the creator.

Strikingly, however, the *Gītā* omits an important item in Prajāpati's creation. According to the *Brāhmaṇas* Prajāpati created the world, creatures and sacrifice through a process of self-sacrifice or self-immolation.[35] The perpetual self-sacrifice of the creator and his reorganisation is symbolically represented by rituals like the *agnicayana.* The omission of this idea in the *Gītā* is very significant in view of its concept of a Supreme God, as we shall see later.

The accommodation of the role of *kāma* in the *Gītā* may also be noted. According to the creation account involving Prajāpati, he created out of *kāma* (desire) and *tapas*(austerity). And he created sacrifice as a cow of desire (*kāmadhuk*).[36] As we have seen, the tendency to excessive desire for material wealth was denounced by the *śramaṇa* teachers. In the brāhmaṇic reaction we noticed the attempts to accommodate *kāma* within the goals and stages of life. The *Gītā* seems to share this concern. So long as there is a recognition of Vedic sacrifice one cannot exclude *kāma* as the prime motive of sacrifice.

(ii) Sacrifice as Effecting Mutual Sustenance between Gods and Human Beings

The *Gītā* continues its reference to the saying of Prajāpati. By sacrifice the gods and humans sustain or foster each other (*parasparam bhāvayantah*). Strengthened by the sacrificial food, the gods will fulfil the *kāma* of the sacrificers. Those who enjoy the benefits of gods but do not give to them in return are thieves (3.11, 12; also 4.12). The earliest form of Vedic sacrifice, namely food offered to gods, is recalled here.[37] Even after sacrifice was developed into a ritual mechanism with autonomous power, the idea of feeding gods continued. We noted how the development of *saṃnyāsa,* which reduced the ritual activities, was thought by a *sūtra* writer to weaken the gods. Here also the concern is expressed that gods, the food-givers, should not be forgotten; no one should rob them of their food, the oblations in sacrifice.

Not only food and material well-being but also greater benefits accrue from sacrifice. By offering food to the gods, one attains the highest good (*śreyah param,* 3.11). Śaṃkara and Rāmānuja interpret *param* here as *svarga* and *mokṣa* respectively. This is in order to set a background for the nature of liberation as they intend to expound.[38] But the word *param* occurs in the *Vedas* to denote the highest world and in the *Upaniṣads* to describe Brahman, the Supreme Reality.[39] Therefore, the intention of the author in putting it in abstract terms 'highest good' seems to point to the highest merit one can gain by performing sacrifice. In 4.12 the word success (*siddhi*) is used. This success comes swiftly when food is offered to gods. This may indicate all sorts of well-being—offspring, wealth, victory in war, etc.—attached to sacrifice in the *Vedas.*

So far the *Gītā* quotes Prajāpati's saying in 3.10–12. As Zaehner and K. Bolle do, it is appropriate to close the quotation with 3.12 and take verses 13–16 as being said by Kṛṣṇa. The leavings of the sacrifice mentioned in 3.13 (also in 4.31) point out another element. It is unique in Vedic sacrifice that the sacrificers have only a share in the leavings after the gods and priests are fed. In many places in the *Vedas*, these leavings are described as a force in which rest all powers including the divine powers of Prajāpati and other gods. It is by the sacred power of the leavings that the sacrificers (*yajamānas*) gain vigour, prosperity, progeny, cattle, fame and glory. Therefore, it is said, one must be careful not to eat before the gods are fed.[40] Here, to eating the leavings of the sacrifice, the *Gītā* attaches one more value, a new meaning, namely freedom from sin and taint (*pāpa* and *kilbaṣaiḥ*, 3.13). Śaṃkara defines sin and taint here as sacrificial offences in ritual performance as well as involuntary acts of injury; others interpret it as attachment to action.[41] With reference to 1.36 where *pāpa* occurs in a general sense of killing, it is appropriate, however, to take it to mean all immoral acts that go against personal integrity and social order. As rewards for eating the leavings of sacrifice, 4.31 has the words *amṛta* and *sanātana brahman*. The word 'brahman' is given a wide range of interpretations.[42] If immortality denotes the Vedic meaning of long life here as well as in heaven, *brahman* may also denote the permanent life in the *brahma loka* as mentioned in the *Upaniṣads*. The verse ends with the statement, "This world is not for him who performs no sacrifice, and much less the other world". Perhaps the author wants to combine the Vedic meaning and the Upaniṣadic meaning of the other world.

Reverting to 3.13, it is said that the opposite of eating the leavings of sacrifice is cooking for one's own sake, which leads to evil (*pāpa*). This seems to attack those who stopped sacrificing, in the belief that the gods had nothing to do with the production of food. To convince such people, the *Gītā* seeks to give an explanation of sacrifice as producing food.

(iii) Yajña as the Cosmic Wheel

As we saw earlier, in its highly elaborated mechanical form, sacrifice was believed to produce power that sustained the universal order and operation. But for the first time, following its insistence on offering food to gods, the *Gītā* introduces a strange scheme of cosmic function centring around sacrifice, i.e., the *yajña cakra*, the wheel of sacrifice. This scheme seems to be a problem by itself and is difficult to explain.

As early as 1928 J.O. Schrader complained that no western scholar had tried to explain the *yajña cakra*. Schrader himself tried to explain it with reference to two Upaniṣadic passages. Actually, however, those passages do not speak about *yajña cakra*; they only allegorise ritual with cosmic forces; and the links they try to make are completely different from that of *yajña cakra*.[43] So far as known to me, T.G. Mainkar is the only scholar who, at least in passing, notes that the idea of the *yajña cakra* calls to mind the *dharma cakra* of the Buddha.[44] This connection is most appropriate because the wheel was a recurrent symbol in the Buddha's teachings, e.g., *dhamma cakka*, *bhava cakka* and *brahma cakka*.[45] When the Buddha preached his first sermon, he set the wheel of *dharma* into motion. Aśoka was invested with the mark of *cakravartin* holding the *dharma cakra*.[46] Gonda notes:

> The wheel is representative of the universality of the spiritual dominion of the Enlightened One, whose secular counterpart is the universal earthly monarch, both of them manifesting the same universal principle, the former on the spiritual and the latter on the secular plane. To roll or move the wheel belongs to a king: "I am that king, that peerless king of *dhamma*: in accordance with *dhamma* I roll my *cakka*" ("Wheel of Truth"). Needless to observe the Buddha is the *cakravartin par excellence*.[47]

The *Mahābhārata* mentions a Nāga king in whose kingdom the wheel of *dharma* was set in motion. One of his virtues is said to have been the performance of sacrifice.[48] The *Gītā*, perhaps adopting the Upaniṣadic style,[49] formulates a new wheel to counter the challenges of the Buddha who had great influence on Aśoka.

According to the *yajña cakra* of the *Gītā*, creatures come into being from food, food from rain, rain from sacrifice, sacrifice from *karman*, *karman* from *brahman*, *brahman* from the Imperishable (*akṣara*). *Brahman*, penetrating everywhere, is based on sacrifice (3.14–15). Both Śaṃkara and Rāmānuja quote Manu III.76 for an explanation of the functioning of the *cakra*. In this passage Manu explains that by performing sacrifice to the gods one supports the entire animal and vegetable world. Then he describes how rain is brought by sacrifice: the oblation duly cast into the flame ascends in smoke to the sun; from the sun it falls in rain; from rain comes vegetable food; and from such food animals derive their subsistence. We find that this scheme explains only the first part of the *yajña cakra* of the *Gītā,* and the second part is more important as it includes some fundamental categories of Indian thought.

As Julius Lipner notes, the text is puzzling on two counts: first, if *yajña* springs from *karman* and *karman* from *brahman,* in what sense is *brahman* based on *yajña* which derives from *brahman*? Second, no link between the first (creatures) and seventh (*akṣara* or Imperishable) members of the wheel is indicated. Reckoning that a great deal hinges on what is meant by *brahman* here, Lipner compares Śaṃkara's interpretation with that of Rāmānuja. He shows that "the structure of the self in Rāmānuja's system shows up through the fabric of his exegesis".[50] For Rāmānuja, *yajña* is that which is born out of *karman,* meaning different activities in ritual performance. He takes *brahman* as *prakṛti* and *akṣara* as the individual self animating a body. For Śaṃkara, *brahman* is the *Vedas, karman* the sacrificial ritual which produces the *apūrva* of *yajña* and *akṣara* the supreme Brahman. For Madhva, Brahman is the supreme Lord, *akṣara* the *Vedas* and *karman* the performance of duties and sacrifice.[51] Commentators generally take either of these explanations or give new explanations which in no way solve the problem. The basic reason for such variety of interpretation is the use of certain terms in the *Gītā* in different senses.[52] On the whole, as far as the *yajña cakra* is concerned, the *Gītā* seems to be more concerned with the *cakra* as symbol than analysing its links.

Thus the wheel of *yajña* is set in motion. The *Gītā* then commands that everybody in this world must turn the wheel (3.16). Otherwise they are evil in nature, sensual in their delight and live in vain. In other words, the worth of human living depends on regular participation in the functioning of the world by generating power through sacrifice. Evil, pleasure-grounded life and life in vain—all these denote selfish living or cooking food for one's own sake.[53]

(iv) Continuation of Sacrifice even in Saṃnyāsa

We discussed in the previous chapter the development of *saṃnyāsa* and its impact on the decline of sacrifice. In the artificial scheme of fourfold *āśrama dharma,* the final stage of *saṃnyāsa* was exempted from the performance of sacrifice though some *śāstra* writers emphasised the performance of *agnihotra* as long as one's life lasts.[54] According to Manu, though the *saṃnyāsin* can give up things like the sacrificial fire he must constantly study that part of the *Veda* which relates to sacrifice and gods.[55] There were diverse opinions about this issue on the one hand and total rejection of the *saṃnyāsa* stage on the other. In such a context in 18.1 Arjuna expresses his desire to know about the nature of *saṃnyāsa* and *tyāga*.

Kṛṣṇa answers: the renunciation of *kāma*-prompted *karman* is *saṃnyāsa* and the abandonment of the fruits of all works is *tyāga*, so the sages understand and the wise declare. Some say all types of action must be given up while others say that *yajña* should not. Learn from me about *tyāga*. The action of sacrifice should not be given up at all, because these acts purify the wise. Attachment to them and their outcome must alone be given up (18.2–6).

What is meant by "purifying the wise" is not clear. The *śramaṇas* taught that *yajña* would contaminate the mind. The *Gītā* reverses this teaching. Rāmānuja understands it as meditation which is worship. He says that "the aspirants after final release who perform such worship throughout their lives, they (i.e. the sacrifices etc.) are the destroyers of the ancient *karma* which obstructs the consummation of such worship".[56] Perhaps meditation on the act of sacrifice, that is, giving oblations into the fire, will help one to give up self-interest for rewards. In any case, playing the role of a *dharmaśāstra* at this point the *Gītā* strongly suggests that in one's life at no moment should the *karman* of *yajña* be given up. This ordinance, coming with supreme authority, may well have contributed greatly to the revival of sacrifice at the time of the *Gītā*.

(v) Minor Corrections in Attitude

In the wake of upheavals in the socio-economic structure, grand *yajña* rituals were possible only for rulers and wealthy people. The *śramaṇas* attacked the pride of the wealthy in their performance of grand rituals. Though the performace of such rituals and ceremonies was acceptable, even the *dharmaśāstra* writers admonished those who boasted about holding them. Manu, for example, says that one should not be proud of rigorously devoted performance of *yajña* and practice of *dāna*.[57] The *Gītā*, in its general description of the cardinal virtues and the deadly sins, says: "The deluded ones in their ignorance say, 'I am rich belonging to a good family; I will perform *yajña* and practise *dāna* by which I will rejoice...'; puffed up with self-conceit, pride and madness in wealth they sacrifice but only in name and not in the way prescribed" (16.15, 17).

The additional concern of performing sacrifice with the appropriate rules is clear in this passage. We shall later point again to the insistence of the *Gītā* on the performance of sacrifice in accordance with the prescribed rules. The primary concern here seems to be the purification of *yajña* from improper social prestige and inappropriate arrogant attitudes.

(vi) Incorporation of New Elements

In course of time many substitutory practices were developed as equally meritorious as sacrifice. While the *Gītā* speaks of only *yajña* in many places (e.g., 3.10–16), in some places it combines those substitutory practices with *yajña*. In one place only *yajña* and *tapas* occur together (5.29); in a few verses *dāna* is added (9.27; 15.25, 27; 18.3, 5); and in some other passages *svādhyāya* is added to the above list (4.28; 8.28; 11.48, 53; 16.1; 17.23, 24); making vows (4.28) and ritual in general (11.48) are also included at two places.

The *tapas* (heat) produced by fire and cooking in the Vedic sacrifice was then interiorised and given the new meaning of actualising the inner forces through *yoga*. *Dāna* was an extended form of priestly *dakṣiṇā* of which the *śramaṇas* and *samnyasins* came to claim a share. Therefore *tapas* and *dāna* were understood as sacred acts along with *yajña* even in the *Upaniṣads*.[58] The study of the *Veda*, or the recitation of Vedic portions in a low voice came to be considered as a sacred act mostly in the *sūtra* and epic times as we noted in the last chapter.[59] New substitutes for sacrifice like *vrata*, *tīrtha* and *pūjā* were prescribed mainly for poor people. The *Gītā*, however, incorporates only the practice of *tapas*, *dāna* and *svādhyāya*—practices seen to be pertinent mainly to the twice-born élite—as equivalent to *yajña*

There is also the incorporation of certain Upaniṣadic ideas of supreme reality. In 17.23–25 we see the appropriating of the triple *mantra*: *Oṃ*, *Tat* and *Sad*; this potent *mantra* is a pointer to *brahman* by which the *Vedas*, *Brāhmaṇas* and *yajña* were ordained. *Mantra* was regarded as generating power. "A *mantra* has an extraordinary potency, a potency out of proportion to its verbal content. It is not devoid of reality. A *mantra* is more effective than a cannon ball. It changes the direction of life".[60] Although for many the passage 17.23–25 has only the value of *mantra,* the *Vedāntins* and commentators have tried to interpret the terms of this *mantra* in different ways.[61] The attachment of these terms for the first time to the act of ritual is quite surprising. While for Otto this is part of the gloss of a brahmin, Modi thinks this is due to some modification of ritual done in the time of the *Upaniṣads.*[62]

The *mantra* is given to be uttered before one begins *yajña, dāna* and *tapas.* First, it points to *brahman.* We have already noticed the development of the idea of Brahman as meaning holy power resting in sacred utterance to meaning the Absolute. In which sense is it to be taken here? It is easy to understand the term in relation to sacred utterance, because it is mentioned in connection with *yajña* etc. Nevertheless, it is not totally irrelevant to construe it as meaning the Absolute. By relating the Absolute to the performance of sacrifice, however, the *Gītā* tries to strip it of its abstract and impersonal connotations. Further, even if the term stands for "all" or "ultimate" it cannot be understood without a pointer, a *mantra,* uttered in sacrifice.Thus this pointing *mantra* is intended not to abolish *yajña* but to give it a new perspective. Śaṃkara takes this *mantra* to purify the ritual and make its nature *sattvic.* For Ānandagiri, the threefold designation of Brahman removes the defects in the acts of *yajña, dāna* and *tapas.*[63]

To clarify further the significant connection of the terms of the triple mantra with ritual, we need to consider them individually. According to the *Brāhmaṇas, Oṃ* was the essence of a long process of sacrifice performed by Prajāpati.[64] This mystic syllable is extolled in the *Upaniṣads* as the embodiment of the totality of reality, or the imperishable Brahman. It is taken as the centre of *dhyāna.* Thus *Oṃ* is the essence of all beings, of the *Vedas* and the quintessence of the Supreme. It springs from the coalescence of *vāc* and *prāṇa.* It is the destroyer of fear and darkness as the weapon of the gods to overcome demons.[65] But even in the *Upaniṣads* sometimes this syllable is attached to the utterance of priests in a ritual performance.[66] The *Gītā* takes this syllable back to its connection with *yajña*. It commands the utterance of *Oṃ* at *yajña, dāna, tapas* by those who speak about Brahman (17.24). Thus the ritual power and cosmic power are conjoined once again.

Like *Oṃ*, the term *Tat* also represents the impersonal reality behind the universe. For Edgerton it suggests "the mystic, magic monism of the *Upaniṣads*".[67] The *Gītā* suggests that those who hunger for *mokṣa* perform *yajña, tapas* and *dāna* by saying *Tat*, but having no thought of *phala* (17.25). *Sad* means the real, truthfulness and existence. When it is used at *yajña* etc., according to the *Gītā*, it means steadfastness (17.27). In 17.28 *Sad* is identified with *śraddhā*, faith which is an important attitude involved in Vedic sacrifice. Without *Sad* in the above sense, the *Gītā* says, *yajña* becomes futile here and hereafter.

It becomes clear from the above that the *Gītā* incorporates into its affirmation of Vedic sacrifice some original ideas like *Oṃ*, *Tat* and *Sad* which in the *Upaniṣads* meant the ultimate. In other words, it counters the Upaniṣadic notion of deritualised reality by bringing back such fundamental categories and terms and using them as a powerful *mantra* at *yajña, tapas* and *dāna*. The attempt is not confined to the *Gītā*. Manu, for example, considers the three *mantras*, *Oṃ*, *Tat* and *Gāyatrī* as meritorious and sin-relieving; they are more powerful than *yajña*.[68] But the *Gītā* succeeds in relating such *mantra* to the performance of *yajña* so that no question of giving it up need arise. Thus the *Gītā*, while affirming Vedic sacrifice, accommodates new practices as equally meritorious and attaches new terms which were once used to indicate the reality beyond ritual sacrifice.

(vii) *Special Emphasis on the Vedic* Dharma *and the Sacrificial War*

We have consistently maintained in this study that *yajña* was central in the Vedic *dharma* with its close association with social stratification. In the wake of the *śramaṇa* movement, at stake was the Vedic class structure, along with this *yajña*-oriented religion. There was a great "confusion" of *varṇa*, which is evident in the repeated injunctions given to the kings that such confusion should not take place in their kingdoms.[69] The *Gītā* in its background has a great deal of emphasis on the preservation of the

Vedic social structure. Belvalkar finds in the text of the *Gītā* a great compromise which, he surmises, took place in order to ward off some uncommon danger threatening society. He says:

> The *Bhagavad Gītā* can then be understood as an effort on a great scale put forth by the older *śrauta* religion with its institutions of *yajña* and *varṇāśrama* to hold its own and to stem the gathering tide of heretic and agnostic speculations. Only so we understand the emphasis laid by the *Bhagavad Gītā* upon *svadharma* or *śāstravihita karman*, when the author probably knew full well that the voice of revolt had already been raised against all those *śāstric* institutions.[70]

In Van Buitenen's words, when "Neither the religious enthusiast nor unsocialised ascetics could offer stability to an expanding society that was badly in need of it", "Kṛṣṇa came to the fore ... who was made to reveal himself as the guarantor of social stability, and the upholder of the *dharma*".[71] In the discussion on Vedic sacrifice we pointed out that sacrifices were the first ordinances (*dharma*) according to the *Vedas* which were supposed to maintain the cosmic and social order.[72] The Buddha redefined the meaning of *dharma* giving it only the ethical content. The revivalist literature emphasised the *yajña*-viewpoint of *dharma* although the ethical dimension was incorporated.

Now Arjuna and Kṛṣṇa are standing in a field of *dharma*. One may find, as Gonda does, in this picture the old friendship between Arjuna, a son of Vedic Indra and Viṣṇu who is incarnate in Kṛṣṇa, has recovered from a breach.[73] The culmination of this friendship in the *Gītā* lies in moral and spiritual assistance towards salvation. But the ethical emphasis of the *Gītā*, which has been extolled in modern interpretations, should be distinguished from ethics in the popular sense. The *dharma* affirmed here, as Austin Creel argues, does not allow for any revision by calculation and evaluation but demands an uncritical obedience.[74] Hence Kṛṣṇa's command not to give up *yajña* and war, the sacrifice of a warrior.

Arjuna is standing in the field of *dharma* and Kuru (*dharma-kṣetre kuru-kṣetre*) as the *Gītā* begins (1.1). In Vedic references to *kurukṣetra*, it is the place of the sacrificial performances of the gods in which Viṣṇu, who is identified with sacrifice, holds supremacy.[75] Therefore it is reasonable to believe that the term *kurukṣetra* originally comes from a *yajña*-ground which was then attributed to a place near the Ganges Valley, the centre of brāhmaṇism. In order to emphasise *yajña* as fundamental to *dharma* it is also called *dharmakṣetra*. Further, *kurukṣetra* has gained now a new significance as the battlefield, the sacrificial ground of warriors. Paul Bowlby, after discussing how the term *yoga* in the *Gītā* is modelled on *yajña* and *dharma*, writes:

> Arjuna must, as he has in the past, fulfil his *kṣatriya dharma*, even at *kurukṣetra*, because it is the setting—the only setting—in which chance can be overcome in the ritual of enactment. The battle is to be seen as a liturgical event, not a means to an end. It is the setting in which Arjuna must, as participant, enact the proper liturgical form—to fight according to the convention of his *varṇa*.[76]

Further, *kṣatriya dharma* would be jeopardised by a complete withdrawal from ceremonial religion because both come from the same source, namely the *Vedas*.[77] The terms *karman* and *dharma*, as we saw, were very much ethicised in the Upaniṣadic period. It was the Buddhists who gave supreme position to *dharma*, which as a moral principle should govern the whole world. King Aśoka was understood as the real elect, dearly loved, to establish *dharma*. He became deeply despondent in the battlefield of Kalinga; this led him to a conversion experience. As a king he tried to bring all sects and all people under an all-embracing umbrella of *dharma* based on common human virtues and values. It was this understanding of *dharma* that disturbed the structure of Vedic *dharma* and created great confusion. By the time of the *Gītā*, Aśoka's reign had ended. In his place Arjuna stands in the same field of *dharma*, which is the field of *yajña*. Like Aśoka, Arjuna also is despondent in his mind on a battlefield. But the supreme command, more supreme than the Buddha, says that Arjuna must not retire from war (as Aśoka did), but face it and contribute to the restoration of the *yajña*-oriented Vedic *dharma*. From a historical point of view, it is not unreasonable in this way to compare Arjuna with Aśoka. More study is needed to clarify the relationship and distinction between the two; even scholars who take the historical milieu of the *Gītā* seriously, do not give sufficient attention to this interesting issue. We have, however, a few clues from various scholars to justify this comparison.[78] Most remarkably Carl Keller in an enlightening essay written in French in 1971 broke the ground for a new perspective in this regard, but this has not been followed up.[79] Keller compares violence and *dharma* in Aśoka's edicts with the teaching of the *Gītā*. Significantly, he calls Arjuna the second Aśoka.[80] He points out that the concern of the

Gītā for a particular *dharma* which it expresses by certain arguments challenges the more universal *dharma* of Aśoka. We shall point out briefly references to this concern in the *Gītā*.

The concern about the maintenance of *dharma* affirmed at the beginning of the *Gītā* may be seen as comparing Arjuna's attitude with that of Aśoka. The despondent Arjuna in the *dharmakṣetra* expresses concern about destruction of family (*kula*), the eternal law (*sanātana dharma*), mixture of *varṇa*, etc. (1.40–44). Kees Bolle observes:

> It could be argued that Arjuna finds himself close to Buddhism in his complaints at the beginning of the *Gītā* and lays out what seems a suitable counterposition to the *dharma -varṇa* system of Hindu tradition. If it is not called Buddhist, it seems implicitly Buddhist in that Arjuna, by abstaining from his duty as a warrior, thinks he opts for a "higher" *dharma* than the tradition calls for.[81]

Kṛṣṇa chides Arjuna for his fickle-mindedness and encourages him to fight for the restoration of *dharma*, even if many are killed in the process. Kṛṣṇa says that it is he who created the four *varṇas*, interpreting their structure in terms of the differentiation and relation of *guṇas* and *karman* (4.13). Then it is implied that the *dharma* of the brahmins is the performance of *yajña* and teaching of the *Veda*, though the *Gītā* makes primary reference to the *kṣatriya dharma*. It says: there is no higher good for a kṣatriya than a fight in accordance with *dharma* which leads him to *svarga* (2.21–37). It repeats the advice of Manu that doing one's own *dharma* even imperfectly is better than doing the *dharma* of others perfectly (3.35, 18.47).[82]

It is true that the *Gītā*, standing "beyond time", talks about extraordinary or special *dharma* also. But there are tensions between them. As Larson points out,

> at least on one level to interpret *mokṣa* in terms of the *dharma* of Arjuna and hence to synthesize or conflate the claims of ordinary and extraordinary *dharma*, there is a dynamic and dialectical tension between *dharma* and *mokṣa* in the *Gītā*; and, although the resolution of the tension in the *Gītā* moves in conservative direction, it is certainly no accident that Gandhi found resources in the text which led in quite a different direction.[83]

As far as the main thrust of the text is concerned, however, "if caste duties or customary duties come into conflict with special duties of non-injury (*ahiṃsā*), then the caste duties are to be followed in preference".[84] Then, for instance, one should not expect that the *Gītā*, with its mention of truth and love would allow a śūdra or a woman to perform *yajña;* its stress would be on the prescribed rules of *yajña* which forbid them.

Likewise, although *ahiṃsā* is one of the special virtues enjoined by the *Gītā* (10.5; 13.7; 16.2; 17.14), according to its teaching, a kṣatriya incurs no sin in killing his enemies in a dharmic war.[85] Like Manu and others it would hold that killing in sacrifice, or in war must be exempted. The idea of *ahiṃsā*, which the Jainas and Buddhists emphasised and which was incorporated into brāhmaṇism, emerged in a context of protest against killing a large number of animals in *yajña*. The Buddha said that a single killing would cause hundreds of births and he was opposed to brāhmaṇical sacrifices that entailed cruel killing of animals.[86] Whether this is doctrinally appropriate to Buddhism or Jainism is a different question. In any case, the Aśokan edicts ban killing of animals in any form. Also, in certain passages of the *Mahābhārata ahiṃsā* is mentioned as a great virtue although it is admitted that killing in some form (e.g. while walking or ploughing) is unavoidable in life.[87]

Does the *Gītā* support killing in sacrifice? Mahadev Desai, who presents the *Gītā* according to the understanding of Gandhi, says that "there is not a trace of it in the sacrifice in the *Gītā* sense".[88] It is true that the *Gītā* does not explicitly speak about the killing of animals in sacrifice. But references to Prajāpati's creation of *yajña* etc. imply killing. The reason why this is not specified is that the *Gītā* is more concerned about the act of sacrifice than its forms. Yet more remarkably, by its repeated reinforcement of the idea of the indestructibility and invulnerability of the soul (2, 17–21, 23–27), it justifies killing. This implies that the *Gītā* has no difficulty in upholding the epic and *śāstra* view of killing in sacrifice. While according to Buddhism, soldiers killed in war cannot but go to hell or be born in an animal species, the *Gītā* promises heaven for them.[89] It is not without reason that Rāmānuja justifies killing in war with reference to 2.31 and supports his view with illustration from Vedic sacrifice. He states:

> In the *agnisomiya* and such other sacrifices, no injury is done to the animal sacrificed, because the *śruti* declares that the giving up (by the sacrificial victim) of an inferior type of body such as that of the goat etc. precedes the attainment of an auspicious body and of *svarga* and such other happy results.[90]

In this connection Rāmānuja refers to *TaiBr,* III.7.2 which addresses a victim in sacrifice saying, "you never die but go through blissful paths to the gods". He also illustrates that just as lancing and such other operations of a surgeon are for the protection of a suffering patient sacrificial slaying is only for the protection of animals.[91] Here Rāmānuja mixes two traditions. In his reference to the *brāhmaṇa* text, for example, there is no mention of the soul; and his second illustration may drift into an unreflective act of killing with dependence entirely on the ever-lasting survival of the soul.

The spiritualised interpretation of war, which is the setting for the *Gītā,* as a war between good and evil and between the higher and the lower faculties of human personality—as given by earlier theosophists and later by people like Gandhi and Radhakrishnan,[92] —merely clouds the main issue of the *Gītā,* whose emphasis is on *dharma* based on *yajña.* The *Mahābhārata* declares that war is necessary for the maintenance of *dharma* and it is the sacrifice of the kṣatriyas which leads them to *svarga.*[93] The *Gītā* also seems to echo the view that war is in some way endemic to the human condition and the absolute abandonment of *hiṃsā* is impracticable.[94] Bazaz contends (without having any sympathy for the context of preserving an eternally designed law) that the *Gītā* enunciates the theory of murder with impunity which has no concern about the killers; for according to Kṛṣṇa they are only instrumental in killing enemies whom he himself has already killed.[95] Hence the difficulty in holding absolute *ahiṃsā* on the basis of the *Gītā.*

The contradiction between the teaching of *ahiṃsa* as a virtue and Kṛṣṇa's command to kill creates a tension between the two. A. Sharma sees the force of this contradiction in Gandhi and Godse, who personify the ethical dilemma of the *Gītā.*[96] Mrinal Das Gupta sees a reversal of the concern of the *bhāgavatas* in the insistence of the *Gītā* on killing because the *bhāgavatas* emphasised non-killing, vegetable offering etc.[97] Jaiswal seems to answer for this complaint when she says that perhaps the setting of the poem in a battleground militated against the principle of *ahiṃsā.*[98] It must be noted, however, that the *Gītā* seems to try deliberately to counter the tendency to look upon war with contempt and renounce it in the name of *dharma,* as is evident from certain passages of the *Mahābhārata.*[99] It also emphasises that in fulfilling a *sanatana dharma,* which is *yajña*-based, killing should not be evaluated from the viewpoint of common virtue. One who worries, about this aspect, it says, only betrays his ignorance of the "self" which never slays and is never slain. Further, as Keller rightly points out, Aśoka's *dharma* is universal and monolithic in comparison with the particular and differentiated *dharma* of the *Gītā.* Aśoka's *dharma* is dynamic and revolutionary; the *dharma* of the *Gītā* is counter-revolutionary and conservative. But Keller does not fail to note that the concern and commitment of the *Gītā* to a particular tradition is more genuine and truthful than Aśoka's concern that precludes any debate and obscures the distinctive nature of each religion.[100] Thus the *Gītā,* standing firm in tradition, recalls the age-long battle between the gods and the *asuras.* It reaffirms with supportive points taken from its own and other traditions, the need for fight which takes the form of war. This is part of the overall reaffirmation of Vedic *dharma* and its *yajña.*

4. Mention of a Variety of Sacrifices

The *Upaniṣads* define the meaning of sacrifice in countless ways. The allegorical interpretation, interiorisation and ethicised interpretation do occur in the Upaniṣads, but together with the continuation of ritual. The major lead was to *yajña* in introspection and inner descent, so that the substratum of reality, the *brahman* or *ātman,* may be reached. Hence the development of *jñāna yajña* and *ātma yajña.* The *Gītā,* on the other hand, mentions various types of *yajña* without caring to explain their nature and final end as originally developed. Let us consider these.

(i) Deva Yajña *and* Dravya Yajña

We have already seen the affirmation of gods who depend on sacrificial food and who in turn fulfil the desire of the sacrificer. As against certain *Upaniṣads* and *śramaṇa* movements, the *Gītā* accepts the independent existence of the gods. The worshippers of the gods, the *Gītā* says, go to the gods (7.23; 9.25). But the *Gītā* brings the gods under the supremacy of Kṛṣṇa, as we shall point out later. Sacrifice to the gods is mentioned as one form of *yajña* and for some adepts the gods are the sole object (4.25).

Sacrifice of substance or wealth (*dravya yajña*) is variously interpreted, such as the practice of generosity and giving away wealth and money to be spent on divine worship.[101] But there is no reason to deny the meaning of *dravya* as materials used in a ritual. In a simple form it is food offered to the gods, in an elaborate form a number of animals sacrificed and other objects used in ritual.

(ii) Adhyāya Yajña

As noted earlier, ritual sacrifice was allegorised as the sacrifice of the study of the *Veda.* Thus, it is said, speech, mind, the eye, mental power, truth, *Ṛg-Yajus-Sāma* texts, precepts, dialogue, *itihāsa, purāṇa* etc. are parts of an *adhyāya yajña*; these are substitutes for spoon, grass, milk-offerings etc. in a ritual performance.[102] The *Dharmaśāstras* regard the study of *Veda* (*svādhyāya*) to be as efficacious as sacrifice.[103] We have already seen how the *Gītā* incorporates this practice along with *yajña* and *dāna.* In 4.28 it mentions it as a particular type of sacrifice.

(iii) Indriya, Prāṇa, Yoga, Tapas *and* Jñāna Yajñas

All these may be classified as one category for the simple reason that in the *Upaniṣads* all these form the common *jñāna yajña.* Curiously enough, the *Gītā* uses the term *jñāna yajña* as one separate type (4.28). We shall discuss the significance of this and its relation to other forms of sacrifice in a later section.

In the *atma yajña* of the *Upaniṣads,* we noticed different layers in the inner journey of a seeker of the self. Sacrificing progressively senses, speech, mind and breath one finally reaches or realises the self. *Tapas* and *yoga* help in the process. But the *Gītā* does not make any attempt to describe the processes of an inner vision through interior sacrifices, and only mentions them individually (4.26–39). Perhaps it carefully avoids the tendency to take the interior vision as the ultimate one. In its description of *dhyāna,* where the process ends, in the place of Brahman or Atman, Kṛṣṇa places himself as the ultimate goal as we shall notice later. Moreover, a new definition of *tapas* is given in 17.14–16 which speaks about the *tapas* of *śarīra, vāc* and *manas.*

Since the *Gītā* does not explain each type of these internal sacrifices, we are not able to know the desired goals in their performance. One clue comes from Manu. Following his insistence on the *pañcamahāyajña* Manu says that some make continual offerings in their own organs of sensation and intellect; some consistently sacrifice their breath in their speech when they contemplate in silence; and in their speech and breath, thus employed, they see the imperishable fruits of a sacrificial offering.[104] Perhaps the *Gītā* wants simply to acknowledge different sacred performances, leaving the question of fruit for each individual, but no one can dispense with the ritual *yajña* in its literal sense.

(iv) Japa Yajña

In 10.25 Kṛṣṇa says that of *yajñas* he is the *japa yajña. Japa* means repeated prayer or *mantra.* Radhakrishnan and Telang interpret it as silent meditation, which etymologically is inaccurate. In developing new substitutes for ritual *yajña* and *śāstra,* writers mention *japa yajña* as one of the forms of sacrifice. This practice would have come from the sacred utterance in the performance of Vedic sacrifice. Kane notes that according to the *śāstra* writers there are three kinds of *japa: vākya* (audibly uttered), *upāṃsu* (inaudibly uttered) and *mānasa* (mentally revolved), each succeeding one being ten times superior. This echoes the different tones adopted for *mantras* in Vedic sacrifice. Kane also points out in connection with sacrifice that the repetition of certain texts, *mantras* and the names of God in *japa* is a means of spiritual power. It purifies heat and helps concentration on God.[105] The connotation "concentration on God" is well applicable to the *Gītā* though the solitary mention of *japa yajña* is given no explanation.

(v) Brahma Yajña

The offering is *brahman,* the ghee is *brahman,* offered by *brahman* in the fire of *brahman.* He who is absorbed in the *karman* of *brahman* goes unto *Brahman* (4.24). Some sacrifice in the fire of *brahman,* "the sacrifice in sacrifce" (4.25). Various are the *yajñas* which are spread out in the mouth or face of Brahman. They all spring from *karman.* Once one knows this one will attain *mokṣa* (4.32).

We faced the difficulty of understanding "Brahman" as mentioned in the *yajña cakra.* In the above verses the difficulty is increased; consultation of various complicated interpretations given by *vedāntins* and commentators does not reduce this difficulty. Instead, we shall observe the cluster of meanings denoted by repetition of the same term to be one of the interpretive techniques of the *Gītā.*

Minor identifies four senses in which the term *brahman* is

used in the *Gītā*: the state of liberated consciousness or peace, *prakṛti* or the lower nature of God, the *Vedas*, and Kṛṣṇa himself as the supreme God.[106] Obviously this classification is based mainly on vedāntic interpretations. Tracing the etymological meaning and different connotations of the term *brahman*, R. Gotshalk gives the following note on its translation in the *Gītā*:

> ... the most common meaning in the *Gītā* is the divine or holy power itself. Although the term developed in this direction early, and gained (for example, in the *Upaniṣads*) numerous technical connotations and references thereby, the *Gītā's* usage, here as with *ātman*, seems free of confinement to a single determinant referent. Thus I have generally translated it simply "holy power".[107]

As we have pointed out earlier, from the *yajña* point of view, one may understand *brahma yajña* as the sum total of different types and dimensions of *yajña*. At least four dimensions are noteworthy here.

First, there is the aspect of ritual sacrifice in which *karman* and *brahman* are two fundamental centres of sacred power. The ingredients in a sacrifice like oblations, ghee and fire become attached to the sacred power. The one who is sunk or absorbed in the *karman* in a sacrificial enclosure, fulfilling a cosmic, eternal *dharma*, becomes the *brahman* or the holy power embodied; persons, utensils and water involved in a sacrifice were thought in the *Vedas* to become 'holy'.

Secondly, *brahman* is the personification of sacred or sacrificial fire. In the *Mahābhārata*, it is said, Brahman is Prajāpati, time, fire and so on.[108] This indicates the identification of *brahman* with all powers. As far as *yajña* is concerned, *brahman* is central. According to Zaehner,

> *Brahman* is not only based on the sacrifice but *is* the sacrifice and everything to do with it, just as Primal Man (*puruṣa*) is in ṚV. 10.90 and Prajāpati or Viṣṇu in the Brāhmaṇas. Brahman, however, is the link between the (sacrificial) action (*karman*) on the one hand and the Imperishable on the other (3.15), the link between the eternal and temporal, hence its presence "penetrating everywhere (s*arvagata*)" links the world of action (whether sacrificial or otherwise) with the imperishable sphere of wisdom.[109]

The terms "going to Brahman" and "spreading in the mouth of Brahman" are variously interpreted. Evaluating them, Hill suggests that the phrase "outspread at the mouth" or "gate of Brahman" "carries on the idea ... of going to Brahman" and all ...

various forms of sacrifice, provided that they are performed by 'knowers of sacrifice', are represented as 'spread out at the gate to Brahman' that each one may adopt for performance the sacrifice he prefers, and nonetheless enter through the door to Brahman".[110] We may, however, recall the original personification of the holy power in Brahman, the officiating priest. Then all sacrifices are outspread in his mouth, since the perfection of a sacrifice depends on his careful utterance. He also stands as a symbol of transcendental wisdom by which one goes beyond the ritual *karman*. Thus Brahman is both the personification of *yajña*, the supreme God, and also the link between ritual *karman* and transcendental wisdom, or between temporal power and the Imperishable.

Third, though the fire of *brahman* and "sacrifice in sacrifice", mentioned in 4.25, is interpreted variously, the element of interiorisation is quite evident in these phrases. Is this the offering of the self by self as Śaṃkara explains? Is it sacrifice with apparatus used in Vedic sacrifice as Rāmānuja thinks? Is it a mental sacrifice in which there is identification of the conditioned self with the Absolute self? A. Sharma suggests that the entire statement may be clearly understood in terms of fire sacrifice. He points out various facets of *agni*: messenger to the gods, link between the worlds of gods and men, and these worlds and nature by the various physical forms of fire, the sun kindled by the gods in heaven and by men on earth, that present in water and brought down by lightning, thunder and rain, latent in streams and ponds and passed into plants, from which fire again could be kindled. "Completing the cycle, Agni in plants was seen as offering himself to himself in fire, rising again in smoke to the clouds".[111] It may be useful to recall here Heesterman explaining the enigmatic Vedic phrase "sacrificing sacrifice in sacrifice" as implying that the sacrificer and the victim are amalgamated into a single identity, namely sacrifice.[112] Hill takes it to mean the performance of ordinary outward ceremonial acts while the mind is fixed not on any god but on the Absolute Brahman.[113] Modi takes it as referring to the Puruṣa whom the gods offered as a sacrifice in the *Ṛgveda*.[114] On the whole, though it may be taken in the Upaniṣadic sense of internalisation, there is no reason to preclude the possibility of it meaning the Vedic experience of ritual sacrifice, particularly the sacrificer's relationship with fire, victim and universe.

Fourth, the *brahma yajña* indicates a liberated state of consciousness. Through *yajña karman* it is possible to achieve what Zaehner calls ecstasy (*samādhi*).[115] It may be defined as mental equanimity against all opposites (2.48) and the abandonment of 'I' ness and 'my' ness (18.53, 54). While one Upaniṣadic strand tries to make absolute this state of consciousness detached from ritual *yajña*, the *Gītā* seems to make it relative and attaches it to *yajña*. Thus, on the whole, the text develops a spirit of accommodation without shaking the foundation of Vedic *dharma*.

5. *Yajña* Interpreted through *Sāṃkhyan* Categories

Some of the fundamental interpretive categories of the *Gītā* come from *Sāṃkhya-Yoga*, the earliest formulation of which is found in the *Mokṣadharma* of the *Mahābhārata*. Kṛṣṇa claims that it is he who first proclaimed it to the ancient *munis* (4.1–3). How far the *sāṃkhya-yoga* categories of the *Gītā* are consistent with the original scheme is a different question which needs separate study in detail. We have already noted the non-Vedic origin of *Sāṃkhya*. As Gotshalk observes, "The *sāṃkhya* to which Kṛṣṇa is appealing ... seems to be an early form of what probably was originally a non-Vedic mode of thought but was gradually assimilated into the Vedic streams in close connection with the *Upaniṣads*."[116]

It is rather far-fetched that the *Gītā* attaches ritual sacrifice to the three *guṇas* of *Sāṃkhya*. J. Neuner notes that by turning a philosophical category towards a ritual system the author of the *Gītā* shows himself as overwhelmingly conservative.[117]

In the *Gītā* divine power is in places identified with "*prakṛti*" seen in a realist sense. This is higher than the material nature characterised by its three *guṇas*. Higher *prakṛti* is *jīvabhūta* (7.5) which becomes manifested in *jīvas*, called *dehīs*, *śarīrīs* and *puruṣas*. This two-foldedness of *prakṛti* seems to do away with the original Sāṃkhyan dualism of *puruṣa* and *prakṛti*. Kṛṣṇa's relationship with *prakṛti* is that of a dialectic; he plants seed in *prakṛti* as the *mahatbrahman* (7.4–15) but stands above it unattached. Then what is the nature of *triguṇa* as understood and related to *yajña* in the *Bhagavad Gītā*?

According to the *Gītā* the three *guṇas—attva, rajas, tamas—* are innate and born of *prakṛti* which in turn fetters the changeless embodied one in the body (14.5). When *sattva* dominates, one becomes spotless, clean, healthy and bound to happiness and knowledge. At the dawn of *jñāna* it dominates and leads to the highest fruits, namely the spotless *brahman,* and uplift. *Rajas* produces passion, craving and attachment, binds the *ātman* to *karman.* It leads to *karma saṃsāra* and its fruit is pain. *Tamas* lacks *jñāna* and produces delusion, heedlessness, indolence and sleep. It leads to rebirth as a fool with the fruit of *ajñāna.* While the paths of *sattva* and *rajas* are upward and middleward respectively, the process of *tamas* is downward (13.6–27). At liberation one passes beyond these *guṇas* (14.26, 27). Though the Lord is imperceivable in his embodiment he is also *guṇa*-bound in a sense (15.7–11).

Arjuna asks about the consequence of these *guṇas* on those who sacrifice with *śraddhā* (17.1). Kṛṣṇa answers: The *sattva*-dominated ones sacrifice to gods for the sake of divine worship, following prescribed rules, yet with no regard for rewards. The *rajas*-dominated ones sacrifice to *yakṣas* and *rākṣasas,* aiming at rewards, and perform with hypocrisy. Those who are overpowered by *tamoguṇa* sacrifice to spirits and ghosts of the deceased ones, lacking faith, ritual prescription, sharing and correct payment of *dakṣiṇā* to priests (17.4, 11–13).

Minor refutes Radhakrishnan's interpretation of the sattvic *yajñas* as dedicated service and philanthropy and argues that they are in the *Gītā* most naturally taken as references to Vedic sacrificial-type ceremonies. He points out that the reward-desiring rajasvic sacrifice is opposed to the later *mīmāṃsā* school which held that the highest justification of sacrifice and other acts was the reward attached to it. From the warning given about performing *yajña* without following rules and not giving *dakṣinā,* which belongs to *tamas,* Minor remarks: "Such sacrifices as the *Gītā* describes as tamasic may be those of the lowest class which was unable to afford such luxuries as having priests in the ceremony."[118] This observation cannot, however, go unchallenged since other categories do not give any clue for an economic analysis. Even if implications to this effect may be derived from them from a socio-economic perspective, at this juncture we are more concerned about the appropriateness of the interpretation of different kinds of sacrifice through the sāṃkhyan category of *triguna* in the *Gītā.*

Yajña is not the only category interpreted in the *triguṇa* scheme, but also cognisance (18.20–22), action (18.7–9, 23–25), intelligence (18.30–32), agent (18.26–28), food (17.8–10), firmness (18.32–35), happiness (18.37–39), *dāna* (17.20–22) and *tapas* (17.17–19). Following these kinds, the *Gītā* tries to relate the three *guṇas* to four *varṇas,* rather unsuccessfully because the numbers do not match. It describes the nature (*svabhāva*) of each *varṇa* and its action accordingly. Only the brahmins and the kṣatriyas are attached to certain peculiar qualities, whereas vaiśyas and śūdras are mentioned in connection with their work (18.40–44). Apparently it is an enthusiastic attempt to connect the Vedic categories with the categories of *Sāṃkhya* without worrying about the analysis of the connections. The *Sāṃkhya* of the *Mokṣadharma* mentions two *mārgas, pravṛtti* and *nirṛtti,* and there is no indication of Vedic *yajña.* Therefore it is an altogether new attempt in the *Gītā* to relate sacrifice to the *triguṇa* scheme of *Sāṃkhya.*

We shall briefly point out some problems in this interpretation of *yajña* in the *sāṃkhyan* categories of *triguṇa.* The *sattvic* type of *yajña, tapas* and *dāna* is marked by the fundamental character of *karma phala tyāga.* The *Gītā* earlier recognises *yajña* as *kāmadhuk.* Here the *sattvic yajña* is directed to the gods. The other two types (*rajasvic* and *tamasvic*) may be taken to oppose the Vedic spirit. But how do we reconcile the indispensable *kāma*-prompted *yajña* with *niṣkāma yajña* of *sattvic* nature? Is an idea of *niṣkāma yajña* taken as a model for *niṣkāma karman,* or is an idea of *niṣkāma karman* imposed on the *karma yajña*? We shall discuss this problem in the next section when we deal with *karma yajña.* In any case here the reward is not denied, since the *sattva yajña* is said to bind one to happiness and to knowledge.

One may argue that the *Gītā* speaks about various levels in understanding an act. But as far as its view is concerned—insisting on Vedic *yajña* to the end of life—there is no clear demarcation of levels. And more fundamentally, even if a particular attitude is operative due to the power of a particular *guṇa* springing out of *prakṛti,* is a person responsible for such an attitude? This problem remains unresolved, as acknowledged by scholars like Dasgupta. Moreover, the *Gītā* elsewhere describes different traits, without any differentiation, where *yajña, dāna, tapas* and *svādhyāya* are included in the divine traits as opposed to the demonic traits (16.1). Thus the *Gītā* can speak about diverse traits and attitudes even without reference to the *triguṇa.*

Another interesting issue related to the above is the attitude of the *Gītā* towards the *Vedas.* On the one hand the *Gītā* accepts uncritically the *sanātana dharma* of the *Vedas*. Kṛṣṇa asks Arjuna to obey the imperative of this *dharma* which leads him to *mokṣa*. On the other hand the *Gītā* tries to transcend the Vedic *dharma*. It says at one point that the *Vedas* have as their subject-matter action divided among the three *guṇas*. And breaking free from them is *sattvic* (2.45). Then the usefulness of the *Vedas* for a true brahmin or *jñāni* is like that of a well in a flood (2.46). In fact the earlier parts of the *Vedas* do not mention the *triguṇa* category; it is found only in a few later *Upaniṣads*.[119] So obviously it was an original attempt of the *Gītā* to find connections between the *sāṃkhyan* categories and the *Vedas*.

6. *Karma Yajña* and *Niṣkāma Karman*

The interpretation of *yajña* in the *Gītā* in relation to action (*karman*) is of great importance as it has shed great influence on the understanding of action in general in Indian thought. Aurobindo rightly observes, "The whole of the *Gītā*'s gospel of works rests upon its idea of sacrifice and contains in fact the eternal connecting truth of God and the world and works."[120] But the greatest difficulty in understanding *karman* in connection with *yajña* lies in the fact that in most of over 105 occurrences of the word '*karman*', apart from the occasional use of terms like *kārya*, it is not at all clear in which sense the *Gītā* uses the term—ritual, ethical or general. Bolle's translation of *karman* as 'ritual' in many places may be seen as untenable, as we have already noted.[121]

R. Panikkar identifies three ideas of *karman* operative in the Indian tradition—(i) the *cosmotheandric karman* of *yajña*, (ii) the path of good works, and (iii) as that which remains as the subtle structure of temporal reality which all existing beings share in common underneath.[122] In the priestly texts *karman* appears as a primordial act, the continuation of which is technically denoted in ritual *yajña*. The *Upaniṣads* interpreted *karman* as every action, as associated with *saṃsāra*. The *śramaṇas* explained *karman* and its effect in different ways. It should be noted, however, that in all interpretations, the power of the action was taken with the meaning that was originally attached to ritual. Accordingly, every minute act is affective. Hence the binding force of *karman*. It is the central concern of the *Gītā* to interpret the nature of *karman* and its binding force or attachment.

18.2–7 indicates *yajña*, *tapas* and *dāna* as acts of *karman*. About the *sāṃkhya* mode of functioning, Kṛṣṇa says that all beings go into his nature (*prakṛti*) at the time of universal destruction and he sends them forth again at the time of universal beginning. This happens at his behest. They are said to be his *karman* who do not bind him (9.7–10). Apart from such an occasional reference to a particular type of *karman*, we do not have a clear indication of the use of the term *karman* with a particular sense. For Gotshalk the *Bhagavad Gītā* seems to deny the traditional meaning of *karman* with overt social and ritual practice. He says, "Instead Kṛṣṇa views action broadly, as the engagement in effort which brings one's active being into play whether in overt action of one sort or another, or in overt inaction but in more subtle and hidden forms of inward effort."[123]

The idea of karmic power which is related to brahmic power originally comes from the context of Vedic ritual. Therefore, here our discussion on *karman* is confined to *yajña* as well as in relation to the subtly different kinds of effort and their accompanying attitudes.

(i) Karman *for* Yajña

In response to Arjuna's confusing question regarding action, and as a prelude to its affirmation of Vedic sacrifice, the *Gītā* declares: This world is in bondage to *karman* unless *karman* is performed for *yajña*; therefore act to this end, free from attachment (3.9). In 4.23, again as a prelude to the description of a variety of sacrifices, it is said: With attachment broken, deliverance won, thoughts fixed on *jñāna*, the *yogi* works for *yajña*, and *karma* entirely melts away. The important question that arises here is, what kind(s) of *karman* are intended or what kind of *yajña* is meant.

Recognising the mysterious idea of *karma* in Hinduism and the transition from ritual *karman* to action in general (which is reversed here) Zaehner observes, "The transition from the idea of 'work' or 'action' to that of 'sacrifice' is, then, given the Vedic background, in no way forced. Arjuna's present work in hand is to go to war, and war itself is a sacrifice."[124]

Śaṃkara's equation of *yajña* here with Viṣṇu is far-fetched. Again, does good *intent* and abandonment of personal interest matter here, as Minor thinks, or is the duality between ends and means abolished, as Nataraja Guru claims?[125] Edgerton points out that the saying "sacrifice has no binding effect" (3.9), which is said in the context of affirming mutual sustenance between gods and human beings (3.12), freedom from sin (3.13) etc., harαly goes with the theory of the ritual *karman* which seems to imply that its whole basis is a matter of selfish interest. He states further that this theory is not brought out clearly in later religious texts, including the *Gītā*, and it is "ignored or slurred over".[126]

R. Otto tries to explain that work for sacrifice in 4.23 is to emphasise knowledge for sacrifice. In his words, "The *jñāna* must be applied to the *yajña*; and then *yajña* is in no sense whatever conceived as a gift to the *Deity*, but in its magical sense as a self-acting or automatic ceremony (*pavitram*) and as a rich store of energy".[127] If we accept Otto's view, then verse 3.9, in which "*karman for yajñá*" finds mention for the first time, should be attached to the *yajña cakra* (3.14–16), skipping the reference to the *kāma*-based sacrifice for gods in 3.10–12. Moreover, the meaning of interest and attachment must be defined in a new way. In any case *karman* for *yajña* here cannot be simplified as a selfless action.

We shall discuss soon the place of personal interest in the performance of *yajña* within a cosmic perspective. Here it should be pointed out that even if one attaches the meaning of detached action to sacrifice, the verses that follow the *yajña cakra* description do not susbcribe to this view. 3.17 says: But the man who can be delighted, satisfied, content in his self (*ātman*) alone, has no obligatory duty (*kāryam*) to do. This is because, 3.18 notes, that person has nothing to gain by action or non-action and he need not depend on action for any advantage. This does not mean abandonment of action but performing it without attachment (3.19). This leads to the Supreme. By action alone Janaka and others ascended to ultimate perfection. Further, the insistence of the *Gītā* on ritual action till the end of one's life gains ample support for asserting non-abandonment of action. But regarding detachment and disregard of fruits the insight seems to come from somewhere else. It is noteworthy that even without reference to *yajña*, at many places the *Gītā* talks about action with detachment in general (e.g. 3.4–8, 31–32).

Tilak holds that the source of unattached action is the *pūrvamīmāṃsā* idea of *yajña*. But he does not explain this with reference to Jaimini. Rather, he insists on the idea that sacrifice cannot be performed without *karman*, therefore *yajña* is nothing but *karman*, created in ancient times. "But, as the sole purpose of this *karman* is *yajña*, and as the *yajña* is the duty of man, therefore, the fruit of this *karman* does not create a bondage for man."[128] The question here is not disregard for results but the unbinding nature of the *yajña karman*, for, as Tilak acknowledges, the type of *karman* done for cosmic well being is non-binding while the other type, performed for the benefit of the doer, is binding.[129] Further, Bazaz points out that the *mīmāṃsā* idea of the non-bindingness of *yajña karman* should be taken in relation to the idea of the categorical imperative of Vedic *dharma*. In his words, "And ordained *karma* is right because it is commanded by the holy scripture; it is a duty performed for its own sake; that it leads to a proper and desired end is only incidental. The essence of life consists in performing Vedic rituals."[130]

It is true that Jaimini's *Mīmāṃsa Sūtra* starts with the statement that its purpose is to explain *dharma*. As we have seen, it asks for an undilutable submission to the duty enshrined in the *Vedas* in terms of ritual action. But, to say that the "desired end is incidental" is not enough. Clooney writes,

> Unlike the *Bhagavad Gītā*, *Mīmāṃsā* is comfortable with the fact that humans desire results and does not ask that the performer be purified or learn to act for the sake of duty alone. It asks only that he admit that when he goes about seeking his own happiness he is nevertheless still part of something larger than himself, something that does not exist for his sake, the sacrifice.[131]

There was no such thing as the problem of binding in connection with the performance of Vedic sacrifice until the *śramaṇas* introduced it. The problem was closely related to their view of material *kāma* as evil. The life of renunciation which they developed affected the *yajña*-based Vedic religion considerably. The *pūrvamīmāṃsakas* countered this development by affirming the unbinding nature of ritual *karman*. If we assume that in the sense of non-desire the *Gītā* mentions the unbinding nature of action done for sacrifice (3.9) it cannot go well with its recognition of Vedic sacrifice, as *kāmadhuk* mentioned in the following verses (3.10-12).[132] Then it seems to share the *mīmāṃsakas'* concern to obey *dharma*. In any case it is a significant point in the hermeneutical process found in the *Gītā*. For *Gītā* such obedient action in sacrifice based on *kāma* is unbinding.

Another important reference for detached and unbinding action in the *Gītā* is to the works of Kṛṣṇa, the supreme Lord. He never renounces action but he acts with detachment in order to set an example for humans to follow (3.21–24). But this reference is of no help for our discussion on unbinding *yajña karman* because nowhere is he said to perform *yajña* as the Vedic gods do.

In the foregoing we have tried to identify the idea of detached action or unbinding *yajña karman* as coming from outside the *Gītā*, and directly or indirectly affecting the standpoint of the *Gītā*. There is, however, reference to bondage and freedom in the text of the *Gītā* itself. Kṛṣṇa says to the bewildered Arjuna that by the natural *guṇas* everyone is bound to act (3.5). *Karman* is accomplished wholly by way of the *guṇas* of nature; yet deluded by the sense of ego a self thinks: "I am the doer". He who knows the truth about the differentiation and relation of *guṇas* to *karman*, thinks, "*guṇas* are concerned with *guṇas*" and does not get attached (3.27, 28). Thus here, not *yajña* but the difference of *guṇa* is mentioned for detachment. Those who are deluded by the *guṇas* of *prakṛti* become attached to the *karman* of the *guṇas* (3.29). What is needed is knowledge; if one is imbued with the intelligence (*buddhi*) addressed in *sāṃkhya-yoga* one will leave behind the bondage of action (*karma bandha*, 2.39). The pictorial presentation of the Vedic tree indicates that it is rooted in *guṇas* and it can be cut off only with the firm sword of non-attachment in order to reach the permanent abode (15.1-3). What trait is required to transcend the *guṇa*-bound Vedic *karman* is not clear. In any case it is one way of interpretation.

While in some places the *Gītā* explains that actions are performed by the compelling force of the *guṇas* of *prakṛti* (3.27;13.29), in other places it gives an analysis of the constituent forces of *karman* (18.15ff). Accordingly, there are five causes for an occurrence of action: body, agent, sense organs, various life functions and biomotor activities and the unknown objective causal elements or the all-controlling power of God (*daiva*). Then can a person determine his action? According to Dasgupta:

> The general implication of the *Gītā* seems to be that, though the action follows necessarily as the product of the fivefold collocation, yet the self can give a direction to these actions; if a man wishes to dissociate himself from all attachments and desires by dedicating the fruits of all his actions to God and clings to God with such a purpose, God helps him to attain his noble aim.[133]

At the same time Dasgupta points out a tension between the *karmic* power that brings automatic fruits (4.9; 6.40-45) and *daiva* effect in rewards (16.19). "The only way in which the two views can be reconciled in accordance with the spirit of the *Gītā*", he says, "is by holding that the *Gītā* does not believe in objective truth of virtue or vice (*puṇya or pāpa*)."[134] Nothing good or bad in an action, but *kāma* and *bandha* matter. This goes well with our earlier observation that if a question of special duty or virtue is in conflict with one's own duty (*svadharma*), it is the latter which should be given preference. Thus far we have argued that *karman* for *yajña* that is unbinding means neither a disinterested act in ritual nor a necessary condition of detachment in it. Rather, it is the obedience to the eternal *dharma*, an idea developed in protest against the claims of the *śramaṇas*. Ritual *yajña* is central to this *dharma*, if it is not *dharma* itself. This will become clearer in our following discussion on *niṣkāma karman* and *karmic saṃnyāsa*.

(ii) Niṣkāma Karman *and* Yajña

This is closely linked with the attachment and binding force of *karman* that we have seen in the previous discussion. The fundamental question with which we are concerned here is whether the ritual *yajña* provides any clue for understanding *niṣkāma karman* in general. How can we understand it in the light of *yajña*? Some commentators try to interpret *nitya-karman* as different from the *naimittika karman* and opposed to *kāmya karman*.[135] Some hold that in the view of the *Gītā*, for instance, "sacrifice must be done in the right spirit of non-attachment to the results".[136] But it is difficult to maintain this on the basis of the text because, first, the above threefold classification of *karman* is not found in it and, second, performance of sacrifice without a concern for its results cannot be maintained with reference to the view of the *Gītā* regarding Vedic sacrifice. As we saw earlier *kāma* is viewed positively in the *Vedas* and the *Gītā* also recognises sacrifice positively as *kāmadhuk*.[137] Therefore, the question needs further analysis.

Buddhism held that *kāma* was the root cause of suffering. Liberation was considered to rest primarily in the destruction of *kāma*. Hence the necessity of *saṃnyāsa* and hard discipline. In the epics and *śāstra* literature a response to the above position may be easily found. On the one hand, *kāma* is viewed as an obstruction in the path of *mokṣa* or at least the lowest goal in the *puruṣārtha*.[138] On the other hand, it is said to be a necessary condition in every act including the performance of sacrifice as ordained in the *Veda*.[139] Manu tries to distinguish between different levels of attitude in a religious performance. A religious act in this world that proceeds from selfish motives such as a sacrifice for rain or a pious oblation in view of a future reward, is declared to be concrete and motivated. But an act performed with a knowledge of God devoid of *kāma* is called abstract and disinterested. The reward for motivated action is a lower *svarga*; for disinterested action, the reward is freedom from bodily existence. Further, a perception of the Supreme Soul in all beings and vice versa with spirit fixed on God leads to one's own effulgence.[140] The *Gītā* does not subscribe to such distinctions. By applying the *triguṇa* category, however, the *Gītā* places the performance of action without desire for reward and passion in the highest category of *sattva karman*; the *rajas* type is marked by desire for reward and egoism; that is *tamasic* which is undertaken out of delusion without regard to consequences of destruction and injury or what is humanly possible (18.23.25); the same is applied to the agent, a constituent entity in action (18.26–28). Where *karman* is specified as *yajña*, *tapas* and *dāna*, the *sattvic* one is said to do one's allotted (*niyatam*) *karman* for duty's sake but giving up reward; the *rajasic* renounces action due to fear of bodily pain, being unable to practise the abandonment of reward; the *tamasic* renounces the allotted *karman* (18.7–9). Actually, according to the original *Sāṃkhya*, the binding force of *karman* comes not so much from *kāma* as from non-discrimination. This idea is closer to the Buddhist and *advaita* position too. Therefore *niṣkāma karman* and *phala tyāga*, according to the *triguṇa*-based interpretation of the *Gītā*, does not mean total absence of any concern about the consequences, but the absence of an egoistic tendency and fearing painful consequences. A verse in the *Mahābhārata* asserts that whatever a man does, it should be taken for the purpose of *yajña*; whatever he earns is for the sake of *yajña*; and if he collects grain it should also be understood to be done for *yajña*.[141] Here also, then, it must imply not so much the absence of interest and desire as egoistic passion and unnecessary worry about consequences.

The importance of action in the *Gītā* is not given due recognition by *vedāntins* like Śaṃkara and Rāmānuja who stand for the definite superiority of knowledge and devotion respectively, though the latter is more inclusive of action. Their interpretation of the *karman* verses of the *Gītā* is coloured by their theological positions. According to Śaṃkara, action is worthily praised for those who are incapable of adopting the perfect means of knowledge; according to Rāmānuja, it is a means of expressing devotion. In minimising the prominence of *karman*, as Upadhyaya says, these *vedāntins* 'twist' the meaning of the *karman* texts.[142] At the same time both show keen interest in interpreting *niṣkāma karman*. For Śaṃkara, it is possible on the ground of *jñāna* which creates equanimity of mind and for Rāmānuja on the ground of *bhakti* which leaves the outcome of an action to God. What is remarkable here is that the *vedantins* do not attempt to interpret *niṣkāma karman* explicitly in relation to *yajña*. In modern times some have attempted to do so. Aurobindo, for example, recognises the inevitable element and force of *kāma* in every action. There is no way to curb it. He makes the following explanation:

> But granting that this cannot be done, the only way is to fix a rule for action outside ourselves, not dictated by anything in our subjectivity, the *nitya karma* of the Vedic rule, the routine of ceremonial sacrifice, daily conduct and social duty, which the man who seeks liberation may do simply because it is enjoined upon him, without any personal purpose or subjective interest in them with an absolute indifference to the doing, not because he is compelled by his nature but because it is enjoined by the Śāstra.[143]

Otherwise, according to the above explanation, a subjective principle of action will be determined by the *guṇas* of *prakṛti*. The tension between the command of the *Veda* and the compulsion of *guṇas*, we have already pointed out. We may highlight here that Aurobindo is right in his argument that the basis of *niṣkāma karman* is not in ritual *yajña*. But his invention of a new grounding for action, namely 'Self' and 'God' is loaded with vedāntic interpretations. About action with focus on God, another emphasis of the *Gītā*, we shall see later, but it should not be confused with the performance of ritual in obedience to an ancient law as asserted in it. Besides, recognising the problem of reconciling obedience to Vedic command and the compulsion of *guṇas* it is the former that dominates the *Gītā* view of *dharma*, as we have seen. In this respect then, *niṣkāma karman* with reference to *yajña* means not an action devoid of any interest in reward but unquestioning obedience without worrying about the outcome. Otherwise where the *Gītā* talks about *niṣkāma karman* as a general principle for all actions there is no reference to *yajña* (e.g. 2.47; 4.19, 20).

As we have pointed out earlier with reference to the bondage of *karman*, Tilak identifies the source of non-binding *karman* in the *mīmāṃsā* doctrine of *yajña*. Tilak also holds that even then one cannot escape obtaining the fruits.[144] Kane observes: "The reward of many religious rites is *svarga* and the *Pūrva-mīmāṃsa Sūtra* refers to numerous Vedic passages where *svarga* is the reward for rites and assumes that the reward goes to the performer."[145]

If one then holds that *phala* is natural and incidental, what is the guarantee that the sacrificer has no thought of reward when he performs a sacrifice? The *Gītā* well recognises Vedic sacrifice is a cow of desire and that its power satisfies human desires. So we are on firm ground in arguing that the idea of *niṣkāma karman* is an independent one which was later used to emphasise the *yajña karman* found in the *Gītā*. Bhandarkar and Upadhyaya point to those Upaniṣadic verses which speak about *niṣkāma karman*, as an outcome of an elevated state of mind.[146] Perhaps the *Gītā* in order to counter the Buddhist views on *kāma* takes this idea and uses it in its interpretation of *karman*.

Even though the *Gītā* extols *niṣkāma karman* it often refers to *kāma* positively. Kṛṣṇa says that in his action he does not yearn for reward (4.15). But this cannot be taken for *yajña* since Kṛṣṇa does not perform it. In 7.11 he says he is the strength of the strong, devoid of *kāma*, but in beings he is the *kāma* which is not at variance with *dharma*. In 10.1 he declares his supreme word out of his *kāma* for the welfare of Arjuna. Saying that he has slain Arjuna's enemies he asks him to win them and enjoy (*bhuṅkṣva*), the kingdom full of wealth (*samṛtdham*, 11.33). Abandonment of action in fear of pain cannot have its reward (18.8). There can be no *bhakti* without some kind of *kāma* or expectation for reward, as we shall point out soon. Therefore, it is correct to hold that the *Gītā* is not antagonistic to *kāma* and *phala* as such. It is also incorrect to hold that the *Gītā* takes *yajña* as a model for *niṣkāma karman*. Even the brāhmaṇic formula in ritual, "I renounce the fruits to the deity" was in fact supposed to bring abundant reward. Thus, the kind of *niṣkāma* it talks about requires a different explanation.

Tilak argues that giving up fruits does not mean giving up all kinds of desire or the enjoyment thereof but giving up personal, selfish attachment (*āsakti*) or insistence (*āgraha*). Therefore, he says, in the name of giving up ambition, attachment or insistence, one should not give up the enthusiasm for doing one's duty with a purpose.[147] This interpretation may be supported by the kind of problem that Arjuna raises at the beginning. In his despondent state Arjuna tells Kṛṣṇa that he and his companions have resolved to commit a great sin (*mahāpāpa*) by undertaking to slay their own kin out of desire for the kingdom and happiness (1.45). He would prefer to be killed by the enemies. In the battlefield, then, there is no indication that Arjuna's mind was clouded with *kāma*. Kaveeshwar builds up his ethics of the *Gītā* on this fact and argues that it was not *kāma* but *moha* that was the problem for Arjuna. "*Moha* means intellectual ignorance, confusion, bewilderment or perverted view".[148] Prithipal traces the meanings of the term *moha* in the *Vedas* as bewilderment, confusion, perplexity, emotional errc or disorder that cause some nuisance to those taking part in a sacrifice. It is a condition that sweeps people away from their tiaditional spiritual norms and their particular paths. Then he applies this meaning to Arjuna's condition in the battlefield:

> He has lost the memory of his own true origin, and that of the other warriors around him. He has even forgotten the real meaning of Kṛṣṇa standing by his side offering him advice and teaching him what is true *dharma*. His duty seems absurd to him; he is bewildered by the tragic contradiction facing him and does not know what to do.[149]

Since this was exactly the problem, in the end Arjuna says he is freed from the confusion or *moha* (18.73). Kaveeshwar writes:

> Arjuna does not say that he has been freed from *kāma*, that he has got rid of all egoistic attachment for the fruit of action, or that he has attained the attitude of inner renunciation. The principal idea ... is that the *moha* (bewilderment) about duty and non-duty of the nature of ignorance, that had popped up in his mind and made him oppose that war which was his essential duty at that moment, was removed and consequently he was ready to perform that duty.[150]

Then the intellectual bewilderment of Arjuna about his duty, Kaveeshwar argues, was related to egoistic attachment "in such an indirect manner" because his desertion of duty was "not born of egoistic attachment, nor was it born exclusively of an aversion for such attachment".[151] The *kāma* was therefore only a possibility caused by *moha*, the source of which was the absence of discrimination not only between self and non-self but also between dharmic war and personal concern for undesirable destruction. Hence the necessity of teaching him about the metaphysical aspects of *kāma*. Kaveeshwar understands, in a broader sense, namely, the desire to have pleasure and to avoid pain. "In a nutshell, *kāma* means narrow egoistic attachment".[152] Then for him the *Gītā* disapproves of only the "*kāma*-natured and *moha*-born desires that include a longing for *svarga* but the desire for *mokṣa* is excluded".[153] Similarly G. Feuerstein argues that the term *phala* is synonymous with inevitable consequence. Then the problem with *kāma*, he holds, is not concern for consequences but the "psychic tension" in action, for it is impossible to work without motivation.[154] It is remarkable, however, that Kaveeshwar and Feuerstein make no reference to sacrifice in their discussions: that factor would have caused many problems for their argument. But their insistence on *dharma* without criticism from personal interest is not irrelevant to the idea of sacrifice, because Arjuna is instructed not to give up sacrifice as such, only its reward. But even if *phala* is understood as attachment and pleasure, nowhere does the *Gītā* say so clearly, least in its affirmation of Vedic *yajña*. Now, we have to look carefully at the *Gītā* view of *saṃnyāsa* and *tyāga*.

(iii) Karmic Saṃnyāsa

There is a link in 6.1 between the giving up of fruits and not giving up of sacrificial fire. This is true *saṃnyāsa*. In other words, the true *saṃnyāsin* is one who does his dharmic action yet does not covet its fruit; not the one who does not build the sacrificial fire and perform the rites. Radhakrishnan comments on this verse, saying that *saṃnyāsa* has little to do with outward works. "It is an inward attitude to become a *saṃnyāsin*, it is not necessary to give up the sacrificial fire and the daily ritual. To abstain from these without the spirit of renunciation is futile". And he says that Śaṃkara's interpretation to the effect that only one type of *saṃnyāsin* is talked about, is unfair to the text.[155] In any case by wishing to take to begging alms rather than waging a war Arjuna already has represented the renouncers' tradition.[156]

The emphasis on *saṃnyāsa* given by the *śramaṇa* movements and its incorporation in the *āśrama dharma* need not be repeated here. At an apparent transitional point from ritual *yajña* to *ātma yajña* the seekers after truth come with sacrificial fire in their hands, as we have seen in the *Upaniṣads*. According to one view, at the stage of *saṃnyāsa* the person concerned must retire to the forest, but with fire, and he may give it up after some days, inhaling the fire by which his conscious *prāṇa* becomes a perpetual *agnihotra*. The *Gītā* is not for giving up "the fire" at any stage, but giving up the fruit of such action. And also here the *Gītā* seems to redefine *saṃnyāsa* as giving up worldly attachment (*saṃkalpa*) at a particular stage; *saṃnyāsa* at any stage should not be justified in the name of *jñāna, mokṣa* or *māya.*[157] P. Olivelle, noting that *saṃnyāsa* occurs in *the Gītā* twenty-two times, focuses his attention on 5.3 which talks about *nityasaṃnyāsin.* He contrasts this with the regular *saṃnyāsin* with reference to ritual activity:

> The meaning of this term becomes clear when we contrast *nityasaṃnyāsin* with the regular *saṃnyāsin.* The latter abandons *karma* once namely during the rite of renunciation, whereas the former is engaged continually in abandoning attachment. For the *Gītā* the *nityasaṃnyāsin* represents the true renouncer.[158]

The immediate concern of the Gītā, however, is not to respond to different understandings of *saṃnyāsa* but to turn Arjuna from his inclination to renounce an action which is central to eternal *dharma.*[159]

Elsewhere Arjuna asks about the true nature of *saṃnyāsa* and *tyāga* (18.1). The answer is, giving up actions that have desire (*kāmyānāṁ karmaṇa*) is *saṃnyāsa* and giving up all fruits of action (*sarva karma phala*) is *tyāga* (18.2). This is a general view of course. The next verse (18.3) mentions the diverse opinions about giving up of actions like sacrifice. Kṛṣṇa's decided opinion is that they should not be given up (18.5). What is to be given up is attachment (*saṅgam*) and reward (18.6). With reference to the usage of the terms *tyāga* and *saṃnyāsa* Olivelle observes:

> Even though *saṃnyāsa* is used more frequently with reference to *karma,* and *tyāga* with reference to *saṅga* and *karma phala,* the two terms are used interchangeably in the *Gītā* as in other literature on renunciation. Nevertheless, the fact that when making the above distinction (18.2) the author of the *Gītā* instinctively chooses *saṃnyāsa* to indicate the abandonment of *karma* is further proof that this term referred primarily to the abandonment of rites.[160]

The abandonment of any obligatory duty (*niyata*) is improper and *ṭamasic,* caused by ignorance (18.7). Abandonment of obligatory duty due to fear of painful outcome is *rajasic*; it strips one of *tyāga phala* (18.8). *Sattvic* is performance of the obligatory duty but with abandonment of attachment and fruits (18.7). We have already seen the problem in this division. What is remarkable is that from the Vedic point of view non-abandonment of sacrifice is taken as a paradigm for all actions; but abandonment of desire and reward is imposed on sacrifice unless it is taken to mean that one should act without worrying about the consequences.

Kṛṣṇa introduces himself as an example of *karmic saṃnyāsa.* He is engaged in constant action, so that humans would follow his path. Were he not engaged in action the world would fall to ruin. But he acts without attachment (3.21-28). If this model is applied to sacrifice one should perform it with a motive of upholding the universal order as expressed in the *yajña cakra.* Whether the *karmic* power generated in sacrifice to uphold the universe is a parallel power of God is a question to be asked. Here it is enough to say that by the insistence of action with vindication from God's action, the *Gītā* once again affirms the karmic power of sacrifice; the idea of truly giving up reward or being unconcerned about it was never part of Vedic sacrifice. On the whole, as Van Buitenen observes, Kṛṣṇa's argument for action in the context of the *Gītā* is at once simple and complex:

> Simple, because he finds cause to propose that act is both necessary and unproductive of rebirth; complex, because he attempts to hold on to the orthodoxy of social action while revolutionizing it from within, and at the same time to demolish the heterodoxy of renunciation-at-any-price without discarding the value of renunciation per se".[161]

As we have seen, it is incorrect to hold that this value is derived from sacrifice; rather the value is imposed on it.

7. Jñāna Yajña

We have pointed out earlier the reference to *jñāna yajña* along with other types of *yajña* (4.28). There the real meaning of the term is not clear. But there is another reference in 4.33 which says that *jñāna yajña* is better than *dravya yajña.* It is related to the idea of *karman* in that all actions find their consummation in knowledge. Remarkably it was the Buddha who once said that *jñāna yajña* is the best of all *yajñas.*[162] In the *Upaniṣads jñāna yajña* occurs as an inclusive term, meaning different stages in the process of interiorisation. But in fact the mention of it by the *Gītā* is unclear as it does not describe it in detail and also it uses the term in different senses. Śaṃkara extols this reference and uses it for his argument for the primacy of *jñāna,* though in 4.28 he interprets *jñāna* as referring to the *śāstras,* the *smṛti* texts.[163] On the contrary, Hill notes, here *jñāna yajña* means the performance of all sacrifices with knowledge and care.[164]

In 18.70 the *Gītā* considers that listening to the dialogue between Kṛṣṇa and Arjuna, i.e., the *Gītā,* is *jñāna yajña.* It is then a religious act like ritual sacrifice into which the *Gītā* incorporates the study of the *Veda, dāna* and *tapas.* In this sense it follows the view that the rewards of this *jñāna yajña* are fortune, wealth, victory and justice as well as the fair worlds of those of *puṇya karman* (18.71, 78). But this is only one meaning.

In chapter 2 Kṛṣṇa talks about *karma* and *jñāna* or *karma-jñāna-samuccaya.* But this is confusing for Arjuna. He asks, if *buddhi* is superior to action why do you enjoin me to do this dreadful action? It is bewildering and confusing (3.1–2). Kṛṣṇa answers, Long ago I proclaimed two paths, *jñāna yoga* to *Sāṃkhyas* and *karma yoga* to *karma yogins;* no one attains freedom from the action and perfection by *saṃnyāsa* . By the natural *guṇas* everyone is bound to act; but self- control is not for non-action and he who acts with self-control excels (3.4-7). It is in the sense that for a proper way of action knowledge is useful, the *Gītā* stresses knowledge. There are problems, however, when we relate it to other forms of *yajña.*

(i) From the Viewpoint of Vedic Yajña

Apart from *jñāna yajña* mentioned along with *dravya yajña* as one type of *yajña* (4.28) and the statement that *jñāna yajña* is superior to *dravya yajña* (4.33), the *Gītā* has a verse (8.28) saying that the *yogin* who knows the sacred teaching goes further and transcends the fruit assigned to *yajña, dāna, tapas* and the knowledge of the *Veda.* Taken out of context, this verse may be misunderstood as minimising the importance of ritual sacrifice. But it should be noted that it is preceded by a teaching on the auspicious time of death. He who knows this secret teaching, in view of his death, transcends the rewards of meritorious acts such as *yajña* and attains to the supreme primeval abode.

As we have pointed out earlier, for the *Gītā* the *saṃnyāsin* is the one who performs action without a desire for reward but not one who is without sacrificial fire in his hand (6.1). According to 18.5 acts like *yajña* and *dāna* purify the mind of the wise. It is strange that *yajña* is newly given the role usually played by *jñāna* and *yoga* in developing a purified state of mind. But how does this happen? Does the act of giving up *dravya* on the fire inspire the performer or does the consecration in preparation for the performance of sacrifice help the sacrificer to develop a new consciousness and unperturbed concentration? As we have already seen, even though there is an attempt in the *Upaniṣads* to present *jñāna yajña* and *ātma yajña* as the logical continuation of ritual *yajña*, conceptually such conclusions are unfounded. Since the *Gītā* does not make its meaning of *jñāna yajña* explicit it is no aid to clarification.

At the same time at certain points in the path of *jñāna* the place of *sabda brahman* or the *Veda* seems to be trivialised (2.46; 6.44). Once again this reflects a kind of tension found throughout the attitude of the *Gītā* to the *Vedas*. What is implied here is perhaps that there are ways of developing a mental attitude of equanimity through *yoga* and *dhyāna*, not necessarily by following the rules or hearing the *mantras* of the *Vedas*. Nevertheless, the purpose of such an attitude is to carry out the obligation of Vedic action both in its ritual and social sense. Then *dravya yajña* is inferior only if it is disturbed by *moha* or bewilderment in the way of fulfilling a primordial obligation that is *yajña*.

(ii) From the Upaniṣadic Perspective

As we discovered earlier, on the one hand the *Upaniṣads* affirm the Vedic sacrifice, on the other they push ritual to the background, emphasising more and more sacrifice of knowledge and sacrifice of self. The apparent transition and logical connection between the two could not however be established because these two operate with entirely different world-views. Instead of a shift of paradigm of conceptual framework, the new views are mixed with the old, a characteristic of the development of Indian thought and hermeneutical process.

In their emphasis on *jñāna yajña* some Upaniṣadic passages denounce the fundamental claims of Vedic *yajña* like *kāma* and *svarga*. Further, all allegorical interpretation, presenting the ritual sacrifice as analogous to the cosmic forces and internal forces in the human personality, is an important principle developed by the *Upaniṣads*. This is taken as the basis of *jñāna yajña*, the way to *ātma yajña*, an interior journey sacrificing the outer and inner layers of the human personality in order to reach to the core, the self, the Absolute. *Yoga* and meditation help in the process. All these form *jñāna yajña.*

Although the *Gītā* incorporates elements of interiorisation it is significant that it nowhere mentions the allegorical interpretation of *yajña.* This is presumably to avoid the drift toward minimisation of the importance of Vedic sacrifice. References to *prāṇa yajña* etc. remain isolated (4.27, 29, 30). But certain other aspects of the *Upaniṣads* find place in the *Gītā* in a peculiar way. According to the *Gītā kāma* and *krodha,* being begotten by *rajoguṇa,* bring sin (*pāpa). Kāma* is a foe on earth. Just as fire is concealed by smoke, mirror by dust, and embryo by membrane, *jñāna* is concealed by *kāma.* The senses (*indriya*), mind (*manas*) and intelligence (*buddhi*) are said to be its seat (3,37–40). Interestingly, the *Gītā* refers to a group of people who say 'control the senses, and slay *kāma*; the senses are superior to the body, the mind and what is superior to the intelligence is *ātman*' (3.41–42). The language of sacrifice is avoided in this reference. In the end (3.43), however, Kṛṣṇa asks Arjuna to know God as higher than the *ātman* and be firm in him; and also Arjuna should vanquish the enemy who is hard to change or conquer. It appears that "enemy" refers either to a group of teachers who taught *jñāna yajña* and *ātma yajña* or to *ātma yajña* itself.

Elsewhere the *Gītā* speaks about different kinds of *jñāna*; it says: know such *jñāna* by humble submission, enquiry and service (4.34); you will cross over by *jñāna* (4.36). The fire of *jñāna* reduces all *karma* to ashes (4.37). He who has *śraddhā,* whose senses are controlled, who is intent upon *jñāna,* gains *jñāna*; he attains the supreme peace (4.39). It may be noted, however, that phrases like "crossing over", reducing or melting and *śraddhā* were described by the Upaniṣadic teachers without ritual connotations. The purpose of such description here seems to set a background for the understanding of *karma* in general, which by *jñāna* becomes unbinding and unproductive of births, because of the sword of *jñāna* (4.41, 42). This we shall consider in greater detail later.

The *Upaniṣads* view elements of *yoga* at random as a discipline to control the senses, direct the internal process and help *ātma darśan.* But the *Gītā* not only talks about yogic action and *jñāna yoga* separately, it also places it above *jñāna yoga,* taking *yoga* as an independent discipline. It says that the man of *yoga* is above the man of *tapas* and even above the man of *jñāna*; he is above the performers of ritual and social action too (6.46). *Yoga yajña* is a type mentioned in 4.28. It should be noted, however, that on the whole the purpose of *yoga* in general is to act with a definite goal. Van Buitenen points out that the use by the *Gītā* of *yoga* cannot be taken in Patañjali's sense. He refers to the literal meaning of *yoga* as yoking of the horse to the chariot for war. It can be applied reflexively to the warrior himself. In 2.38 Kṛṣṇa tells Arjuna to yoke himself to the battle. Van Buitenen observes that this reflexive usage is usual in the *Gītā*, meaning a particular effort to win a goal even if it is mentioned in a complex way. He says,

> *Yoga* is always somebody, in something, with something, for some purpose; *yoga* in an absolute sense hardly occurs in the *Gītā* at all... When *yoga* occurs by itself it is often times an abbreviation of *karma* or *bhakti-yoga*. *Yoga*, then, implies (1) the process of a difficult effort; (2) a person committed to it; (3) the instrument he uses; (4) the course of action chosen; and (5) the prospect of a goal.[165]

We have already examined the *yoga* and goal of Arjuna as a kṣatriya within the framework of the Vedic *dharma*. Here the point to be highlighted is that *jñāna yajña* and *yoga yajña*, which scarcely occur in the *Gītā*, should be taken as preparation for this *yoga* and goal.

Like the *Upaniṣads* the *Gītā* speaks in many verses about the final end of the yogic action as the attainment of *Brahman*, *śānti*, firm standing, supreme joy, absorption of the self into the self, freedom from *kāma* or *krodha* and having the senses subdued (2.50–72; 5.6, 7, 10, 12, 17, 18, 21–26; 6.27, 28). Whether this end is ultimate or inferior to the God-experience is a different question. One outcome of this state of consciousness is equanimity or sameness. Thus men of insight view with equal eye a brahmin of knowledge and good breeding, a cow, an elephant, and even a dog and an outcaste (5.18). In short, one is indifferent to all differences and opposites (6.8, 9). But the implications of developing such mental attitude seem to support not the interior journey of the Upaniṣadic teachers but intense devotion and proper action.

(iii) From the Viewpoint of Karma

Kṛṣṇa tells the despondent Arjuna he grieves for those who are not to be grieved for, yet speaks words about wisdom (*prajña*). The learned (*paṇḍita*) do not grieve for the living or for the dead

(2.11). This is an initial response to Arjuna, chiding him for his unnecessary grief. Then there is an analysis of the development of such confusion: in a man intent upon matters of sense, attachment to such matters is born. From attachment *kāma* is born. From *kāma, krodha* is born. From *krodha* deluding confusion (*samoha*) is born. From that confusion remembrance (*smṛti*) is dispersed and from such dispersal comes destruction of *buddhi.* Because of the destruction of *buddhi* a man is lost (2.62, 63). Does this explain the origin of *ajñāna*? No, it simply tries to trace the development of confusion within an *a priori* view of ignorance. As Dasgupta points out, "the *Gītā* was not interested to trace the origin of attachments and desires and was satisfied to take their existence for granted and urged the necessity of expiation for peace and equanimity of mind".[166] Thus freedom from *ajñāna* and *kāma* means to attain *samādhi* (2.54), self-contentment, undisturbed mind in both pleasure and pain, and absence of passion, fear or anger. The one who has attained this state is a *sthitaprajña* and *muni* (2.55, 57, 58). This in no way should lead to the abandonment of action but to action with a steady mind, realising the imperative of *dharma* in the first place and the inevitable condition of *prakṛti* to act in the second place. The most important emphasis is on *smṛti,* tradition remembered, which should not be confused.

We have already discussed the meaning of *kāma* and bondage from the perspective of the *Gītā.* Here our focus is on *jñāna* as it helps to effect *niṣkāma karman* in the right sense. To avoid subjective impulses and critical questions about the outcome of an action (i.e., what Arjuna required) there should be developed a mental attitude which considers all opposites equal.[167] This is the precise meaning of action in non-action and vice versa (4.16ff). This is the spirit of *samatva.* But it must not be misinterpreted as mechanical indifference towards everything or devoid of every feeling. It means, as Feuerstein observes, "a positive state of mind in which we are able to look with balanced serenity on all the many things that would ordinarily upset us and stir up unwholesome emotions and becloud our judgements".[168] In the view of the *Gītā,* of course, the focus of this attitude is obedience to *dharma.*

The same idea is related to the practice of *yoga.* Kṛṣṇa says we should aspire for neither fruit-bound action nor non-action, but action with *yoga*. It helps to have equilibrium in opposites (2.48). Action impelled by concern about outcome is inferior to *buddhi yoga* (2.49). One whose *buddhi* is yoked in *yoga* leaves behind good and evil even while here on earth. Effort with *yoga* is skilfulness or power in action (2.50). Thus *yoga* is taken from its connotations of mental and physical discipline in solitude and given the meaning of dynamic action. Even where the *Gītā* speaks about *yoga* as a meditative act to be done in solitude following the yogic principle (e.g. 6.10-15), its final goal, according to its interpretation, is to do action with steady mental attitude without any confusion or bewilderment. The term *jñāna yajña* thus could be related to a number of ideas although the *Gītā* does not give its exact sense.

8. *Bhakti Yajña* and its Focus

Thus far we have discussed the affirmation of Vedic sacrifice in the *Gītā* and its interpretation of sacrifice in relation to various types of sacrifice, *triguṇa* category of *Sāṃkhya, karma* and *jñāna*. Despite some problems in understanding the nature of this interpretation, we have argued that indirectly or directly, the ideas of *triguṇa, karma* and *jñāna* support the observation of Vedic *dharma* in which *yajña* has a central place. In this section we will discuss the interpretation of *yajña* in relation to *bhakti*, devotion to supreme personal God, the teacher of the *Gītā*. It will nevertheless become clear that once again a supreme person appears to unify and integrate various powers, both personal and impersonal, and give the ultimate focus for a religious act like sacrifice. Biardeau emphasises that it is *bhakti* that integrates the opposites—world affirmation and renouncement, pure and impure, etc.[169] On the other hand, we will observe a certain tension in this integration.

In the last chapter we dealt with the development of the Kṛṣṇa cult and Bhāgavatism. Kṛṣṇa was identified with heroes, seers and gods; and particularly with reference to the minimum use of terms like Kṛṣṇa and Viṣṇu, the *Gītā* appears to be supra-sectarian.[170] M.R. Yardi identifies in this text the first "ecumenical effort" to bring the different Hindu theological systems under one banner.[171] Majumdar points out that the important outcome of the amalgamation of bhāgavatism with brāhmaṇism is the identification of Vāsudeva-Kṛṣṇa with two prominent Vedic gods, namely Viṣṇu and Nārāyaṇa; and this assured a permanent position to Viṣṇu but gave an altogether new turn to the latter. Then the amalgamated form of brāhmaṇism and bhāgavatism which came to be called Vaiṣṇavism formed the main plank of the orthodox religion in its contest with Buddhism.[172] Jaini notes that this development must have come as a great relief to those who were excluded from Vedic sacrifice and who were not able to comprehend the impersonal Absolute of the *Upaniṣads*; further, he says, it stabilises the duties of rank and household life and in this sense in adopting Kṛṣṇa the orthodox brāhmaṇism was clearly fulfilling a need for an all-comprising personal God and saviour.[173] In order to counter the influence of the Buddha who was called teacher (*sattha*) and Lord (*bhagavān*) and was believed to have taken many former births (*jātaka*) in which he had preached his *dharma*, the ingenious people of the brāhmaṇic fold took a human hero, Kṛṣṇa, already legendary and revered among the Vṛṣṇis, and made him an authoritative teacher of *dharma* and Lord of the universe, and also ascribed to him various other religious strands.[174] Another extraordinary success of the *Gītā* was its new doctrine of *bhakti* which was mainly the intensification of sacred awareness found in different forms in the time of the *Vedas* and the *Upaniṣads*. We may recall the appearance of the Ādipuruṣa and Prajāpati in the *Vedas* as supreme beings related to sacrifice. The relationship of Kṛṣṇa with *yajña*, however, has unique features.

(i) Kṛṣṇa as Recipient and Enjoyer of Sacrifice

In 5.29 Kṛṣṇa says: "Knowing me as the proper object or enjoyer of *yajña* and *tapas*, the Lord of all the worlds and the friend of all beings, the *yogin* attains *śānti*." This is the first reference to *yajña* related to the supreme God, apparently a transition from *karma-jñāna yajña* to *bhakti yajña*, occurring at the end of a chapter. "This very abrupt introduction of the personal God", Zaehner comments,

> as the only true recipient and experiencer of sacrifice and religious practices in general is surprising, as it does not seem to fit in with the rest of the chapter which is otherwise quite coherent. Perhaps we should interpret the verse in connection with 4.24 where Brahman is described as the offering.[175]

By declaring himself as the receiver of the offering and making reference to various types of *yajña*, Kṛṣṇa claims to excel all holy power, even the *brahman,* for as 9.24 puts it, he is the enjoyer of and presides over all sacrifices.

In the *Vedas* the receivers of sacrifice are the gods who subsist by sacrificial food. Earlier, the *Gītā* recognises this (3.10-12) and speaks of the independent existence of gods in different places (4.12; 7.23; 9.23, 25). On the other hand Kṛṣṇa's supremacy over the gods is asserted by declaring worship of gods as inferior or identifying himself as their inner self (10.2, 14; 11.15, 52; 17.4; 18.40). It is certain that the *Upaniṣads* and the *śramaṇas* lowered the position of the Vedic gods, subjecting them to the process of *karma saṃsāra.* This is countered by the projection of Kṛṣṇa as the God of all gods. Yet, on the whole the continuation of gods independently receiving sacrifice is acknowledged in the *Gītā.* This reflects the tension in reconciling the Vedic gods with the absolute claim of Kṛṣṇa as the only receiver of sacrifice.

(ii) Kṛṣṇa Identifying Himself with the Sacrifice

Kṛṣṇa says: "I am the *adhiyajña* appertaining to sacrifice or the governor of sacrifice (7.30; 8.2, 4). I am the ritual action (*kratu*); I am the sacrifice (*yajña*); I am the ancestral oblation; I am the healing herb; I am the sacred *mantra;* I am the butter; I am the fire and I am the offering" (9.16). Besides this direct identification he identifies with the essence of the prominent entities related to sacrifice. Thus he says "Of the Āditiyas I am Viṣṇu; of gods I am Vāsava (Indra); of the Yakṣas and Rākṣasas I am Kubera; of the *vāsus* I am *pāvaka* (*agni*); of the chief household priests I am Bṛhaspati (the Lord of prayer or sacred utterance); of utterances I am *Oṃ;* of *yajñas* I am the *japa yajña;* of spiritual men I am Kapila; of cows I am *kāmadhenu;* of demons I am Prahlada; of metres I am *Gāyatrī*" (10.21-35). These are some of the important "I am" sayings of Kṛṣṇa. They seem to reflect the Upaniṣadic style of making identifications. It is not easy to find the exact meaning of these sayings, since the identification includes demons, *yakṣas* and *rākṣasas* who are denounced in other places. One may, however, take this as meaning that Kṛṣṇa is the foremost of all.

Rāmānuja interprets *adhiyajña* as meaning that the Lord is the essence and supreme object of worship through sacrifices. He is the self of Indra and other gods. In this sense *adhiyajña* is to be meditated on by the three classes of qualified aspirants at the time of the performance of rites like *pañcamahāyajña.*[176] For Śaṃkara

The *Adhiyajña* is He who identifies himself with all acts of sacrifice, the deity named Viṣṇu; the *śruti* says: *yajña* is verily Viṣṇu ... He is verily Myself. I am the Deity concerned with all acts of sacrifice in the body. As an act of sacrifice (*yajña*) has to be performed by the body, it is said to be inherent in it, and as such it may be said to rest *in the body*".[177]

Śaṃkara's reference to Viṣṇu as *yajña* may remind us of many such phrases like "Prajāpati is *yajña*" that occur in the *Vedas.* Jordens observes that by identifying himself with *yajña,* Kṛṣṇa is fulfilling a long tradition started in the Ādipuruṣa and continued in Prajāpati and Brahman who are said to be the victims of sacrifice.[178] Because of their self-sacrifice they could not find a permanent place in the minds of people. It must be noted here that Kṛṣṇa is never in favour of being sacrificed like Puruṣa and Prajāpati. Hence his supremacy remains unquestioned. Kṛṣṇa's special identification with Viṣṇu is not without reason. Viṣṇu is said to be sacrifice but never in the sense of a sacrificial victim like Prajāpati and Puruṣa, but rather in the sense that he is the Lord of sacrifice. In this position he plays Prajāpati's role in resolving the fight of *devas* and *asuras.*[179] Therefore Kṛṣṇa's identification with sacrifice is not in the sense of a victim but in the sense of being invulnerable and the Lord of sacrifice.

For the claim of Lordship, Kṛṣṇa not only identifies with sacrifice which is the primordial field of karmic power but also with various power centres like natural elements, *tapas, yoga, jñāna,* ethical principles and Brahman or Ātman (7.8–11, 29–30; 8.3, 4, 8–10, 11–13, 14, 16–22; 10.4, 5; 12.7–11, 13-20; 16.1–5). Identification with 'Brahman' is especially remarkable. The supreme Brahman of the *Upaniṣads* is subdued by Kṛṣṇa. Thus Kṛṣṇa provides a relational centre in himself for all such powers.

(iii) Bhakti *Transcending* Yajña

Kṛṣṇa says that the *soma* drinkers, trusting the *Vedas,* worship him with sacrifice. The reward is only an enjoyment in *Indraloka* (9.20). After this enjoyment they have to come down to the world of mortals (9.21). But sure and permanent release lies with God which is to be attained through devotional worship, no matter what be the worth of offerings. "He who offers to me with *bhakti* a leaf, a flower, a fruit or water, I accept that offering of devoted self" (9.26).

With reference to this verse some scholars are of the opinion that image-worship was prevalent in the time of *Gītā*.[180] But, further, the *Gītā* widens the horizon of offering. Now whatever one does, eats, performs as sacrifice, *dāna* or *tapas*, Kṛṣṇa accepts them as an offering. Released from all bondage and evil in *yoga*, one goes to him. It is *bhakti*, not some ethical quality nor social position, that matters (9.28ff). It is interesting to notice that even in the context of emphasising *bhakti* and simple offering, sacrifice becomes one form of offering (9.27, 34). Whether its intrinsic value is stripped, is not clear.

In bhāgavatism the killing of animals in sacrifice seems to be condemned. In its place various oblations like grain and fruit are suggested. When the *Gītā* talks about such simple offerings the *bhāgavata* cult is echoed.[181] Hence the prominence of *bhakti* in the *Bhagavad Gītā*.

(iv) Inadequacy of Yajña *for the Vision of God*

Viśvarūpa darśana is decisive in the understanding of *bhakti* by the *Gītā*. This moment is central in the dialogue between Kṛṣṇa and Arjuna. In the *Vedas viśvarūpa* is a god representing sacrifice who with his three heads consumes the *soma* and other oblations.[182] But the cosmic theophany of Kṛṣṇa appears to be all consuming, all containing, yet transcending all. He shows this divine form purely out of his *yoga* power (11.5ff).

After this vision Kṛṣṇa tells Arjuna: Neither by the *Vedas*, nor by *yajña*, nor by *dāna*, nor by *tapas* can I be seen with this form, but by *bhakti* as you have had (11.48, 53, 54). This verse resembles a passage in the *Nārāyaṇīya* section of the *Mahābhārata* in which it is said that Nārāyaṇa, the supreme God, cannot be seen by performance of *yajña*, *tapas* etc. but only by intensive devotion. Even the seven *ṛṣis* could not see him. He shows himself to the devout ones out of his grace.[183] In his comment on 11.53, 54 Rāmānuja says the same with an additional emphasis, echoing the emphasis of the *Kaṭha* and *Muṇḍaka Upaniṣads*: the Supreme Self is known only by the one whom he chooses for his revelation.[184] In the *Atharva Veda*, *viśvarūpa* is applied to certain gods, meaning their association with creation, their identification with self and their omniscience.[186] Mainkar notes that this is reminiscent of the *mahāyāna* doctrine of different bodies of a *bodhisattva*.[186] According to 4.1-6 Kṛṣṇa was always there revealing himself in different forms. This is one of such revelations. "Kṛṣṇa is God born as man:

it is, indeed, only in his human form He is friendly and kind, or laughing (2.10), that He comforts Arjuna or confides to him the entrancing secret of his love for his devotees".[187] Nevertheless, by occasional *viśvarūpa darśana* he evokes an awesome wonder and outpouring devotion from his devotees before which actions like *yajña* and *tapas* have no longer absolute value as before.

(v) Bhakti Yajña *in Relation to other* Yajñas

Projecting God as the central focus of all actions and all holy powers the *Gītā* tries to embrace various types of sacrifice, as we have found in this chapter. In other words, God is said to integrate and unify various positions and powers. Aurobindo calls this an absolute reconciliation.[188] Such are the repeated statements made about the God-centre of the *Gītā*. Nevertheless, from the *yajña* point of view the integration of all strands of the meaning of God-centre is not without problems.

Like the Vedic gods Kṛṣṇa also receives sacrifice and enjoys it. He claims supremacy over gods, as the Lord of all gods as well as their innermost self (8.4). At the same time the independent existence of gods and their right to receive sacrificial food and their power to fulfil the desire of the sacrificers is recognised (3.10–12; 4.12). In 9.25 he says, "to the gods their devotees go ... to me my devotees come". We cannot hold that benefits of sacrificing to gods are inferior because in 9.20, 21 Kṛṣṇa says, "those who worship me by sacrifice will enjoy heaven and come back to earth again". Thus the *Gītā* affirms the Vedic gods and supreme God Kṛṣṇa side by side.

By accepting the Vedic sacrifice and identifying with the essence of it Kṛṣṇa basically accepts the power of ritual action. There are references, however, to the effect that he transcends the Vedic sacrifice. It is sigificant to note that at such transitional points as found in 2.42–44 the Lordship of Kṛṣṇa is indirectly demanded. Thus, that passage says: The undiscerning who delight in the *Veda* say that there is nothing beyond this; those who are characterised by *kāma* and have *svarga* as their chief aim; their minds are seduced by flowery words; and they delight in Vedic lore; they cling to pleasure and power which can be achieved by ritual. Here Kṛṣṇa seems to address those brahmins who were reluctant to accept him in their fold, as we pointed out in connection with the *Mahābhārata*; or he criticises the attitude of pride that undergird some sacrificers. In any case as long as he is the source of the *Vedas* and essence of the sacrifice, he cannot replace sacrifice and *Vedas.*

Apart from the idea of mutual sustenance between gods and human beings found in sacrifice, another important idea is that sacrifice upholds the universal order and brings rain. It is a sin not to turn the cosmic wheel of sacrifice. This is said by Kṛṣṇa himself. At the same time, he is the Īśvara standing in the heart of all beings by his *māyā* power, causing all beings mounted on a wheel or machine (*yantra*) to revolve (18.61). He identifies with the essence of all beings and all natural entities (15.12-150). He says, "I, the supreme self, having entered the three worlds, sustain them" (15.17). This claim certainly counters the claims of not only automatic functioning of the universe as held by the *śramaṇas,* but also the *yajña*-oriented world-view of the brahmins. We have seen that *yajña* with prescribed rules and *dakṣiṇā* to priests, are insisted on by Kṛṣṇa. The autonomous power of ritual and the supreme power of Kṛṣṇa are recognised side by side.

A more significant point of departure from Vedic sacrifice in the *Gītā* concerns the question of vision and authority. The *Vedas* and sacrifices were originally "seen" by a group of primordial *ṛṣis,* the number of whom is traditionally put as seven. One of the motives in Vedic sacrifice was to become identified with these ancient *ṛṣis.* Now Kṛṣṇa identifies on the one hand with those *ṛṣis, kavis* or *munis* as variously called. Thus the royal sages know the *yoga* (4.2); the ancients who desired release were active (4.15); even the great sages (*mahārṣis*) and four ancients (*pūrvai*) had their being from the Lord (10.16); of great *ṛṣis* he is Bhṛgu (10.25) and of divine *munis* he is Nārada (10.26) and Vyāsa (10.37) and of *kavis* he is Uśana (10.37); and his knowledge has been sung many times by *ṛṣis* (13.4). Consequently their authority recedes to the background and Kṛṣṇa is supreme and more authoritative than the *ṛṣis.* Thus even *kavis* are perplexed about action and non-action (4.16); those *ṛṣis* who attain extinction only in Brahman are freed from sin (5.25); even the great *ṛṣis* do no know the Lord's origin (10.2); all *ṛṣis* including Nārada and Vyāsa say, he is supreme (10.13); in the *viśvarūpa* Arjuna sees the *mahārṣis* praising the Lord with songs (11.21). Neither the multitude of gods (*suragaṇa*) nor the great sages know his origin, for he is their beginning (10.2).

W.K. Whillier compares the *viśvarūpa darśana* with the vision of the Vedic seers. "Seers had a direct intuitive insight into duty. They, by oral instruction, handed out hymns to later generations who were destitute of the direct intuitive insight".[189] Whillier identifies the manifestation of *vāc* to regulate ritual, transcendental consciousness, giving of *nāma rūpa*, power of *māyā* and intimate relationship as the chief elements in the mode of comprehension of their vision. It is a non-personal mode of consciousness which penetrates throughout. The truth of this reality, like a wife, remains an enigma, shrouded in poetic mystery just as the power that generates vision and *vāc* remains essentially incomprehensible.[190] The rationalisation of this mystery, Whillier holds, forms a transition from Vedism to classical caste ideology. It became a special privilege for the brahmin priests to continue the ancient *darśana* and handle the mechanism of ritual *yajña* which is the actualisation of the unseen mystery, though 'seen' by the ancient ones. Further, the interdependence of seers or the communality of brotherhood, as pointed out by Whillier, must have contributed to a collective priesthood. But the *Gītā* provides a link as well as discontinuity with this idea. Whillier writes:

> In the *Bhagavad Gītā* the model of the dialectic between the Lord and the adulant, one who knows and one who knows not, is continuous with the dynamic characterised by the *brahmodaya* in the *Ṛgveda*. Both are "dialectic" in the sense that both teaching situations initially involve a queston and answer exchange which, having exhausted discursive logical categories of thought in the attempt to reconcile empirical contradictions, culminates in the vision of a higher order of reality which is beyond common understanding.[191]

Whillier points out that the vision of the Vedic seers was received corporately whereas Arjuna stands alone—that was never seen before. In order to have this vision the seers performed sacrifice, but for Arjuna it is listening to the teaching of the Lord which produces a proper state of mind for a vision. "In this higher form of enlightenment Arjuna is drawn into solitary intimacy with the transcendent".[192] It is significant to note, however, that Arjuna receives this vision in the battlefield, which is, as a warrior, his sacrificial ground within the Vedic *dharma*. Thus there is transcendence within a tradition, not outside of it.

Besides, the *yajña*-oriented religion was exclusive in attaching sacred importance to a particular *varṇa* and accommodating a particular class. For example, women, śūdras, a black bird and a dog were abhorred in the vicinity of a *śrauta* ritual. Buddhism and Jainism accepted women monks though their position in the Buddhist monasteries was lower than that of men. But early law books assessed a woman's position as equivalent to that of a śūdra and child, whatever her class.[193] Manu does not allow sacrifice or even a rite like *vrata* for woman whose exalted position in heaven rests on honouring her husband, her lord.[194] But Kṛṣṇa in his love, embraces all beings including a man of evil conduct if he has *bhakti* (9.29, 30). Even those who are believed to be low-born like vaiśyas, śūdras and women, he accepts (9.32). It is important to see that the vaiśyas who had been among the twice-born were considered base-born along with śūdras and women in the time of the *Gītā*. In the wake of socio-economic changes in the pre-*Gītā* period they lost many benefits in trade and agriculture and slipped into the position of śūdras. In any case, unlike *yajña*, *bhakti* makes all people equal. The opposites of pure and impure or low and high are absorbed in the totality of *bhakti*.[195] But if this development cannot replace sacrifice with all its rules and notions the opposites may continue to exist in a subtle way, as we see in the *Gītā* itself.

Regarding the variety of sacrifices (4.24-32), Kṛṣṇa relates himself with them. *Deva yajña* then becomes Kṛṣṇa *yajña*, without of course denying that the gods can receive offerings independently. *Dravya yajña* in various forms, including simple *dravyas*, is directed to God. As Kṛṣṇa is the essence of all the *Vedas* and *mantras*, *svādhyāya* has effect only with reference to him. *Prāṇa yajña*, *jñāna yajña*, *yoga yajña* etc, which indicate the aspect of interiorisation, find their ultimate meeting point in this supreme God. *Japa yajña* is interpreted as identification with God, without any explanation. *Brahma yajña*, whatever may be its meaning, is either superseded or identified with God. Thus, in a *bhakti* interpretation of sacrifice various forms of it find integration in God though they do not lose their independent significance.

Kṛṣṇa takes the sāṃkhyan world-view for his interpretation of the types of sacrifice. Perhaps *sāṃkhya*, originally a non-Vedic system of thought, was popular among the *bhāgavatas*. Once we accept the sāṃkhyan view of a self-potent or *puruṣa*-dependent *prakṛti*, there need not be any place for sacrifice as the support of the world, in the Vedic sense. But in the *Gītā* both are accepted side by side; the writer of the text probably thought that sacrifice could find its own place in an all-embracing cosmic process. More importantly, Kṛṣṇa claims that the *triguṇa* is from him (7.12-15). Its exact meaning is difficult to understand because he applies it to various attitudes in sacrifice. The *yajña* undergirded by *sattva guṇa* and abandonment of desire for reward cannot easily be fitted into *bhakti* because Kṛṣṇa could not but promise supreme rewards for his devotees. Then in fact it becomes a refined *rajoguṇa yajña* in which reward is admitted. The *tamoguṇa yajña* is interpreted as the improper performance in which *dakṣiṇā* to the priest is not duly made. Actually in a *bhakti*-oriented, simplified form of worship there need not be concern for ritual rules. The statement "not by sacrifice but by devotion" indicates this. Water and flowers should become equally valid offerings as sacrifice. Further, if the *triguṇa* theory can be significantly applied to *yajña* it may be applied to *bhakti* too; but for this there is no reference in the text. Yet on the whole, our earlier comment is relevant here: if *triguṇa* comes from God or *prakṛti* it is difficult to evaluate different attitudes involved either in *yajña* or in *bhakti*.

In centring all *karman* on the one sovereign God, De Smet argues, a Copernican revolution is wrought by the *Gītākāra*.[196] In contrast to the *śramaṇa* teachers, he points out, the *Gītā* portrays God as an example and focal point for human action. The radical reinterpretation of all *karman* as an offering to God brings a sacrificial dimension to action.

> The sacrificial dimension brings about three results: (1) it makes man devote himself to his duties; (2) it makes his actions totally *niṣkāma*; (3) it ushers in the culmination of his *bhakti* as loyal and loving service to his Lord.[197]

We might ask, however: to what duties does the sacrificial dimension make one devoted? As we saw earlier, Arjuna was asked to contribute to the Vedic *dharma* without worrying about his personal likes and dislikes or about the outcome. As an individual he had no choice but to obey the ordinance. But in *bhakti* he becomes one with greater worth, 'dear' to the Lord. Does this new development replace the former? It seems not. In this case both obedience to *dharma* and devotion to God seem to be held together in spite of the tension between them. Moreover, the central act of *yajña* in Vedic *dharma* (both for mutual sustenance between gods and humans and for the functioning and preservation of the cosmos) is not given up even after the whole of *karman* is directed to God.

The problem of understanding the idea of *niṣkāma karman* has already been discussed in detail. It was made clear that this idea does not negate desire and concern for consequence as the condition of any act. Even *bhakti* is not presented in such a way that it strips off all the feeling and aspiration of a devotee. The primary need that *niṣkāma* attempts to resolve is an intellectual bewilderment (*moha*) about the outcome of a *dharmic karman*. It should not be evaluated from a conventional point of view; instead, it should be uncritically accepted as an eternal command. When this command comes from a divine person it carries more weight even though devotion to that person brings freedom and joy in the devotee. One may expect that this freedom must break the rigidity of ritual rules. But Kṛṣṇa does not indicate a stage at which this could happen. Because of this, the ritual *karma yajña* and *bhakti yajña* remain conceptually unrelated. Actually being mindful of a Supreme Lord helps one renounce all one's *karma* to God and become free of possessiveness and craving; Arjuna is asked to fight with this attitude (3.30). Moreover, *puṇya karma* is said to abolish one's sin and help one to be devoted to God (7.24–28). Conversely, to have a *darśana* of God's *viśvarūpa* is purely out of his grace, but it makes the devotee perform *karman* for him, completely give over to him, be devoted to him, without attachment and without enmity to any being, and go to him (11.55; 12.6). Hence there is a mutual interaction between *karma* and *bhakti*. Though the *Gītā* is not always clear about the sense in which it uses the term *karma*, certainly it primarily refers to the duties of Vedic *dharma* including the duty of sacrifice in order to sustain gods and the cosmos.

Though the *Gītā* does not develop the idea of *jñāna-yajña*, its mention of it has something to say about its relationship to *bhakti-yajña*. Insights are taken from Manu and the *Mahābhārata* for *jñāna* to be perceived as the highest form of comprehending God and his nature.[198] Kṛṣṇa says: "He who knows my divine birth and *karma* comes to my being (*bhava*) having killed *kāma*, *krodha*, etc. by *jñāna* (4.6–10); some sacrifice to me with *jñāna yajña* and worship me as one and manifold" (9.65). Thus *jñāna yajña* is a way to *bhakti yajña* (see also 12.3, 4). At the same time Kṛṣṇa dispels the ignorance of his devotees by the shining lamp of *jñāna* (10.11). Of those with *jñāna* he is their *jñāna* (10.38). Likewise he is identical with the *Veda* and *Vedānta* which alone provide *jñāna* (15.15).

Reaching or becoming Brahman is one point in the process of *jñāna* and *yoga*. But God is beyond that. He is the dwelling place of *brahman* (14.26, 27; 15.18, 19); he is the *Uttama Puruṣa* and *Paramātman*, who is beyond and other than not only the perishable world and beings but also the imperishable or the immovable (15.16, 17). Attaining the supreme perfection and becoming Brahman by the help of *jñāna*, however, further leads to *bhakti* for the supreme Lord (18.49–56). Zaehner's interpretation of the *Gītā* is dominated by this emphasis: monistic experience, which is one strand of the *Upaniṣads*, is penultimate and the ultimate is theistic experience, the other strand of the *Upaniṣads*. After a detailed discussion on this he sums up:

> It can be said that in the *Gītā* Brahman is the 'All', both temporal and eternal, while the highest Brahman is identical with the personal God, Kṛṣṇa who transcends both.[199]

On this basis Zaehner developed critical points about the experience of absorption into an "ambiguous" entity which is inferior to the numinous experience. Some other critics have gone to the extent of saying that the monistic trend is self-exterminative and suicidal, which is counter-balanced by theism.[200] Following the experience of oneness with the innermost self and of the liberated consciousness or a fixed, still state which is a conditioned mode of being, Feuerstein says,

> In a last act of self-surrender, the liberated being must open himself to the eternal love of God. Wisdom (*jñāna*) has helped him to cross over the ocean on unconditioned existence and transcend space and time—now love (*bhakti*) must unite him to the Supreme Being.[201]

In 9.15 Kṛṣṇa says, "Others with *jñāna yajña* worship me as one and yet as manifold, with face turned every way". Jordens finds in this verse the combination of *brāhmaṇic* sacrifice, Upaniṣadic knowledge and devotion. "*Yajña* thus becomes penetrated by the fulness of *bhakti*: knowledge and love of the Lord. Detached knowledge becomes attached knowledge. The vacuum of intention left by detachment is filled with the positive intention of the love of the Lord."[202] True, Jorden does not recognise the specific sense in which the *Gītā* understands the ideas of knowledge and detachment, but the connection he makes between them and *bhakti* is remarkable. Moreover, one may find a similarity between Vedic Prajāpati who appeared to save the *yajña* from its impersonal potency with Kṛṣṇa who appears to save the *ātma yajña* from self-extinction which was developed by one strand of Upaniṣadic thought and *śramaṇa* movement.

As we pointed out earlier, the *Gītā* often mentions *yoga* (i.e. *yoga yajña*) as different from *jñāna*. Although *yoga* originally emerged as a means of *ātma yajña*, later it came to be thought of as an end itself. But the *Gītā* gives it a new direction with its God-dimension as its ultimate end although for Arjuna the immediate implication is to do his duty. It talks about the supreme joy and realisation of the self in all in the process of *yoga* (6.29, 32). But in 6.30, 31 the self is replaced by God; Kṛṣṇa says: He who sees me everywhere and sees all in me, I am not lost to him, and he is not lost to me. That man of *yoga* who, taking his stand upon oneness, is devoted to me standing in every creature, exists in me, whatever directions the turns of his existing take him in. Likewise in 6.47 *yoga* is placed above *karman* and *jñāna* and in the previous verse it is said, "of all the men of *yoga* he who is possessed of faith and devotes himself to me with his inner self given over to me, I consider him to be the most disciplined" (also, see, 7.1-3). In *yoga* there is direct concentration on God. In certain places *bhakti* and *yoga* are combined with *jñāna*. Thus, it is said, of four classes of man, the man of *jñāna* who has *yoga* and *bhakti* excels (7.16, 17). Besides, Kṛṣṇa says: "noble are all these (*yogins*) without exception; but to my mind the man of *jñāna* is my very *ātman*. The *yogi* takes his stand upon me alone, the unsurpassed way" (7.18). Nevertheless in the context of the *Gītā* all these have an immediate purpose. As a *smṛti* the *Gītā* gives rules for the acts of *dharma* based on *śruti*, an ancient revelation. In Van Buitenen's words, "what it says about the human soul, God, and their interrelations has some purpose only as a sort of *arthavāda* to the injunction Fight. The notions of the *Gītā* about the avoidability of the consequences of acts is at least questionable. But by and large, as long as the text does not imply that the injunctions originated with a person, Kṛṣṇa, at a specific time, or that of the *Mahābhārata*, but simply reaffirms *Veda*-based *smṛti*, it is not in contradiction with *śruti*".[203] Although the central concern of the *Gītā* is the sacrifice of warriors, it is applicable to ritual sacrifice as well. Besides, we have considerable references to the reaffirmation of the ritual sacrifice although its scope is extended to include many other elements and to relate to many other ideas.

9. Conclusion

From a historical point of view the *Gītā* shares the common concern of the *Pūrvamīmāṃsā*, *Mahābhārata* and the *Dharmaśāstras* in reviving Vedic religion and sacrifice. Of the orthodox *darśanas* which, in an indirect way, contribute to this revival the *Gītā* takes *sāṃkhya* which provides categories for the interpretation of Vedic sacrifice. Sharing in the common characteristics of the above mentioned revival, the *Gītā* incorporates many elements from the *śramaṇa* movement. Hence there is *dāna, tapas, svādhyāya,* etc. sharing equal status with *yajña.* The mention of various types of *yajña* like *prāṇa yajña, jñāna yajña* and *yoga yajña* along with *dravya yajña* echoes the Upaniṣadic concerns of a new interpretation of *yajña.* Further, the interpretation of *karma* and *jñāna* could be taken, in the final analysis, to support the Vedic *dharma* and *yajña,* both directly and indirectly. Therefore the *Gītā* makes a significant contribution in a distinctive way, addressing with the authority of a supreme person in a situation in which the brāhmaṇic religion and sacrifice needed saving.

The *Gītā* affirms some of the fundamental aspects of Vedic sacrifice; for instance, sacrifice is the cow of desire, it feeds the gods and it upholds the operation of the universe. The leavings of sacrifice are said to remove evil and sin. In fact, in comparison with certain *śāstra* writers the *Gītākāra* seems to be more conservative in his emphasis on sacrifice. He insists on proper performance of sacrifice with all the prescribed rules, including due distribution of *dakṣiṇā.* He speaks for the continuation of sacrifice even in *saṃnyāsa.* His main concern of course is to support dharmic war, the sacrifice of the kṣatriyas. Apart from such direct indications, he supports the Vedic religion through new interpretations.

The interpretive categories of *karma, jñāna, bhakti* and *triguṇa* in the *Gītā* serve implicitly the purpose of the text to uphold the brāhmaṇic religion. The real tension arises when the brāhmaṇic ritual and *bhāgavata bhakti* stand together. Those who do not see the position of the *Gītā* from the viewpoint of its context have tried to solve this tension by saying that Vedic sacrifice in the text should be considered as this-worldly and preliminary (Minor), as of lower order (Tilak), as one manifestation of the Divine leading to an identification with him (Aurobindo), as an interpolation (Garbe), symbol of selfless service (Gandhi, Radhkrishnan, Belvalkar, Modi), and as a *karman* of *nitya* variety opposed to *kāmya karman* and so on.[204] This is because the text at certain places appears to transcend the Vedic ritual and it uses terms like *brahman, karman, jñāna* and *yoga* in different senses. Direct references to Vedic sacrifice are relatively few; but the sacrifice of the kṣatriyas is central. And a long tradition of interpreting *karman* in generally ethicised forms with the interpretive use of technical philosophical terms colour the interpretations.

Upadhyaya contends that the *Gītā* "seeks to combine the knowledge of *sāṃkhya* dualism and Upaniṣadic absolutism, along with the method of *yoga* and *bhakti,* with Brāhmaṇical ritualism by giving the latter a new meaning, and advocating thereby a new doctrine of *niṣkāma karma*".[205]

But as we have shown, the *niṣkāma* in the context of the *Gītā* denotes mainly the mental attitude of equanimity and detachment for action in the sense of avoiding any confusion and bewilderment in fulfilling the demands of an eternal law. The *Gītā* mentions *kāma* positively in many places. Relatedly, it is a common notion developed by many that there is a spiral movement or complex dialectics that culminates in *bhakti,* pushing all else to the background. Modi's passing suggestion that the first edition of the *Gītā* gave prominence to action before it was revised in favour of *bhakti* lacks evidence.[206] Further, the *carama sloka,* "giving up all *dharmas*, surrender to me" (18.66) is often quoted for the point of the culmination of *bhakti.* This verse is taken as containing a most secret teaching which should be spoken only to those who have the qualifications of *tapas, bhakti* etc (18.67, 68). There have been different opinions about the meaning of this verse. Madhva, for example, takes it to mean "giving up only the fruits" but not the *dharma* as such, which would contradict the main thrust of the teaching of the *Gītā.* Viewed in context, however, this verse may be taken to mean something else. It may reflect the attempt of bhāgavatism to overcome brāhmaṇism at a certain point in the process of amalgamation, emphasising its *bhakti* to which the

Vedic *dharma* should be surrendered. It is not a loss for brāhmaṇic tradition because Kṛṣṇa's Lordship upholds the *sanātana dharma.* Moreover, at the culminative point of *bhakti* if the command for the performance of Vedic sacrifice applies only to a lower category of people there is hardly any clue available to confirm this. And if the command appeals to all for the sake of mutual satisfaction of desire of both gods and human beings as well as the movement of the cosmic wheel, then it is difficult to hold *bhakti* and the supremacy of God as culminative. Rather, different strands are held together.

It is easy to discern an attempt at synthesising divergent trends into a harmonious whole by the author of the *Gītā.* But those different trends have their own paradigms or world-views. Then what is the new framework of all these paradigm, what is the central focus? Tilak's *Gītā Rahasya* has come to the conclusion that the text teaches *jñāna mūlaka-bhakti pradhāna-karma yoga,* a life of activism grounded upon knowledge and centred on the adoration of the Lord as the way of salvation.[207] But this formulation does not take *karma yoga* as meaning that *yajña karman* which is central and fundamental to all actions in general.

The lone statement "*jñāna yajña* is superior to *dravya yajña*" is pushed to its maximum by the *advaitins.* In the *Gītā,* however, the Upaniṣadic *jñāna yajña,* which is the way to *ātma yajña,* is given only lip-service. Just the same, it could be argued that first, the *jñāna yajña* does not replace *dravya yajña;* second, *jñāna* is interpreted mostly as being in support of it indirectly, i.e., as a mental state to perform action, including ritual action, without fickleness of mind, without confusion and worry about the consequences; hence the idea of *niṣkāmu karma.*

From the perspective to *bhakti* God is the integrative focus of all actions guided by knowledge. But if it is accepted that ritual sacrifice, an indispensable action, carries its Vedic notions, as we have already indicated, the relationship between the karmic power of ritual sacrifice and the supreme power of the Lord is placed side by side. And even if ritual sacrifice, along with knowledge etc, could be converted to one form of divine worship, the cosmic significance of sacrifice would have to be discarded, which the *Gītā* is reluctant to do.

Further, the affirmation of sacrifice as mutually sustaining gods and human beings and references to gods in the third person as receiving the oblations side by side with the supreme Lord, raise doubts whether according to the *Gītā* Kṛṣṇa has complete supremacy over gods and other beings like *rāksaṣas* who also are said to receive oblations from their devotees. As a result, his claim of supremacy over creation, function of the world and all beings and his emphasis on *bhakti,* which may be expressed by simple offerings like water and flowers, remain exclusive, not inextricably integrated.

In addition, in his identification with the world on the ground of the *sāṃkhya* framework, and his acknowledgement of the natural *guṇas,* Kṛṣṇa leaves certain problems unsettled. The natural force of *guṇa* is taken along with a supreme God, the creator and controller of the whole universe, who in his human form asks people to do their duty properly.[208] We have pointed out the problem in applying the *triguṇa* category to different types and attitudes of action. In fact, without making such connection the *Gītā* could present its concern more clearly.

The only key, however, to understand such problems in the *Gītā* is to have a historical perspective. As we noted earlier, the text emerged in the context of a brāhmaṇic revival, characterised by assimilation of new ideas and amalgamation with alien cults. Hence the synthesis of the *Gītā.* But nowhere in the study of Hinduism is opinion more divided than regarding the question of synthesis found in the *Gītā.* Thus there are those who hold that the synthesis of the *Gītā* is grand, comprehensive, perfect and so on.[209] On the contrary, there are others who find contradictions and inconsistency, and even a "cunning literary synthesis of the non-Aryan lore of Kṛṣṇa".[210] At another level, there are those who see "a deliberate appropriation, adjustment and synthesis",[211] while there are others who observe that the *Gītā* achieves "a kind of spontaneous synthesis".[212] As a piece of literature arising from a context of conflicting religious views, one may see the *Gītākara* "as a mere ecumenical creed-splicer" whose desire to accommodate many viewpoints is evident in the text.[213] It is more reasonable to say, however, that the *Gītā* shares the epic nature of the fluidity of thought, presenting many options together.[214] In other words, "the *Gītā* shares in the ambiguity of the tradition on the question of the univalency and/or multivalency of scriptural texts".[215] Sometimes when scholars make different claims about the synthesis of the *Gītā* they choose particular themes and do not show clearly its nature. Modi, for example, holds that each chapter of the *Gītā* develops one *yoga* or aspect of the central theme, i.e., disinterested action suiting people of a particular temperament. But his description of the message of the *Gītā* appears more complicated than that of the *Gītā* itself. He in fact makes cross references between chapters in a complex way.[216]

From the perspective of Vedic sacrifice, as in the *Mahābhārata*, we see a poly-paradigmatic position in the *Gītā* as it brings together different frameworks known as different *yajñas*. We have, however, identified a conscious effort to emphasise the central concern of Vedic *dharma* with the help of other types of *yajña* which are either simply mentioned or taken as interpretative categories. The main principles adopted in supporting Vedic *dharma*, including ritual sacrifice and the sacrifice of battle by the authority of a supreme God, seem to be that of affirmation, identification and assimilation. One may find these principles consistently maintained in the dynamic process of the brāhmaṇic religious tradition over the ages.

Notes

1. Eric Sharpe, *The Universal Gītā*, London, 1985, p.106.
2. F. Edgerton, *The Bhagavad Gītā*, Cambridge, 1944, part 2, p.77.
3. Rudolf Otto suggests for the *Ur-Gītā* and the interpretation of eight treatises in his *Original Gītā*, London, 1939. In his view, the glosses of *Bhagavad Gītā* 3.9-18 and 4.24-32 were inserted by a theologian concerned with sacrifice; they are foreign to the tenor of *yoga*. But we find similar views of these glosses in other sections also, for instance, in 6.1 and 7.30. and the statement "not by sacrifice but by devotion" occurs both in 11.48 and 11.53; but in Otto's classification, these verses are distributed to the *Ur-Gītā* and treatise no. 1; see, *ibid.*, p.148ff. Similar discrepancies are noticeable in Garbe's classification too; for instance, the passage 4.24-34 speaks of different types of sacrifice; Otto takes it as one gloss but his teacher Garbe takes only 4.24, 31 as included in the second redaction: for Garbe's suggestion for redactions, see Robert Minor, *Bhagavad Gītā*, New Delhi, 1982, p.xxxivff. In his three-author theory, Khair takes the verses that affirm *yajña* with modifications such as 3.9-16 and 4.23-33 as coming from the first author who counteracts the reaction against *yajña* by widening the scope of its meaning; the second author emphasises ceremonial duties since objectionable features are gone; but 8.28 which, in his view, comes from the second author, says that a *yogi* transcends sacrifice and so

on; further, he does not take into account *yajña* being identified with Kṛṣṇa and Kṛṣṇa asking to sacrifice for him which, for Khair, a section of devotion, is different from the two. See G.S. Khair, *Quest for the Original Gītā,* Bombay, 1969, p. 61ff.

4. E.g. for a dialogue between F.O. Shrader and S.K. Belvalkar on the so-called Kashmir recension, see Schrader "An Implication of the *Bhagavad Gītā* Riddle", *NIA,* I (1938-39), pp. 62-8; Belvalkar, "The So-called Kashmir Recension of the *Bhagavad Gītā, NIA,* II (1939-40), pp.211-51.
5. For a discussion on this elevation see Aghehānanda Bharati, "Hinduism and Modernization", in *Religion and Change in Contemporary Asia,* ed. R. Spencer, Bombay, 1971, p. 85f.
6. R.N. Minor, *Modern Indian Interpreters of the Bhagavad Gītā,* Albany, N.Y.,1986, p. 227.
7. E.J. Sharpe, *The Universal Gītā - Western Images of the Bhagavad Gita,* London, 1985, p. xiii: of course the Vedantic approaches already took this position.
8. See B.G. Tilak, *Srimad Bhagavadgītā Rahasya or Karma Yoga Sastra,* Bombay, 1935, pp.402,919; Mahadev Desai, *The Gospel of Sẹlfless Action or the Gītā According to Gandhi,* Ahmedabad, 1946, p.130. See also P.M. Modi , *BhG.*; Notes , p. 83f.
9. R.N. Minor, *op.cit.,* p.111; Bhaktivedanta, *Bhagavad Gītā As It Is,* New York, 1972, pp.172,176.
10. Quoted by E.J. Sharpe, *op.cit.,* p.10.
11. S.N. Dasgupta, *A Histroy of Indian Philosophy,* II, Delhi, 1975, p.485.
12. *ibid.,* p.520.
13. R. Panikkar, *The Vedic Experience - Mantra-Manjari,* London, 1977, p. 424.
14. *ibid.,* p. 425..
15. He continues: in the first it leads to hell, in the second to heaven and in the third to final salvation. K.N. Upadhyaya, *Early Buddhism and Bhagavad Gītā,* Delhi, 1983, p.108.
16. D.D. Kosambi, *The Culture and Civilization of Ancient India,* New Delhi, 1976, p.207. But elsewhere Kosambi points to the *Gītā* verse 3.14 in which sacrifice is admitted to be the generator of rain without which food and life would be impossible. And he calls this a slippery opportunism that characterises the whole book. See Kosambi, *Myth and Reality,* Bombay, 1962,p.17.
17. See Belvalkar, "*Bhagavad Gītā*: A General View of its History and Character" in *CHI,* II,p.149f.
18. D.S. Sarma, *The Bhagavad Gītā,* Madras, 1930,p. 20.
19. S.C. Roy, *The Bhagavad-Gītā and Modern Scholarship,* London, 1941, p.178.
20. K.W. Bolle, *The Bhagavad Gītā, A New Translation,* Berkeley, 1979, p. 240.

21. See R.C. Zaehner, *The Bhavgavad Gītā*, Oxford, 1969, p. 20.
22. R.N. Minor, *op.cit.* p. 207.
23. Jordens, "*Yajña*", p. 291.
24. *ibid.*, p. 292.
25. For a survey of opinions and arguments, see R.N. Minor, *BhG an Exegetical Commentary*, New Delhi, 1982, p. XLIIIff.
26. *Ibid.*, p. xlix.
27. See K.N. Upadhyaya, *op. cit.*, p. 29.
28. R. De Smet, "A Copernican Reversal: The Gītākara's Reformulation of Karma", *PEW*, XXVII/1(1977), p. 53.
29. Van Buitenen, *The Bhagavad Gītā in the Mbh.*, Chicago, 1981, p.11.
30. *ibid.*, p. 7.
31. See R.N. Minor, *Bhagavad Gītā*, p. xxiff; Tilak, *Gītā*, 2, pp.720-39; K.N. Upadhyaya, *op. cit.*, pp. 4-9.
32. V.S. Sukthankar, *On the Meaning of Mahābhārata*, Bombay, 1957, p.119.
33. S.K. Belvalkar, "*Bhagavad Gītā*: A General View of its History and Character", *CHI*, 1962, II, p.153.
34. See *ŚB.*, II, 1.8.2-3; *Manu*, I.22,23.
35. R. Panikkar calls this "an alienation of the cross"; *Hermeneutics*, p.172.
36. In myths *kāmadhuk* is associated with Indra. Its another name is *kāmadhenu*. It is *kāma* personified as the prime motive of sacrifice. See *ŚB.*, IV.2.3.6; *AV.*, XIX, 52; XI, 2.1,5.
37. See *ŚB.*, III, 4.2.6,7; A.B. Keith, *The Religion and Philosophy of the Veda and Upanisads*, Cambridge, 1925, p.460.
38. See R.C. Zaehner, *BhG.*, p.165.
39. E.g.. *ṚV*,X, 18.11 *AV* XII, 2.21; *ŚvU*, I, 12; III, 7; *MaiU.*, VI, 24.
40. E.g. *AV*, IX, 6; XI, 7.
41. See R.N. Minor, *BhG.* p.116f.
42. *ibid.*, p.173f; R.C. Zaehner, *BhG*, p.194; Tilak, *Gītā*, p.960f.
43. See J.O. Schrader, "The Sacrificial Wheel taught in the *Bhagavad Gītā*", *IHO*, V/2(1929), pp.173-81; cf. *BṛU*, VI.2.9-13and *ChU*, V.4-9.
44. T.G. Mainkar, "Some Thoughts on the Brahma Sutras and the *Bhagavad Gītā*", *ABORI*, LVIII-LIX(1977-78), p.750.
45. See C.A.F. Rhys Davids, *A Manual of Buddhism*, London, 1932, p.175; T.W. Rhys Davids, *Buddhist Suttas*, Oxford, 1900, p.153f; S.N. Dasgupta, *A History of Indian Philosophy*, I, p. 84ff; J. Gonda, *Indian Kingship from the Religious Point of View*, Leiden, 1969, p.125.
46. Romila Thapar, *Aśoka and the Decline of the Mauryas*, Delhi, 1973, p.146.
47. J. Gonda, *Ancient Indian Kingship*, p.125f.
48. *Nārāyaṇīya*, 356.
49. See *AiĀr*, II.1-3.

50. J.J. Lipner, "Applying the Litmus Test: A Comparative Study in Vedāntic Exegesis" in *A Net Cast Wide,* Newcastle upon Tyne, 1987, p. 59.
51. See M.R. Sampatkumaran (tr.), *The Gītābhāṣya of Rāmānuja*, Bombay, 1985, p.79; R.C. Zaehner *BhG,* p.167.
52. E.g. There are three or four senses in which the term *brahman* is used in the *Gītā*; see R.N. Minor, *BhG,* p.98.
53. *BhG.* 3.13.
54. See *HDhś,* II, p.425.
55. *Manu,* VI .83.
56. M.R. Sampatkumaran, *The Gitabhāṣya,* p.431.
57. *Manu,* IV.236, 237.
58. *BṛU,* VI.2.16.
59. See J. Gonda, *Vedic Ritual - The Non-Solemn Rites,* Leiden, 1980, p.469.
60. Vinoba Bhave, *The Steadfast Wisdom,* Varanasi,1973, p.150f.
61. See R.N. Minor, *BhG,* p.457f; M.R. Sampatkumaran, *Gitabhāṣya,* p.422f.
62. P.M. Modi, *BhG,* p.655.
63. See Douglas Hill, *The Bhagavad Gītā,* London, 1928, p.254.
64. See *AiB,* V.32ff.
65. *ChU,* I.1.1ff.
66. E.g. *TaiU,* I.8.1.
67. Edgerton, *BhG,* p.458.
68. *Manu,* II.76f.
69. See A.L. Basham, *The Wonder that was India,* London, 1956, p.147.
70. Quoted by A. Michael, "Ethical Action in the World-view of the *Gītā*", *JSBHG,* II(1982), p.22; cf. S.K. Belvalkar, *BhG,* p.lxxxivf.
71. Van Buitenen, *BhG,* p.13.
72. See *ṚV,* X.90.16; J.M. Koller, "*Dharma*: An Expression of Universal Order", *PEW,* XXII/2(1972), p.134.
73. For a discussion on this friendship see J. Gonda, *Aspects of Vaiṣṇuism,* Utrecht, 954, pp.151ff.
74. See A.B. Creel, "*Dharma* as an Ethical Category Relating to Freedom and Responsibility", *PEW,* XXII/2(1972), p.166f.
75. See S.N. Dasgupta, *A History of Indian Philosophy,* II, p. 536; cf. *ŚB,* XIV.1.1.18-24; it is also the place of battles of *devas* and *asuras,* later of Pāṇḍavas and Kauravas.
76. Bowlby, "Tradition in the *Bhagavad Gītā*", *SR,* XVII/2(1988), p.167f.
77. See E. Deutsch, *The Bhagavad Gītā,* New York, 1968, p.180.
78. Vinoba Bhave mentions antithetically the attitude of Arjuna with Aśoka in the battlefield. See G.W. Kaveeshwar, *The Ethics of the Gītā,* Delhi:, 1971, p.109. De Smet pictures vividly the background of the *Gītā* with special reference to the *śramaṇa* movement and

Aśoka, though comparison is not specifically made; see De Smet, "The *Gītā* in Time and Beyond Time", in *The BhG and the Bible*, ed. B.R. Kulkarni, Delhi, 1972, p.7ff.

79. For one such attempt recently, see I. Selvanyagam, "Aśoka and Arjuna as Counter-figures Standing on the Field of *Dharma*: A Historical-Hermeneutical Perspective", *HR*, Aug. 1992, pp.59
80. C. Keller, "Violence et Dharma chez Aśoka et dans la *Bhagavad Gītā*:, *AS/EA*, XXV(1971), p.189.
81. K.W. Bolle, *BhG*, p. 242.
82. *Manu*, X,97.
83. G.J. Larson, "The Tirūmurti of *Dharma* in Indian Thought: Paradox or Contradiction?", *PEW*, XXII/2(1972), p.151f.
84. S.N. Dasgupta, *A History of Indian Philosophy*, II, p.514.
85. *ibid.*
86. G.S.P. Misra, *Development of Buddhist Ethics*, New Delhi, 1984, p. 90.
87. See *Mbh*, XII.261-265, 272, 277; XIII.32.
88. M. Desai, *op. cit.*, p.130.
89. See K.N. Upadhyaya, "The Impact of Early Buddhism on Hindu Thought (with special reference to the *BhG*)",*PEW*, XVIII/3(1968), p.169.
90. M.R. Sampatkumaran, *Gitabhāṣya*, p. 38.
91. *ibid.*, p.39.
92. See E.J. Sharpe, *Gītā*, p.105.
93. See *Mbh*, V.139; XII.97-99.
94. See K.N. Upadhyaya, "The *BhG* on War and Peace", *PEW*,XIX/2(1969), pp.159-69. For elements of warrior ethics in the *Gītā*, see M.C. Smith, "Warrior Ethics in the *BhG*", *JSBhG*, IV(1984), pp.32-46; Tilak, *Gītā*, p.42ff.
95. P.N. Bazaz, *The Role of BhG in Indian History*, New Delhi, 1975, pp.259ff.
96. Sharma, *Hindu Gītā*, London: Duckworth, 1986, p.xv.
97. M. Das Gupta, "Early Viṣṇuism and Narayaniya Worship", *IHQ*, VIII(1932), p.80f.
98. See S. Jaiswal, *The Origin and Development of Vaiṣṇavism*, Delhi, 1967, p.115.
99. See S.N. Dasgupta, *A History of Indian Philosophy*, II, p. 508.
100. C. Keller, "Violence et *dharma*," p.193ff.
101. See R.N. Minor, *BhG*, p.170f.
102. *ŚB*, XI.5.6.3ff.
103. *HDhś*, IV, p.47f.
104. *Manu*, IV.21-23.
105. See *HDhś*, IV, p.44ff; *Manu*, II.85; R.N. Minor, *BhG*, p.320.
106. See R.N. Minor, *BhG*, p.98.
107. R. Gotshalk, *BhG*, Delhi, 1985, p.148.
108. See R.N. Minor, *BhG*, p.97.

109. R.C. Żaehner, *BhG*, p.191f.
110. Hill, *BhG*, p.145; see also *ibid.*, p.195.
111. Sharma, *Gītā*, p.47; cf. T.J. Hopkins, *The Hindu Religious Tradition*, Belmont, 1977, p.18.
112. J.C. Heesterman, "Self-sacrifice in Vedic Ritual", in *Gilgul: Essays on Transformation, Revolution and Permanence in the History of Religion*, eds. S. Shaked and others, Leiden, 1987, p. 92.
113. Hill, *BhG*, p.142.
114. Modi, *BhG*, 'Notes', p.140.
115. See R.C. Zaehner, *BhG*, p.192.
116. Gotshalk, *BhG*, p.84. For a discussion about the different views of scholars on the origin and nature of *sāṃkhya* found in the *BhG*, see p.170f; see also Modi , *BhG*, p.62f.
117. J. Neuner, "Religion und Riten Die Opferlehre der *BhG*", ZKT, 93 (1951), p.192f.
118. R.N. Minor, *BhG*, p.454.
119. *ŚveU*, V.7; *MaiU*, VI.10.
120. Aurobindo, *Essays on the Gītā*, Pondicherry, 1970, 13, p.117.
121. Killingley's comments on K.W. Bolle's translation, see *Religion* , X/ 2(1980), p.235.
122. See R. Panikkar, "The Law of *Karman* and the Historical Dimension of Man", *PEW*, XXII1(1972), p.31.
123. Gotshalk, *BhG*, p.100.
124. R.C. Zaehner, *BhG*, p.165; cf. *BhG*, 2.47.
125. See R.N. Minor, *BhG*, p.164f; N.Guru, *BhG*, p,185.
126. Edgerton, *BhG*, p.77.
127. Otto, *Gītā*, p.232.
128. Tilak, *Gītā*, p, 632.
129. See *ibid.*, p.72f.
130. Bazaz, *BhG*, p.56.
131. F.X. Clooney, "Jaimini's Contribution to the Theory of Sacrifice as the Experience of Transcedence", *HR*, 25/3 (1986), p.211; also see Keith, *Karma Mīmāṃsā*, Calcutta, 1921, p.74 and S.N. Dasgupta, *A History of Indian Philosophy*, II, p.405.
132. Jaini points out that the *Gītā* steers a Hindu middle path as it were between the *karmic brāhmaṇa* and *śramaṇa* renunciation traditions. He further notes: "In advocating disinterested action" the *Gītā* had achieved a major objective of the brāhmaṇical revival, *viz.*, the consolidation of the *āśrama* and *varṇa* discipline". Jaini, "*Śramaṇas:* Their Conflict with Brahmanical Society", in *Chapters in Indian Civilization*, p.74.
133. S.N. Dasgupta, *op. cit.*, p.516.
134. *ibid.*,p.522.
135. See Tilak, *Gītā*, p.73f; Hill, *BhG*, p.46f. S.N. Dasgupta notes the qualification for the study of *vedanta* as not having given up the

nitya and *naimittika karman* but only the *kāmya karman* and *nisiddha karman*, the prohibited acts. See S.N. Dasgupta, *A History of Indian Philosophy*, I, 489.

136. R.N. Minor, for example, expresses this view; R.N. Minor, *BhG*, p.113.
137. E.g. '*Kāma* is the very substance of human living', *ŚB*, XIV.7.2.7; *BhG*, 3.10.
138. See *Mbh*, XII.180,181; *HDhś*, II, p.8f.
139. See C. Malamoud, "On the Rhetoric and Semantics of Puruṣārtha", in *Way of Life*, 1982, p.45; cf. *Manu*, II.2-5,94ff.
140. *Manu*, XII.89-91.
141. Quoted by Tilak, *Gītā*, p.72.cf. *Śanti Parvan* 26.25.
142. K.N. Upadhyaya, *Early Buddhism and BhG*, Delhi, 1983, p. 481f.
143. Aurobindo, *Gītā*, p.102f.
144. See Tilak, *Gītā*, p.634f, 917f.
145. *HDhś*, V, p.1206.
146. See R.G. Bhandarkar, *Vaisnavism, Saivism and Minor Religious Systems*, Strassbourg, 913, p. 27; K.N. Upadhyaya, *Early Buddhism and Gītā*, p.109. For a reference in *Mbh* to *niṣkāma karman* and *bhakti*, see p.136f.
147. See Tilak, *Gītā*, p.451f.
148. G.W. Kaveeshwar, *The Ethics of the Gītā*, Delhi, 1971, p.57. He points out the verses: 2.7, 13, 52; 4.35; 11.1; 18.72, 73.
149. D. Prithipal, "*Moha*: The Study of a Human Religious Thought", *SR*, 4/4(1974-75), p.364.
150. Kaveeshwar, *op.cit.*, p.40.
151. *ibid.*, p.76.
152. *ibid.*, p. 56.
153. *ibid.*, p.52ff.
154. See Feuerstein, *BhG*, p.156f.
155. Radhakrishnan, *BhG*, p.187; also see Modi, *BhG*, 'notes' p.66f.
156. See Modi, *ibid.*, chapter 1, p.7.
157. For references from the scriptural context of the *Gītā*, see Tilak, *Gītā*, p.420ff.
158. Olivelle, "Contributions to the Semantic History of Saṃnyāsa", *JAOS*, 101/3 (1981), p.269.
159. See Kaveeshwar, *op. cit.*, pp.15ff.
160. Olivelle, *op. cit.*, p. 270.
161. Van Buitenen, *BhG*, p.16f.
162. See K.N. Upadhyaya, *op. cit.*, p.129.
163. See Zaehner, *BhG*, p.195.
164. Hill, *BhG*, p.110, note:1.
165. Van Buitenen, *BhG*, p.18.
166. S.N. Dasgupta, *Philosophy*, II, p.500.
167. Most of the opposites the *Gītā* mentions, such as pleasure and pain

(2.14,15,36; 6.32; 10.4,5; 13.20; 14.24), gain and loss (2.36), success and failure (2.48; 4.22; 18.26), honour and dishonour (6.7) and enemies and allies (6.9), reflect the context in which Arjuna was placed.

168. Feuerstein, *BhG,* p.158.
169. See M. Biardeau and C. Malamoud, *Le Sacrifice dans l Inde Ancienne,* Paris, 1976, , p.138.
170. See Van Buitenen, *BhG,* p.28; also see S.N. Dasgupta, *A History of Indian Philosopbhy,* II, p. 538.
171. See W.M. Callewaert and H. Shilanand, *Bhagavadgitānuvāda, A Study in the Transcultural Translation,* Ranchi, 1983, p.67.
172. R.C. Majumdar, *Ancient India* , Delhi, 1982, p.174f.
173. See Jaini, "Śramaṇas", p.74f.
174. De Smet, "*Gītā* in Time and Beyond Time",p. 29; "Integrative Doctrine of God of the *BhG*" in *Prayer and Contemplation,* ed. Vadakkekara, Bangalore, 1980, p.151ff.
175. R.C. Zaehner, *BhG,* p. 217.
176. See, M.R. Sampatkumaran, *The Gitabhāṣya,* p. 205; R.C. Zaehner and R.N. Minor accept Rāmānuja's interpretation.
177. Alladi Mahadeva Sastri, *The BhG with the Commentary of Śri Śaṅkaracharya,* Madras, 1977, p.224.
178. See Jordens, "Yajña in the BhG", p. 289.
179. *ŚB,* I.2.4.
180. See Modi, *BhG,* Notes, p. 399.
181. See K.N. Upadhyaya, *Early Buddhism and BhG.,* p.144f; R.G. Bandarkar, *Vaisnavism and Saivism and Minor Religious Systems,* p.7.
182. See J.C. Hesterman, *Inner Conflict* , p.47.
183. See S.C. Roy, *Mbh,* VI, pp. 531f, 542.
184. See M.R. Sampatkumaran, *op. cit.,* p.304f.
185. See D.Srinivasam,"The Religious Significance of Divine Multiple Body Parts in the Atharva Veda", *Numen,* XXV/3(1978), pp.193-225.
186. T.G. Mainkar, "Some Thoughts on the Brahmasutras and the *BhG*", p.750.
187. De Smet, "The *Gītā* in Time and Beyond Time", p.27f.
188. Aurobindo, *Gītā,* p.118.
189. W.K. Whillier, "Vision and Authority", *JSBhG,* V-VII(1985-87), p.151.
190. *ibid.*; p.153.
191. *ibid.*, p.155.
192. *ibid.*, p.157.
193. A.L. Basham, *The Wonder that was India,* p.179.
194. *Manu,* V.155.
195. Biardeau and Malamoud, *Le Sacrifice dans l Inde Ancienne,* Paris, 1976, p.138.
196. De Smet, "A Copernican Reversal", p.58.

197. *ibid.*, p. 62.
198. See *Manu,* XII.87; S.C. Roy, *Mbh,* VI, p. 558.
199. R.C. Zaehner, *BhG,* p.38; also see p.105f.
200. E.g. see Feuerstein, *BhG,* p.14.
201. *ibid.*, p.161.
202. Jordens, "Yajña in the BhG", p.292.
203. Van Buitenen, *BhG,* p. 9.
204. See R.N. Minor, *BhG,* p.151; Tilak, *Gītā,* p.634; Aurobindo, *Gītā,* p.104f; Belvalkar, "BhG: General View", p.139f.
205. K.N. Upadhyaya, *Early Buddhism and BhG,* p.107.
206. Modi, *BhG,* 'Notes', p. 384.
207. Tilak, *Gītā,* p.480; for vindication, see S.K. Belvalkar, "*BhG*: General View", p.149.
208. For a discussion on this problem, see S.N. Dasgupta, *A History of Indian Philosophy,* II, p. 533.
209. E.g. see Radhakrishnan, *BhG,* p.13f.
210. S.K. Bhattacharya, *Kṛṣṇa-Cult,* New Delhi, 1978, p.184.
211. K.N. Upadhyaya, *op. cit.*, p.115.
212. A. Sharma, *Gītā,* p. xxvi.
213. N. Hein, "Monotheism in the *BhG*: A Stylistic Clue", *SHR,* XXXI(1975), p. 251.
214. See A. Sharma, *Gita,* p. 254f.
215. *ibid.*, p. 255.
216. See Modi, *BhG,* ch. 2, p. 37.

Conclusion

This study has been an investigation into the nature of developments in the understanding of *yajña* (sacrifice) in the post-Vedic period and the teaching of the *Bhagavad Gītā* in response to these developments. With a recognition of the shortcomings involved in the various approaches to the religious texts which reflect these developments an historical-hermeneutical approach had been attempted in this study. In view of the distinctive characteristics of the Vedic *yajña* as action with cosmic significance we have not confined the analysis to the mere performance of ritual *yajña* but have taken along with it related ideas and connected factors. Therefore, on the whole, the discussion centres around the interaction and interrelatedness of a primordial vision and practice, tradition and interpretation.

The first chapter outlined the major aspects of Vedic *yajña*: its form, power and meaning. Vedic sacrifice cannot be restricted to a simple act of offering to the deities. Most probably, from this early form, it developed into an elaborate system bearing cosmic significance. The ritual act was believed to have hidden correspondences with the cosmic functioning; it was homologous with the 'other' or heavenly world. But this act became very complex , involving rules for minute details and a variety of personnel (priests) and oblations including a great number of animals. *Karman, brahman* and *tapas* were thought to generate sacred power as potency of ritual action, sacred utterance and heat of fire, as well as cooking, respectively. The meaning of sacrifice lies not in the cognisance and comprehension of everything in it, but the relationship and communication it makes and in the construction and integration it effects. Sacrifice has its intrinsic potency to create and sustain the cosmos. In relation to the sacrificers, the meaning of *yajña* lay in their participation in upholding the universal order, which includes feeding the gods, transcendent self-awareness and regeneration. From the expressed intentions of sacrifice it becomes clear that *kāma* is the undergirding attitude. Moreover, *yajña* is the primordial *dharma*, according to the *Vedas*, around which Vedic society was structured with, for example, the division of four *varṇas*. It is this *dharma* which is the unifying force in society, and to which the deities including the supreme deities like Prajāpati are subordinated. Finally, there are glimpses of symbolic correlation of ritual with the structure of the universe and human personality, found especially at the later stages of Vedic development.

The *Upaniṣads* carried further the interiorisation and symbolic interpretation of sacrifice which we have mentioned in the second chapter. Although the *Upaniṣads* contain a radical reinterpretation of sacrifice along with a new world-view, it is significant to note that they do not eradicate the ritual *yajña*. The emphasis, however, is on unified vision and self-realisation that are the fundamental aspects of an *ātma yajña*. The inferiority or the futility of ritual *yajña* and the impermanence of its results, including *svarga*, are established with a new doctrine of *karma saṃsāra*. Further, *brahman* is taken to mean the sum total of reality, *karman* as action in general, and *tapas* as interior heat. Cosmic vision and self realisation are achieved by the actualisation of inner powers for which *yoga* is formulated as the way. In an interior descent *kāma*, senses and the vital forces, like *prāṇa*, are sacrificed. The goal is self-sacrifice and an experience of oneness with the Supreme Reality. The *Upaniṣads* talk about this reality both in personal and impersonal terms. The ritual *yajña* is not, however, at all related to this reality except that a new kind of *yajña* is substituted for the former. Yet on the whole, we have noticed a fusion of the ritual and ethical, interior and exterior, that is correlated to the microcosmic and macrocosmic dimensions of reality. Accordingly, new terms emerged like *karma yajña, jñana yajña, brahma yajña* and *ātma yajña*. But conceptually, we have argued, there is a paradigm shift in the *Upaniṣads* though the continued persistence of Vedic ritual seems to obscure this shift.

Along with and following the *Upaniṣads*, Vedic religion underwent great changes which find brief description in the third chapter. The discussion covers a period of about four hundred years beginning from the sixth century B.C. Development of monarchy, centralised economy and inter-cultural encounters of social life are pointed out as greatly contributing to a decline in Vedic sacrifice and to the emergence of alternative perceptions, although there is no clear indication in the texts about the nature of this interaction. It is obvious, however, that the role of the *śramaṇa* movement, especially manifested among the Buddhists, Jainas and the *Ājīvikas,* was substantial in giving metaphysical shape to such perceptions. The *śramaṇas* ridiculed belief in the innate potency of the *yajña* ritual, opposed the elaborate performance of sacrifice in which large number of animals were killed and challenged brāhmaṇic support for the monarchic structures and rulers who still patronised grand performance of *yajña.* Further, they propounded alternative world-views to counter the *yajña*-based world-view. In place of Vedic authority they posited enlightenment and direct perception. *Kāma* was for them the arch enemy in the spiritual path. They replaced ritual rules by ethical rules for a new society conducive to authentic living. *Ahiṃsā* that was developed in the context of their protest against animal killing in sacrifice became one of their cardinal virtues. In due course, however, the *śramaṇa* movement lost its vigour, mainly because of its strong structures and inevitable allowance for some form of ritual in the religious life of its communities. Yet its influence on the political ideologies of the Mauryas, especially that of Aśoka, is considerable. Though Aśoka banned animal-killing in sacrifice he showed tolerance to all religions. Nevertheless the brāhmaṇic reaction to the challenges of the *śramaṇa* movement found an opportunity to revive the Vedic religion of sacrifice in taking advantage of the developments complemented by further political changes in its favour.

A revival in the brāhmaṇic religion at the turn of the second century B.C. is noticed in the history of ancient India. This is marked by the establishment of the Suṅga dynasty by Puṣyamitra, a staunch supporter of brāhmaṇism. Hence the decline and revival of sacrifice, perhaps as symbolised in the epic stories in the exile and return of the guardians of *dharma.* The orthodox *darśanas,* especially the *Pūrvamīmāṃsa,* boosted this revival by reaffirmation of the authority of the *Vedas* and the inherent potency of *yajña* ritual while the *Dharmaśāstras* attested it by law codes. But it is significant that the revival brought with it new elements to the Vedic religion derived mainly from the insights of the *śramaṇa* movement. Thus a process of assimilation is part of the revival of brāhmaṇism. Practices like *dāna, tapas* and *tīrtha* which became prominent during the time of decline in the sacrifice were incorporated into brāhmaṇic religion, as practices equivalent to sacrifice. The new scheme of fourfold *āśrama dharma* tried to combine *saṃnyāsa* and *vānaprastha* with the Vedic stages of *brahmacārya* and *gṛhastha.* Likewise, the fourfold *puruṣārtha* tried to combine ethical *dharma* and ultimate *mokṣa* with *artha* and *kāma,* the main motivating factors of Vedic sacrifice; so also the scheme of the four *yugas.* But it is important to note that these new formulations could not be clearly defined. The advocates of revival had different opinions about the number and order of the components of these formulations. Particularly, *saṃnyāsa* and *mokṣa* were taken with great reluctance as they appeared to obscure the meaning of Vedic sacrifice. Hence a strained synthesis.

The same is true in the greater synthesis of *bhāgavata* and brahmin elements which was achieved in the amalgamation of these two cults effected by the socio-religious situation at the time of revival. Some tensions are evident at the beginning of the process of this amalgamation. But things were worked out well in the process, thus giving birth to the later vaiṣṇavism of the pan-Hindu tradition. Bhāgavatism contributed *bhakti* to a personal God, Kṛṣṇa, who was interpreted by the orthodox thinkers as one of the *avatārs* of the chief Vedic god Viṣṇu and who is identical with all gods, the receivers of Vedic sacrifice. Ultimately, however, brāhmaṇism seems to have absorbed bhāgavatism, using its supreme God for teaching the Vedic *dharma* authoritatively as well as giving an integrative focus to all new forms of sacrifice like *karma* and *jñāna yajñas.* Further, new practices like *pūjā, dāna, tapas* and the study of the *Veda* were introduced and regarded as meritorious as sacrifice. Such a synthesis and assimilation, however, provided tools to reaffirm Vedic sacrifice in new ways, as we find in the *Gītā.*

All these developments were taken by the *Bhagavad Gītā* in an attempt to give a new interpretation of sacrifice without rejecting the Vedic vision. The *Gītā* reflects very much the concerns of the epics, especially the *Mahābhārata* and the *śāstra* writers (particularly Manu), with regard to the revival in Vedic religion and the process of synthesis. The text also takes insights from the *Upaniṣads,* Buddhism and *sāṃkhya-yoga* and tries to synthesise these into its combined perception of brāhmaṇism and bhāgavatism . Thus the

Gītā tries to counter a number of conflicting trends by attempting a compromise or reconciliation.

First of all, the *Bhagavad Gītā* reaffirms the fundamental assumptions and beliefs related to Vedic sacrifice. It affirms the primordial nature of Vedic sacrifice as part of the original creation, its mutual supporting power between gods and human beings and its sustaining power for the orderly functioning of the cosmos. Over against the *dharma cakra* developed by the Buddhists the *Gītā* sets a *yajña cakra* demanding indispensable participation of humans in setting the wheel in motion. Reacting to the liberal attitude taken by some law-givers that *saṃnyāsins* can give up ritual and other acts, the *Gītā* insists on their continuation by *saṃnyāsins.* What is needed is only the renunciation of *kāma* or attachment or confusion. It also incorporates the new substitutes like *dāna* and *tapas* as equivalent to *yajña.* It attaches the sacred terms of *oṃ, tat, sad* to the performance of sacrifice. Further, a note of correction is made for a right attitude in the performance of ritual *yajña:* avoidance of pride and confusion about its outcome. But there is no voice for deritualisation, not even a glimpse of allegorical interpretation or clear statement of *ātma yajña.* This picture obviously challenges some of the observations made by scholars about the *Gītā's* attitude to Vedic sacrifice, as we noted at the beginning.

Moreover apart from the direct affirmation of Vedic sacrifice, the *Gītā* indirectly supports the Vedic *dharma* by taking up the question of war, the sacrifice of warriors. In protest against a tendency to retire from the everyday life in the world and an aversion to war, Kṛṣṇa, a counter-image of the Buddha, encourages Arjuna, a counter-image of Aśoka, to fight. Kṛṣṇa justifies killing in sacrifice, i.e. war, by pointing out the categorical imperative of the *sanātana dharma,* the inevitability of death and the invulnerable nature of the soul. *Varṇa dharma* is upheld by saying that it was created by God himself for the establishment of order in society. Performance of sacrifice with prescribed rules, including liberal *dakṣiṇa* to priests, is insisted upon. Thus the supreme Lord is portrayed as supporting every cardinal principle of the ancient system of sacerdotalism. Hence brāhmaṇism is reintroduced through the authority of God. One may recognise the hand of a brahmin genius in this interpretation.

The *Bhagavad Gītā* mentions several types of sacrifice like *deva yajña, brahma yajña* and *jñāna yajña,* which had been understood in specific senses in the earlier period. It is not easy to find the exact sense in which the text uses terms like *brahman* and *jñāna* which were once used for a new interpretation of sacrifice as different from the idea of Vedic sacrifice. Perhaps it is too much to expect from a text like the *Gītā* which combines new ideas with old, a consistent view of sacrifice. Further, from an Upaniṣadic viewpoint the *Gītā* seems to pay only lip service to *jñāna yajña* because in the *Upaniṣads jñāna yajña* is identical with *ātma yajña* which has a distinctive conceptual framework. In this respect the single statement that "*jñāna yajña* is superior to *dravya yajña*", remains in isolation without in any way affecting the *Gītā's* affirmation of Vedic sacrifice. Likewise, the *Gītā* attempts a novel interpretation and classification of *yajña* using the sāṃkhyan scheme of *triguṇa.* This attempt, which appears artificial on the whole, helps to insist on the performance of sacrifice in a perfect way as it is related to the best, i.e., the *sattva guṇa* type.

By relating *yajña* to action, the *Gītā* tries to provide profound insights for authentic action though the sense(s) in which the term *karman* occurs in the text is not always clear. The famous idea of *niṣkāma karma* propounded by the *Gītā,* from the viewpoint of *yajña,* means neither disinterested action nor dispassionate detachment, as often understood. It is the performance of action, both ritual and general, with undivided concentration on carrying out of a mandatory duty required by *sanātana dharma.* The idea of action without a desire for reward is, however, attached to sacrifice in some places. Actually this idea cannot be taken to originate in the Vedic idea of sacrifice but is imposed upon it. Further, in the view of the *Gītā, karma yajña* may include all types of *yajña* mentioned earlier. *Jñāna yajña* is made subservient to *karma yajña,* thus presumably avoiding the Upaniṣadic tendency of understanding *jñāna* as a path to an 'abstract goal'.

The integrative point of the Gītā in interpreting sacrifice is found in *bhakti yajña.* Kṛṣṇa claims that he is the Lord, enjoyer of all sacrifices. Even the offerings made to the Vedic gods finally go to him for he is the 'self' of those celestial beings. There are, however, references to *devas, bhūtas* and other beings receiving sacrifice from their devotees as their goals in the end. There is, then, a tension between Kṛṣṇa taking the place of the ancient gods and allowing them their traditional dominion in limited measure. Further, the Lord identifies with *yajña* as its essence and cause in the style of the chief Vedic gods like Prajāpati. But the difference made is that Kṛṣṇa can never be the victim of sacrifice as was Prajāpati; he is its governor and saviour, like Viṣṇu. In the approach to the supreme God it is *bhakti* which is necessary and with that God accepts all offerings, however simple they are. The most beautiful expression is, "You do everything as an act of sacrifice to the Lord". This *bhakti* orientation gives a new significance to Vedic sacrifice. Besides, the Vedic vision is subordinated if not contradicted by a new vision, i.e., the *viśvarūpa darśana* which could be experienced not by the performance of *yajña* or *dāna* but by divine grace and *bhakti*. In this new framework there develops a new outlook for society in which *all*, including *śūdras* and women, who were previously precluded from Vedic *yajña*, are embraced. *Jñāna*, (not with reference to *jñāna yajña* in the Upaniṣadic sense) is taken to be instrumental for a perfect relationship with a loving God. He is the integrative power of all vital forces whether in nature or in human personality. But all these interpretations are directed to the fulfilment of Vedic *dharma*.

The brāhmaṇization of the epic stories is applicable to the *Gītā* as well. A brahmin writer seems to have produced the *Gītā* with an immediate purpose. Perhaps the writer thought that the *bhāgavata* vision of the Supreme would provide a solid ground to counter the heterodox challenges and integrate the diverse strands of thought found in the *Mahābhārata*. Apparently he was a liberal person strongly supporting the amalgamation of bhāgavatism and brāhmaṇism. Thus he combined the ideas prevalent in diferent traditions. Wherever he thought he could make a connection of different ideas, so he did. Consequently the text appears very complex, which is rather typical of the sections where he brings together divergent trends without bothering about the strange tensions they might cause. While giving rather isolated statements about matters like *jñāna yajña* and curious connections such as *triguṇa* with *yajña*, however, the author does not deviate from his primary purpose, which is to reaffirm Vedic *dharma*, which includes both ritual sacrifice and the sacrifice of warriors, i.e., war. Seen from the *bhakti* emphasis, the sacrifices of action and knowledge in a specific sense could be taken as supporting devotion to a supreme God. But the greatest difficulty lies in solving the tension between the affirmation of Vedic *yajña* with its cosmic significance by the *Gītā* and its *bhakti* emphasis. It is true that the scope of sacrifice is widened to include new aspects such as different types of sacrifice and even every action as sacrifice. In certain places the *bhakti* tends to transcend Vedic *dharma.* In the final analysis the *karmic* power of Vedic ritual seems to continue as a parallel to the supreme power of God. Using again the language of scientific developments, instead of opting for a paradigm shift, the *Gītā* has taken a form of "poly-paradigm" which is characteristic of later brāhmaṇic Hinduism as well. A study of the post-*Gītā* literature from this perspective will make this distinctive character clearer.

Today in Hindu religious traditions we see mostly temple, *pūjā* and the *āgamic* ritual in place of Vedic fire-altar and complicated *yajña* ritual though the notions of Vedic ritual continue. At the same time it should be acknowledged that "Vedic sacrifices survived, especially in Brahmaṇic circles, for many centuries after the Vedic period and in particular cases to the present day."[1] Apart from the occasional performance of or call for a grand sacrifice, especially in the context of present-day Hindu revival movements, many domestic rituals are practised especially in the *vaiṣṇava* brahmin circles with rigid rules as prescribed in the *Gṛhya Sūtras.*[2] In this connection the report of P.H. Prabhu in his study of Hindu social organisation is noteworthy. He writes about the *yajña parampara* that has been preserved through the ages.

> A very pointed instance of the persistence of this *parampara,* social heritage or tradition, is the fact that even today, the term *yajamāna* (sacrificer) is very commonly used to denote the head of the house, or the householder, or the husband of a woman, according to the context in which it appears... This is how the socio-religious heritage of the Vedic India has persisted in the cultural consciousness of the Hindu even to this day.[3]

Thus the ritual tradition on the whole has a remarkable continuity despite many challenges and new focuses like *bhakti* and *jñāna.* Even where *bhakti* or *jñāna* is given prominence, ritual in most cases continues in the name of tradition. As in the *Gītā,* conceptually the inter-connectedness between them is not analysed. In this situation it would be interesting to see how this inter-connectedness is analysed or ignored in modern interpretations of the *Gītā* and the consequence for cultic life of Hindus. It needs a new approach with new interpretative procedure, which admittedly lies beyond the scope of this study.[4] We bring this study to a close by highlighting certain unique features in the hermeneutical process which we have examined.

1. A living religion is characterised by its dynamic process. It is a historical-hermeneutical process which involves interaction between core vision and social changes. As far as brāhmaṇic Hinduism is concerned *yajña* is one of the best examples for the study of this process, as it is a fundamental category in its vision and tradition.

Every process is unique, as is its core vision and hermeneutical pattern, even though there may be certain resemblances between the patterns of different religious traditions. For example, the Judeo-Christian tradition also has the idea of sacrifice. It has its own history of development. "Several prominent scholars are of the opinion that many of the sacrificial rites in the Old Testament developed as the Israelites came into contact with neighbouring heathen, particularly Canaanite, cults and, thus, they were products of a lengthy and complex development."[5] The ideas of praise, thanksgiving, atonement etc. were attached to the performance of sacrifice but all such ideas were taken on the basis of "the reciprocal commitments implied in the original covenant" that God had made with his people.[6] Comparing this basic idea with the understanding of sacrifice in brāhmaṇic Hinduism, Clooney writes:

> the Biblical idea of sacrifice is always God-oriented, based in the fact and value of God's relationship with his people, his covenant with Israel, whether the sacrifice constitutes or reflects or restores that covenant. There does not seem to be any part of the Bible which values sacrifice in and of itself, and certainly no trend which would value sacrifice more than God.[7]

There were, however, shifts in emphases of meaning, e.g. from cult to morality: God demands not sacrifice but love, knowledge and obedience (1 Sam.15.22; Hos. 6.6); from cult to inner relationship between an individual and God: no delight in sacrifice but accepting the broken spirit and contrite heart (Ps. 51.16,17). One may find in the Old Testament occasions of priestly resistance to the moving away from sacrificial cult (e.g. Ps. 51.19, cf 51.16; 17). In the New Testament the cruel death of a "criminal" i.e. Jesus, is interpreted in terms of an end to cultic sacrifice, a permanent act of atonement, making a new covenant, giving up life for others, public acknowledgement of God's supremacy, the sinfulness of humanity, and so on (e.g. Mt. 26.26ff; MK. 10.45; Jn. 1.29; Rom. 3.24f; Heb. 9.23ff; 1 Jn. 4.10). The efficacy of this divine sacrifice has been understood in the Church in terms of God's demand for living sacrifice (Rom.12.1), the continued sacrifice of Christ in an unbloody manner in the eucharist,[8] spiritual sacrifice of praises (Rom. 13.15f; 1 Pet. 2.5), and so on. The interpretation continues. In the Indian Church, for example, there are different opinions about the sacrifice of Jesus, whether it has or needs to have atonement value or moral influence.[9] In all these interpretations there is no clue in this tradition for the understanding of ritual act which is effective in itself, creative, universally potent, its result latent wihtin it, as in the case of Vedic sacrifice. There is, then, a unique process of change and interpretation on the basis of distinctive core vision and the development of its tradition. This fact should challenge the assumptions of a phenomenology of religion which synchronises religious traditions and tries to see the common essence of institutions like, for instance, sacrifice. One needs to go beyond the typological description and evolve a critical analysis of a historical process which is a hermeneutical process too.

From a diachronic outlook the changing process is a complex one. External impact and internal development imperceptibly get fused. The succession of innumerable individual cases of changes, influences etc. cohering into a process, as far as the post-Vedic developments are concerned, is chronologically almost undefinable; and the developments are never uniform and unilinear. Nevertheless, radical changes in dominant ideas are discernible. For example, in the *Upaniṣads* directions for a new understanding of sacrifice are clearly identifiable. These directions reach their head in the *śramaṇa* movement which was a great force effecting changes in the understanding of sacrifice. Challenging ritual sacrifice, suggesting alternative ways of making offerings to gods and providing new frameworks for religious life marks the approach of this movement.

2. Even though the vital aspect of a primal vision continues as in the case of ritual action, revision and change of perceptions are part of

a hermeneutical process. The idea of a God related to sacrifice, for example, which provides a focal point of potent action and unifying force, has changed fast in early times. The Ādipuruṣa, the first image of a supreme God in the Vedic tradition, later became a sacrificial vicitim at the time of the creation of this universe. When the brāhmaṇic ritual became highly elaborate and complex, with a belief in the innate potency of a ritual act, in order to save the sacrifice from an impersonal and arbitrary functioning of sacrifice, Prajāpati appeared. But soon the name Prajāpati was changed into the question, who is Prajāpati? In the *Upaniṣads* Prajāpati is brought to a lower position as teacher and the supreme Brahman introduced as reality. But in the name of realising this one reality in one's own self, internal powers were actualised through *tapas* and *yoga,* which often threatens self-destruction and the destruction of the world. The presentation of this supreme reality as a person was introduced in certain *Upaniṣads* as a focal point for devotion and knowledge. But it did not become popular. The popularity is achieved in the person of the many faced Kṛṣṇa. This, however, is not the final stage as far as the scriptural tradition is concerned, even though Kṛṣṇa is identified with the personal Brahman and subjugated to the perception of an impersonal reality. Later literatures seem to question the supremacy of Kṛṣṇa. Yet somehow the process of perceiving the ultimate reality and giving it a name and form in Hindu tradition stops with the figures of Śiva, Viṣṇu and Kṛṣṇa—goddesses are incorporated mostly as their consorts, and popular deities, mostly as their manifestations.

3. In every hermeneutical process there are distinctive ways of interpretation. In the post-Vedic developments in the understanding of sacrifice the following principles are prominent: (i) Apart from direct affirmation of Vedic authority and tradition, novel ways of doing it: e.g., the wheel of sacrifice found in the *Gītā* with a view to counter the wheel of *dharma* developed by the Buddhists. (ii) Allegorical interpretation: e.g., forces of nature forming a horse-sacrifice as developed in the *Upaniṣads.* (iii) Interiorisation that gave birth to a new type of sacrifice: e.g., the *ātma yajña* of the *Upaniṣads.* (iv) Development of ethical principles in place of a religious practice: e.g., kindness to all beings as an authentic form of sacrifice as preached by the *śramaṇas,* which had great influence on the *dharmic* reforms of Aśoka. (v) Giving new definitions for old ideas: e.g., who is brahmin or brāhmaṇa? The *śramaṇa* teachers define brahminhood

not in terms of priestly power but ethical qualities. (vi) Development of new substitutes for old practices that became ambiguous and difficult: e.g., *pūjā, tīrtha* and *vrata* in place of sacrifice; offering water or flowers instead of animals. (vii) Making new identifications and connections: e.g., Kṛṣṇa as the sacrifice and the ideas of sacrifice of action, of knowledge and of devotion. (viii) Use of categories taken from other traditions as conceptual tools for new interpretations: e.g., interpretation of sacrifice through the *triguṇa* category of *Sāṃkhya.* Apart from these principles there are arguments and dialogues in support of a particular view-point as we have seen regarding war and the question of killing animals in sacrifice.

4. Logical continuity and consistency in the use of terms need not be expected in every interpretation. We have pointed out a wide range of meanings assigned to the terms *brahman, karman, tapas* and *dharma.* These terms mean different things for different people in different contexts.[10] But when scholars use these terms today, they do not always seem to acknowledge the specific senses in which certain terms (e.g. *dharma*) are used in the scriptures. This sets the greatest difficulty for a clear understanding of the religious traditions of India.

5. In a process of inter-cultural or intra-cultural interaction, the formulation of new ideas and counter ideas may leave loopholes in the subsequent process. We have a clear example for this. The idea of the soul as an entity is developed probably by *śramaṇas* or *munis* and introduced in the *Upaniṣads.* Originally it was to challenge the ritual sacrifice and point out its impermanent goal of *svarga*: whether god, *ṛṣis* or human being, all die even in *svarga* and all have to come down for new forms of birth. This idea was developed further by the *śramaṇas* in different ways. In the Buddhist framework of dependent origination, for example, no permanence is given even to the soul. At the same time, Buddhism protested against killings in sacrifice and preached *ahiṃsā.* But this seems to lack doctrinal foundation. If everything is in a flux and there is no such entity as the soul what is the harm in killing? Presumably using this advantage, in the time of the brāhmaṇic revival, it was held that killing in sacrifice is not *hiṃsā;* even more interestingly, the *Gītā* justifies "sacrificial" killing with the support of the idea of the invulnerability of the soul. Then Rāmānuja is right in his view that by killing in sacrifice we create an opportunity for the victim to gain a higher form of birth. As long as the *saṁsāra*

of the soul is maintained there can be no substantial move from this position. In fact, the self-torture of certain *śramaṇas* appeared to the sacrificers as worse than sacrificing animals. Besides, a modicum of *hiṃsā* was unavoidable for maintaining discipline in a monastery or in a state; this was evident in the rules supported by the *śramaṇas*. Taking advantage of this fact, the sacrificers asked for exemption of sacrificial slaughter from the general ban on killing animals.

The same may be said about the fourfold *āśrma dharma* and the *puruṣārtha* schemes also. They were formulated with a view to contain *śramaṇa* influence and incorporate its ideas. Since there was no clear-cut thinking about their logical connections and coherence they invited divided opinions about their form, number and meaning. This may be the reason why *āśrama dharma* and *puruṣārtha* remained dead letters even though they give some insights and options to understand the nature of human life and its goals. From the viewpoint of structural science this process makes the development more complex as fundamental aspects of one paradigm are taken to support a paradigm contrary to it.

6. Despite modification and refinement, the fundamental traits of an ancient vision persist as a stubborn fact. Ritual, for example, inextricably related to the Vedic vision, institution and experience, has never been replaced despite sharp criticisms levelled against it. Although the *śramaṇas* allowed simple forms of ritual, they never accepted its Vedic presupposition such as that ritual has innate power. In the course of time, however, the influence of the brāhmaṇic ritual was seen in the *śramaṇa* tradition too. Hence the development of an elaborate and rigid form of ritual, for instance, in the Jaina and Buddhist traditions. They could dispense with gods, and even a supreme God, but not with ritual. Even alongside the emphasis on *bhakti* ritual has continued. *Bhakti*, at certain points converted the intrinsic value of ritual into instrumental value, but seems to have maintained it as a power parallel to the supreme power of God. This is evident in the forms of worship in Hindu temples. Even devotional śaivism, which preserves the tradition of Śiva disturbing the brāhmaṇic ritual and becoming mad on account of his love for his devotees, is not able to transcend ritual rigidity. Likewise, those who emphasise knowledge and meditation are hardly able to surpass ritual. Hence the mixture of ritual, devotion and meditation in the religious life of many Hindu thinkers.

7. Relatedly, there seems to be a tension between the universal and the particular in a hermeneutical process. There is a tendency in the modern period, for example, to generalise, moralise and universalise the Vedic idea of *dharma. Yajña* was the key of primordial *dharma* according to the *Veda.* In the process of change there has been a sustained effort to preserve this *dharma* while allowing slight modifications. For a strict follower of the *Gītā, dharma* means the Vedic *dharma* with sacrifice at its centre, which also includes the duties of different *varṇas.* At one point Kṛṣṇa calls for giving up all *dharmas* and surrender to him; this, however, does not mean the abandonment of the *dharmic* action, only performing them in surrender to him or in obedience to his command without questioning about their consequences. Arjuna has to perform the sacrifice of war, the duty of a kṣatriya. It is difficult to find a universal *dharma* unless one takes in isolation certain teachings which are applicable to all.[11] Gandhi, for example, took the references to *ahiṃsā* more seriously than the command to kill in the *Gītā,* which appeared to be meaningful for those who fought violently for the freedom of India. Similarly, the idea of *niṣkāma karma* occurs in the *Gītā* primarily in the sense of undivided and unbewildered obedience to an eternal *dharma.* But those who take this as meaning a desirable common human mental attitude to action in general, do not take the original meaning seriously. A common human attitude without any reference to a supreme authority, a law or God, is far from the concern of the *Gītā.* Thus, there is obviously a tension between the particular and the universal which is taken on the basis of the particular.

8. Tolerance, accommodation and synthesis are some fundamental aspects of the hermeneutical process we have inquired into. As we pointed out, the kind of tolerance developed in brāhmaṇic tradition was not so much based on a broad spiritual vision and thought as in the light of certain exigencies. In a context of challenging trends the brāhmaṇic tradition incorporated many ideas from other traditions but without diluting its original vision. Moreover, the spirit of tolerance was motivated by a compromising political policy adopted by Aśoka at a crucial moment of tensions. In this sense his position may be comparable to that of Solomon, Constantine and Akbar. But in all these cases the compromise was short-lived.

In the process of assimilation "a deliberative, thoughtful and careful analysis" is not evident.[12] Consequently, there are uncertainties and artificiality in formulations, as we have pointed out with reference to the fourfold *āśrama* and *puruṣārtha*. Likewise, there are tensions as between ritual rigidity and loving devotion, between *ahiṃsā* and killing, and so on. The same may be found in the *Gītā* which tries to synthesise not simply ideas but more fundamentally a distinctive world view of Vedic religion, Upaniṣadic thought, sāṃkhya framework and *bhāgavata* cult. Seen from the distinctive visions of these traditions, the *Gītā* seems to develop a poly-paradigmatic framework, though its emphasis on Vedic *dharma* in various ways is consistent. This is characteristic of the hermeneutical process of Hinduism in general. It is not only incorporation of some ideas and interpretation of an idea in a new way but accommodation of fundamentally different frameworks.

9. Changing attitudes to traditional religious texts are another aspect of the hermeneutical process, as we have noticed in our inquiry. Of course, more detailed and extensive study is called for to compehend the exact position of the *Upaniṣads* as the end or goal of the *Vedas*, of the epics and law codes as well as different philosophical systems which claim to accept the authority of the *Vedas* and their tenet as a primary source. Sacrifice is the quintessence of the Vedic texts. In the *Upaniṣads*, claims for the authority of the *Veda* are mixed with counter-claims. The same tendency may be noted in the *Mahabharata*, which is also called the fifth *Veda*. Particularly the *Purvamīmāṃsa* developed not only exegetical principles but also principles to affirm the authority of the *Veda* and to evaluate the validity of a text with reference to its use for the performance of sacrifice. This approach is, not however, applicable to all schools and *smṛti* texts. On the whole, although brāhmaṇic Hinduism is inextricably tied to the legitimising authority of the *Vedas*, as Brian Smith points out, "in post-Vedic times the subject matter of the *Veda* is largely unknown by those who define themselves in relation to it".[13] Renou's *Destiny of the Veda in India* is a profound attempt to identify this paradox in the later phases of Hinduism.[14]

The above paradox is evident in the *Gītā*. For the *Gītā*, on the one hand the *Vedas* are *guṇa*-bound (2,45), of limited use for an aspirant of liberation like that of a well in a flood (2,46), *saṃsāra*-bound (9.20.21), of no value for having a vision of God (11.48.53,54) and so on. On the other hand, Kṛṣṇa is identified with the *Sāman* hymns and *Gāyatrī* metre (10.35); Kṛṣṇa alone is to be known from all the *Vedas* (15.15); one should obey the commands of the *Vedas* in this life (16.23f); study of the *Vedas* is equivalent to sacrifice; recitation of it is the *tapas* of speech (17.15). On the whole the *Gītā* seems to reflect a dialectical tension between the *apauruṣeya* value of the *śruti* and the concrete aspect of a changing culture. It presents a renewed vision of the *sanātana dharma* but on its base it builds new superstructures in order to keep the *dharma* more dynamic and the form of the culture more fluid.

Originally, the *Gītā* comes under the category of *smṛti*, representing a tradition remembered and interpreted. But the vedāntic and modern approaches to it have given it the position of *śruti.* Perhaps a more systematic approach to the scriptures is needed so that the original place of particular texts may be clearly understood in the light of their context. The only voice to this effect seems to be that of Swami Dayananda Sarasvati, a great Hindu revivalist in the modern period who with his watchword "back to the Vedas" accepted only the *saṃhitā* part of the *Vedas* as true revelation, bypassing even great texts like the *Upaniṣads* and the *Gītā.* Being true to its nature as dynamic and everchanging, Hinduism needs to present its attitude to the scriptures more clearly.

10. Finally, despite tension between various trends in a synthetic process, the aspect of "spilling seeds" or "scattering sparks" should be recognised in a dynamic process. Though the *Gītā* reaffirms the Vedic *dharma* with sacrifice at its cente, in its process of assimilation and new interpretation, certain ideas occur so outstandingly that they could be picked out in isolation and used to approach the text in a selective way with a view to find its relevance for changing contexts. Two such ideas are remarkable. First, the *Gītā* states, "Sacrifice of knowledge is superior to sacrifice of objects". This statement is repeated by those who want to challenge a kind of religious obsession with ritual. Second, Kṛṣṇa says, "Whatever you do, do it as a sacrifice to me". This statement is often highlighted as giving a profound insight for meaningful action and devotion. This has currently been taken to mean a dedicated participation in the movement of social transformation and national integration, as emphasised by many Hindu thinkers. The above statements are spilling seeds that emerge out of the process of a struggle to interpret an ancient vision in a new circumstance. Those who magnify these statements within an interpretative tradition need to evaluate how such ideas are integrally related to other dimensions of religious life.

And since they use the sacrificial language, the religious acts of ritual and sacrifice should be paid special attention.

NOTES

1. J. Gonda, *Change and Continuity in Indian Religion*, New Delhi, 1985, p.16; for the origins of the development of *pūjā*, see T. J. Hopkins, *The Hindu Religious Tradition*, Belmont, 1971, p.110.
2. For certain routine of rituals practised in *vaiṣṇava brāhmaṇa* communities, see D.B.K. Rangachari, *The Śrī Vaishṇava Brāhmaṇas*, Delhi, 1986.
3. P.H. Prabhu, *Hindu Social Organization*, Bombay, 1979, p. 64.
4. For a useful suggestion, see G.J. Larson, "The *Bhagavad Gītā* as Cross-Cultural Process: Towards an Analysis of the Social Locations of a Religious Text", *JAAR*, XLIII/4(1975), pp.651-69.
5. J. Thachil, *The Vedic and Christian Concept of Sacrifice*, Alwaye, 1958, p. 219.
6. M.F.C. Bourdillon and Meyer Fortes(ed.), *Sacrifice*, London, 1980, p. xv; also see G. Ashby, *Sacrifice: Its Nature and Function*, London, 1988, p. 36.
7. F.X. Clooney, "Sacrifice and Spiritualization", *Harvard Theological Review*, 78/3-4 (1985), p. 365.
8. See Thachil, *op. cit.*, pp.300ff.
9. For Chakkarai's view, for instance, see Robin Boyd, *An Introduction to Indian Christian Theology*, Madaras, 1975, p.177.
10. For a discussion on this issue, see J. Gonda, *op. cit.*, pp. 70, 198.
11. For a scholarly dialogue on the question of universal and particular with reference to Kṛṣṇa's command for killing, see Paul Weiss, "The *Gītā*: East and West", *PEW*, IV/3(1954), pp. 253-8 and Haridas Chaudhuri, "The *Gītā* and its Message for Humanity", *PEW*, V/3(1955), pp. 245-53.
12. P.H. Prabhu, *op. cit.*, p. 345. Prabhu makes this comment on social systems in Hinduism which may be applicable to religious institutions also.
13. B.K. Smith, "Exorcising the Transcedent: Strategies for Defining Hinduism and Religion", HR, 27/1 (1987), p. 45.
14. For a clear statement of the problem, see L. Renou, *Destiny of the Veda in India*, Delhi, 1965, p.1.

Bibliography

TEXTS, BOOKS AND MONOGRAPHS

Aguilar, H., *The Sacrifice in the Ṛgveda—Doctrinal Aspects*, Delhi: Bharatiya Vidya Prakashan, 1976.

Aiyar, P., "Imitations of the Bhagavad Gītā and Later Gītā Literature", *CHI*, Vol. II, 1962, pp. 204-19.

Ashby, G., *Sacrifice: Its Nature and Function*, London: SCM Press, 1988.

Aurobindo, Sri, *Essays on the Gītā*, Pondicherry: Sri Aurobindo Birth Centenary Library, 1970, Vol.13.

Baird, R.D., *Methodological Issues in Religious Studies*, Chicago: New Horizons Press, 1975.

Barth, A., *The Religions of India*, London: Kegan Paul, 1891.

Basham, A.L., "Jainism and Buddhism" in *Sources of Indian Tradition*, compiled by Wm. Theodore de Bary and others, New York: Columbia University Press, 1964, pp.37-202.

————(ed.), *A Cultural History of India*, Oxford: Clarendon Press, 1975.

————*History and Doctrines of Ājīvikas*, Delhi: Motilal Banarsidass, 1981.

————*The Wonder that Was India*, London: Sidwick and Jackson, 1956 (Reprint by Rupa Publications, 1982).

————*The Sacred Cow: The Evolution of Classical Hinduism* (ed. and annotated by K.G.Zysk), London: Rider, 1990.

Basu, J., *India of the Age of the Brāhmaṇās*, Calcutta: Sanskrit Pushtak Bhandar, 1969.

Bazaz, P.N., *The Role of Bhagavad Gītā in Indian History*, New Delhi: Sterling Publishers, 1975.

Belvalkar, S.K. *Miscarriage of the Attempted Stratification of the Bhagavad Gītā*, Bombay: Karnatak Printing Press, 1937.

————*The Bhagavad Gītā*, Poona: The Bilvakunja Publishing House, 1943.

————"Bhagavad Gītā: A General View of its History and Character", *CHI*, 1962, Vol. II, pp.135-57.

————and R.D. Ranade, *History of Indian Philosophy*, Vol.II; *The Creative Period*, New Delhi: Oriental Books Reprint Corporation, 1974.

Bergaigne, A., *Vedic Religion*, Tr. by V.G.Paranjpe and indexed by Maurice

Bloomfield, Vols. I-IV bound in one, Delhi: Motilal Banarsidass, 1978.

Bhagat, M.G. *Ancient Indian Asceticism,* New Delhi: Munshiram Manoharlal, 1976.

Bhaktivedanta Swami Prabhupāda, A.C., *Bhagavad-Gītā As It Is,* New York: Collier Books, 1972.

Bhandarkar, R.G., *Vaiṣṇavism, Śaivism and Minor Religious Systems,* Strassburg: Verlag Von Karl J. Trubner, 1913.

Bharati, A., "India: Hinduism and Modernization", in *Religion and Change in Contemporary Asia,* ed. Robert F. Spencer, Bombay: Oxford University Press, 1971, pp.67-104.

Bhattacharyya, N.N., *Ancient Indian Rituals and their Social Contents,* Delhi: Manohar, 1975.

Bhattacharya, S.K., *Kṛṣṇa-cult,* New Delhi: Associated Publishing House, 1978.

Bhide, V.V., *The Cāturmāsya Sacrifices,* (With Special Reference to the Hiranyakesi Srauta Sūtra) Pune: University of Poona, 1979.

Bianchi, U., "History of Religions", *ER,* ed. by Mercea Eliade, New York; Macmillan Publishing Company, 1987, Vol.6, pp. 399-408.

Biardeau, M., "The Salvation of the King in the Mahābhārata" in *Way of Life, King, Householder, Renouncer,* ed. T.N. Madan, New Delhi: Vikas Publishing House, 1982, pp. 75-97.

———— and Charles Malamoud, *Le Sacrifice dans l'Inde Ancienne,* (Science Religieuses—Volume LXXIX), Paris: Presses Universitaires de France, 1976.

Bloomfield, M., *Hymns of the Atharva-Veda,* Oxford: Clarendon Press, 1897. *Sacred Books of the East,* Vol. XLII.

Bolle, Kees W., *The Bhagavad Gītā, A New Translation,* Berkeley: University of California Press, 1979.

Bourdillon, M.F.C. and Meyer Fortes (ed.), *Sacrifice,* London: Acdemic Press, 1980.

Boyd, R., *Introduction to Indian Christian Theology,* Madras: CLS, 1975 (rev. edn.).

Brockington, J.L., *The Sacred Thread: Hinduism in its Continuity and Diversity,* Edinburgh: University Press, 1981.

Brown, W.N., *Man in the Universe—Some Continuities in Indian Thought,* Berkeley: University of California Press, 1966.

Callewaert, W.M. and Shilanand, H., *Bhagavadgītānuvāda, A Study in Transcultural Translation,* Ranchi: Satya Bharati Publication, 1983.

Casa, C.D., "Jainism" in *Historia Religionum,* eds. C. Jouco Bleeker and Geo Widengren, Leiden: E.J. Brill, 1971. Vol.II ("Religions of the Present"), pp. 346-71.

Chakraborti, H.P., *Vedic India: Political and Legal Institutions in Vedic Literature,* Calcutta: Sanskrit Pustak Bhandar, 1981.

Chattopadhyaya, S., *Evolution of Hindu Sects—up to the time of Śaṃkaracarya,*

New Delhi: Munshiram Manoharlal, 1970.

Conze, E., *Buddhism, Its Essence and Development,* Oxford: Bruno Casirer, 1974.

Coomaraswamy, A.K., *The Vedas—Essays in Translation and Exegesis,* Kent: Prologos Books, 1976.

————*Hinduism and Buddhism,* New York: Philosophical Library n.d.

Cowell, E.B. and W.H.D. Rouse, (Tr and ed.), *The Jātaka or Stories of the Buddha's Former Births,* Delhi: Cosmo Publications, 1978, 6 Vols.

Crim, K. (Gen.ed.), *Abingdon Dictionary of Living Religions,* Nashville: The Parthenon Press, 1981.

Dandekar, R.N., "Brahmanism" in *Sources of Indian Tradition,* Compiled by Wm. Theodore de Bary and others, New York: Columbia University Press, 1964, pp.1-36.

————"Hinduism" in *Historia Religionum,* eds. C. Jouco Bleeker and Geo Widengren, Leiden: E.J.Brill, 1971. Vol.II("Religions of the Present"), pp. 237-345.

————*Insights into Hinduism,* Delhi: Ajanta Publications, 1979.

Das, V., "Kama in the Scheme of Puruṣarthas: the Story of Rama" in *Way of Life,* 1982, pp.183-203.

————*Structure and Cognition—Aspects of Hindu Caste and Ritual,* Delhi: Oxford University Press, 1982.

Dasgupta, S.N., *A History of Indian Philosophy,* Delhi: Motilal Banarsidass, 1975. 5 Vols.

———— *Hindu Mysticism,* Delhi: Motilal Banarsidass, 1976.

Dell, D. J., Thomas Hopkins and others, *Guide to Hindu Religion,* Boston: G.K. Hall & Co., 1981.

Derrett, J.D.M., *Dharmaśāstra and Juridical Literature,* ed. Jan Gonda (Part of Vol.IV), Wiesbaden: Otto Harrassowitz, 1973.

Desai, M., *The Gospel of Selfless Action or the Gītā According to Gandhi,* Ahmedabad: Navajivan Publishing House, 1946.

De Smet, R.V., "Gītā in Time and Beyond Time", in *The Bhagavad Gītā and the Bible,* ed. B.R. Kulkarni, Delhi: Unity Books, 1972, pp.1-30.

———— "Highlights of the Life of Faith (*Śraddhā*) in India", in *God's World Among Men,* ed. by G. Gispert-Sauch, S.J. Delhi: Vidyajyoti, 1973, pp.39-58.

———— "The Integrative Doctrine of God of the Bhagavad-Gītā" in *Prayer and Contemplation,* ed. C.M. Vadakkekara, Bangalore: Asirvanam Benedictine Monastery, 1980, pp.139-57.

Deussen, P., *The Philosophy of the Upaniṣads,* (Tr. A.S.Geden), Edinburgh: T.&T. Clark, 1906.

————*Sixty Upaniṣads of the Veda,* Translated from the German by V.M. Bedekar and G.B. Palsule, 2 parts, Delhi: Motilal Banarsidass, 1980.

Deutsch, E., *The Bhagavata Gītā,* New York: Holt, Rinehart and Winston, 1968.

Devasthali, G.V., *Religion and Mythology of the Brāhmaṇas with Particular*

Reference to the Śatapatha-Brāhmaṇa, University of Pune: The Bhan Vishnu Ashtekar Vedic Research Series No.1, 1965.

Dhavamony, M., *Phenomenology of Religion*, Rome: Gregorian University Press, 1973.

——— *Classical Hinduism,* Rome: Gregorian University Press, 1982.

Drury, N., *The Sacrificial Ritual in the Śatapatha Brāhmaṇa*, Delhi: Motilal Banarsidass, 1981.

Dumont, L., *Religion/Politics and History in India*, The Hague: Mouton Publishers, 1970.

Dutt, R.C., *The Early Hindu Civilization*, Calcutta: Punthi Pustak, 1963.

Dutt, S., *Early Buddhist Monachism,* Bombay: Asia Publishing House, 1960.

Edgerton, F., *The Bhagavat Gītā*, Cambridge: Harvard University Press, 1944.

——— *The Beginnings of Indian Philosophy*, London: George Allen & Unwin, 1965.

Eggeling, J., *The Śatapatha-Brāhmaṇa* (according to the text of the Madhyandina School) in *SBE,* in 5 parts; Vols. XII, 1882; XVI, 1885; XLI, 1894; XLIII, 1897; XLIV, 1900.

Eliade, M., *Yoga: Immortality and Freedom,* London: Routledge & Kegan Paul, 1958.

Eliot, S.C., *Hinduism and Buddhism,* New York: Barnes & Noble, Inc., 1957 (3rd print). Vols. 3.

Feuerstein, G.A., *Introduction to the Bhagavad-Gītā—Its Philosophy and Cultural Setting,* London: Rider & Company, 1974.

Garbe, R., "Bhagavad-Gītā" in *ERE,* II. pp.535-8.

Geden, A.S., "Asceticism (Hindu)", *ERE,* Vol.II, pp. 87-96.

Ghurye, G.S., *Indian Sadhus,* Bombay: Popular Prakashan, 1964.

——— *Vedic India,* Bombay: Popular Prakashan, 1979.

Gispert-Sauch, G., "Sacrifice in Hinduism" in *The Eucharistic Mystery,* ed. J. Dupuis, Darjeeling: St. Mary's College (Now Vidyajyoti) 1968, pp.131-47. (Unpublished papers bound).

———, "An Inquiry into the Upanishadic Prayer 'From Lead Me to the Real ...' in *Dialogue in Action,* Essays in honour of Johannes Aagaard, eds. Lars Thumberg, Moti Pandit, and Carl Vilh. Fogh-Hansen, New Delhi: Prajna Publications, 1988, pp.179-213.

Gonda, J., *Notes on Brahman,* Utrecht: J.C. Beyers, 1950.

——— *Aspects of Early Viṣṇuism,* Utrecht: N.V.A.Oosthoek's Uitgevers Mij, 1954.

——— *Ancient Indian Kingship from the Religious Point of View,* Reprinted from 'NVMEN'III and IV with addenda and an index, Leiden: E.J. Brill, 1969.

——— *Selected Studies: Vol. IV: History of Ancient Indian Religion,* Leiden: E.J. Brill, 1975.

———*HIL,* Wiesbaden: Otto Harrassowitz, Vol.I, fasc. 1: *Vedic Literature*

(Saṃhitās and Brāhmaṇas), 1975: Vol. II, fasc.1: *Medieval Religion*: Literature in Sanskrit, 1977.

——— *Vedic Ritual—The Non-Solemn Rites*, Leiden: E.J.Brill, 1980.

——— *Change and Continuity in Indian Religion*, New Delhi: Munshiram Manoharlal, 1985.

——— *Prajāpati's Rise to Higher Rank*, Leiden: E.J. Brill, 1986.

——— *Mantra Interpretation in the Śatapatha-Brāhmaṇa*, Leiden: E.J. Brill, 1988.

Gopal, R., *India of Vedic Kalpasūtras*, Delhi: National Publishing House, 1959.

Gotshalk, R., *Bhagavad Gītā, Translation and Commentary*, Delhi: Motilal Banarasidass, 1985.

Grierson, G.A., "Bhakti-Marga" in *ERE*, Vol.II, pp. 539-51.

Griffith, R.T.H., *The Hymns of the Sāma Veda*, Benares: E.J. Lazarus and Co., 1907.

——— *The Hymns of the Atharva-Veda*, Benares: E.J. Lazarus and Co., Vol.I, 1916; Vol.II, 1917.

——— *The Hymns of the Rigveda*, Benares: E.J. Lazarus and Co., Vol.1, 1920; Vol. 2, 1926.

Griswold, H.D., *The Religion of the Rigveda*, London: Oxford University Press, 1923.

Gupta, S.K., *Madhusūdana Sarasvatī on the Bhagavad Gītā, Being an English translation of his Commentary Gūdhartha Dipika*, Delhi: Motilal Banarsidass, 1977.

Halbfass, W., *Tradition and Reflection—Explorations in Indian Thought,* New York: State University of New York Press, 1991.

Harbans Singh (ed.), *Approaches to the Study of Religion,* Patiala: Guru Gobind Singh Department of Religious Studies, n.d.

Hardy, F., "The Classical Religions of India" in *The World's Religions*, eds. Stewart Sutherland, Leslie Houlden, Peter Clarke and Friedhelm Hardy, London: Routledge, 1988. pp. 569-659.

Harvey, V.A., "Hermeneutics" *ER*, 1987. Vol.6, pp. 279-87.

Harzer, E., "Sāṃkhya", in *ER*, Vol.13, pp. 47-51.

Haug, M., *The Aitareya Brahmanam of the Rigveda*, Bombay: Government Central Book Depot, 1863. 2 Vols.

Haughton, G.C.(ed.), *The Institutes of Manu*, New Delhi: Cosmo Publications, 1982. 4 Vols (1-2 text, 3-4 translation).

Heesterman, J.C., "Householder and Wanderer", in *Way of Life*, pp. 251-98.

——— *The Inner Conflict of a Tradition—Essays in Indian Ritual, Kingship and Society*, Delhi: Oxford University Press, 1985.

——— "Self-Sacrifice in Vedic Ritual", in *Gilgul: Essays on Transformation, Revolution and Permanence in the History of Religion*, ed. S. Shaked and others, Leiden: E.J. Brill, 1987, pp. 91-106.

——— *The Broken World of Sacrifice—An Essay in Ancient Ritual*, Chicago: The University of Chicago Press, 1993.

Henninger, J., "Sacrifice", in *ER*, Vol. 12, pp. 544-57.

Herman, A.L., *The Bhagavad Gītā, A Translation and Critical Commentary*, Springfield: Charles C. Thomas Publisher, 1973.

Hill, W.D.P., *The Bhagavad Gītā*, London: Oxford University Press, 1928.

Hiltebeital, A., *The Ritual Battle—Krishna in the Mahābhārata*, London: Cornell University Press, 1976.

Hinnels, J.R. and E.J. Sharpe (eds.), *Hinduism*, England: Oriel Press, 1972.

Hiriyanna, M.A., *Outlines of Indian Philosophy*, London: George Allen & Unwin, 1968.

Hopkins, E.W., *The Religions of India*, London: Edward Arnold, 1896.

Hopkins, T.J., *The Hindu Religious Tradition*, Belmont: Wadsworth Publishing Company, 1971.

Hubert, H. and M. Mauss, *Sacrifice: Its Nature and Function*, Tr. by W.D. Halls, London: Cohen & West, 1968.

Hume, R.E., *The Thirteen Principal Upaniṣads*, London: Oxford University Press, 1921.

Jacob, C.J.A., *A Concordance to the Principal Upaniṣads and the Bhagavadgītā*, Delhi: Motilal Banarsidass, 1963.

Jacobi, H. (Tr.), *Gaina Sutras, SBE*, Vols. XXII(1884). XLV (1895).

Jain, J.C., *Life in Ancient India as Depicted in the Jaina Canons* (with Commentaries), Bombay: New Book Company, 1947.

Jain, K.C., *Lord Mahāvīra and His Times*, Delhi: Motilal Banarsidass, 1974.

Jaini, P.S., "*Śramaṇas*: Their Conflict with Brahmanical Society" in *Chapters in Indian Civilization*, pp.41-81.

——— *The Jaina Path of Purification*, Delhi: Motilal Banarsidass, 1979.

Jaiswal, S., *The Origin and Development of Vaiṣṇavism*, (From 200 B.C.E. to 500 A.D.), Delhi: Munshiram Manoharlal, 1967.

James, E.O., "Sacrifice (Introductory and Primitive)", *ERE*, vol.11, pp.1-7.

——— *Origins of Sacrifice — A Study in Comparative Religion*, London: J.. Murray, 1933.

——— *Sacrifice and Sacrament*, London: Thames and Hudson, 1962.

Jayatilleke, K.N., *The Message of the Buddha*, London: George Allen & Unwin, 1975.

Kalathil, J., *The Development of the Gītā Concept of God*, Trichy: St. Joseph's Industrial School Press, 1950.

Kane, P.V., *History of Dharmaśāstra*, Poona: Bhandarkar Oriental Research Institute, 1974. Vol.II, Part II and Vol. III.

Kaveeshwar, G.W., *The Ethics of the Gītā*, Delhi: Motilal Banarsidass, 1971.

Keith, A.B., *The Karma-Mīmāṃsā*, Calcutta: Association Press, 1921.

——— *The Religion and Philosophy of the Veda and Upaniṣads*, Cambridge: Harvard University Press, 1925 (first half: Chapter 1-19, pp.1-312;

second half: chapter 20-29, pp. 313-683).

——— *Rigveda Brāhmaṇas: The Aitareya and Kauṣītaki Brāhmaṇas of the Rigveda*, Cambridge: Harvard University Press, 1920.

——— *The Veda of the Black Yajus School entitled Taittirīya Samhita*, 2 Parts. Delhi: Motilal Banarsidass, 1967.

——— *The Aitareya Āraṇyaka*, Oxford: Clarendon Press, 1969.

Khair, G.S., *Quest for the Original Gītā*, Bombay: Somaiya Publications, 1969.

Killingley, D., "OṂ: The Sacred Syllable in theVeda" in *A Net Cast Wide: Investigations into Indian Thought in Memory of David Friedman*, ed. J. Lipner, Newcastle upon Tyne: Grevatt & Grevatt, 1987, pp.14-33.

Kinsley, D.R., *Hinduism —A Cultural Perspective*, New Jersey: Prentice-Hall, 1982.

Kloppenborg, R. (ed.), *Selected Studies on Ritual in the Indian Religions, Essays to D.J. Hoens*, Leiden: E.J. Brill, 1983.

Knipe. D.M. *In the Image of Fire—Vedic Experience of Heat*, Delhi: Motilal Banarsidass, 1975.

Koller, J. M., *The Indian Way*, New York: Macmillan Publishing Company, 1982.

Kosambi, D.D., *An Introduction to the Study of Indian History*, Bombay: Popular Prakashan, 1975.

——— *Myth and Reality*, Bombay: Popular Prakashan, 1983.

——— *The Culture and Civilization of Ancient India in Historical Outline*, New Delhi: Vikas Publishing House, 1976.

Kuhn, T.S. *The Structure of Scientific Revolutions*, 2nd edition enlarged, Foundations of the Unity of Science, The University of Chicago Press,1970.

Lal, R.B., *The Gītā in the Light of Modern Science*, Bombay: Somaiya Publications, 1970.

Larson, G.J., *Classical Sāṃkhya*, Delhi; Motilal Banarsidass, 1979.

Leeuw, G.V., *Religion in Essence and Manifestation* (Tr. J.E. Turner and new foreword by Ninian Smart), Princeton: Princeton University Press, 1986.

Levi, S., *La Doctrine du Sacrifice Dans Les Brahmaṇas*, Paris: Ernest Leroux, Editeur, 1898.

Ling, T., *The Buddha —Buddhist Civilization in India and Ceylon*, London: Temple Smith, 1985.

Lipner, J.J., *The Face of Truth, a Study of Meaning and Metaphysics in the Vedantic Theology of Ramanuja* . London: Macmillan Press, 1986.

——— "Applying the Litmus Test: A Comparative Study in Vedantic Exegesis" in *A Net Cast Wide: Investigations into Indian Thought in Memory of David Friedman*, ed. J. Lipner, Newcastle upon Tyne: Grevatt & Grevatt, 1987, pp. 54-73.

——— "Theology and Religious Studies" in *The Threshold of Theology*, ed. Paul Avis, Hants: Marshall Pickering, 1988.

Lott, E.J., *Vision, Tradition, Interpretation—Theology, Religion and the Study of Religion*, Berlin: Mouton de Gruyter, 1988.

Luke, K., "The Ṛgvedic Conception of Dharma" in *God's Word among Men*, ed. G. Gispert-Sauch, S.J., Delhi: Vidyajyoti, 1973, pp. 25-37.

Madan, T.N., *Non-Renunciation—Themes and Interpretations of Hindu Culture*, Delhi: Oxford University Press, 1987.

Mahadeva, S.A., (Tr.) *The Bhagavad Gītā with the Commentary of Sri Sankaracharya*, Madras: Samata Books, 1977.

Mahadevan, T.M.P., (ed.), *Indian Philosophical Annual*, Vol. 1, Madras: The Centre of Advanced Study in Philosophy, Madras University, 1965.

Majumdar.B., *Kṛṣṇa in History and Legend*, Calcutta: University Press, 1969.

Majumdar, R.C., *Ancient India*, Delhi: Motilal Banarsidass, 1982.

———, R.C. Raychaudhuri and Kalikinkar Datta, *An Advanced History of India*, London: Macmillan and Co., 1950.

——— (ed.), *The History and Culture of the Indian People*, Vol.1, *Vedic Age*, London: George Allen & Unwin, 1951, and Vol. 2, *The Age of Imperial Unity*, Bombay: Bharatiya Vidya Bhavan, 1960.

Malamoud, C."On the Rhetoric and Semantics of Purusartha" in *Way of Life*, 1982, pp. 33-54.

Maliekal, L., *Yajña and Eucharist*, Bangalore: Dharmaram Publications, 1989.

Minor, R.N., *Bhagavad Gītā, an Exegetical Commentary*, New Delhi: Heritage Publishers, 1982.

——— *Modern Indian Interpreters of the Bhagavad Gītā*, Albany: State University of New York Press, 1986.

Misra, G.S.P., *Development of Buddhist Ethics*, New Delhi: Munshiram Manoharlal, 1984.

Misra, P., *Evolution of the Brahman Class*, (In the Perspective of Vedic priesthood), Varanasi: Banaras Hindu University Press, 1978.

Mitchiner, J.E., *Traditions of the Seven Ṛṣis*, Delhi: Motilal Banarsidass, 1982.

Modi, P.M., *The Bhagavad Gītā, A Fresh Approach*, Bhavnagar: Anand Printing Press, 1955.

Monier-Williams, M., *Brāhmaṇism and Hinduism*, London: J. Murray, 1887.

——— *Indian Wisdom*, London; Luzac & Co., 1893.

——— *A Sanskrit-English Dictionary*, Oxford: Clarendon Press, 1899.

——— *Buddhism in its Contrast with Christianity*, Varanasi: The Chowkhamba Sanskrit Series Office, 1964.

Mookerji, R., *Aśoka*, London: Macmillan and Company, 1928.

Moore, C.A. (ed.), *The Indian Mind: Essentials of Indian Philosophy and Culture*, Honolulu: University of Hawaii Press, 1967.

Nagatomi, M., B.K. Matilal, J.M. Mason and E.C. Dimock J. (eds.) *Sanskrit and Indian Studies*, Dordrecht: D. Deidel Publishing Company, 1980.

Nataraja Guru, *The Bhagavad Gītā*, Bombay: Asia Publishing House, 1961.

Nikam, N.A. and R. Mckeon (eds. & tr.), *The Edicts of Aśoka*, Chicago: University of Chicago Press, 1959.

O'Flaherty, W.D., *Śiva The Erotic Ascetic*, Oxford: University Press, 1973.

——— (ed.), *Karma and Rebirth in Classical Indian Traditions*, Berkeley: University of California Press, 1980.

——— and J.D.M. Derrett (eds.), *The Concept of Duty in South Asia*, New Delhi: Vikas Publishing House, 1978.

Olivelle, P., *Vāsudevāśrama Yatdharma-Prakāśa: A Treatise on World Renunciation*, Vienna: Indological Institute, University of Vienna, Part I (Text), 1976; Part II (Tr.), 1977.

——— "Samṇyasā", *ER*, Vol.13, pp. 51-3.

Oman, J.C., *The Mystics, Ascetics and Saints of India*, London: T.F. Unwin, 1903.

Otto, R., *The Original Gītā*, London: George Allen and Unwin, 1939.

Pande, G.C., *Śramaṇa Tradition—Its History and Contribution to Indian Culture*, Ahmedabad: L.D. Institute of Indology, 1978.

——— *Studies in the Origins of Buddhism*, Delhi: Motilal Banarsidass, 1983.

Panikkar, R., *The Vedic Experience—Mantra-Manjari*, London: Darton, Longmann & Todd, 1977.

——— *Myth, Faith and Hermeneutics*, New York: Paulist Press, 1979.

Paradkar, M.D. (ed.), *Studies in the Gītā*, Bombay: Popular Prakashan, 1970.

Parrinder, G., *The Bhagavad Gītā: A Verse Translation*, London: Sheldon Press, 1974.

Potter, K.H. (ed.), *The Encyclopedia of Indian Philosophies*, Delhi: Motilal Banarsidass, Vol. I, 1974; Vol. II, 1977; Vol. III, 1981.

Prabhu, P.H., *Hindu Social Organization, A Study in Socio-psychological and Ideological Foundations*, Bombay: Popular Prakashan, 1979.

Radhakrishnan, S., *The Philosophy of the Upaniṣads*, London: George Allen & Unwin, 1924.

——— *The Bhagavadgītā*, London: George Allen and Unwin, 1948.

——— *The Principal Upaniṣads*, London: George Allen and Unwin, 1953.

——— *Indian Philosophy*, London: George Allen and Unwin, 1971; Vol.I.

Raghavan, R. and R.N. Dandekar, "Hinduism" in *Sources of Indian Tradition*, compiled by Wm. Theodore de Bary and others, New York: Columbia University Press, 1964, pp. 203-366.

Ramanathan, A.A., *The Saṃnyāsa Upniṣads*, Madras: The Adyar Library and Research Centre, 1978.

Rangachari, D.B.K., *The Śrī Vaishnava Brahmans*, Delhi: Gian Publishing House, 1986.

Rangaswamy Mudaliar, A. and Sons (ed.), *Nālāyiradivyaprabhandam* (Tamil), Madras: Poomagal Press, 1929.

Rapson, E.J. (ed.), *The Cambridge History of India,—Vol.I: Ancient India*, Cambridge University Press, 1922.

Raychaudhuri, H., *Materials for the Study of the Early History of the Vaishnava Sect*, University of Calcutta, 1936.

Renou, L., *Religions of Ancient India*, University of London, The Athlone Press, 1953.

——— *The Destiny of the Veda in India*, Delhi: Motilal Banarsidass, 1965.

Rhys Davids, C.A.F., "Asceticism (Buddhist)", *ERE*, ed. James Hastings, New York: Charles Scribner's Sons, 1960. Vol.XI, pp. 7-8.

——— *A Manual of Buddhism*, London: The Sheldon Press, 1932.

Rhys Davids, T.W., *Dialogues of the Buddha*, London: Oxford University Press, 1899. 3 Vols.

———*Buddhist Suttas, Sacred Books of the East*, ed. by Max Muller, Oxford: Clarendon Press, 1900.Vol.XI.

——— *Buddhist India*, London: T. Fisher Unwin, 1903.

Rice, E.P., *The Mahābhārata—Analysis and Index*, Madras: Oxford University Press, 1934.

Roy, P.C., *The Mahābhārata*, English Translation, Calcutta: Datta Bose & Co., 1928. 6 Vols.

Roy, S.C., *The Bhagavad-Gītā and Modern Scholarship*, London: Luzac & Co., 1941.

Rustagi, U., *Darṣapūrṇamāsa*, Delhi: Bharatiya Vidya Prakashan, 1981.

Sampatkumaran, M.R., (Tr.) *The Gītābhasya of Rāmānuja*, Bombay: Ananthacharya Indological Research Institute, 1985.

Sarma, D.S., *The Bhagavad Gītā*, Madras: The Current Thought Press, 1930.

Sastry, A.M., (Tr.), *The Bhagavad Gītā with the Commentary of Sri Sankaracharya*, Madras: Samata Books, 1977.

Sharma, A., *The Puruṣārthas: A Study in Hindu Axiology*, Michigan: Asian Studies Centre, Michigan State University, 1982.

——— *The Hindu Gītā, Ancient and Classical Interpretations of the Bhagavadgita*, London: Duckworth, 1986.

Sharma, H.D., *Contributions to the History of Brāhmanical Asceticism* (Saṃnyāsa), Poona: Oriental Book Agency, 1939.

Sharpe, E.J., *Comparative Religion—A History*, London: Duckworth, 1975.

——— *The Universal Gītā—Western Images of the Bhagavad Gītā,—a Bicentenary Study*, London: Duckworth, 1985.

Smart, N., *The Phenomenon of Religion*, London and Basingstoke: Macmillan Press, 1973.

——— *The Science of Religion and the Sociology of Knowledge*, Princeton University Press, 1973.

Smith B.K., *Hinduism and Vedic Ritual—Reflections on Resemblance, Ritual and Religion*, New York: Oxford University Press 1989.

Smith, V.A., *The Oxford History of India*, Oxford: Clarendon Press (third edition ed. Percival Spear and revised by M.Wheeler, A.L. Basham, J.B. Harrison and Spear), 1964.

Staal, F., *Agni, A Vedic Ritual of the Fire-Altar*, Delhi: Motilal Banarsidass, 1983. 2 Vols.

——— *The Science of Ritual*, Poona: Bhandarkar Oriental Research Institute, 1982.

Stutley, M. and James, *Harper's Dictionary of Hinduism*, New York: Harper & Row, 1977.

Subba Rau, S., *The Bhagavad Gītā According to Sri Madhwacharya's Bhashyas*, Madras: The Minerva Press, 1906.

Sukthankar, V.S., *On the Meaning of the Mahābhārata*, Bombay: The Asiatic Society of Bombay, 1957.

Tambiah, S.J., "The Renouncer: His Individuality and his Community", in *Way of Life*, 1982, pp. 299-320.

Tapasyananda, S. (tr.), *Śrīmad Bhāgavata, The Holy Book of God*, Madras: Sri Ramakrishna Math, 1980. 3 Vols.

Telang, K.T., *The Bhagavadgītā with the Sanatsugātīya and the Anugītā* (2nd rev. edn.), Oxford: Clarendon Press, 1898.

Thachil, J., *The Vedic and the Christian Concept of Sacrifice*, Alwaye (Kerala): Pontifical Institute of Theology and Philosophy, 1985.

Thapar, R., *A History of India (Vol. I)*, Harmondsworth: Penguin Books, 1968.

——— *Aśoka and the Decline of the Mauryas*, Delhi: Oxford University Press, 1973.

———"The Householder and the Renouncer in the Brahmanical and Buddhist Traditions" in *Way of Life*, 1982, pp. 273-98.

——— *Ancient Indian Social History, Some Interpretations*, New Delhi: Orient Longman, 1978.

Thite, G.U., *Sacrifice in the Brāhmaṇa—Texts*, University of Poona, 1975.

Tilak, B.G., *Śrīmad Bhagavadgītā Rahasya or Karma-Yoga-Śāstra*, Bombay: Bombay Vaibhava Press, 1935. 2 Vols.

Upadhyaya, K.N., *Early Buddhism and the Bhagavadgītā*, Delhi: Motilal Banarsidass, 1983.

Vadakkekara, C.M., (ed.), *Divine Grace and Human Response*, Bangalore: Asirvanam Benedictine Monastery, 1981.

Van Buitenen, J.A.B., *The Pravargya*, Poona: Deccan College Postgraduate and Research Institute, 1968.

———"Vedic and Upaniṣadic Bases of Indian Civilization" in *Chapters in*

Indian Civilization, Vol.1: Classical and Medieval India, ed. Joseph W. Elder, Iowa: Kendall/Hunt Publishing Company, 1970, pp. 3-38.

———*Rāmānuja on the Bhagavad Gītā*, Delhi: Motilal Banarsidass, 1974.

———*The Mahābhārata*, Chicago: The University of Chicago Press, 1. The Book of the Beginning, 1973.

———*The Bhagavad Gītā in the Mahābhārata*, Text and Translation, Chicago: The University of Chicago Press, 1981.

Vesci, U.M., *Heat and Sacrifice in the Vedas*, Delhi: Motilal Banarsidass, 1985.

Vinoba, A., *Talks on the Gītā*, Kashi: Akhil Bharat Sarva Seva Sangh Prakashan, 1959.

——— *The Steadfast Wisdom*, Varanasi: Sarva Seva Sangh Prakashan, 1973.

Wach, J., *The Comparative Study of Religions*, Edited with an Introduction by J.M. Kitagawah, New York: Columbia University press, 1976.

Walker, B., *Hindu World*, London: George Allen and Unwin, 1968.

Wardenburg, J., *Reflections on the Study of Religion, Including an Essay on the Work of Gerardus van der Leeuw*, The Hague: Mouton Publishers, 1978.

Warder, A.K., *Indian Buddhism*, Delhi: Motilal Banarsidass, 1970.

Wayman, A., "Buddhism" in *Historia Religionum*, eds. C.J. Bleeker and G.Widengren, Leiden: E.J. Brill, 1971.Vol.II("Religions of the Present"), pp. 372-464.

Weber, A., *The History of Indian Literature* (Translated from German by J. Mann and T. Zachariah), Varanasi: Chowkhamba Sanskrit Series Office, 1961.

Whaling, F. (ed.), *Contemporary Approaches to the Study of Religion* (in 2 Vols.), Berlin: Mouton Publishers, 1983.

Winternitz, M. *A History of Indian Literature*, University of Calcutta, 1927. Vol.I.

Zaehner, R.C., *Hinduism*, London: Oxford University Press, 1962.

——— *The Bhagavad-Gītā*, Oxford: Clarendon Press, 1969.

Periodicals

Aiyangar, N., "Śramaṇas", *IA* , X(1881), 143-45.

Albright, W.F. and P.E. Dumont, "A Parallel Between Indic and Babylonian Sacrificial Ritual", *JAOS*, 54(1934), 107-28.

Anand, S., "The Opening Verse of the Gītā", *ABORI*. LXVI(1985), 175-83.

Apte, K.V., "Contradictions in the Bhagavad Gītā", *Journal of the Asiatic Society of Bombay*, New Series, 39-40 (1964-65), 105-24.

Banerji, A., "Foreign Elements in Hindu Ritual and Practice", *IHQ*, XXVIII (1952), 257-64 and *IC*, XVI(1949), 31-8.

Basham, A.L., "The Rise of Buddhism in its Historical Context", *AS*, IV/3 (1966). 395-411.

Bedekar, D.K., "Primitive Society and Yajña", *ABORI*, XXXI (1950),70-99.

Belvalkar, S.K., "The So-called Kashmir Recension of the Bhagavad Gītā", *NIA*, II (1939-40), 211-51.

Berg, R.A., "The Bhagavad Gītā on War: The Argument from Literature", *JSBhG*, V-VII(1985-87), 25-35.

——— "Theories of Action in the Bhagavad Gītā", *ibid.*, 36-50.

Bilmoria, P. and J.V. D'Cruz, "The Bhagavad Gītā: A Perspective of Text, Tradition and Transformation", *ibid.*, 51-81.

Bhattacharjee, U.C., "External Evidence about the Teacher of the Upaniṣads", *IA*, LV(1926), 31-5.

——— "The Home of the Upaniṣads", *IA*, LVII(1928), 166-73; 185-89.

Bolle, K., "Sat and Asat in the Bhagavad Gītā ", *JSBhG*, IV(1984), 1-31.

Bowlby, P.W.R., "Tradition in the Bhagavad Gītā", *SR*, 17/2(1988),159-68.

Carpenter, D., "Language, Ritual and Society—Reflections on the Authority: The Vedas in India", *JAAR*, LX/1 (1992), pp.52-77.

Chakrabarti, S.C., "On the Transition of Vedic Ritual Lore", *IIJ*, XXI/3 (1979), 181-8.

Chaudhuri, H., "The Gītā and its Message for Humanity" (Comment and Discussion), *PEW*, V/3 (1955), 245-53.

Chaudhuri, J.B., "The Wife in the Vedic Ritual", *IHQ*, XVI(1940), 70-98.

Clooney, F.X., "Sacrifice and its Spiritualization in the Christian and Hindu Tradition: A Study in Comparative Theology", *Harvard Thelogical Review*, 78/3-4(1985), 361-80.

——— "Jaimini's Contribution to the Theory of Sacrifice as the Experience of Transcendence", *HR*, 25/3 (1986), 199-212.

Coburn, T.B., "Scripture in India: Towards a Typology of the Word in Hindu Life", *JAAR*, LII/3(1984), 435-60.

Coomaraswamy, A.K., "Ātmayajña: Self-Sacrifice", *HJAS*, 6(1941), 358-98.

Creel, A.B., "Dharma as an Ethical Category Relating to Freedom and Responsibility", *PEW*, XXII/2 (1972), 155-68.

Dandekar, R.N. "The Theory of Puruṣārthas: A Rethinking", *ABORI*, LXVIII(1987), 661-71.

Dasgupta, S., "Is Sāṃkhya Non-Vedic?", *IC*, I/1-4 (1934-35), 79-80.

De, S.K., "Bhagavatism and Sun-Worship", *Bulletin of the School of Oriental Studies*, VI(1930-32), 669-72.

——— "Some Aspects of the Bhagavad Gītā ", *IC*, IX(1942), 21-35.

———"The Vedic and Epic Kṛṣṇa", *IHQ*, XVIII(1942), 297-301.

Deshmukh, G.H., "On Hindu Sacrifices", *The Journal of the Anthropological Society of Bombay*, 1/1(1886), 106-18.

De Smet, R., "A Copernican Reversal: The Gītākāra's Reformulation of Karma", *PEW*, XXVII/1 (1977), 53-63.

Dhammaratana, U., "Buddha and Asceticism", *IHQ*, XXXIII (1957), 129-38.

Eck, D.L., "India's Tirthas: 'Crossings' in Sacred Geography", *HR*, 20/4 (1981), 323-44.

Edgerton, F., "Sources of the Philosophy of the Upaniṣads", *JAOS*, 36 (1917), 197-204.

———"Dominant Ideas in the Formation of Indian Culture", *JAOS*, 62(1942), 151-6.

Ewing, A.H., "The Hindu Conception of the Functions of Breath—A Study in Early Hindu Psycho-Physics", *JAOS*, 22(1901), 249-308.

Farquhar, J.N., "The Organization of the Sannyasis of the Vedanta", *JRAS*, 1925, 479-86.

Gispert-Sauch, G, "Vedic Sacrifice: Recent Studies and Theological Questions", *Vidyajyoti*, L/9 (1986), 478-89.

Goman, T.G. and R.S. Laura, "A Logical Treatment of Some Upaniṣadic Puzzles and Changing Conceptions of Sacrifice", *Numen*, XIX/1 (1972), 52-67.

Gonda, J., "Ascetics and Courtesans", *ALB*, XXV/1-4 (1961), 78-102.

——— "The Indian Mantra", *Oriens*, 16 (1963), 244-97.

——— "The Vedic Mantra and the Epic Dharma", *JRAS*, 1971, 122-33.

——— "The Significance of the Right Hand and the Right Side in Vedic Ritual", *Religion*, II/1 (1972), 1-23.

——— "Some Notes on the Use of Vedic Mantras in the Ritual Texts of the Vaikhānasas", *IIJ*, XXV/1-2 (1972), 1-31.

———"A propos of the Mantras in the Pravargya Section of the Ṛgvedic Brāhmaṇas", *IIJ*, XXI/4 (1979), 235-71.

——— "The Popular Prajāpati", *HR*, 23/2 (1982), 129-49.

——— "Prajāpati and Prāyaścitta", *JRAS*, 1983, 32-54.

———"Vedic Gods and the Sacrifice", *Numen*, XXX/1(1983), 1-34.

Gopalan, S., "The Concept of Duty in the Bhagavad Gītā: An Analysis", *JSBhG*, V-VII(1985-87), 1-13.

Grierson, G.A., "The Narayaniya and the Bhagavatas" *IA*, XXXVII (1908), 251-62, 373-86.

Das Gupta, M., "Early Viṣṇuism and Nārāyaṇīya Worship", *IHQ*, VII(1931), 93-166, 343-58, 655-79; VIII(1932), 64-84.

Hara, M., "Note on Two Sanskrit Religious Terms — Bhakti and Śraddhā", *IIJ*, VII (1963-64), 124-45.

Hecht, R.D., "Studies on Sacrifice, 1970-1980", *RSR*, 8/3 (1982), 253-9.

Heesterman, J.C."Reflection on the Significance of the Dakṣiṇā", *IIJ*, III (1959), 241-58.

——— "Vrātya and Sacrifice", *IIJ*, VI (1962-63), 1-37.

——— "Review: Madeleine Biardeau et Charles Malamoud, *Le Sacrifice dans l'Inde Ancienne*, *IIJ*, XXI/1 (1979), 47-9.

Hein, N., "Monotheism in the Bhagavadgītā: A Stylistic Clue", *SHS*, XXXI (1975), 250-60.

Hiltebeital, Alf., "The Mahābhārata and Hindu Eschatology", 12/2 (1972), 95-135.

——— "Kṛṣṇa and the Mahābhārata (A Bibliographical Essay), *ABORI*, LX (1979), 65-107.

——— "Towards a Coherent Study of Hinduism", *RSR*, 9/3(1983), 203-12.

——— The Two Kṛṣṇas in One Chariot: Upaniṣadic Imagery and Epic Mythology", *HR*, 24/1 (1984), 1-26.

Holck, H.F., "Some Observations on the Motives and Purposes of Asceticism in Ancient India", *AS/EA*, XXIII/1-2(1969), 45-57.

Hooykaas, C., "Pañca-Yajñas in India and Bali", *ALB*, XXXIX(1975), 240-59.

Hopkins, E.W., "The Social and Military Position of the Ruling Caste in Ancient India, as Represented by the Sanskrti Epic", *JAOS*, XIII (1889), 57-76.

——— "Yoga-Technique in the Great Epic", *JAOS*, 22(1901), 333-79.

——— "A Buddhistic Passage in Manu", *JAOS*, 43 (1923), 244-6.

Jacobi, H., "The Dates of the Philosophical Sūtras of the Brahmans", *JAOS*, XXXI (1911), 1-29.

Johnsen, G., "Varuṇa and Dhṛtarāṣṭra", *IIJ*, IX(1965-66), 245-65.

Jordens, J.T.F., "Yajña in the Bhagavad Gītā", *AS*, III/2 (1965), 283-92.

Kaelber, W. O., "The 'Dramatic' Element in Brāhmaṇic Initiation: Symbols of Death, Danger and Difficult Passage", *HR*, 18/1 (1978), 54-76.

——— "Tapas and Purification in Early Hinduism", *Numen*, XXVI/2 (1979), 192-214.

——— "The Brahmacārin: Homology and Continuity in Brāhmaṇic Religion", *HR*, 21/1 (1981), 77-99.

Kane, P.V., "The Pūrva-Mīmāmsā System", *ABORI*, V/1(1924), 1-40.

Kapferer, R., "Contradiction and the Logic of Conversion in the Bhagavad Gītā", *JSBhG*, V-VII (1985-87), 127-37.

Keller, C.A., "Violence et Dharma, chez Ashoka et dans le Bhagavad Gītā" AS/EA, XXV (1971), 175-201.

Kesarcodi-Warson, I., "Varṇa-Jāti and Ideal Society with Reference to the Bhagavad Gītā", *JSBhG*, II(1982), 44-88.

Knipe, D.M., "One Fire, Three Fires, Five Fires: Vedic Symbolism in Transition", *HR*, 12/1 (1972), 28-41.

Koller, J.M., "Dharma: An Expression of Universal Order", *PEW*, XXII/2 (1972). 131-44.

Kosambi, D.D., "Early Stages of the Caste System in Northern India", *JBBRAS* (New Series), 22 (1946), 33-48.

——— "Early Brahmins and Brahmanism", *JBBRAS*, 23 (1947), 39-46.

——— "The Avatara Syncretism and Possible Sources of the Bhagavad Gītā", *JBBRAS*, 24-25 (1948-49), 121-34.

——— "Combined Methods in Indology" *IIJ*, VI (1962-63), 177-202.

Laine, J.W., "Hinduism and Mahābhārata", *WZKSAIP*, XXX(1986), 73-81.

Larson, G.J., "The *Trimurti* of Dharma in Indian Thought: Paradox or Contradiction?", *PEW*, XXII/2, (1972),145-53.

——— "The BhG as Cross-Cultural Process", *JAAR*, XLIII/4 (1975), 651- 69.

——— "The Song Celestial: Two Centuries of the Bhagavada Gītā in English", *JSBhG*, III, 1983, 1-55.

Law, N.N., "The Antiquity of the Four Stages of Life (Asramas)", *IA*, LII, 1923, 272-8.

Mainkar, T.G., "Some Thoughts on the Brahmasūtras and the Bhagavad Gītā ", *ABORI*, LVIII-VIX, (1977-78), 745-55.

Mehta, R., "Asceticism in Pre-Buddhist Days", *IC*, III (1936-37), 571-84.

Michael, A., "Ethical Action in the World-View of the Gītā", *JSBhG*, II (1982), 1-24.

Minor, R.N., "The Bhagavad Gītā and Modern Scholarship: An Appraisal of Introductory Conclusions", *JSBhG*, I (1981), 29-60.

——— "The Quest for the Gītākara: Multiple Authorship Revisited", *ABORI*, LXIII (1982), 29-42.

Monier-Williams, M., "On Buddhism in its Relation to Brahmanism", *JRAS*, 18(1886), 127-56.

Nakamura, H., "Upaniṣadic Tradition and the Early School of Vedanta as Noticed in the Buddhist Scripture", *HJAS*, 18(1955), 74-104.

——— "Yajñavalkya and Other Upaniṣadic Thinkers in a Jain Tradition", *ALB*, 31-32 (1967-68), 216-28.

Nandi, R.N., "Client, Ritual and Conflict in Early Brahmanical Order", *IHQ*, VI/1-2(1979-80), 64-118.

Neuner, J., "Religion und Riten Die Opferlehre der Bhagavad Gītā", *ZKT*, 73 (1951), 170-213.

Nilakanta Sastry, K.A., "Jaimini and Badarayana" *IA*, L(1921), 167-73.

——— "The Mīmāṃsa Doctrine or Works", *IA*, L (1821) 240-6.

Olivelle, P., "The Notion of Āśrama in the Dharmasūtras", *WZKSAIP*, XVIII (1974), 27-35.

——— "A Definition of World Renunciation", *WZKSAIP*, XIX (1975), 75-83.

——— "The Integration of Renunciation by Orthodox Hinduism", *JOIUB*, XXVIII/1 (1978), 27-36.

——— "Contributions to the Semantic History of Samṇyāsa", *JAOS*, 101/3 (1981), 265-74.

——— "King and Ascetic—State Control of Asceticism in the *Arthaśāstra*", *ALB*, 51 (1987), 39-59.

Olson, C., "The Existential, Social and Cosmic Significance of the Upanayana Rite", *Numen*, XXIV/2 (1977), 152-60.

Panikkar, R., "Indology as a Cross-Cultural Catalyst—A New Task of Indological Studies: Cross-Cultural Fertilization", *Numen*, XVIII (1971), 173-9.

———"The Law of *Karman* and the Historical Dirmension of Man", *PEW,* XXII/1 (1972), 25-43.

Preciado-Solis, B., "Some Problems Concerning the Origin of Saṃnyāsa", *ABORI,* LXVIII (1987), 359-69.

Prithipaul, D., "*Moha*: The Study of a Human Emotion in Hindu Religious Thought", *SR,* 4/4 (1974-75), 357-66.

Ray, A., "Śrīkṛṣṇa and the Source of the Bhagavad Gītā", *IHQ,* IX (1933), 188-96.

Raychaudhuri, H.C., "The Aśoka Chakra—Its Symbolism", *IC,* XV (1948-49), 179-83.

Reat, N.R., "Karma and Rebirth in the Upaniṣads and Buddhism", *Numen,* XXIV/3 (1977), 163-85.

Renou, L., "La Valéur du Silence dans le Culte Vedique", *JAOS,* 69(1949), 11-18.

Rhys Davids, C.A.F., "The Relations Between Early Buddhism, and Brahmanism", *IHQ,* X(1934), 274-87.

Rhys Davis, H., "Cremation and Liberation: The Revision of Hindu Ritual", *HR,* 28/1(1988), 37-53.

Rupwate, D.D., "A Versatile Significance of *Ṛta*'", *ABORI,* LX III(1982), 1-13.

Schrader, F.O., "Ancient Gītā Commentaries", *IHQ,* X (1934), 348-57.

——— "The Sacrificial Wheel Taught in the Bhagavadgītā", *IHQ,* V/2 (1929), 173-81, 790-91.

——— "An Implication of the Bhagavad Gītā Riddle", *NIA,* 1(1938-39), 62-8.

Selvanayagam, I., "Aśoka and Arjuna as Counter-figures Standing on the Field of Dharma: A Historical-Hermeneutical Perspective", *HR* (1992 Aug.), 59-75.

Senart, M.E., "Introduction to the French Translation of the Bhagavad Gītā", *ABORI,* VIII (1926-27), 305-21.

Sharma, A., "The Role of the Anu Gītā in the Understanding of the Bhagavad Gītā", *RS,* 14/2 (1978), 261-7.

——— "Some Misunderstandings of the Hindu Approach to Religious Plurality", *Religion,* VIII/2 (1978), 133-54.

——— "Ancient Hinduism as a Missionary Religion", *Numen,* XXXIX/2 (1992), pp.175-92.

Sharpe, E.J., "Some Western Interpretations of the Bhagavad Gītā", *JSBhG,* I (1981), 1-28.

——— "The Early Theosophists and the Interpretation of the Bhagavad Gītā", *JSBhG,* IV (1984), 47-67.

Shendge, M.J., "The Interdisciplinary Approach in Indian Studies", *ABORI,* LXIII (1982), 62-98.

Shideler, E.W., "The Meaning of Man in the Bhagavad Gītā", *The Journal of Bible and Religion,* XXVIII/3 (1960), 308-16.

Skurzak, L., "Indian Asceticism in its Historical Development", *ALB*, 31-32 (1967-68), 202-10.

Smith, B.K., "Vedic Field Work", *RSR*, 11/2 (1985), 136-45.

——— "Gods and Men in Vedic Ritualism: Towards a Hierarchy of Resemblance", *HR*, 24/4 (1985), 291-307.

——— "Sacrifice and Being—Prajāpati's Cosmic Emission and its Consequences", *Numen*, XXXII/1 (1985), 71-87.

——— "The Unity of Ritual — The Place of the Domestic Sacrifice in Vedic Ritualism", *IIJ*, XXIX/2 (1986), 79-96.

——— "Ritual, Knowledge and Being", *Numen*, XXXIII/1 (1986), 65-89.

——— "Exorcising the Transcendent: Strategies for Defining Hinduism and Religion", *HR*, 27/1 (1987), 32-55.

——— "Review of Heesterman's *The Inner Conflict* etc.", *RSR*, 14/1 (1988), 1-10.

——— "Canonical Authority and Social Classification: *Veda* and *Varṇa* in Ancient Indian Texts", *HR*, 32/2 (1992), 103-25.

Smith, M.C., "Warrior Ethics in the Bhagavadgītā", *JSBhG*, IV (1984), 32-46.

Srinivasan, D., "The Religious Significance of Divine Multiple Body Parts, in the *Atharva Veda*", *Numen*, XXV/3 (1978), 193-225.

Staal, F., "The Meaninglessness of Ritual", *Numen*, XXVI/1 (1979), 2-22.

Strug, C., "Kuhn's Paradigm Thesis: A Two-Edged Sword for the Philosophy of Religion", *RS*, 20 (1984), 269-79.

Tadapatrikar, S.N., "The Kṛṣṇa Problem", *ABORI*, X (1929), 270- 344.

Thite, G.U., "Animal Sacrifice in the Brāhmaṇa Texts", *Numen*, XVII/2 (1970), 143-58.

———"The Magico-religious Elements in the Principal Upaniṣads", *JOIUB*, XXVI/1 (1976), 11-17.

Upadhyaya, K.N., "The Impact of Early Buddhism on Hindu Thought (with special reference to the Bhagavadgītā", *PEW*, XVIII/3 (1968), 163-73.

——— "The Bhagavad Gītā on War and Peace", *PEW*, XIX/2 (1969), 159-69.

Utgikar, N.B.(tr.), "Garbe's Introduction to the Bhagavadgītā", *IA*, XLVII (1918), Supplementary, 1-33; Appendix 34-5.

Van Buitenen, J.A.B., "Dharma and Mokṣa", *PEW*, VII, (1957), 33-40.

———"A Contribution to the Critical Edition of the Bhagavad Gītā", *JAOS*, 85, (1965), 99-109.

Vira, R., "Implements and Vessels Used in Vedic Sacrifice", *JRAS*, 1934, 283-305.

Wadhwani-Shah, Y., "Sacrificial Ritual and Upaniṣads", *ABORI*, LXVI (1985), 47-61.

Weiss, P., "The Gītā: East and West", *PEW*, IV/3 (1954), 253-8.

Werner, K., "Yoga and the Ṛg Veda: An Interpretation of the Kesin Hymn (RV 10, 136)", *RS*, 13(1977), 289-302.

Wheelock, W., "A Taxonomy of the Mantras in the New and Full-Moon Sacrifice", *HR*, 19/4 (1980), 349-69.

Whillier, W.K., "Vision and Authority", *JSBhG*, V-VII (1985-87), 151-60.

Wilson, H.H., "On the Sacrifice of Human Being as an Element of the Ancient Religion of India", *JRAS*, 13, 1852, 96-107.

Wyatt, N., "Asvamedha and Puruṣamedha in Ancient India", *Religion*, 19/1 (1989), 1-11.

Young, D.N. DE L., "The Saṅgha in Buddhist History", *RS*, VI (1970), 243-52.

Index